Mary Fedden

Enigmas and Variations

Christopher Andreae

Mary Fedden

Enigmas and Variations

Lund Humphries

Published in 2007 by

Lund Humphries
Gower House
Croft Road
Aldershot
Hampshire GU11 3HR

and

Lund Humphries
Suite 420
101 Cherry Street
Burlington
VT 05401-4405
USA

Lund Humphries is part of Ashgate Publishing

www.lundhumphries.com

British Library Cataloguing in Publication Data:

Andreae, Christopher
Mary Fedden: enigmas and variations
1. Fedden, Mary 2. Fedden, Mary – Criticism
and interpretation
I. Title
759.2

Library of Congress Control Number: 2006940412

ISBN 978-0-85331-953-5 (hardback)
ISBN 978-0-85331-954-2 (limited edition)

Designed by Yvonne Dedman
Copy-edited by Howard Watson

Printed in Singapore under the supervision of
MRM Graphics

Contents

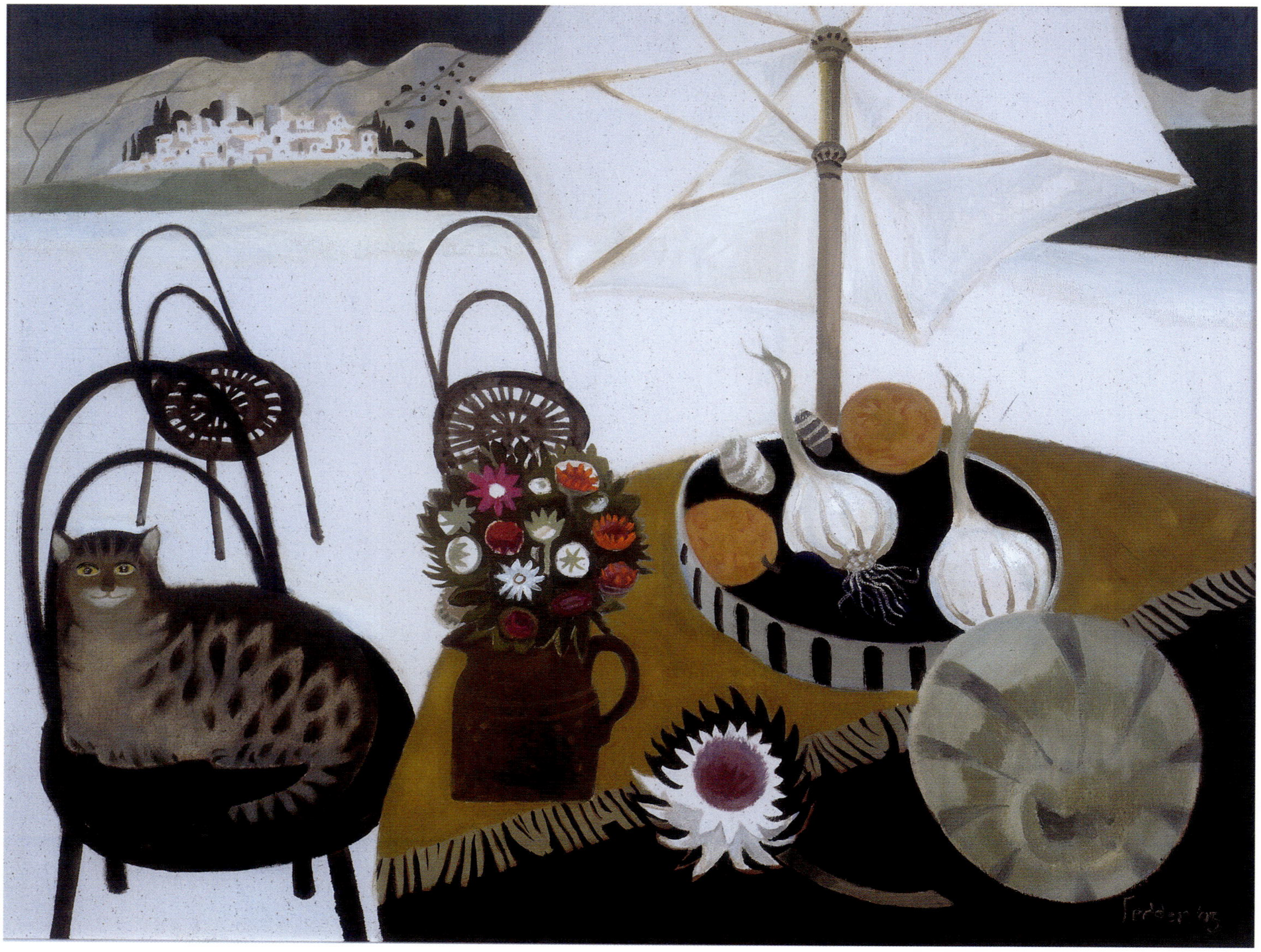

The White Umbrella, 2005
Oil on canvas
61 x 81.2 cm (24 x 32 in)
Private collection

Thanks and Acknowledgments

Primary thanks, of course, go to Mary Fedden herself who has been unfailingly encouraging, helpful, welcoming and generous with her time.

Her friends and admirers have been no less generous, informative and enthusiastic – to a man and woman, each has rooted for this to be a book worthy of her. Inevitably, some people have been pestered by the author even more than others and deserve particular thanks: John Iddon, Pat Jordan-Evans, Joanna Carey, Bill Clark and Lena Boyle. Extraordinary degrees of help have also been given by Suzette Mitchell, Jayne I. Hanlin and Mike Fear (an exemplary and affable photographer). Appreciative thanks also to Lucy Myers and everyone else involved at Lund Humphries.

Without the kindness and willing cooperation of very many others, this project would not have been feasible. I hope that I have not overlooked a single one of them:

Pamela Aitchison, Susannah Amoore, John A. Anderson, Mark and Kate Anderson, David Attenborough, Primrose Bell, Jane Blunden, Matthew Bradbury, Allan Christea, Ian Collins, Jane Corbett, Susie Cox, Sue Daly, Georgina David, Andrew Davison, Jane Denton, Robert and Lucy Dorrien Smith, James Druce, Nigel Farrow, Anna Fedden, Eleanor Fein, Anna Ford, Michael Forgacs, Julian Francis, Andrea Fredericksen, Melanie Gardner, Bamber and Christina Gascoigne, Charlotte Grant, Simon Grant, Richard Gault, Marie Goodwin, Patricia Haitink, Philip Harley, Jason de Mendes Harris, Robert Hartford, Jane and Edmund Haviland, Rachel Hidderley, Hazell Hills, Trine Hougaard, David Howard, Kate Howe, Sarah Hue-Williams, Jackie Hughes, Victoria Huxley, Holly Johnson, Rachel Kent, Susan Kent, Pat Lousada, Penny Madden, Michael Manser, Simon Martin, Ken Mellon, Barbara Moller, Susan Morris, Jovan Nicholson, Nicholas Polunin, Shafiq Rehman, Jenny Roland, Graham Ross, Peter de Rougement, Adrian Rowe, Andrew Scott, Hugo Scott, James Scott, Graham Smith, Don Stein, Paul and Roser Strachan, Sallie Thomas, Johnathan Messum, Joanna Varcoe, Paul and Kathy Wade, Chris Wadsworth, Nicholas Watson, Tom West, Ian Weston, Paul Whitfield, Andrew Wills, Brenda Woods, Muriel Woodward, Paul and Sybella Zisman.

Mary Fedden: Themes, Variations and Enigmas

Mary Fedden describes painting as, more than anything else, a 'passion'. She emphasises the word not only with due feeling but with a note of finality in her voice which cuts through the nonsense that too easily surfaces when people talk – or write – about art.

The first time I met her, she made a similarly apt and brief remark about her work. 'It makes people feel happy,' she said. 'I don't know why, but it does.'[1] It all seems very matter-of-fact and good-natured. One of her collectors confirms her point. He is principally a keen connoisseur and buyer of small sculptures, yet he has acquired a number of particularly simple and also small paintings by Fedden that complement the three-dimensional works (see Illustrations 1–4). One of his Feddens hangs comfortably near where his Matisse bronze stands. A friend was apparently somewhat aghast at this turn in his collecting interests, as if Fedden might be too 'light' in such weighty sculptural company. This surely misconceives the conviction of her work and her seriousness through a lifelong career, and overlooks her persistent determination to make each painting a fresh discovery, however similar it may appear to be at first sight to some other pictures by her. It is also a sorry (or snobbish) failure to recognise the indelibly individual character of her painting. This collector was not fazed anyway. He countered by asking: 'How many artists can you say paint happiness? She does. And it is needed.' He can't find 'a trace of angst in her work,' he says. In much of his sculpture collection, he certainly can.

In researching this book, I have found collector after collector saying much the same thing about Mary Fedden. They find something satisfying, almost nourishing, about the Feddens they live with, and these pictures turn out not to be quite so straightforwardly realistic or literal as they seemed at first. They are continually intriguing. They belong in a domestic environment – the dining room, the bedroom, or on the stairs. They might well be summed up by a term once much bandied about: 'life-enhancing'.

The artist Eleanor Fein, a close friend of Fedden, puts it this way: 'People love her work because her character just shines through it.' That strong character is marked by openness, an uncomplicated generosity, warmth, bonhomie and frankness. She has a heartfelt concern for others. Frustrating circumstances are often interrupted by her sense of merriment, by a funny story, a genre of which she is a master, or by plain common sense. She also has an appealing relish for the absurd. She delights, for instance, in Edward Lear's touching, self-effacing nonsense. In quite funny ways, she feels an affinity with him (Ill. 5). Illogicalities and absurdities occur surprisingly often in her paintings and drawings without compromising their seriousness as art (Ills 6 and 7). 'When a painting of mine comes out a bit quirky, I'm always very *pleased.*' Then she adds: 'It doesn't happen often enough.'

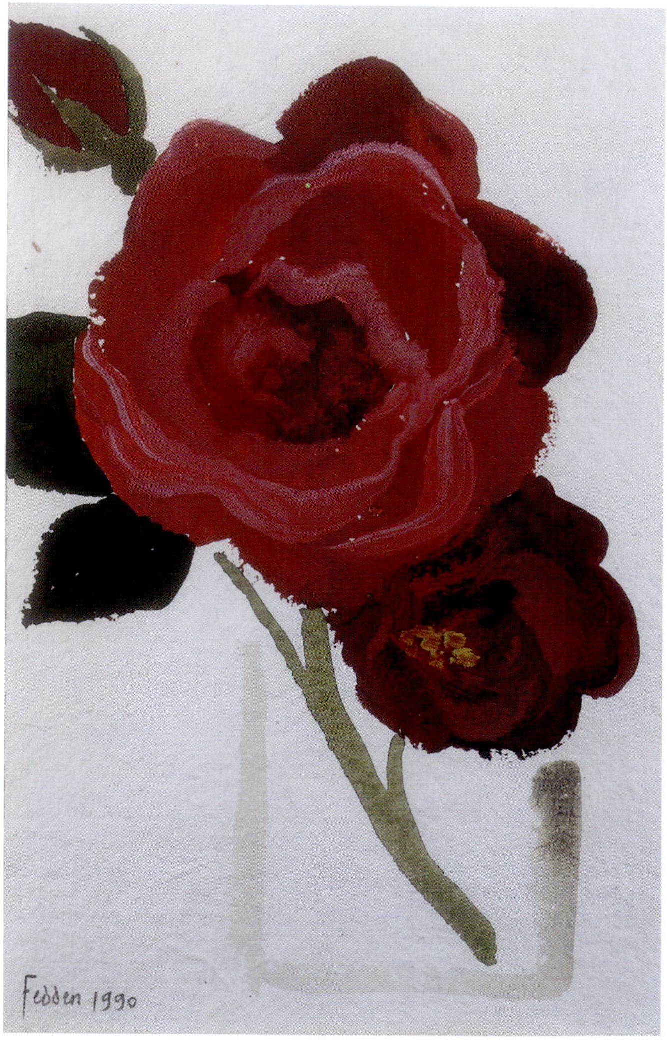

1
Rose, 1990
Gouache
18.8 x 12 cm (7⅜ x 4¾ in)
Private collection

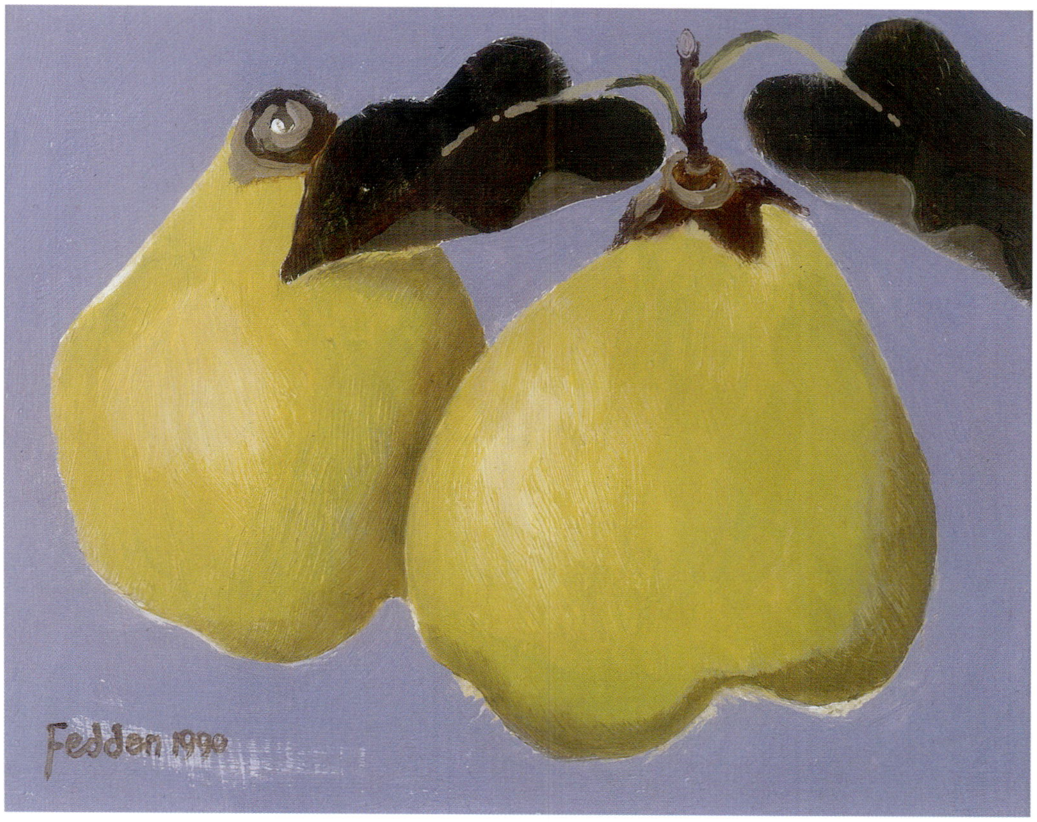

2
Quinces, 1990
Oil on board
14.8 x 19 cm (5¾ x 7½ in)
Private collection

3
Anemones, 1990
Oil on canvas
29.5 x 39.3 cm (11⅝ x 15½ in)
Private collection

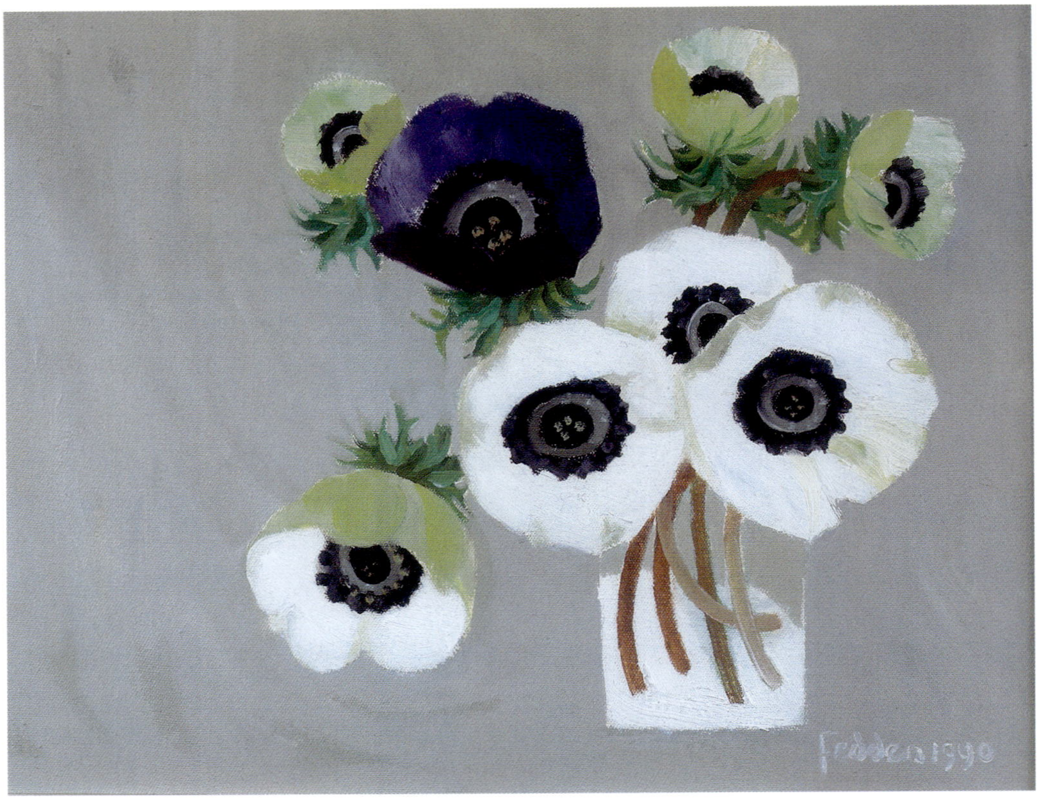

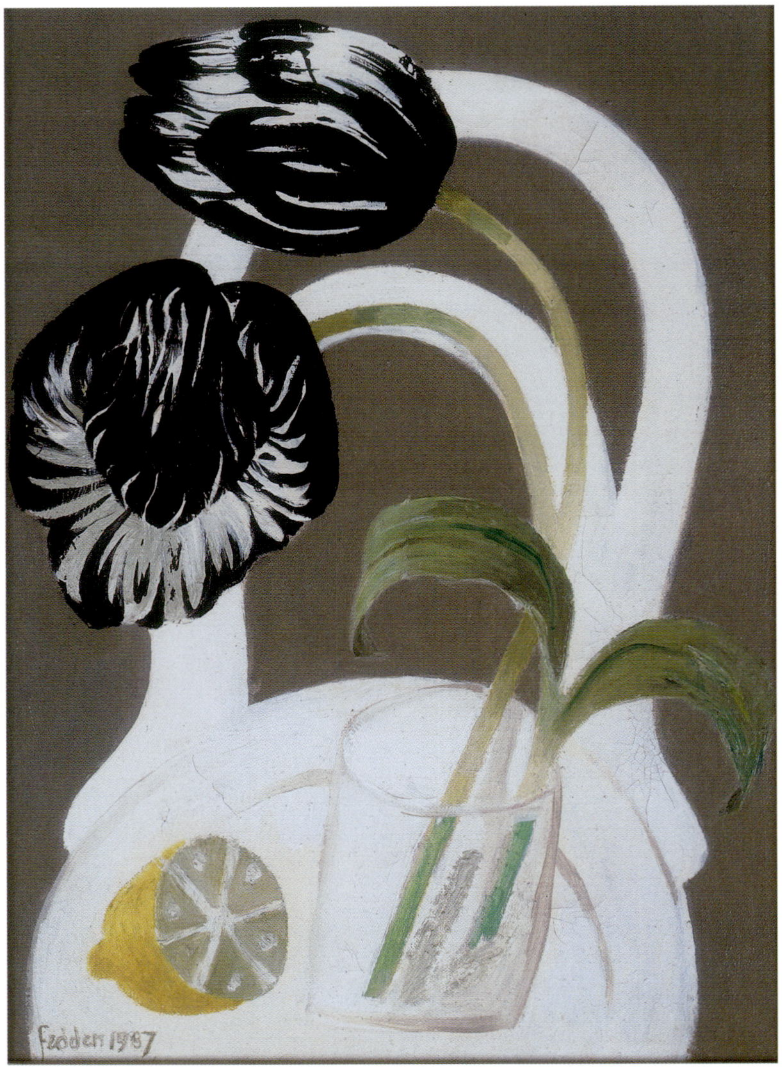

4
Black Tulips, 1987
Oil on canvas
38.8 x 28.8 cm (15¼ x 11⅝ in)
Private collection

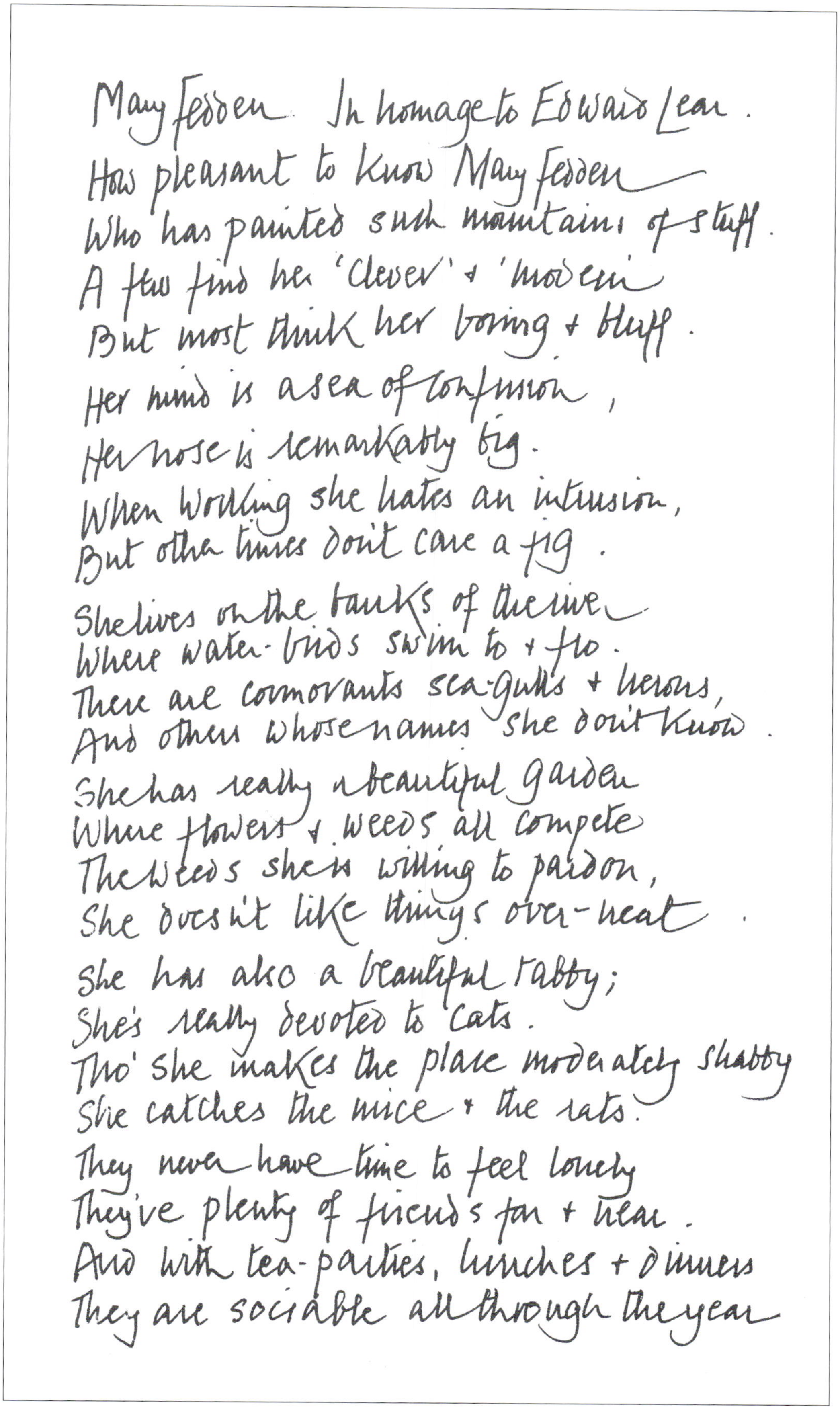

Mary Fedden In homage to Edward Lear.

How pleasant to know Mary Fedden
Who has painted such mountains of stuff.
A few find her 'clever' + 'modern'
But most think her boring + bluff.

Her mind is a sea of confusion,
Her nose is remarkably big.
When working she hates an intrusion,
But other times don't care a fig.

She lives on the banks of the river
Where water-birds swim to + fro.
There are cormorants sea-gulls + herons,
And others whose names she don't know.

She has really a beautiful garden
Where flowers + weeds all compete
The weeds she is willing to pardon,
She doesn't like things over-neat.

She has also a beautiful tabby;
She's really devoted to cats.
Tho' she makes the place moderately shabby
She catches the mice + the rats.

They never have time to feel lonely
They've plenty of friends far + near.
And with tea-parties, lunches + dinners
They are sociable all through the year

5
Mary Fedden's handwritten 'In homage to Edward Lear'

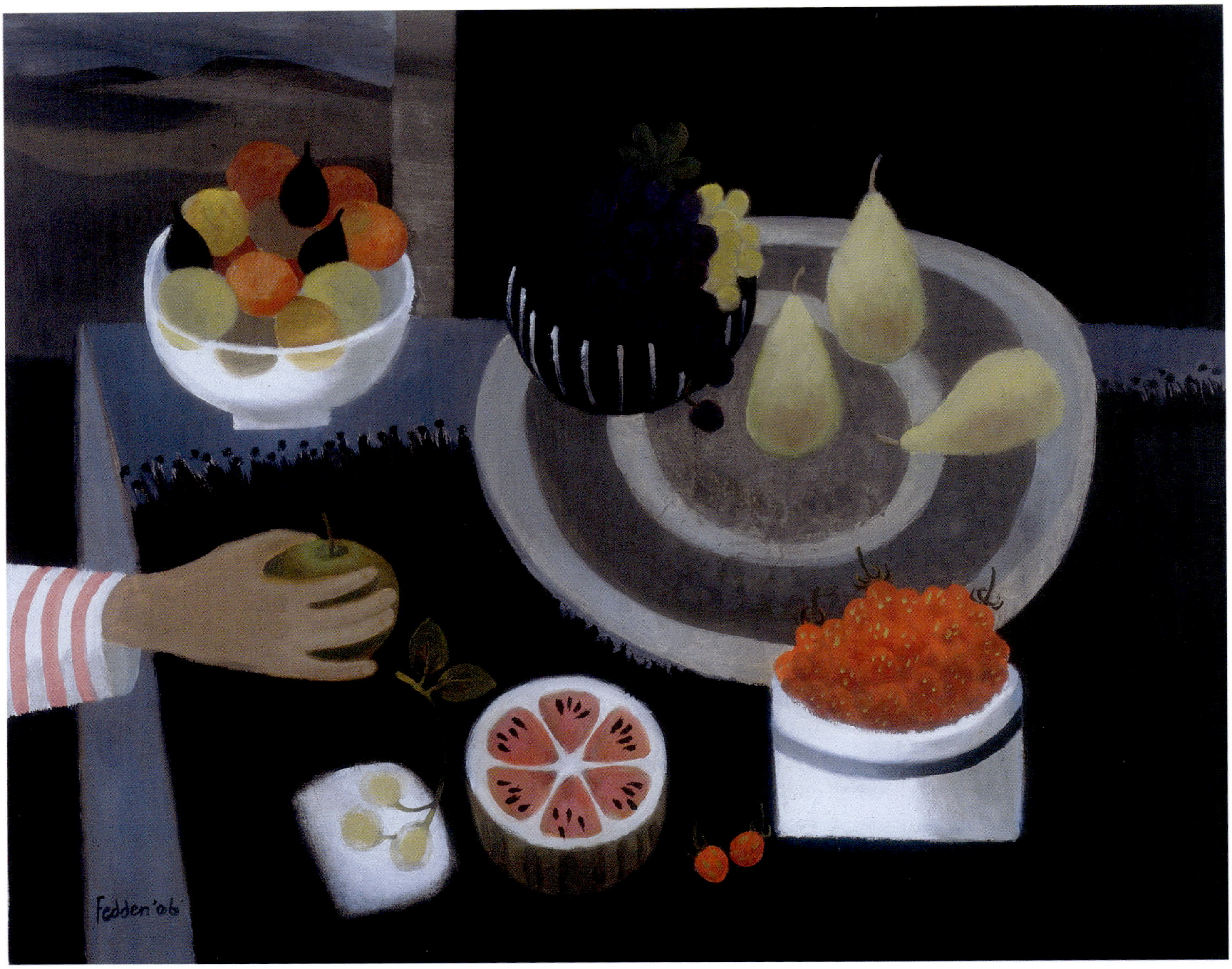

6
Stealing an Apple, 2006
Oil on canvas
70 x 90 cm (27½ x 35⅜ in)
Private collection

For Fedden's most avid collectors, the only word is 'fan'. Some of them have one or two Feddens, but there are others who confess that they find it hard to stop collecting her pictures. Her work can become something of an addiction. More than one collector has been known to sleep on the pavement outside a gallery all night so as not to miss the opportunity of buying a new favourite. And her collectors do have their favourites. They are usually quite clear about which of her works they like – and do not like. This prolific artist is actually much wider in her themes and variations than the usual description of her as basically – or even exclusively – a still-life painter would suggest (Ills 8–14). In the preferences and selectiveness of her collectors, there is an echo of her own disarmingly straightforward self-appraisal. 'I can look round my studio,' she told me, 'and I know exactly which of my pictures I don't like, which ones I like – and the few that I love.'

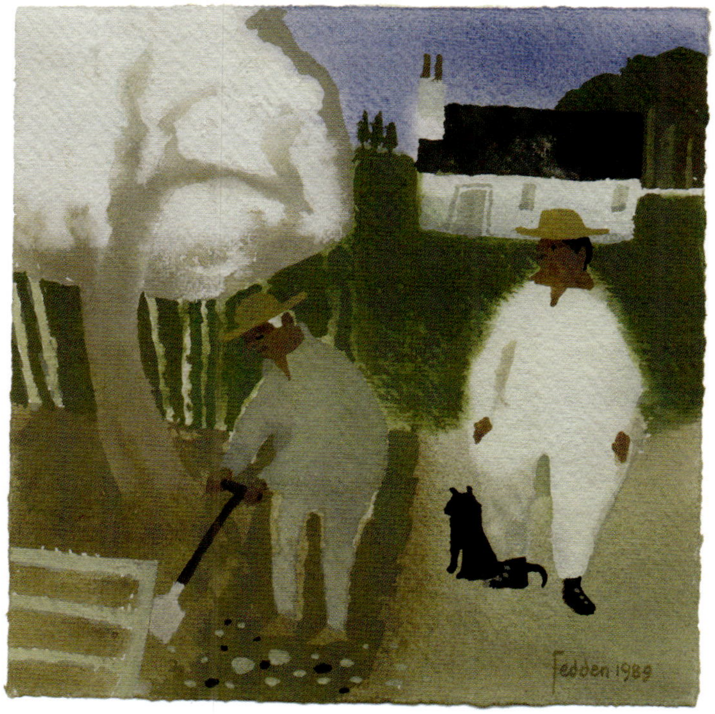

7
The Gardeners, 1989
Gouache
19.5 x 19.5 cm (7⅝ x 7⅝ in)
Private collection

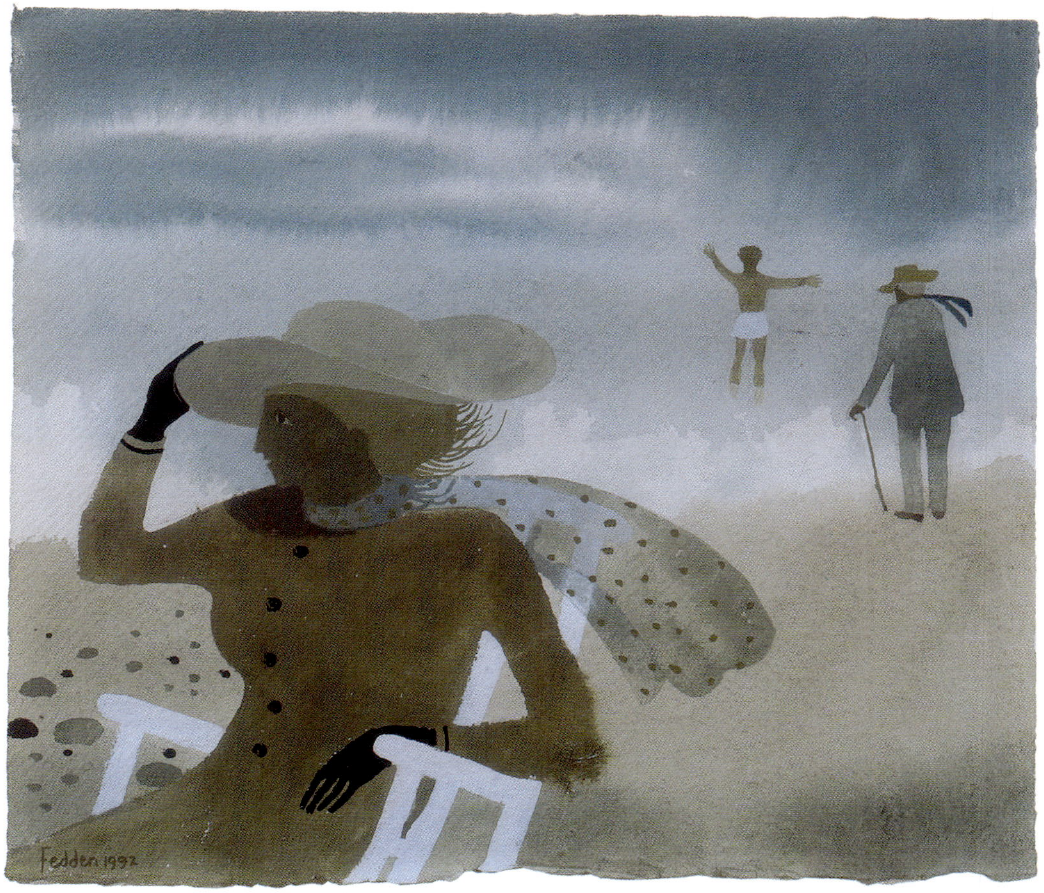

8
Death in Venice, 1992
Gouache
28 x 33 cm (11 x 13 in)
Private collection

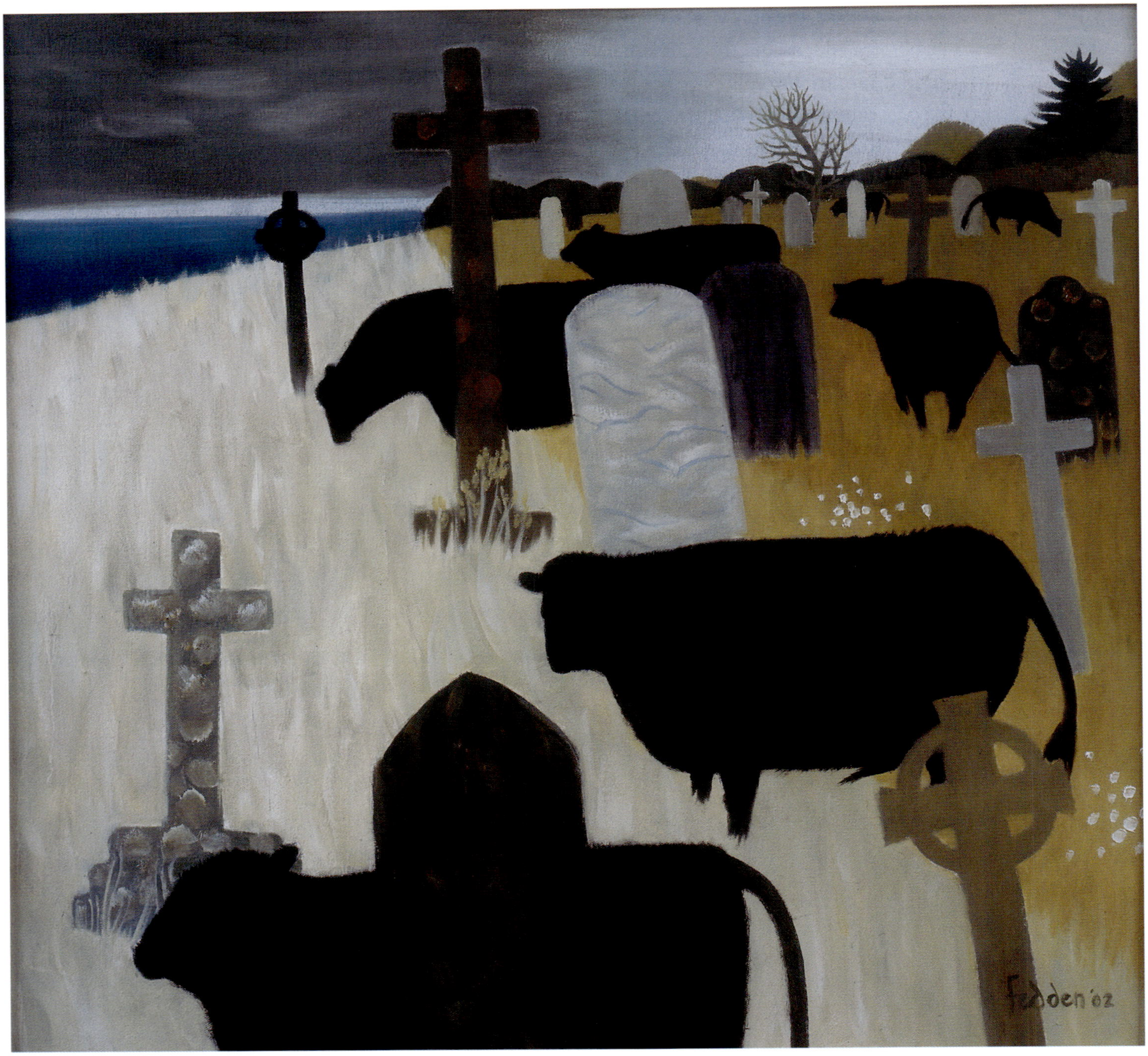

9
Cows in the Church Yard, 2002
Oil on canvas
62 x 66 cm (24½ x 26 in)
Private collection

Mary Fedden and Raleigh Trevelyan were visiting this Cornish graveyard filled with knee-high grass when it was invaded by cows. To them it was a field day. One of them knocked over a large gravestone. When Raleigh revisited the place months later, the stone was still fallen.

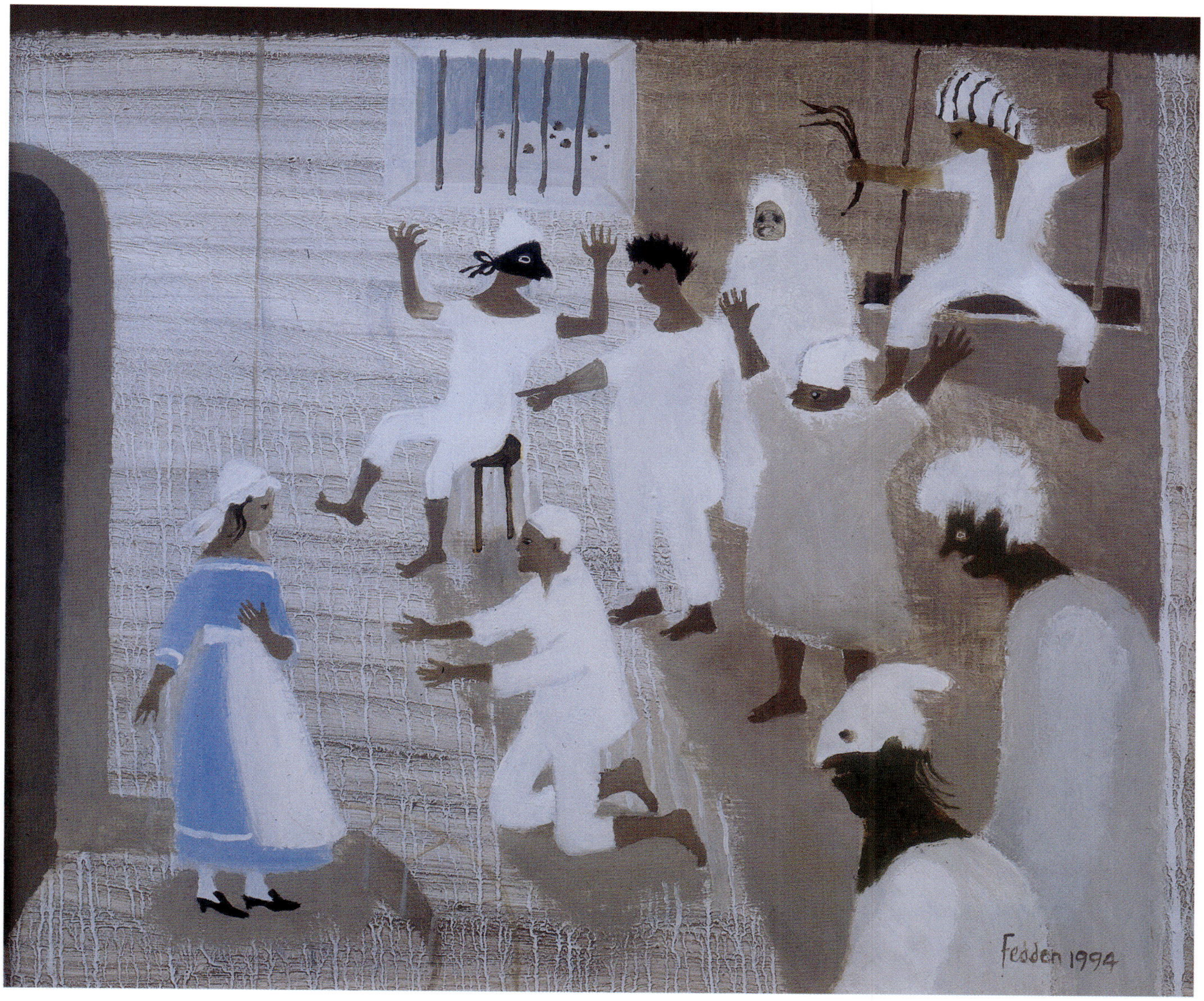

10
The Rake's Progress, 1994
Oil on board
49 x 59 cm (19¼ x 23¼ in)
Private collection

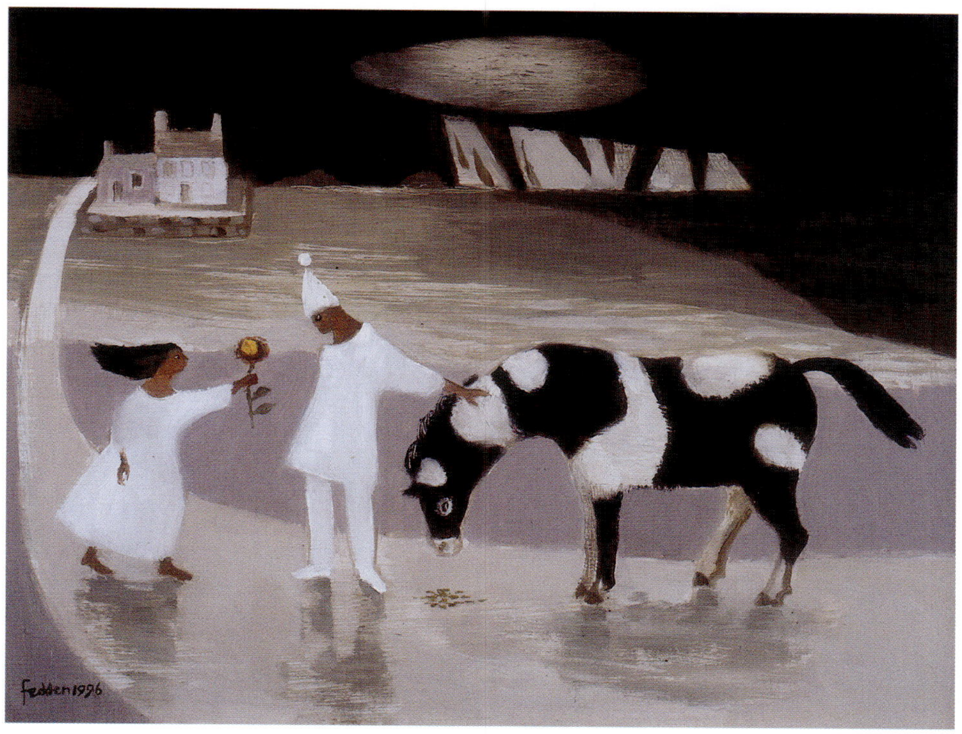

11
Love, 1996
Oil on board
30 x 40 cm (11¾ x 15¾ in)
Private collection

Fedden told Tom West, who owns this painting: 'She loves the man. The man loves the horse. The horse loves its food.'

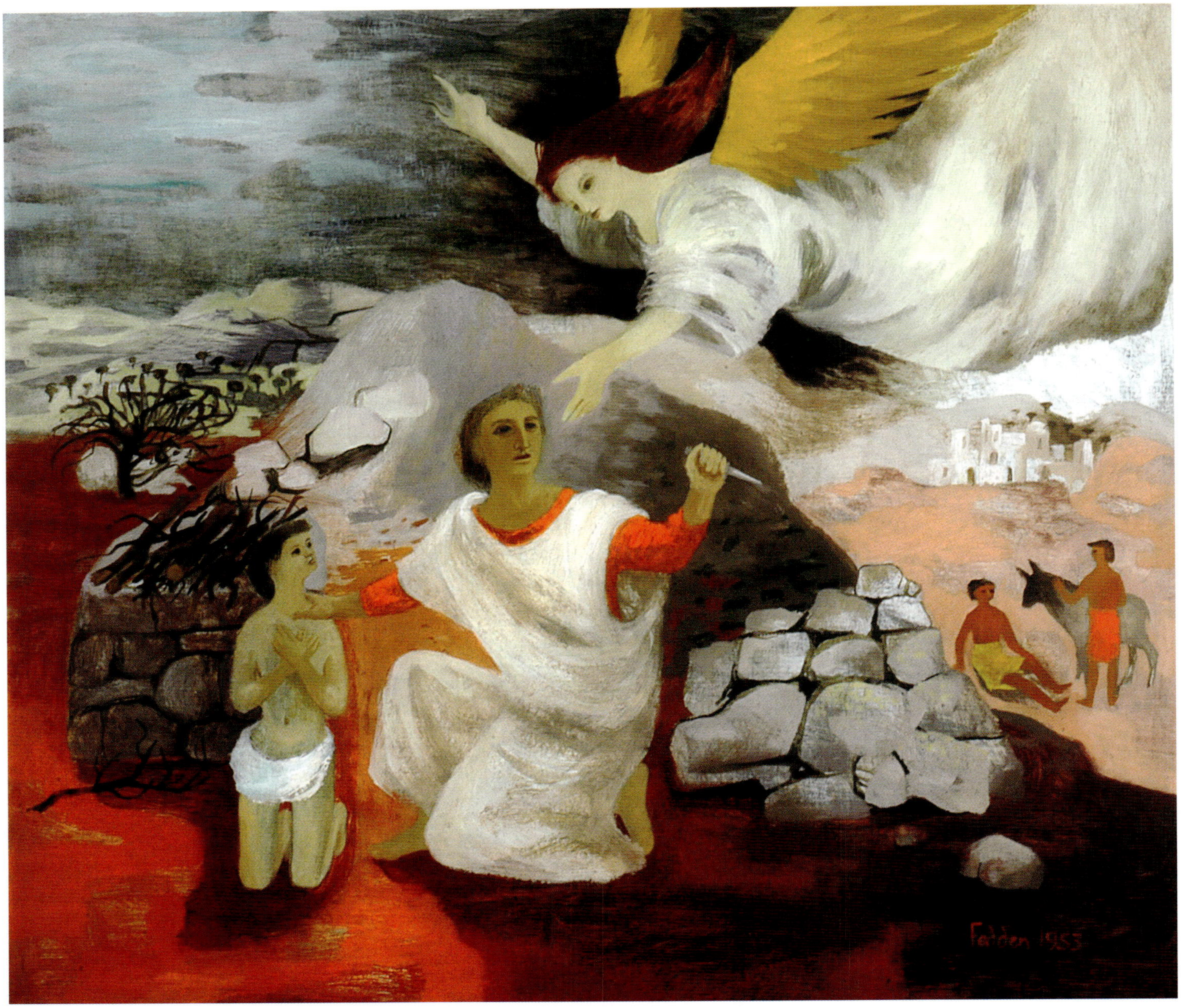

12
Abraham and Isaac, 1953
Oil on board
64 x 75 cm (25⅛ x 29½ in)
Art Consultancy Services

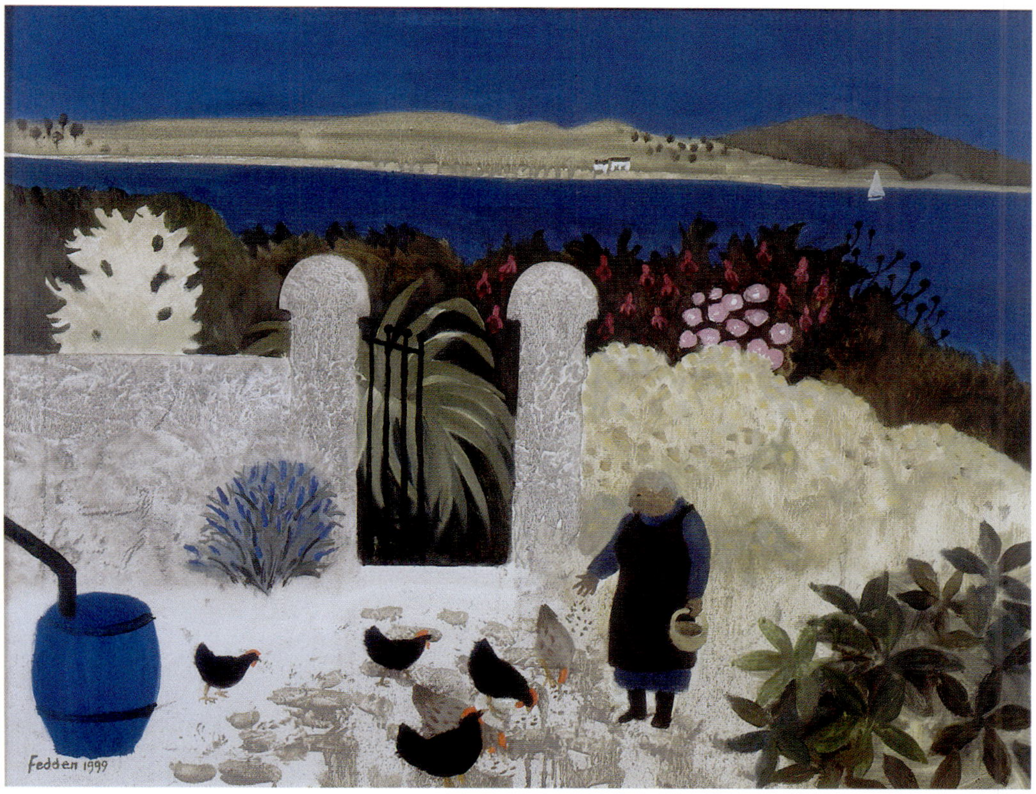

13
A Garden in West Cork, 1993
Oil on canvas
45.7 x 61 cm (18 x 24 in)
Private collection

14
Summertime, 1955
Oil on canvas
60 x 75 cm (23½ x 29½ in)
Private collection

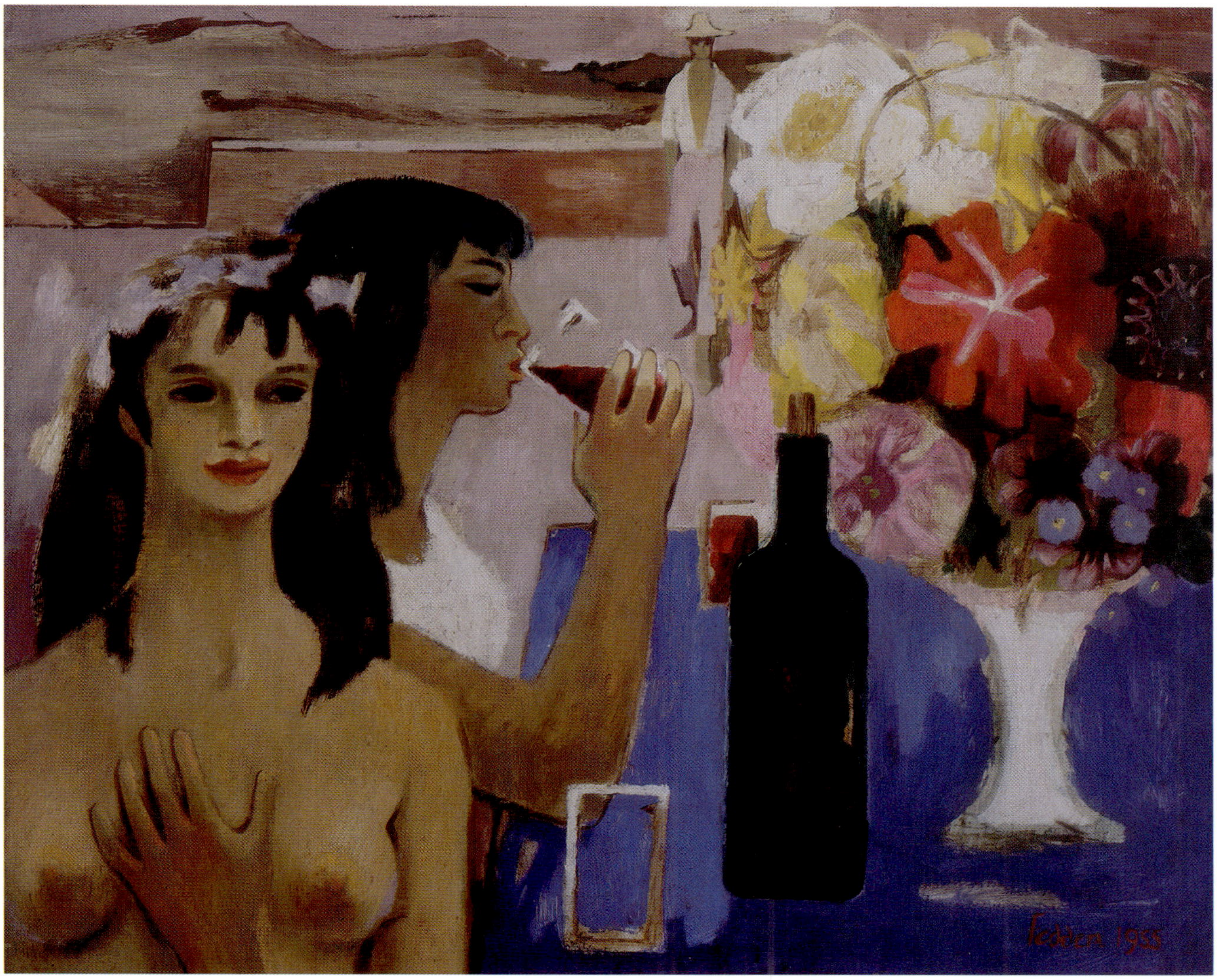

Fedden's self-appreciation and self-criticism balance out. She is sometimes obviously happy that a painting has worked. During one visit to her studio, she pointed out to me *Poppies* (2006) (Ill. 15), a striking painting of Iceland poppies, recently completed. It was larger than life and luminous, painted with absolute simplicity and clarity. It was a jubilant thing, and she was unaffectedly as pleased as punch with it. On the other hand, during a phone call one time, she mentioned just finishing a painting she had been working on. She knew it was finished because adding to it would belabour and ruin it. Yet finishing it did not necessarily mean that she was completely satisfied. 'Oh no!' she said quite sharply. 'If I was ever completely satisfied with anything, I'd probably give up painting!'

She is reluctant to sell certain paintings. She says that as she grows older, she finds herself increasingly wanting to hold on to the ones she loves. These are the pictures that have succeeded in some surprising way that she herself can't quite put her finger on. Something new has shown up in them. This will feed her subsequent pictures. With understatement – she often voices her concern that people might think her too pleased with herself – she will say of one of her break-through paintings, 'I think that one is *quite* good; don't you?'

Her popularity, though, is such that she often has to fight vigorously to stop someone buying a painting she really wants to keep – *Poppies* for instance. This is not easy because she is notorious among her friends for a distinct reluctance to say no.

Fedden's works, rather like bunches of good garden flowers in a vase or of grapes in a bowl, ask simply to be enjoyed. They are immediately and wholly appreciable – you might even say, rather aptly, *edible*. Food, after all, is one of her main subjects. This is in the long tradition of 'still-life' painting. (Ills 16 and 17)

The viewer of a Fedden painting is being presented with 'objects of desire'. You cannot actually eat her apples and melons, of course, and her grapes cannot be popped in the mouth. The viewer is enticed but not fed. He is not like the man described with such sensate vividness by John Keats in his 'Ode on Melancholy': '… whose strenuous tongue/Can burst Joy's grape against his palate fine'.[2] Nevertheless, both the eyes and the taste buds are excited. The inner orange cleft of a cut melon, the segmented cross section of a lemon, the stone still snug in the nest of a halved avocado, all elicit hungry anticipation, but the pleasure is finally visual. So her still lifes both conjure up and deny the delight of beautiful food. These paintings are a consumer culture on their own account. (Ills 18, 19 and 20)

Although she could not for a moment be labelled a 'Pop Artist', it cannot be entirely overlooked that when she taught painting at the Royal College of Art, among the students were some of the rising stars of the late 1950s and early 1960s who rightly or wrongly came to be identified with Pop Art: David Hockney and Patrick Caulfield, for example. Today she states categorically that she learnt as much from them as they did from her.

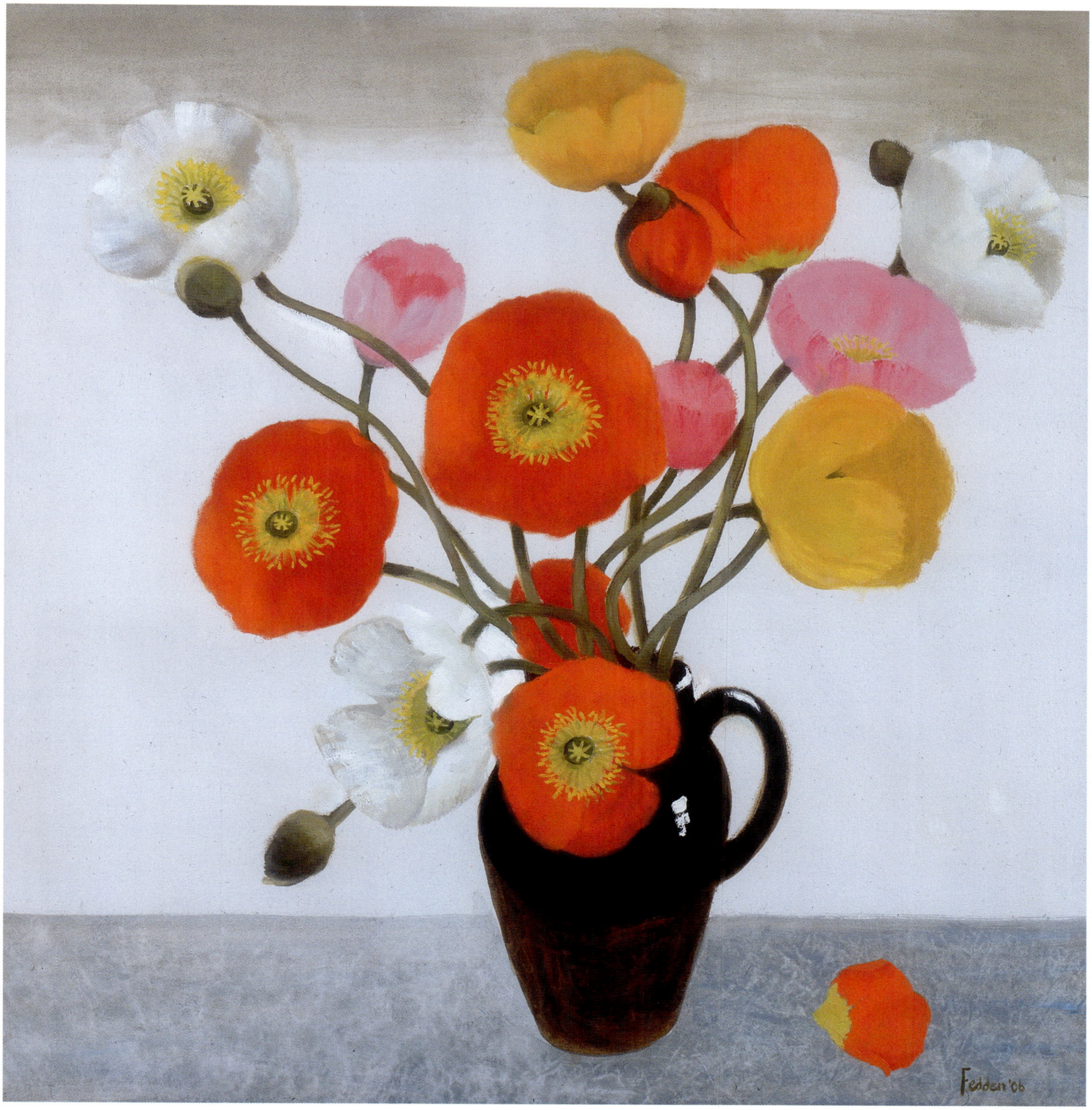

15
Poppies, 2006
Oil on canvas
79.5 x 79.5 cm (31¼ x 31¼ in)
Credit: The Artist

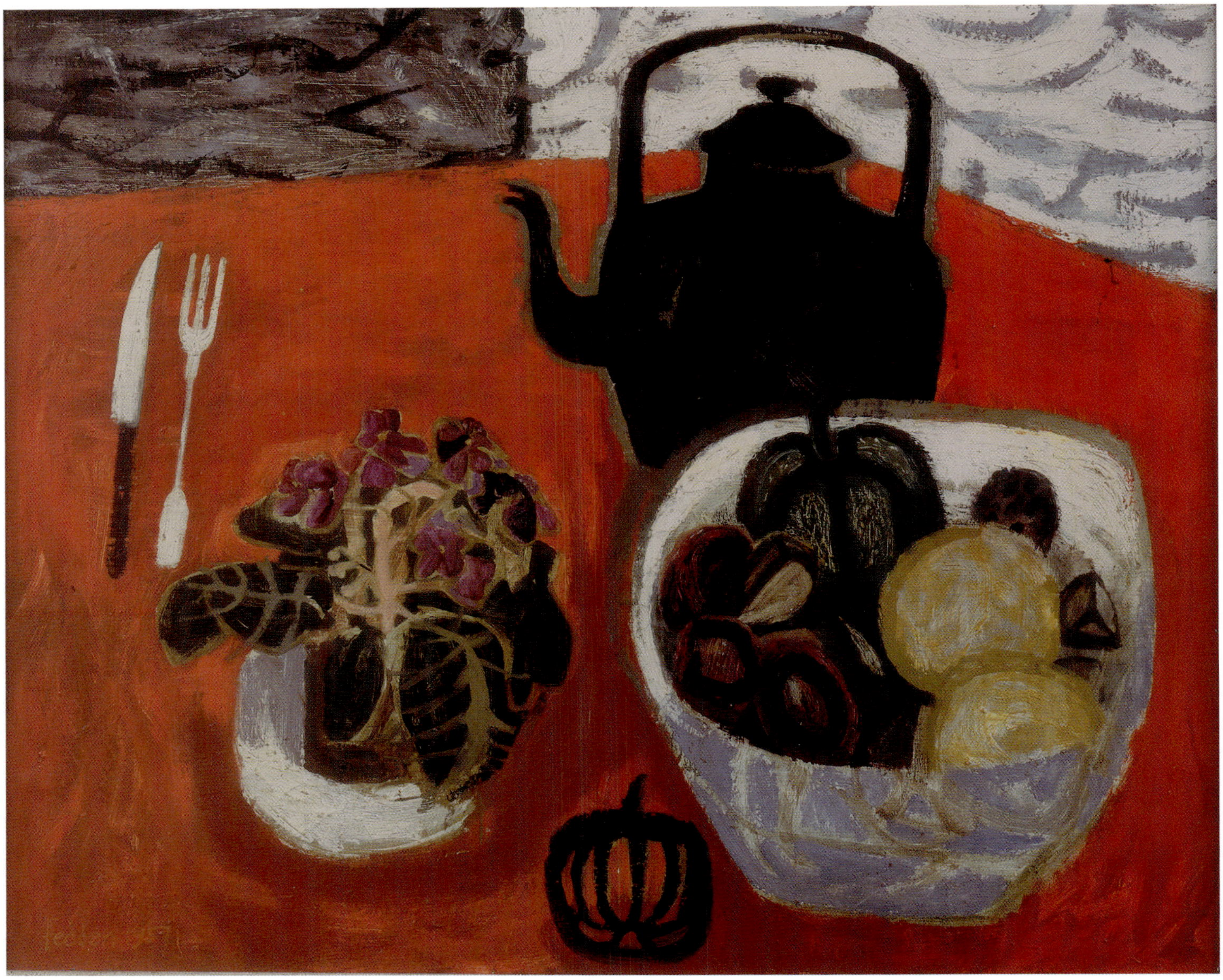

16
The Red Table, 1957
Oil on canvas
60 x 75.2 cm (23⅝ x 29⅝ in)
Private collection

17 (opposite)
Lunch in Sardinia, 1956
Oil on canvas
75.3 x 60.5 cm (29⅝ x 23¾ in)
Private collection

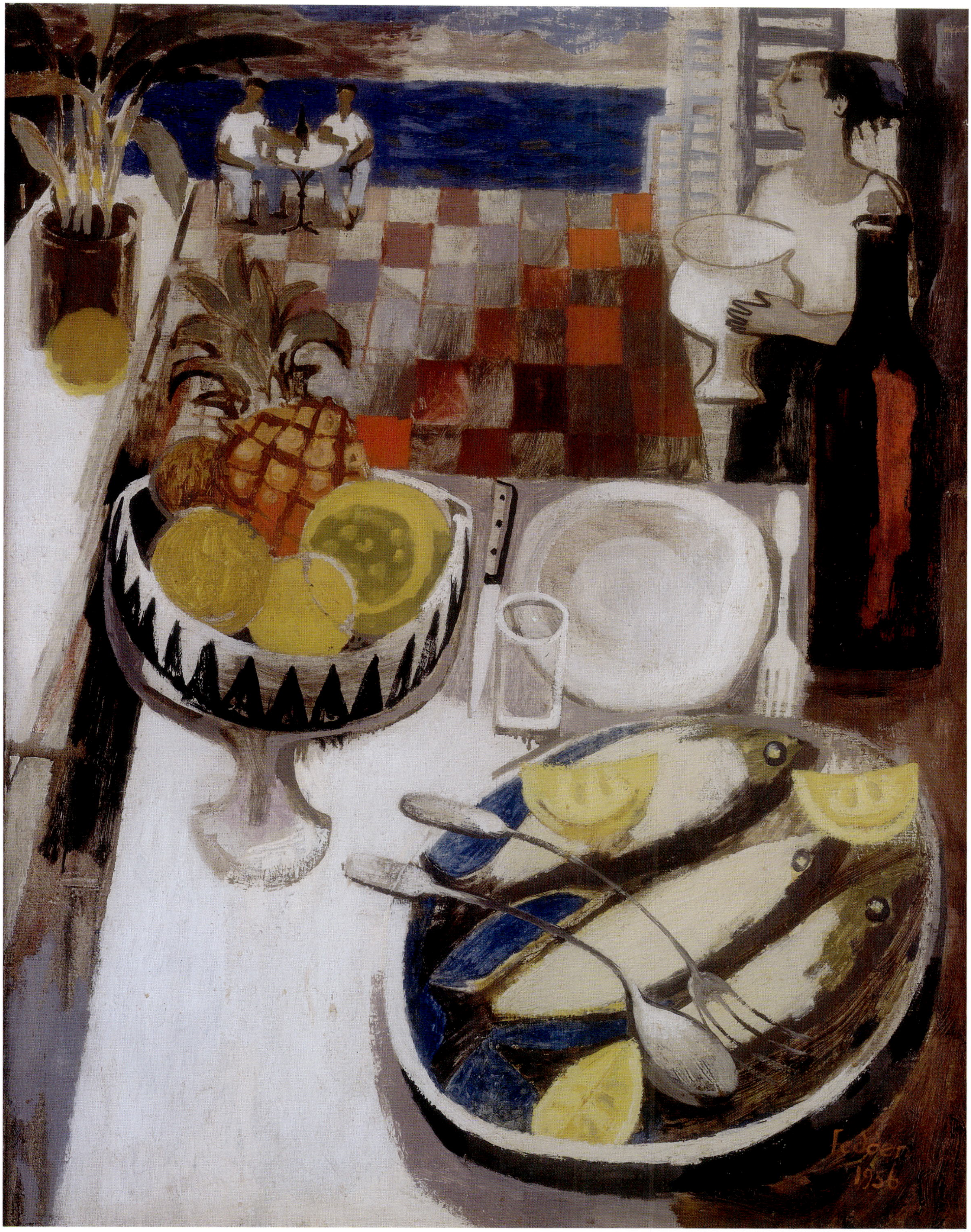
1956

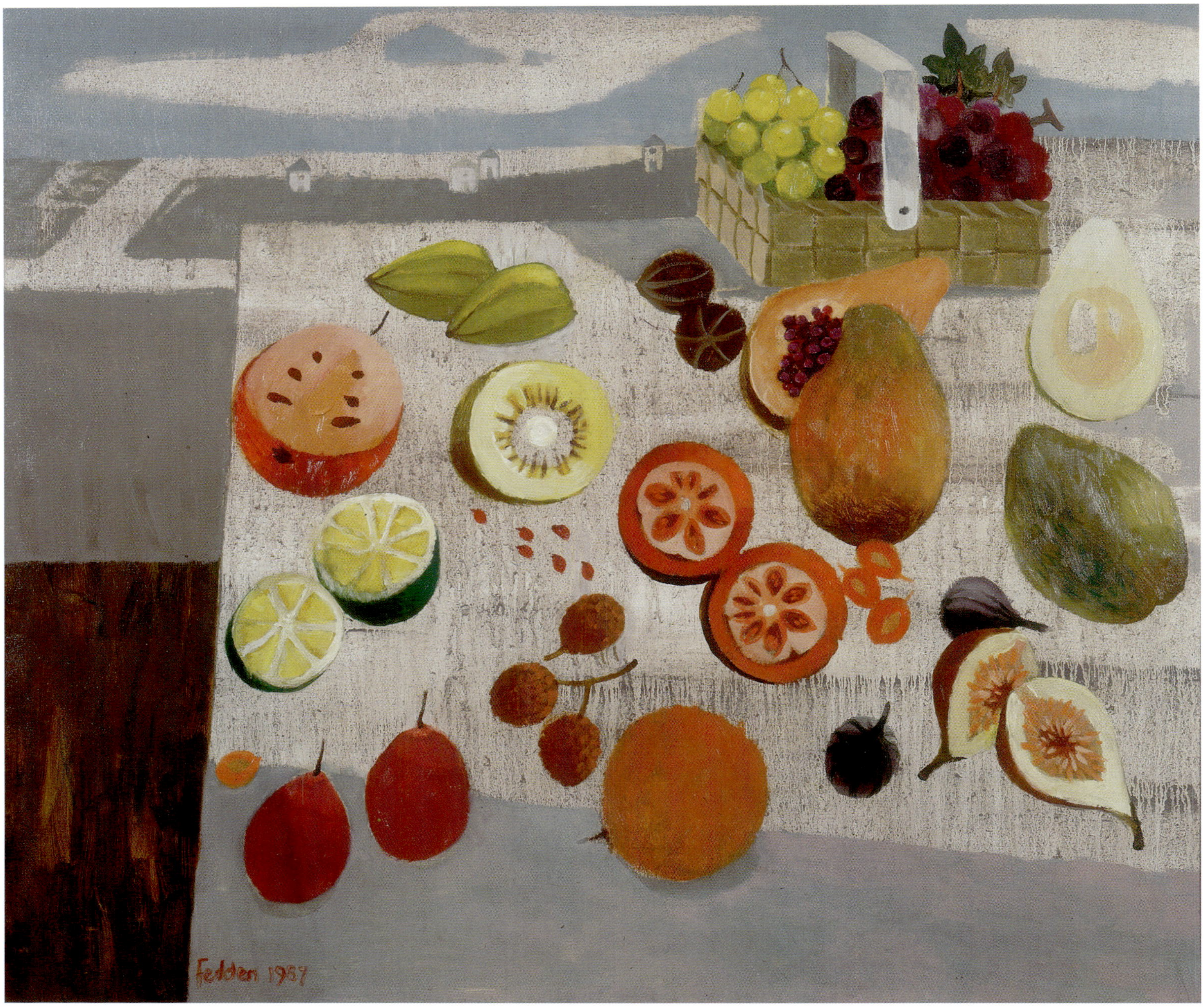

18
Tropical Fruit, 1989
Oil on canvas
76.2 x 91.5 cm (30 x 36 in)
Private collection

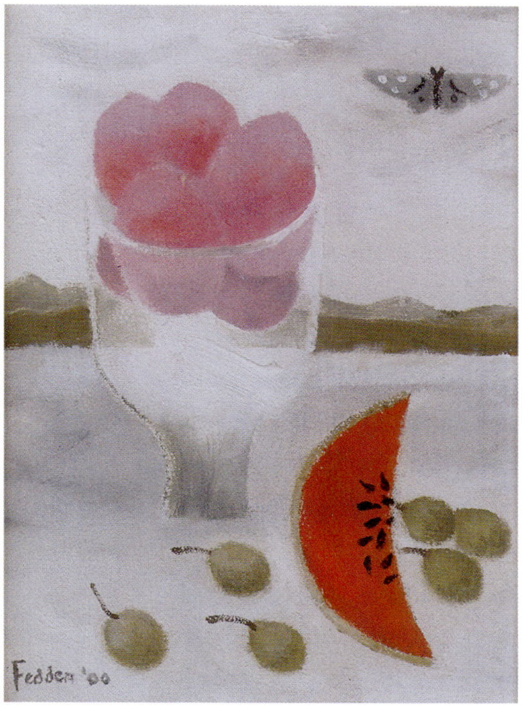

19
Melon, 2000
Oil on board
23.9 x 18.2 cm (9⅜ x 7⅛ in)
Private collection

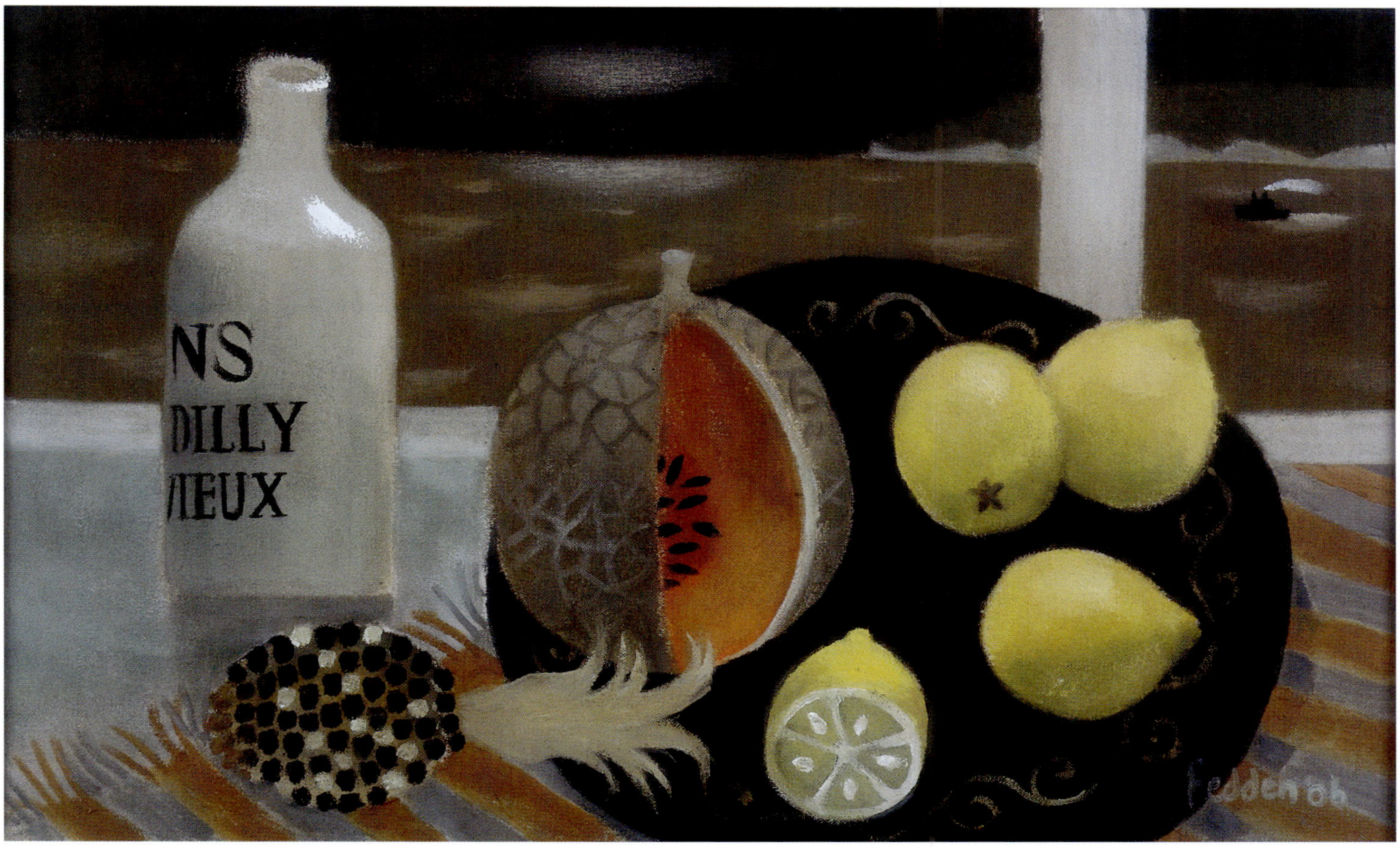

20
The Brown Sea, 2006
Oil on canvas
29.5 x 49.8 cm (11⅝ x 19¼ in)
Private collection

Caulfield's still-life images are precise and calculated. They appear to exist in a cool netherworld of debased pictorial clichés, but they subtly redeem these clichés. Feelings are somehow contained by his hard edges. Fedden likes Caulfield's work, but she now criticises her own for being 'hard-edged', virtually against her wishes. She does delineate her domestic objects with exactness – but never with the apparent impersonality of Caulfield. She brings to her objects, which some may find merely banal, a humorous affection. From Hockney, much admired, she gleaned a freedom of attitude to the whole business of being a painter but, stylistically, they have nothing in common.

Pop Art simultaneously parodied and celebrated the images and objects of consumerism. Fedden's imagery is of the celebratory kind. It is surprising that more of her pictures have not been adopted by the advertising world, though one was used to promote 'French Country Holidays'. Glyndebourne Opera House, with which she has a long and friendly association, recognises a stylish connection between her work and the high culture of *Così fan tutte* and summer-garden picnics: Glyndebourne paper napkins are printed with a Fedden painting *of* a picnic. The '*fêtes champêtres*' of Jean-Antoine Watteau find here an unpretentious, modern equivalent. In another continuation of still-life tradition, bottles of wine, gin, beer and cider frequent her pictures: objects of desire! (Ills 21–25)

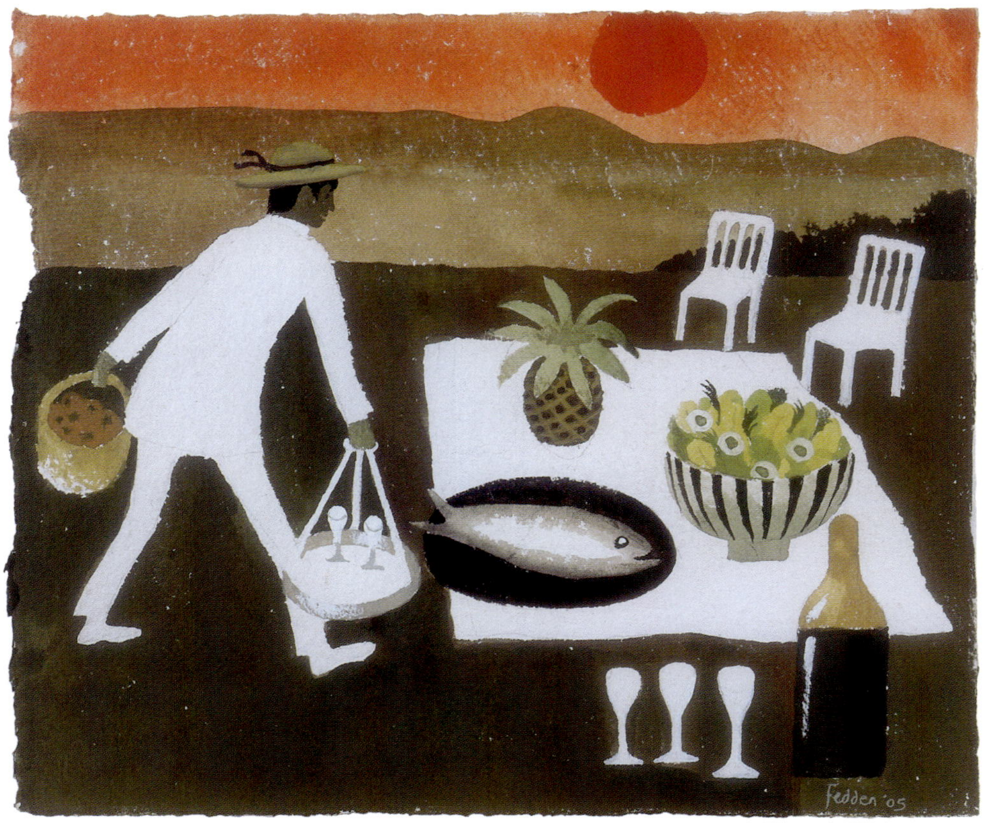

21 (left)
The Aegean Tray, 2005
Gouache
23.2 x 28.5 cm (9⅛ x 11¼ in)
Private collection

22 (opposite)
Lamplight, 1990
Oil on canvas
90 x 75.2 cm (35⅜ x 29⅝ in)
The Arts Club, London

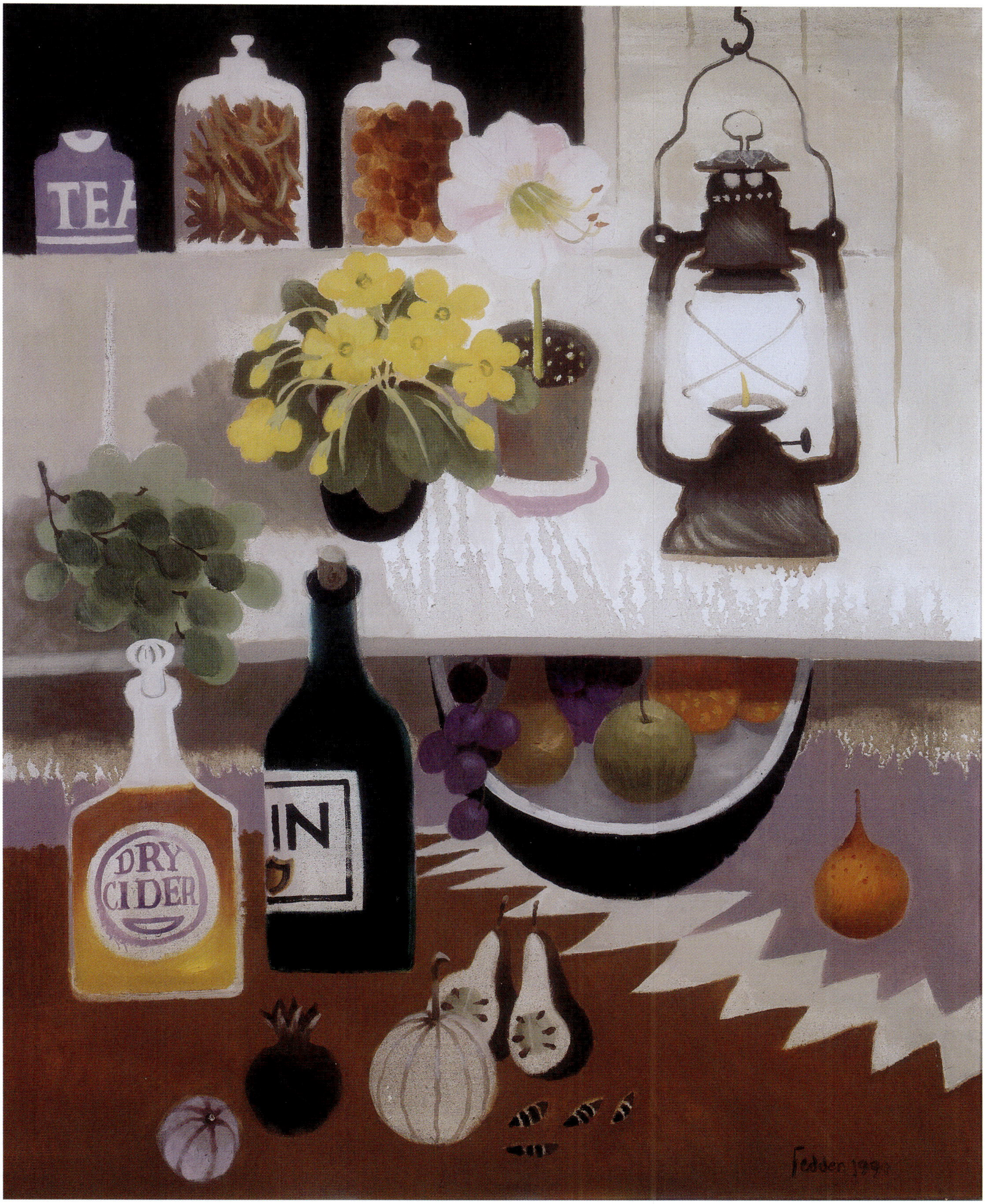
TEA
DRY CIDER
IN
Fedden

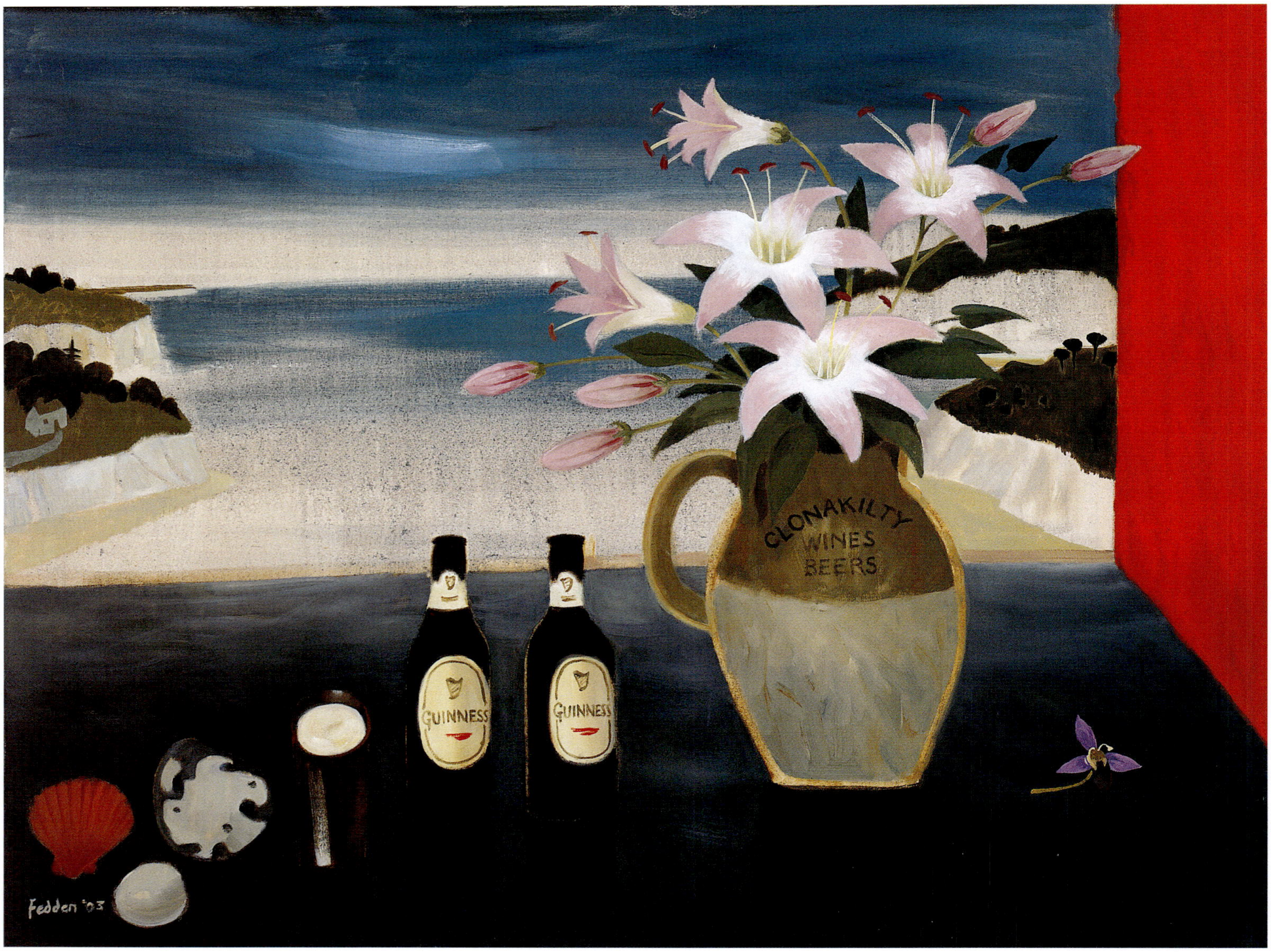

23
Casey's Bar, 2003
Oil on canvas
89.5 x 120 cm (35¼ x 47¼ in)
Private collection

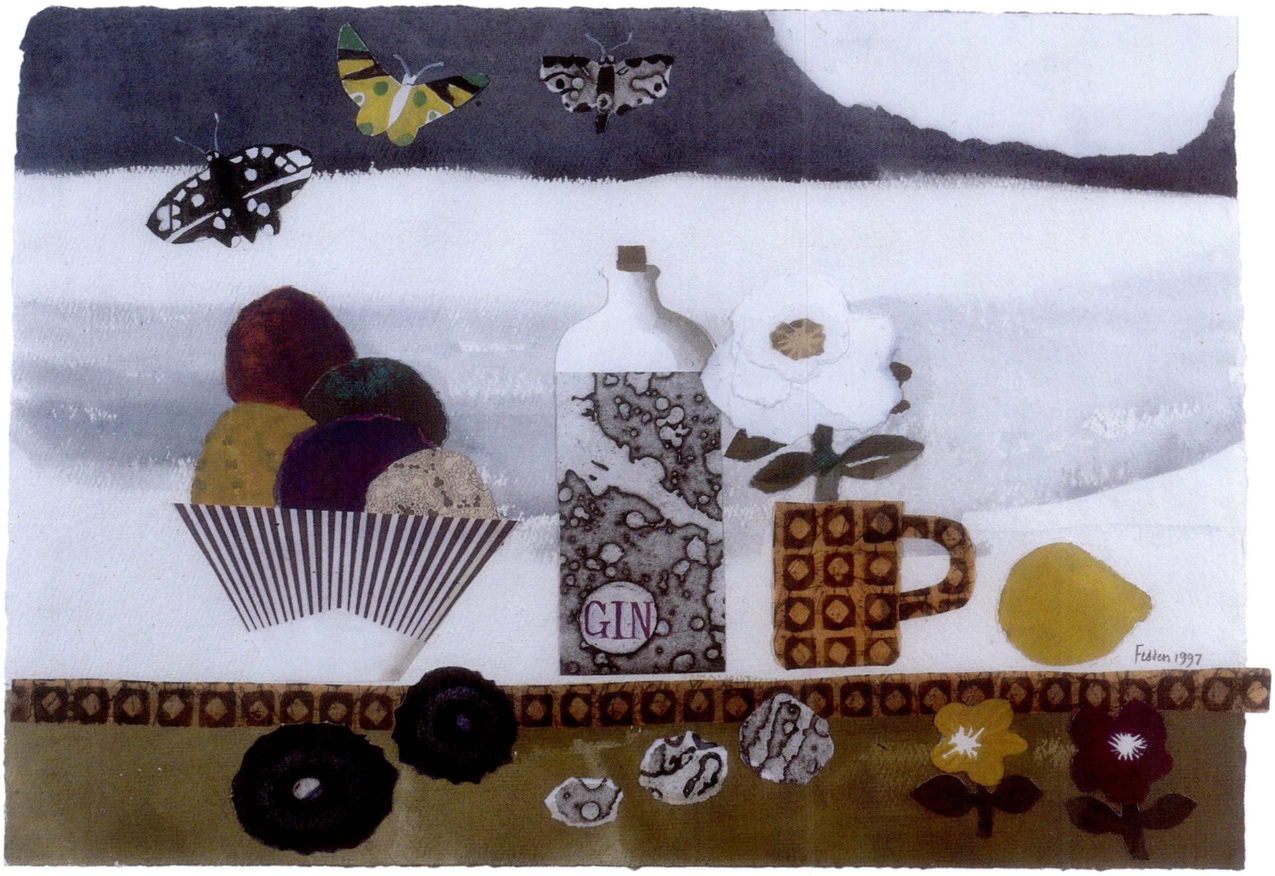

24
The Gin Bottle, 1997
Collage and gouache
39.7 x 56.8 cm ($15\frac{5}{8}$ x $22\frac{3}{8}$ in)
Private collection

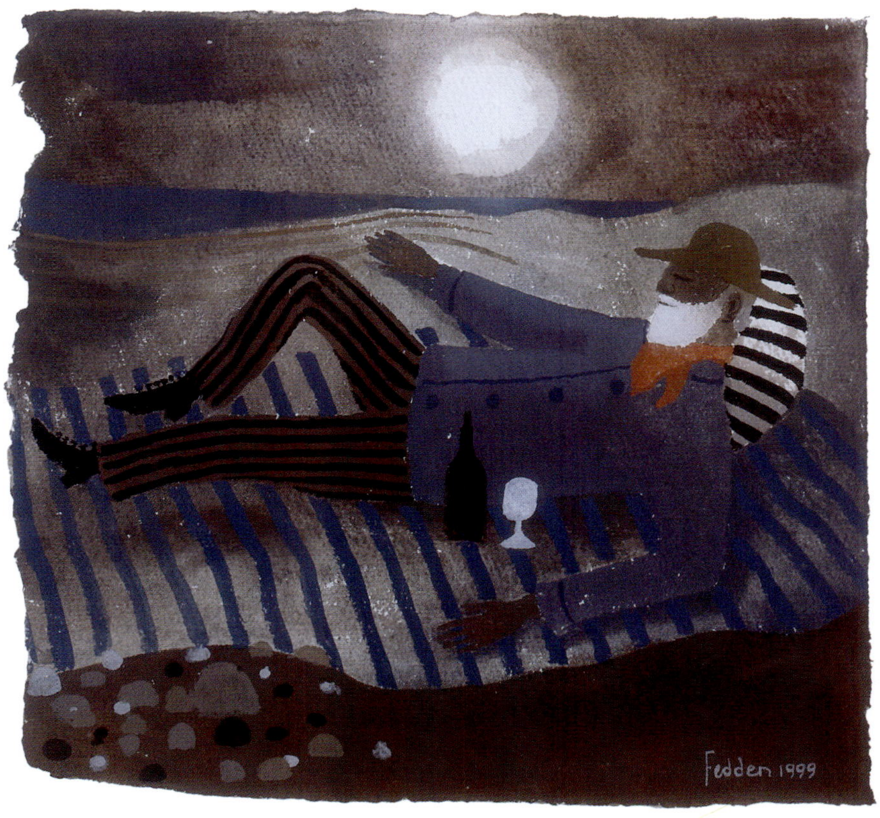

25
Sleeping on the Shore, 1999
Gouache
26.1 x 28.8 cm ($10\frac{1}{4}$ x $11\frac{3}{8}$ in)
Private collection

This phrase, *Objects of Desire*, was the title of an exhibition staged in New York and London in 1997–8, examining the 'modern still life'. Fedden, an accomplished still-life painter for some five decades by then, would have been an appropriate inclusion. For whatever reason, she was not represented. Indeed, her name rarely crops up in exhibition surveys or histories of twentieth-century British painting. Reputation is an impenetrably mysterious issue, and the art world busily and endlessly pigeonholes, espouses or ignores artists. Popularity achieved outside or beyond the reach of the curatorial community may even work subtly against an artist. G.K. Chesterton once ironically touched on this paradox: 'By a curious confusion, many modern critics [or curators] have passed from the proposition that a masterpiece may be unpopular to the other proposition that unless it is unpopular it cannot be a masterpiece.'[13]

If Mary Fedden is to be classed as now decidedly 'popular', her art-world reputation may arguably need to catch up. The Tate has been a beneficiary of gifts from her but has hardly rushed, on its own initiative, to add her works to its collection. A good selection of her prints is the honourable exception. She is represented in a number of public collections across Britain (Ills 26 and 27) but, in recent years, the charts she has shot up have not been dictated by museum taste.

26 (oppcsite)
Girl in a Brown Hat, 1958–9
Oil on canvas
110 x 90 cm (43¼ x 35½ in)
Reading Foundation for Art Collection, Reading Museum Service

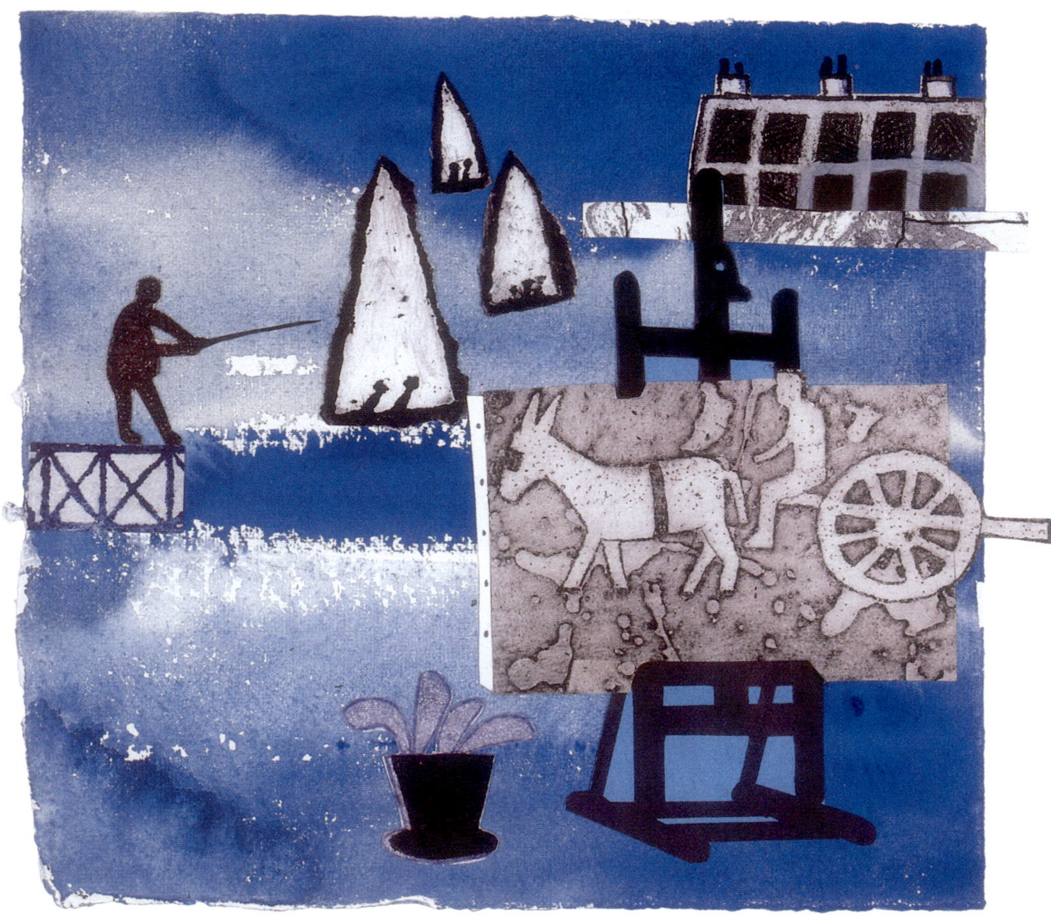

27
The Easel, c.1990
Collage and gouache
25.4 x 35.5 cm (10 x 14 in)
Tullie House Museum and Art Gallery, Carlisle

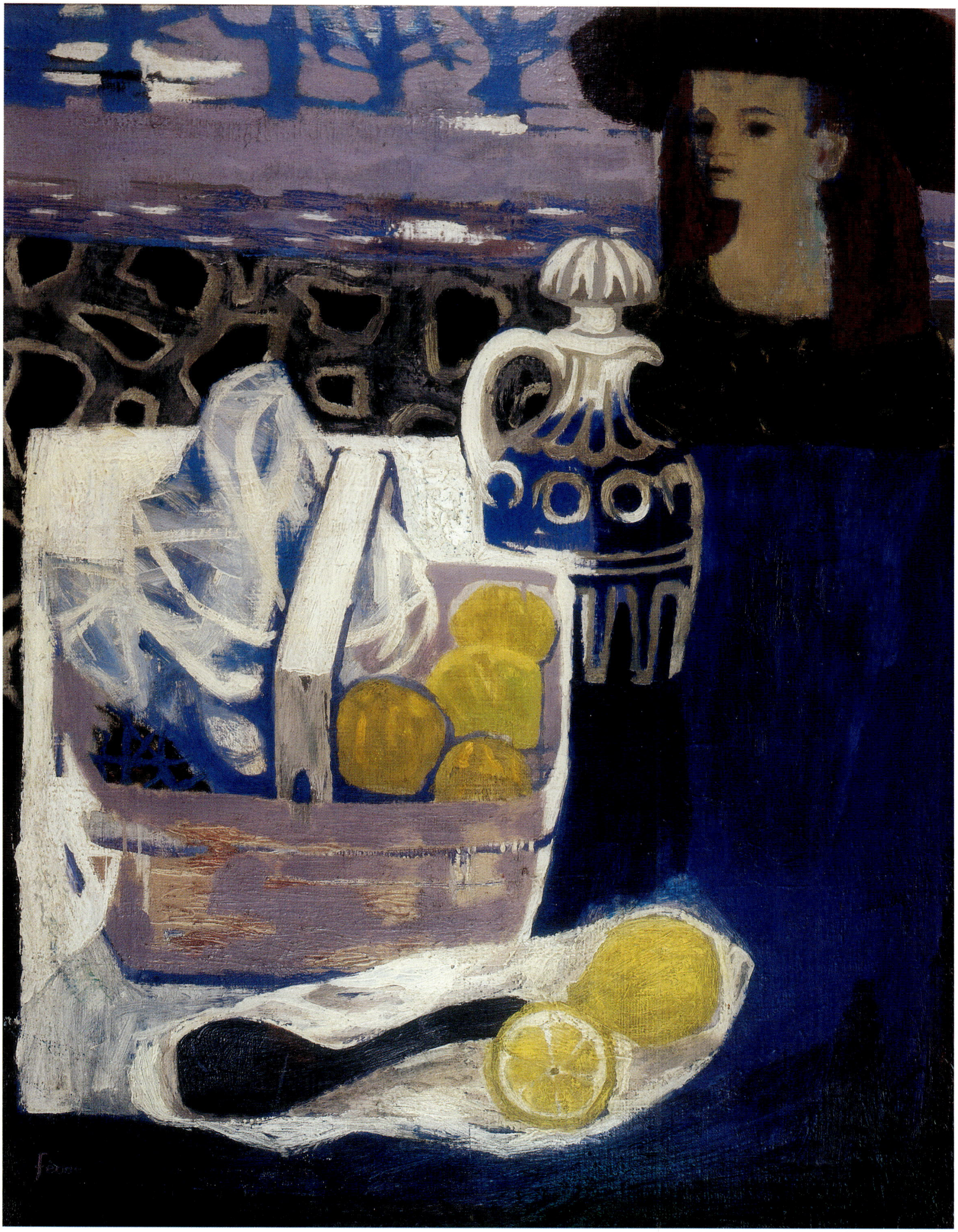

Her ubiquity on the internet (not a technology with which she has any contact herself) is remarkable. This is partly the result of her prolific outpouring of work, but also evidence of her saleability – a kind of Fedden diaspora or bandwagon. Its main cause is surely her determination not to be monopolised by a single gallery or dealer. Compare her presence on the internet with that of, say, Mary Newcomb (an artist she greatly admires) and it tells the story. Newcomb has been very successfully and almost exclusively represented by only one London gallery. Fedden's spread has helped her to be available not just in London but all over provincial England. The prices attached to her works are escalating dramatically at auction. Even older, forgotten pictures are resurfacing and now fetching respectable prices as their owners bequeath or hand them down to younger family members who need injections of cash more than they want Feddens on their walls. A new generation of Fedden fans are, however, at the ready. These reappearing works are making it possible to get a much clearer and broader idea of Fedden's variousness and development. This development extends over many years, given her special capacity for longevity. Lately, dealers, scrupulous and unscrupulous, have also found her ever more saleable at ever higher prices.

Fedden herself has often voiced her distaste for this escalation, wanting people to own her works because they love them and not only because they can afford them. She defies this situation in her own way when she can – by asking very low prices – although this does lead to her being exploited sometimes. In fact, she has for many years sold virtually everything she produces (except the few she manages to keep) – paintings, drawings and collages – with most of them ending up in eager private hands. It's the high prices that are new.

Popularity is a nebulous thing, and one can only guess at some of its causes. Fedden's images have certainly found their way into many people's homes in the form of what she probably thinks of as spin-offs. The shop at the Royal Academy of Arts in London has evidently done a roaring trade in postcards and Christmas cards, calendars, mugs and jugs, even at one time a jigsaw, and reportedly will soon be marketing a 'throw' of a Fedden design. Such spin-offs have doubtless increased the breadth of her popularity but, by the same token, may well have suggested to some people a lack of commitment to the solemn intensity of high art. There is a silliness about such an assumption, though, when you consider that Constable has been used to sell chocolates, and museum shops do everything they can to increase revenue by selling Rembrandt postcards, Monet tea towels, or Mondrian tee-shirts.

Fedden is modest about her work. She does not make stupendous claims for it. It does not make great claims for itself. Perhaps this is partly because of her being English. Perhaps it is partly because, in the welter of self-promotion by shock tactics that typifies certain aspects of the art world today, apparently simple pictures of objects on a canvas look quiet and unexceptional. Yet this lack of pretension might also, subconsciously, have something to do with the history of still life. In past centuries, it was relegated by the art world to the lowest level in the hierarchy of painting genres (history painting was the highest). Still life was considered too close to the kitchen or to 'women's work' – not quite a 'politically correct' attitude today!

Maybe still lifes – and Fedden's in particular – do continue to explore the domestic and the ordinary, but they hold their own remarkably, speaking directly to people's shared experience. Fedden's still lifes strongly exemplify this directness and accessibility.

It isn't helpful that Fedden's paintings have not always been reproduced with absolute faithfulness, and she is particularly vulnerable to the flattening processes of less-than-perfect reproduction. The roughness and vigour of her brushwork, her sensitivity to surfaces, are too often lost completely – smoothed out – and this gives a wrong impression of her touch and uniqueness. It is a kind of shock when, after looking at reproductions of her work, you re-encounter the genuine article – a refreshing shock to realise how good she actually is, how much of a downright, honest-to-goodness *painter*. (Ills 28, 29 and 30)

28
Quinces (detail from Ill. 2, p.9), 1990

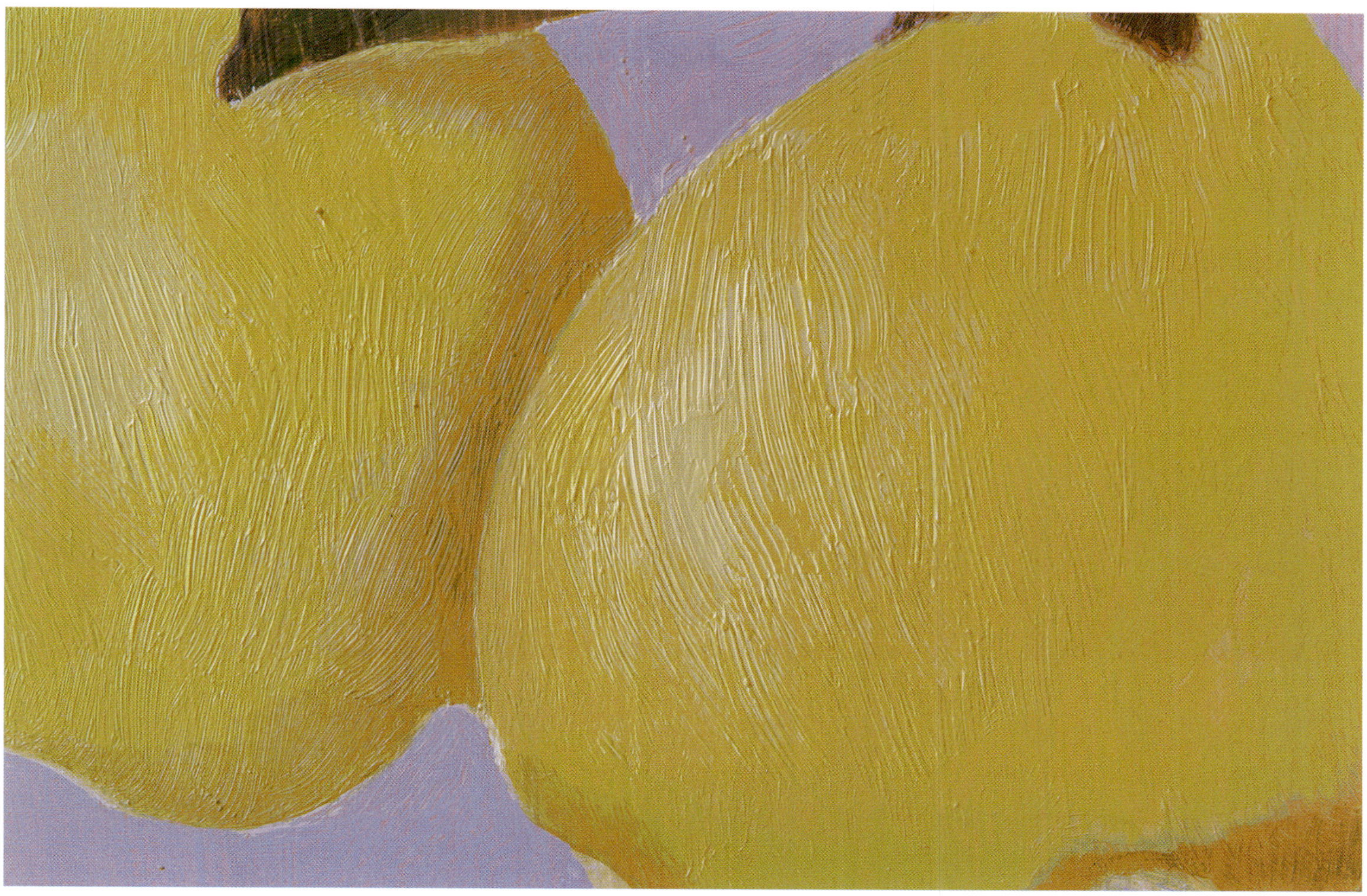

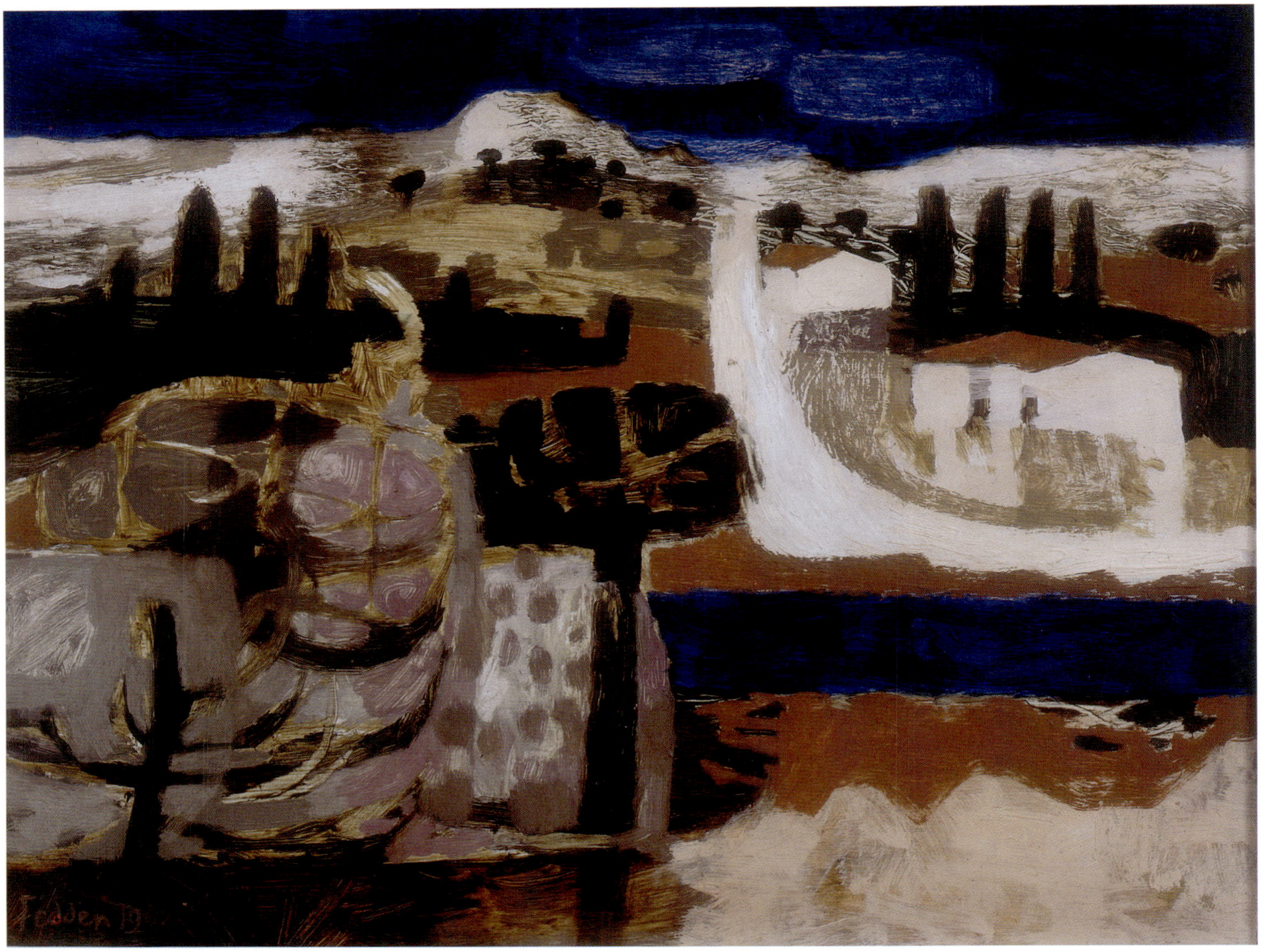

29
Landscape, 1962
Oil on canvas
44 x 58 cm (17¼ x 22⅞ in)
Private collection

30 (opposite)
Landscape (detail from Ill. 29), 1962

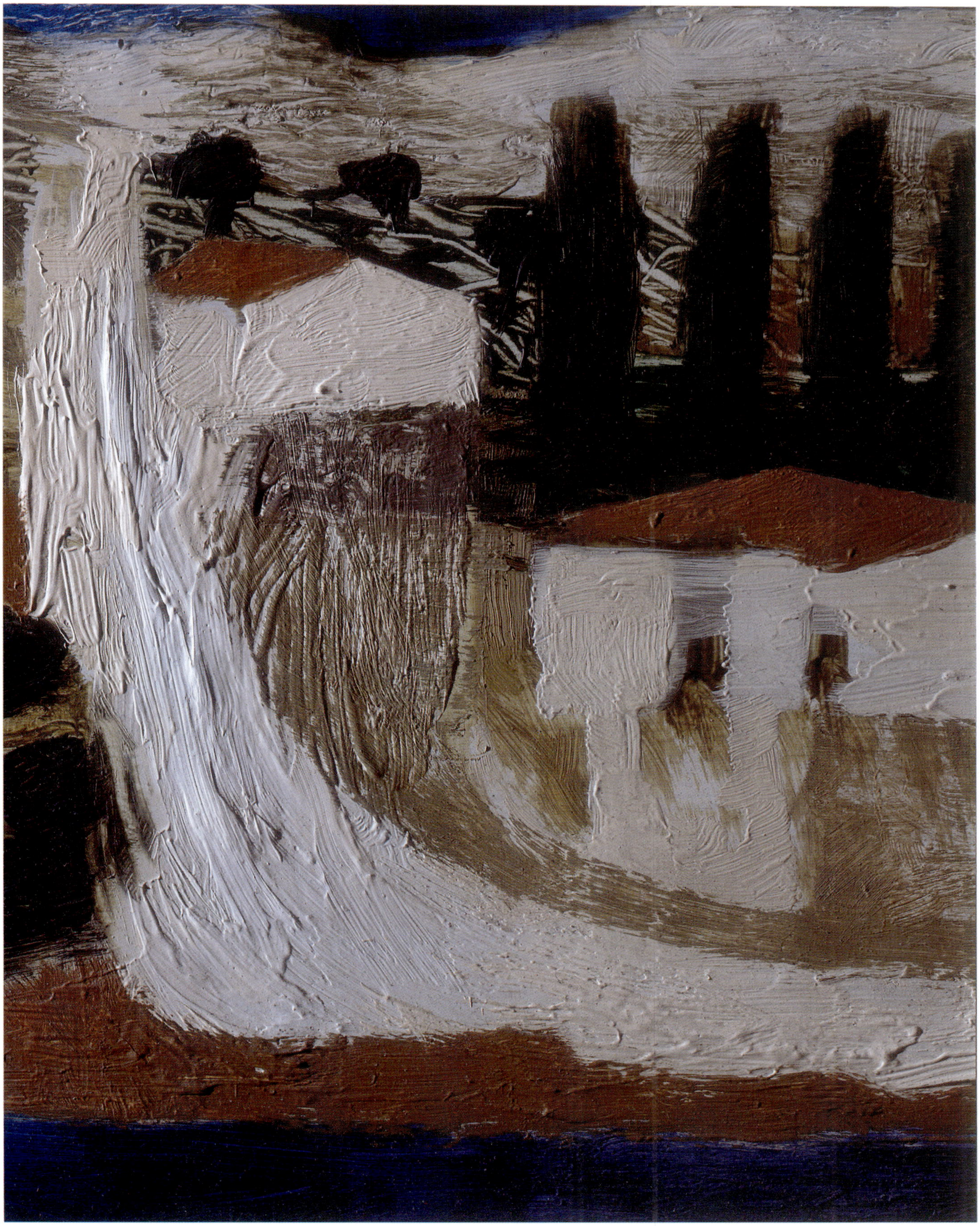

The composition of her paintings is also, for instance, crucial in its relationship to the edges of the canvas or paper. The intervals between objects and their surrounding spaces are integral to a painting (Ills 31–35). Unfortunately, it is not unknown for a card made from one of her pictures to be crudely trimmed and cropped to fit the format of the card. It could be argued that this hardly matters to someone buying a greetings card. Nevertheless, this treatment is actually an insensitive distortion. It is also surprisingly disrespectful if the cards are being sold in an art institution that presumably puts art first and commercialism second.

Motifs from her pictures are lifted to form new patterns – not *her* patterns – on sugar bowls or teapots. These artefacts can be tasteful, but their connection with

31
The Black Chair, 1996
Oil on canvas
48.8 x 59.2 cm (19¼ x 23¼ in)
Private collection

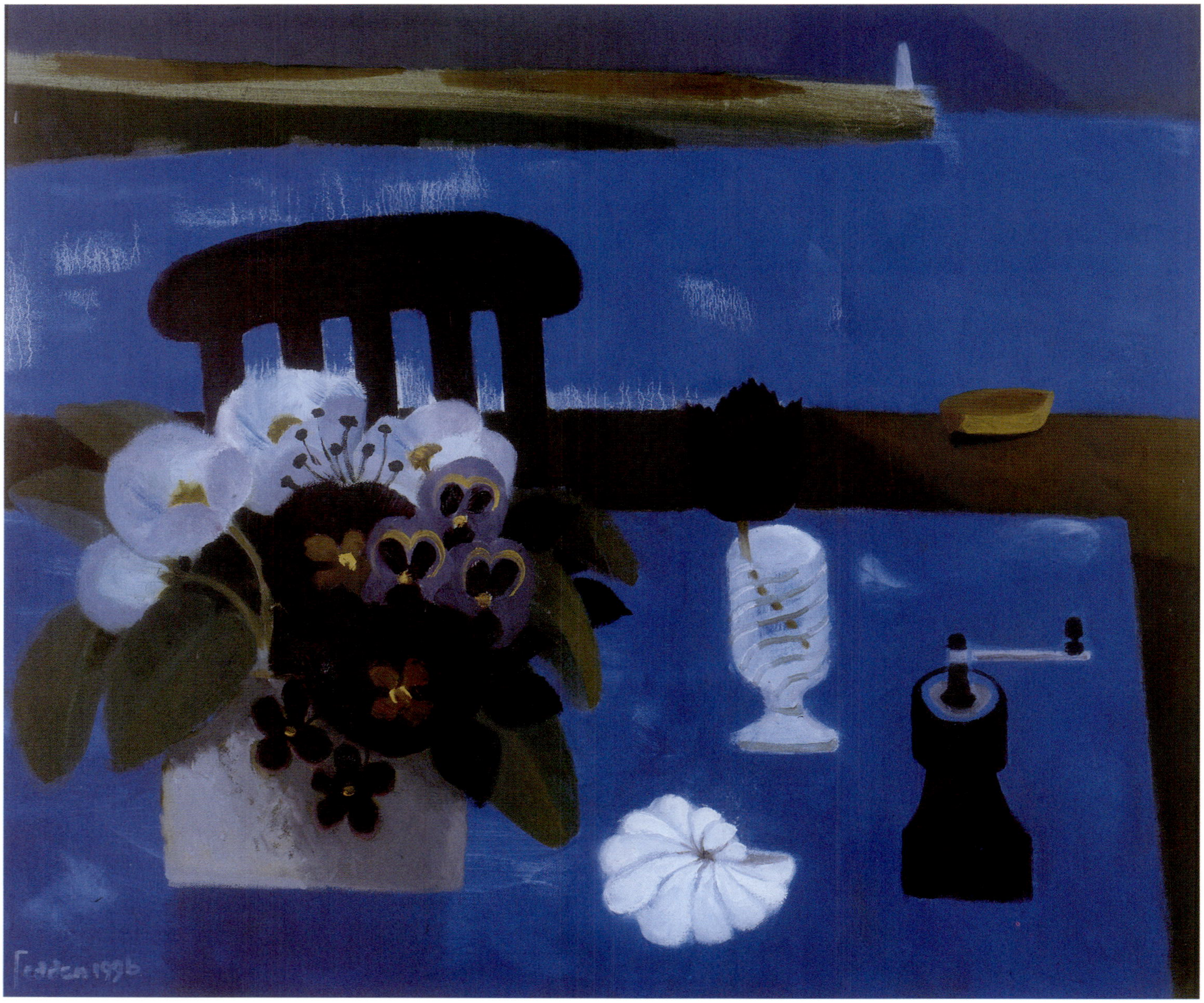

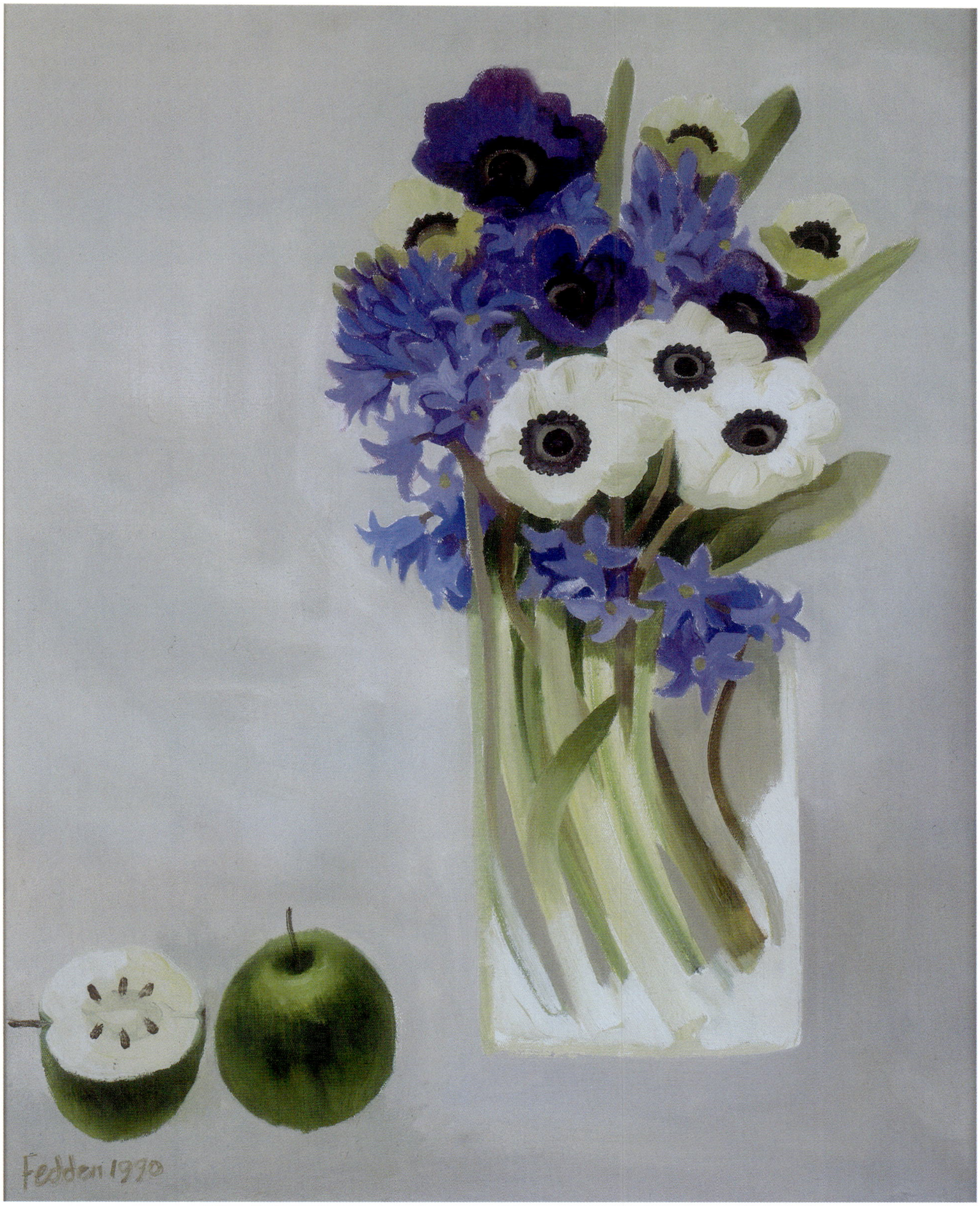

32
Anemones & Hyacinths, 1990
Oil on canvas
58.8 x 48.7 cm (23¼ x 19⅛ in)
Private collection

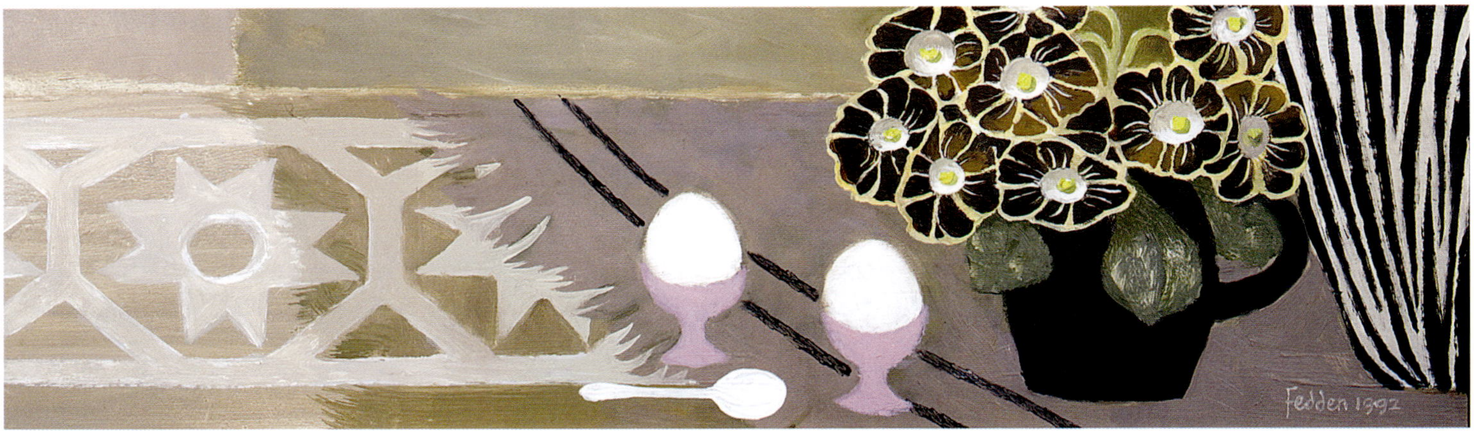

33
Still Life with Egg Cups, 1992
Oil on board
19 x 61 cm (7½ x 24 in)
Credit: Bill Clark

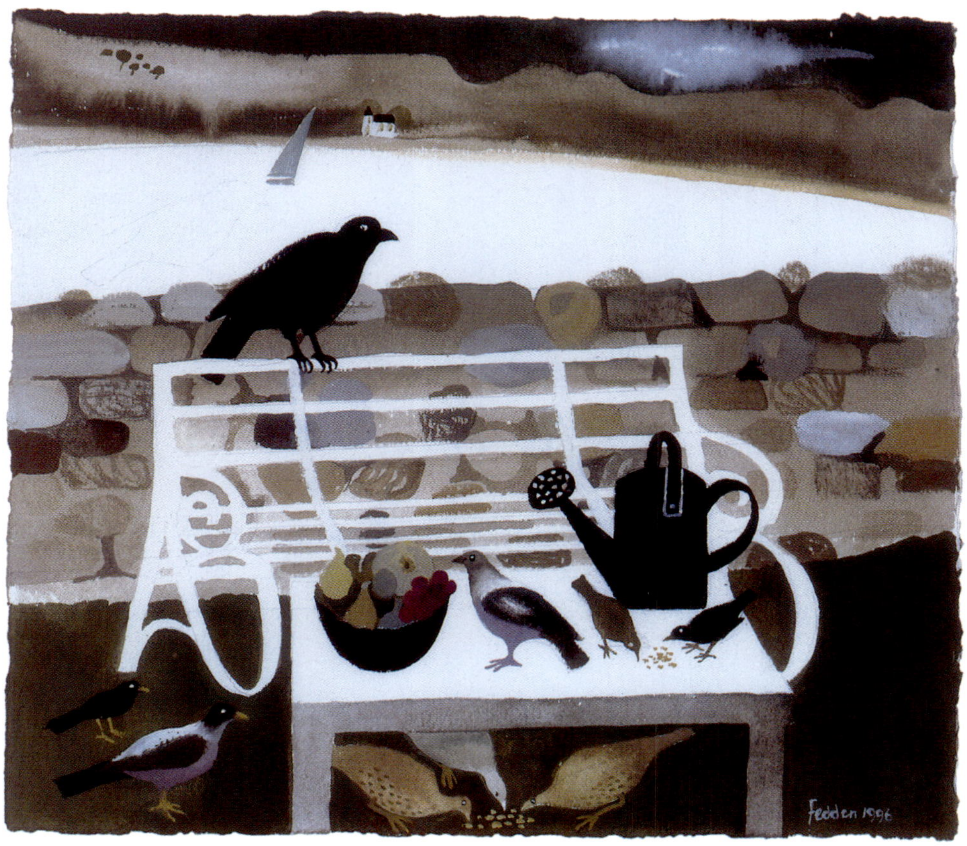

34
The Raven, 1996
Gouache
24 x 28 cm (9½ x 11 in)
Private collection

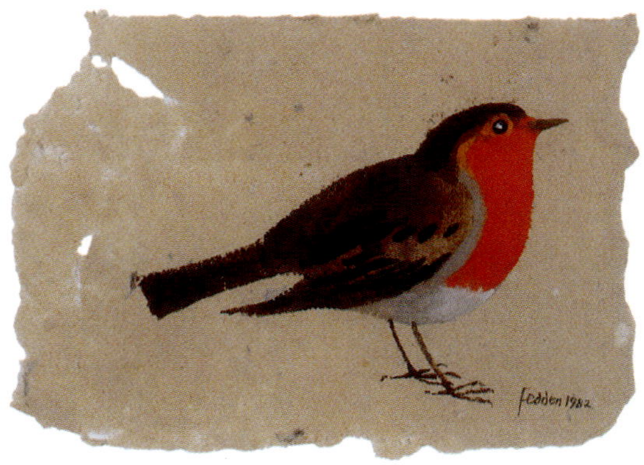

35
Robin, 1982
Gouache
10.6 x 15.1 cm (4⅛ x 6 in)
Private collection

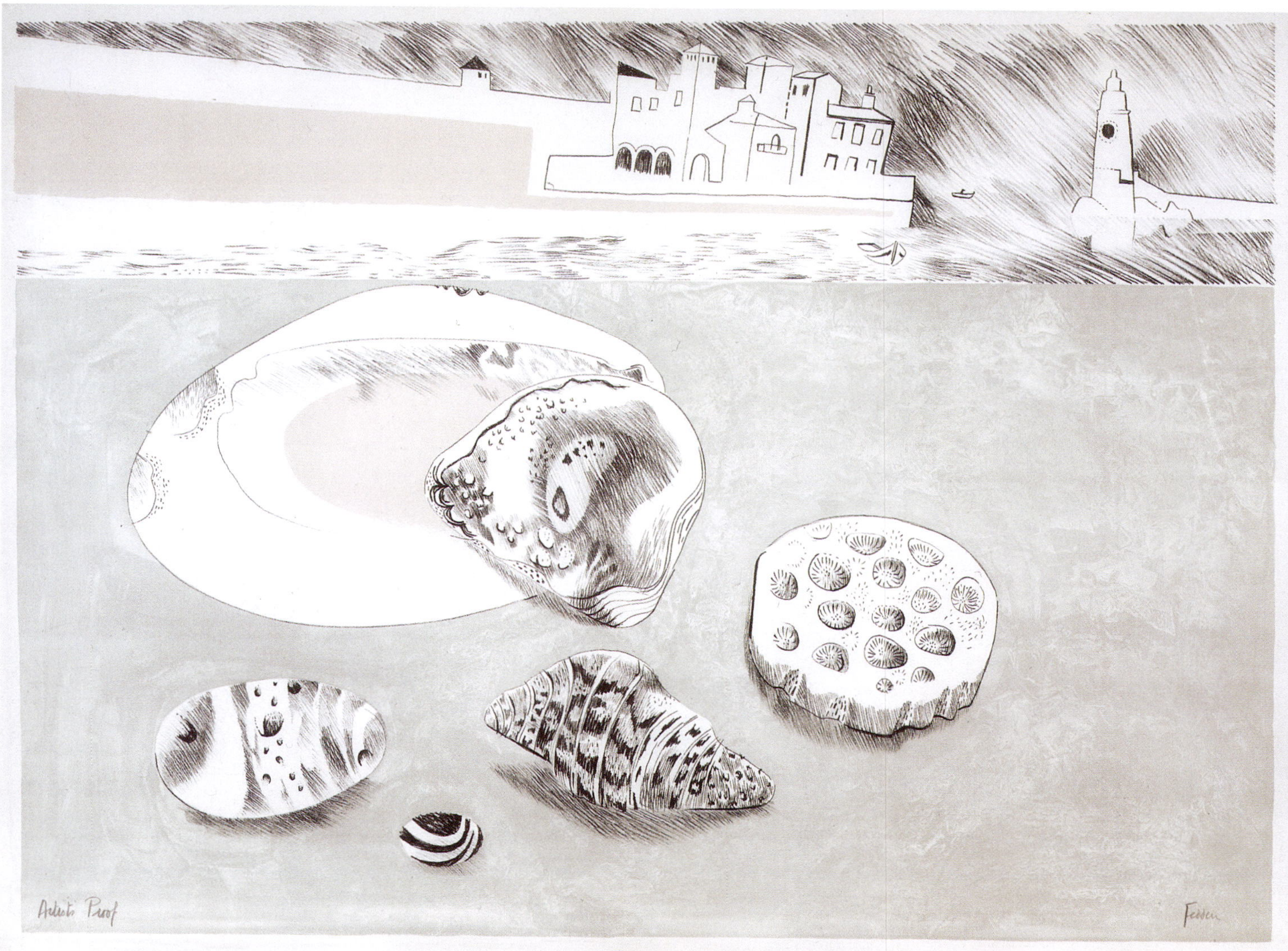

36
Shells and Pebbles, 1971
Lithograph
54.6 x 74.9 cm (21½ x 29½ in)
Credit: The Artist

Fedden's paintings – her art – is tenuous. And so it goes. It should be pointed out that such things are done with her permission (often for charitable purposes), if not her complete willingness, and perhaps she sees such peripherals as a legitimate way of making her art available to people who can't afford her originals. These peripherals have also extended her popularity.

She has made, or had made for her, some fine prints, mainly lithographs, yet even these she sees as a tangent (Ill. 36). Her main business is painting: 'I don't consider myself a printmaker at all.' She knows what she is talking about. Her husband Julian Trevelyan was definitely a hands-on, limited-edition printmaker

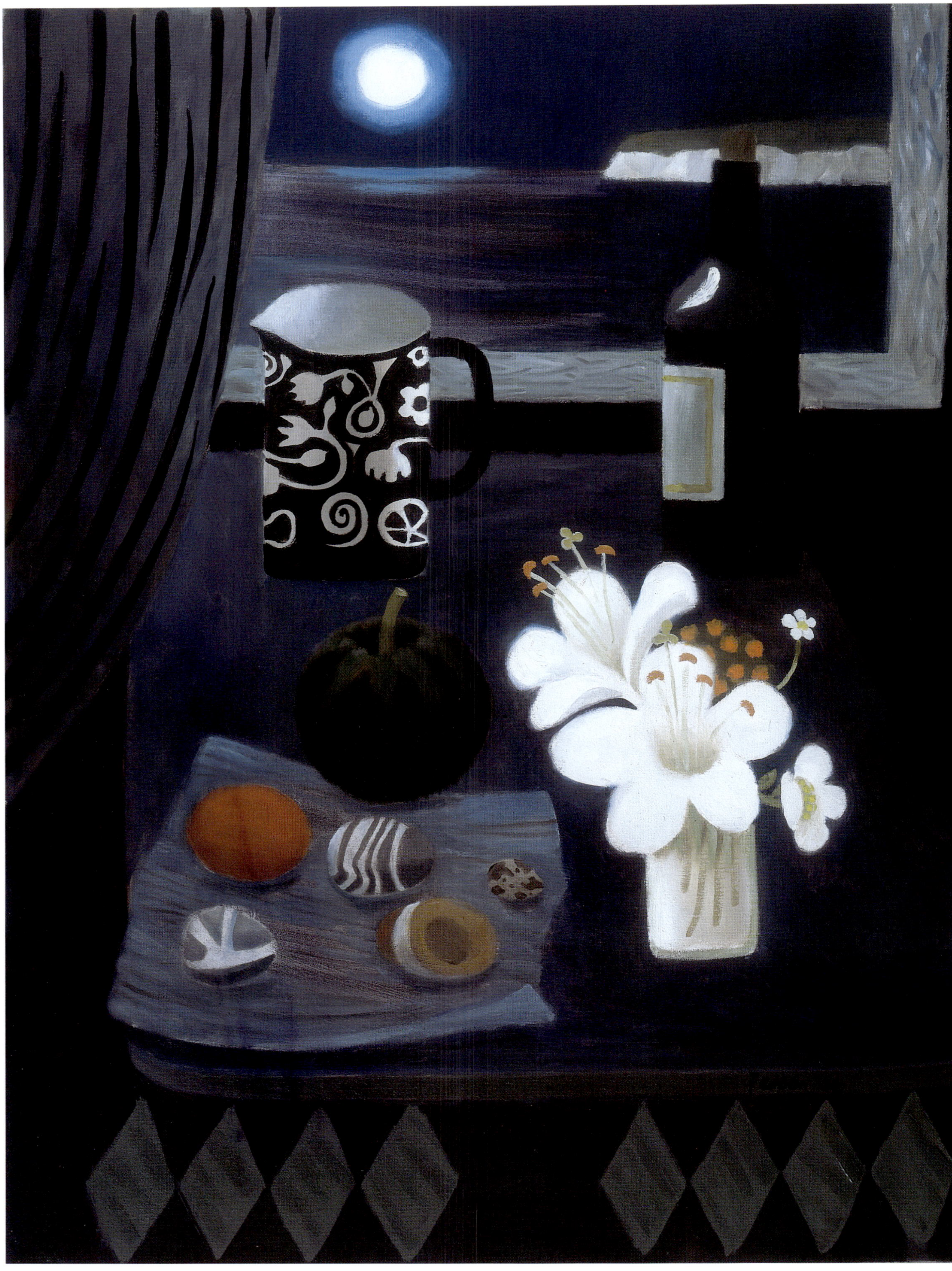

37 (opposite)
Irish Lilies, 2006
Oil on canvas
90 x 70 cm (35⅜ x 27½ in)
Private collection

(he was also a painter), and she is fully aware of the exigencies and niceties of that pursuit. But, she says, 'I always wanted just to paint. I enjoy working alone. I find it difficult to work with a team. You know – you have to compromise all the time.'

There are other possible factors in the growth of her popularity that are not of her own making. In the last few decades, women painters have been given more attention and accorded greater respect. Her work may well be riding that wave. There is also a resurgent interest in 'Modern British Art' as it is categorised in auction catalogues. Along with it come some of those neo-Romantics of the 1940s and 1950s – people like John Minton, John Craxton and the young Graham Sutherland, inspired by Samuel Palmer, the nineteenth-century visionary. Fedden's own vision was fostered by that time and still retains much that could be seen as contributing to a current need for some kind of romantic return or newness. Is it possible in the new century to paint moonlight and lilies (Ill. 37) without absurdity or cynicism? Without laughable nostalgia but with bold conviction? John Piper, in his book *British Romantic Artists*, summarised his subject in a way that fits a certain aspect of Fedden:

> *Romantic art deals with the particular. The particularisation of Bewick about a bird's wing, of Turner about a waterfall or a hill town, or of Rossetti about Elizabeth Siddall, is the result of a vision that can see in these things something significant beyond ordinary significance: something that for a moment seems to contain the whole world; and when the moment is past, carries over some comment on life or experience besides the comment on appearances.*[4]

Mary Fedden is undeniably fascinated with the particularity of, for instance, a bird's feather (Ill. 38) or a hill town (Ill. 39). There is a streak of neo-Romanticism that has run through her work since the 1950s (Ill. 40). Her still lifes also, in and of themselves, contain a 'whole world', to use Piper's words.

As a painter of still life, Mary's fascination for *things* as the elements of a painting is in line with the idea of 'particularisation'. And pattern is also integral. In the same series of books as Piper's *British Romantic Artists*, H.J. Paris wrote about another woman painter, Frances Hodgkins, referring to her:

> *harmonies and shapes which have a highly personal and emotional appeal, and which sometimes suggest the inspired designer of tiles and textiles.*
>
> *The study of shapes and patterns leads naturally to the study of things, of the world made up of a variety of things, which it has also been the business of science to analyze. 'Thinginess,' and the free association of the ideas and feelings which things arouse in the mind, forms the next stage in the evolution of the contemporary idiom, and the basis of a new kind of imaginative art.*[5]

This perceptive linking of things and patterns virtually prophesies Mary Fedden's future paintings.

38
Robin and Feather, 2000
Gouache
21 x 15 cm (8¼ x 6 in)
Private collection

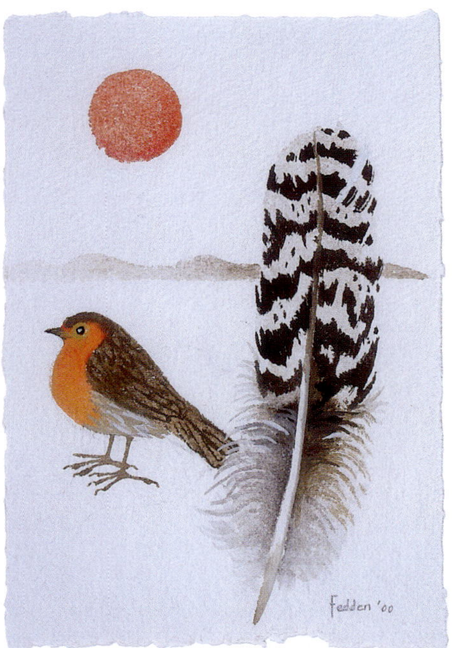

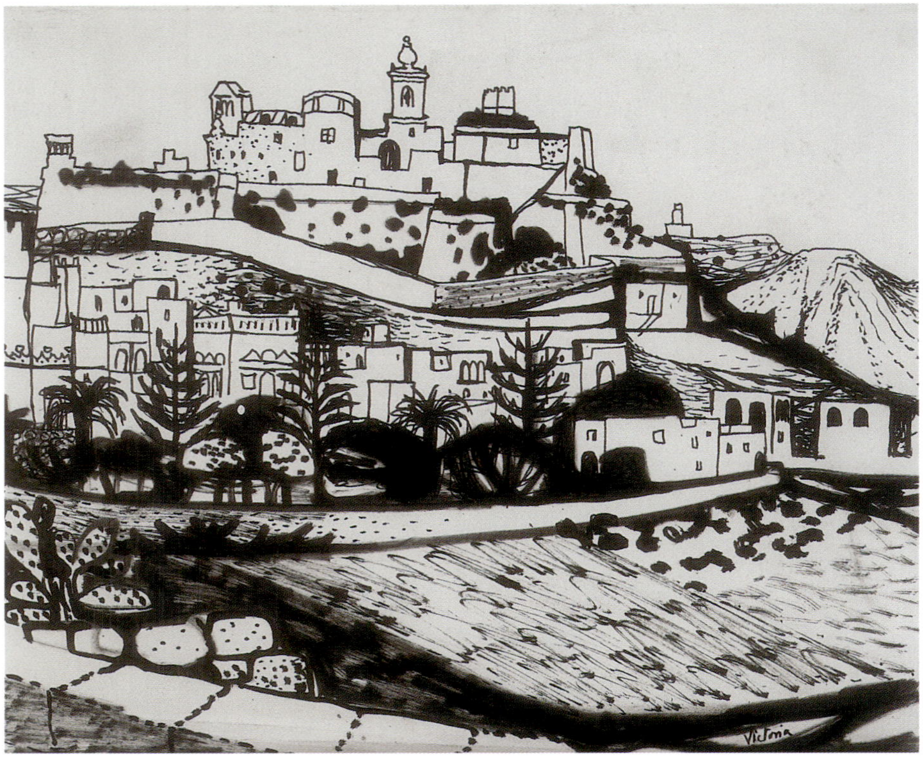

39
Gozo, date unknown
Pen and ink
Dimensions unknown
Credit: The Artist

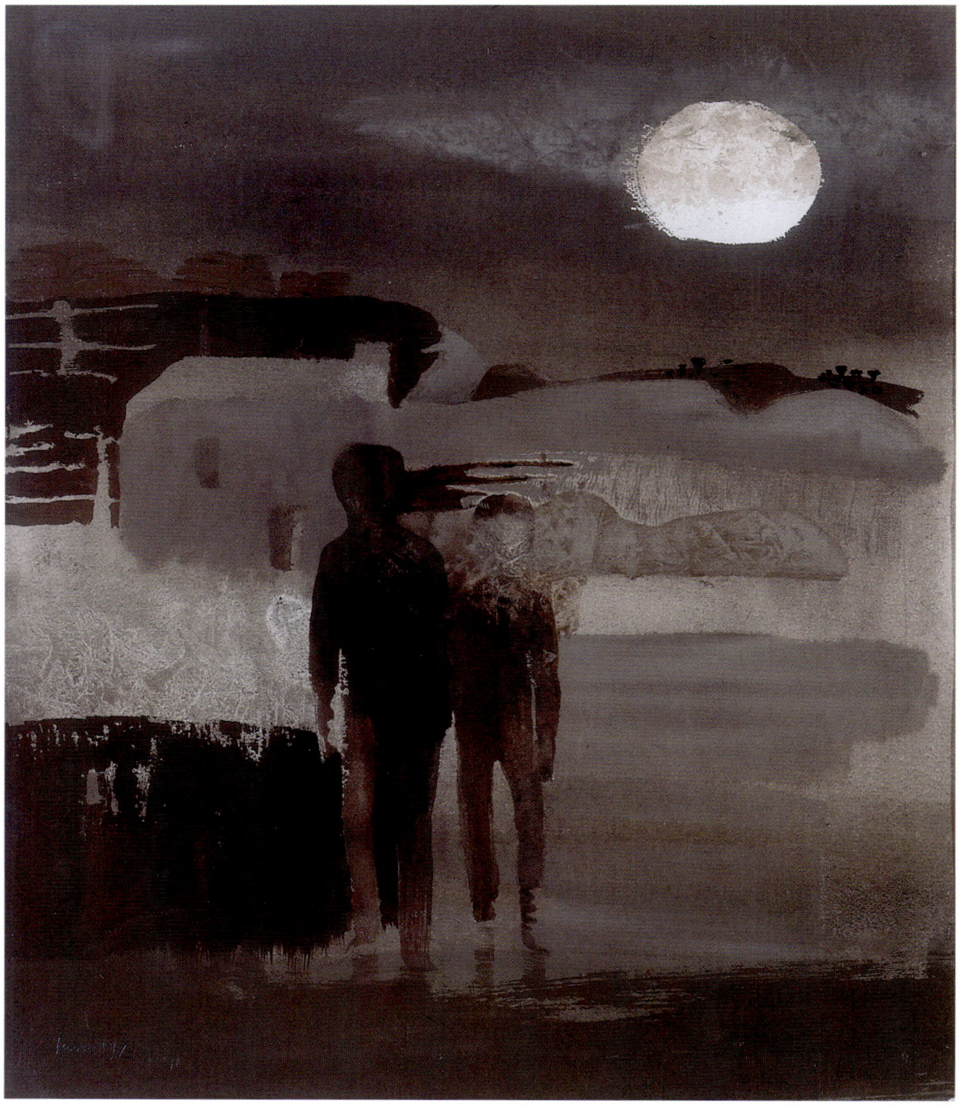

40
Figures in Moonlight, 1973
Gouache
30.3 x 26.4 cm (11⅞ x 10⅜ in)
Private collection

There could be a danger in attempting to pin down Fedden's paintings and drawings and subject them to a wordy investigation they might not bear. They don't invite analysis or discussion. They are intuitive and spontaneous (or appear to be). In fact, they are quite strong and original enough to take in their stride such writerly treatment, aimed not at 'explaining' her work but at encouraging the sort of inspection and close looking that it unquestionably warrants. Fedden is, however, aware of this danger perpetrated by writers and (with a touch of mischief) points out that someone writing a book about her work can't just say he loves it and leave it at that. 'He *has* to write more!' Yet she hints that 'more' could mean speculative interpretation or complex psychological theorising. She feels that writers look for meanings and connections that she herself does not see in her art or intend. 'All *I* am trying to do is simply paint good pictures.'

This is a very English attitude. The English do love words – and Fedden is herself an enthusiastic word-wielder in conversation and letter-writing. (Reading is one of her listed hobbies in *Who's Who.*) But words applied to paintings can sometimes seem unnecessary.

Fedden's husband, Julian Trevelyan, wrote in his early memoirs, *Indigo Days*:

> *In comparison with the French, the English painter is a lazy individual intellectually, undemonstrative and unwilling or incapable of exchanging ideas, and relying very much on the light of nature to lead him. Each time I go to Paris I am astonished afresh at the intellectual curiosity of painters; hours are passed turning over theories and propositions, and though much of it may be hot air, yet the mere exercise of the thinking muscles must lead to some mental agility and suppleness …*[6]

Trevelyan was, of course, also an English painter, though he had worked in France. No one could possibly accuse him or his wife of being 'lazy' – but it is true that her endless energies are concentrated on the *act of painting* rather than the act of talking about it.

It seems Trevelyan was much the same. She still considers he was her best critic. Since he died in 1988, she says 'I miss his bright discerning eye every day'.[7] His comments on her work were succinct and practical. Yet his effect on her work, after they set up together at the end of the 1940s, was nothing short of a radical (and, she felt, *needed*) transformation. It led, essentially, to the way she paints even now. He painted in the studio she now occupies and she painted in the adjacent room. 'At lunchtime he used to come and see what I'd done. And he stood behind me – I remember it quite well – and if he thought it was coming on, he'd say, "that's OK" or "that's better". Or he'd say, "Take out all that left part."' She would whine, 'That's my favourite part!' And he would come back with, 'Well, take it out; it ruins the picture.' 'And at that stage,' she says, 'I did just exactly what he told me, and he was always right.' She also for a while made landscape paintings – paintings of places – very similar to those of Trevelyan. (Ill. 41)

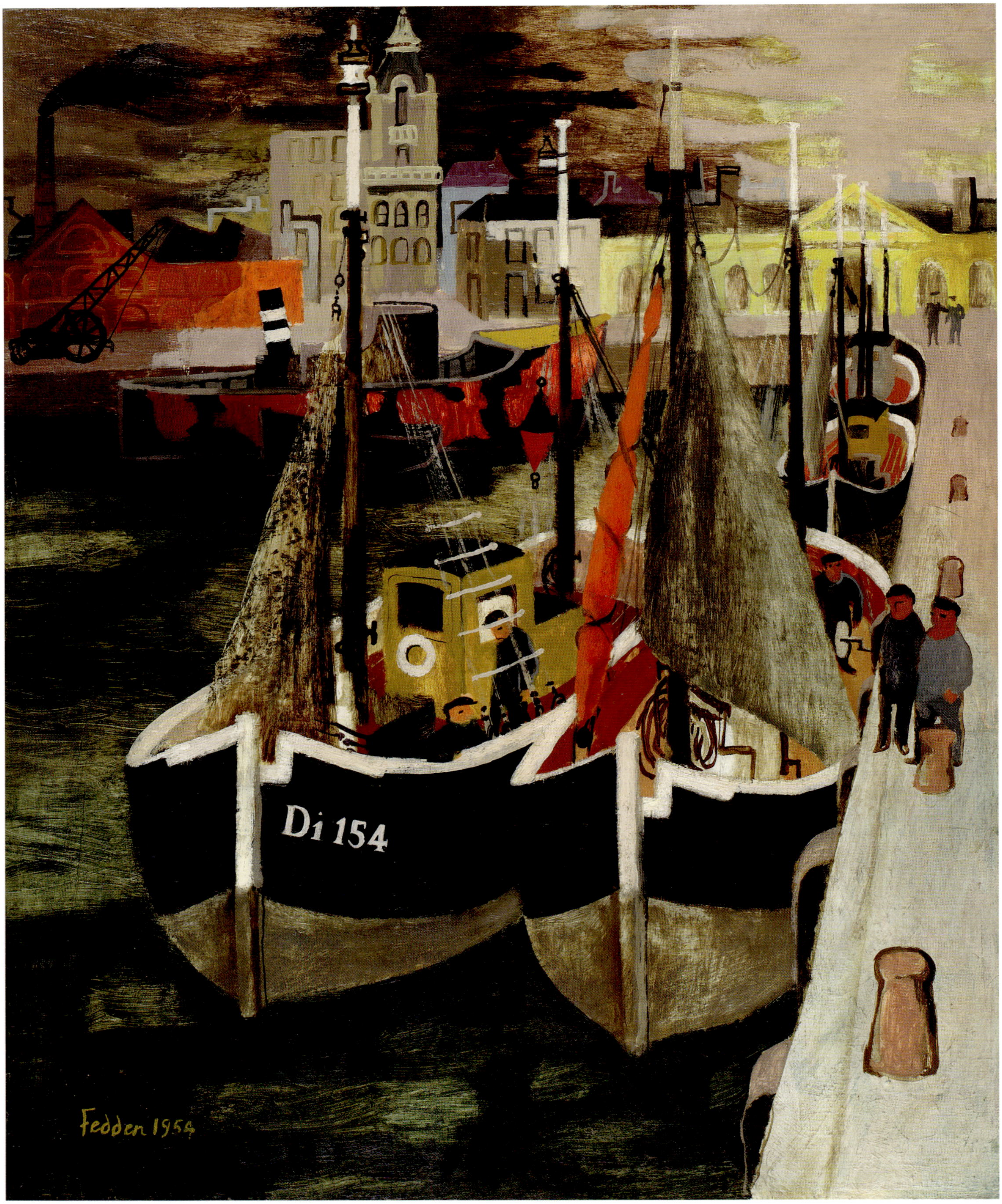
Di 154
Fedden 1954

Fedden explains her motivation in the most unfussy and direct manner. What evidently matters most is the feeling a painting gives out, its mood. She is strong in her opinion that her paintings are not symbolic or full of hidden meanings, but she does also admit that her art may, after all, contain associations and enigmas that are bound to mean different things to different people. When friends – or writers – point out something they have noticed in one of her paintings that she hasn't considered at all (even though she painted it!), her surprise is tinged with pleasure.

On the other hand, she is quick to dismiss any extravagant idea that the array of unusual objects inhabiting her studio and their apparently uncontrived juxtaposition on her canvases carry any significance whatever. They are just objects she loves to paint – over and over again, in different ways. Her representation of them develops and changes over the years; for instance, she paints 'Charlotte's Jug' (given to her by one of her god-daughters) quite differently today from the way she first painted it. The actual jug is not large and has a small pattern. Fedden has not only enlarged it and made the pattern bigger, she has also changed its shape from one painting to another – as can be seen by comparing *Charlotte's Jug* of 2000 (Ill. 43, overleaf) with *Irish Lilies* (Ill. 37, p.38), painted six years later.

From her point of view, the only common factor the objects have is her almost obsessive fondness for them as motifs. They are idiosyncratic; she knows that. Some are 'found objects'. Many are gifts from friends 'who know the sort of things I like'. They are her visual vocabulary. They keep her painting attached to the 'real world' and are the chief reason why her work does not float off into abstraction (Ill. 42).

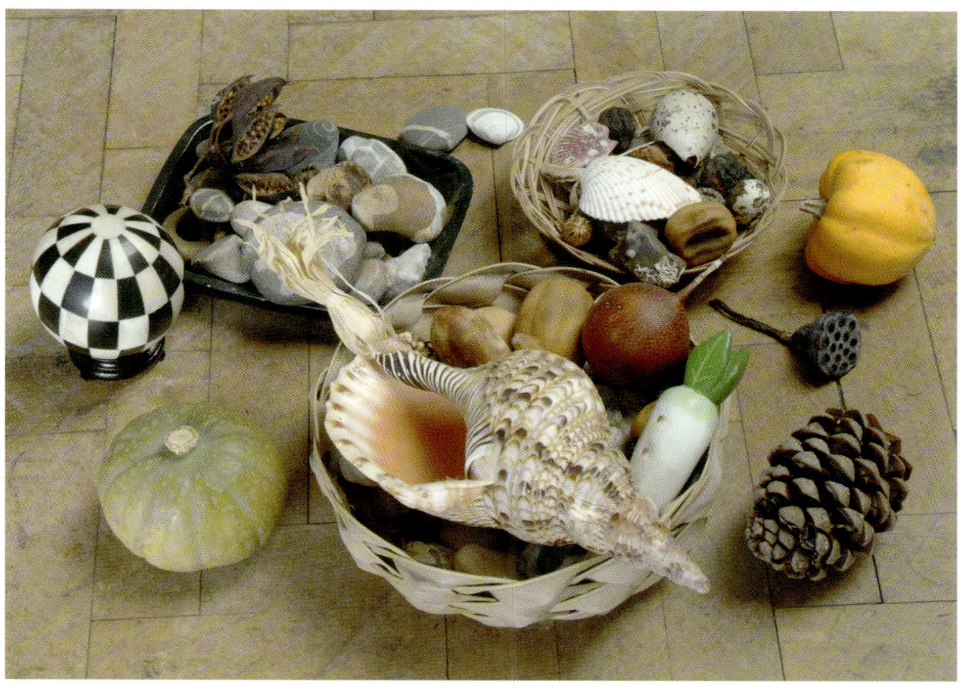

41 (opposite)
Dieppe, 1954
Oil on canvas
76.5 x 64 cm (30 x 25¼ in)
Richard Green Gallery, London

42 (right)
Objects in Mary Fedden's studio
Photograph by Mike Fear

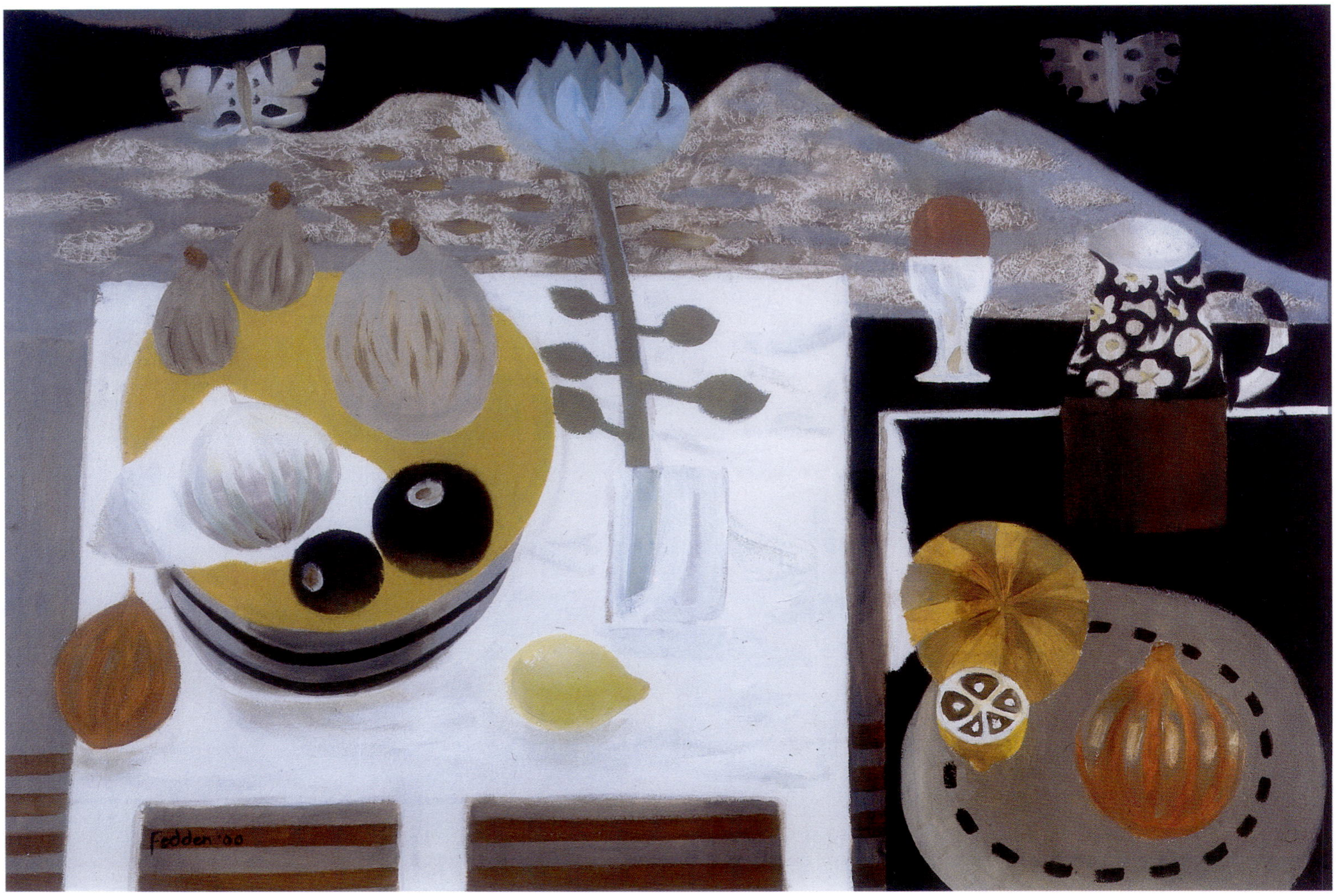

42
Charlotte's Jug, 2000
Oil on canvas
59.2 x 89 cm (23⅜ x 31⅞ in)
Private collection

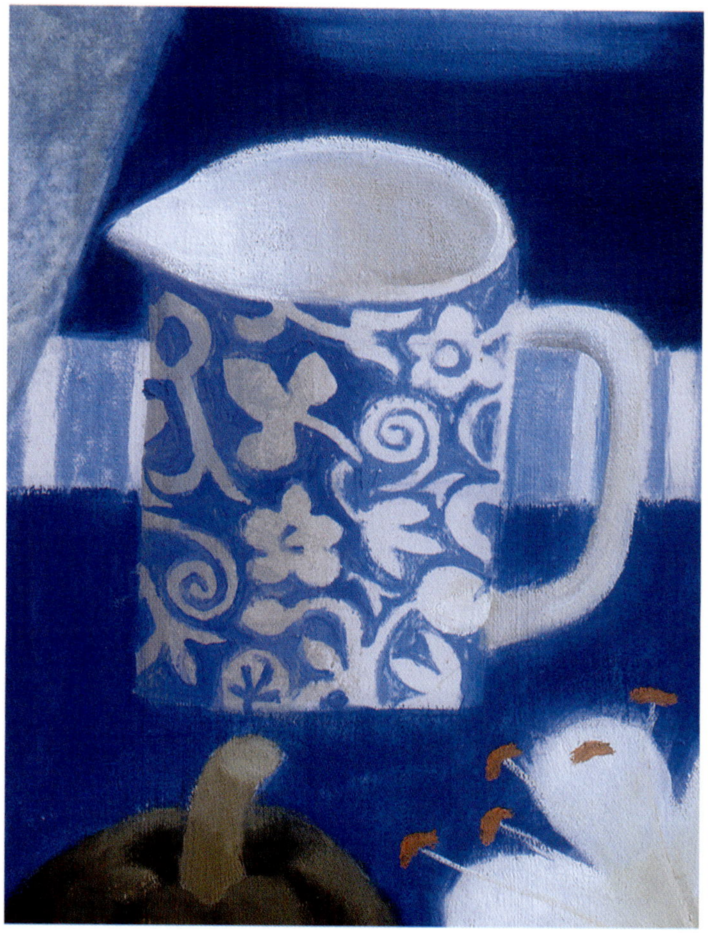

Black Bottle by Moonlight
(detail from Ill. 72, p.70)

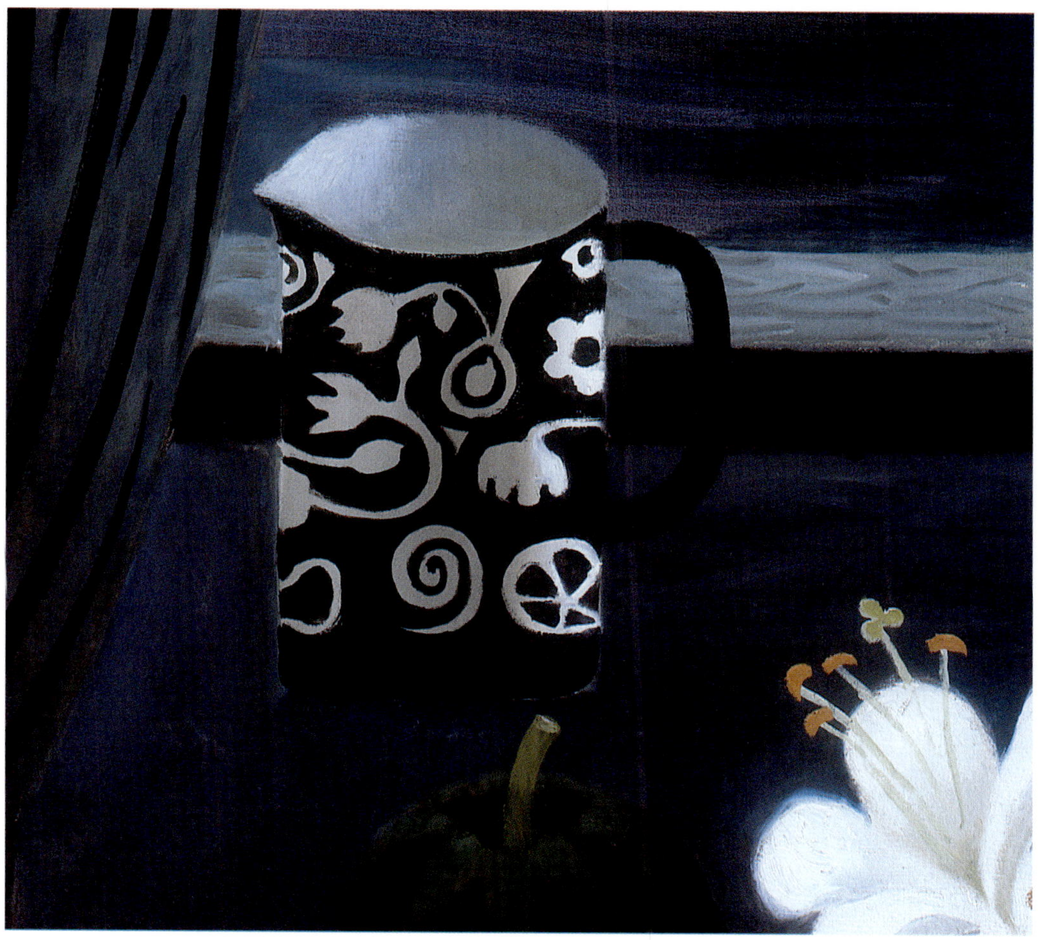

Irish Lilies (detail from Ill. 37. p.38)

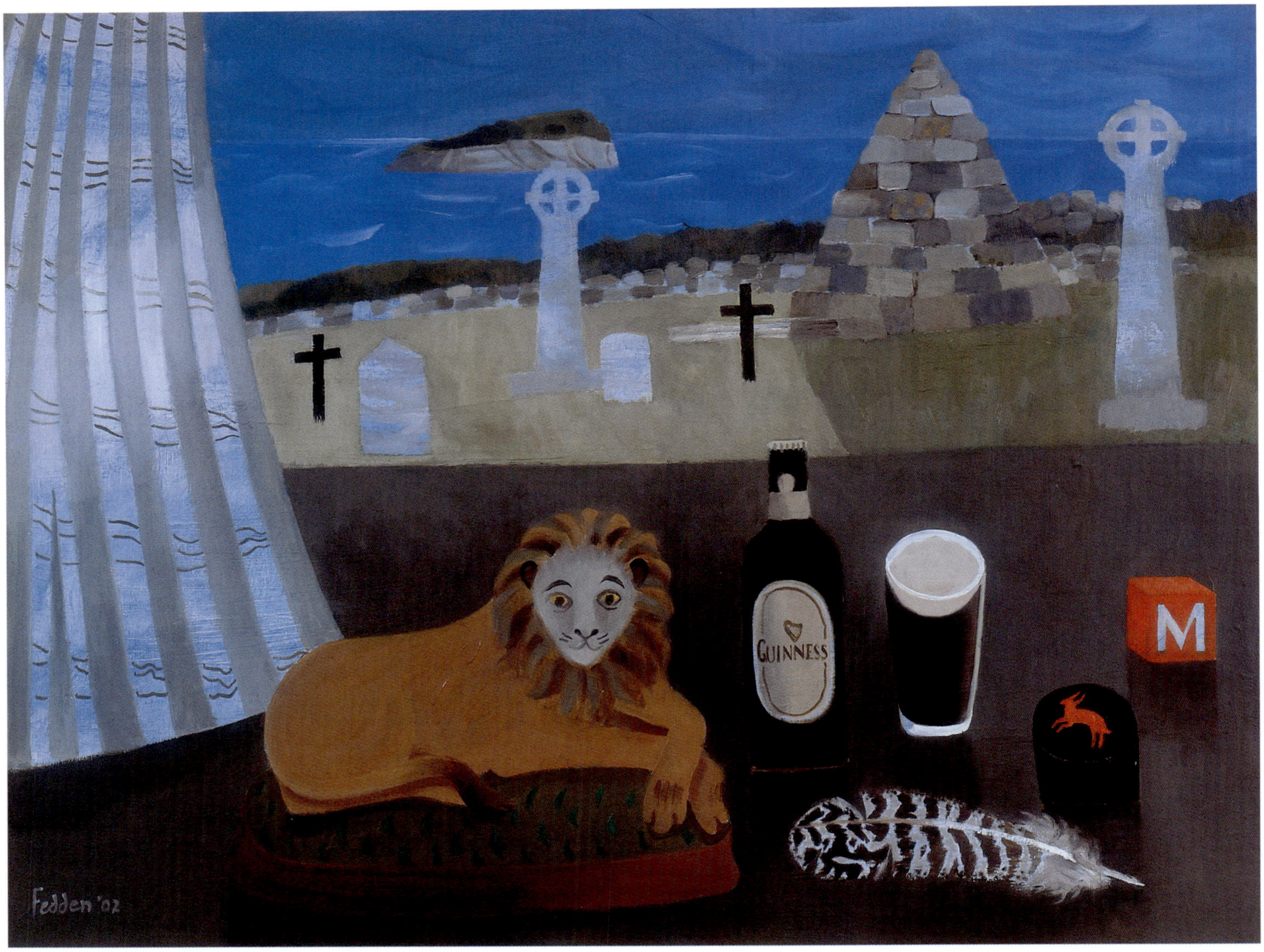

44
Irish Lion, 2002
Oil on canvas
75.1 x 100.5 cm (29½ x 39¼ in)
Private collection

All the same, she admits that her still lifes are not at all just objective descriptions. They comprise an imaginative, ideal world – a world she explores only in her studio and only with paintbrush or pencil. She often stresses that her art, however literal it may seem to be in its accurate depiction of her objects, in fact fully engages the imagination. She teasingly subjects her work to casual remarks such as 'I just strew things on the canvas, mostly off the top of my head.' 'Strew' suggests haphazard abandonment. Actually, her compositions are often taut, controlled and even classical. They involve a much-practised intuition rather than accident. Yet it is also true that the Surrealists had, in the 1920s and 1930s (when she was at school and then a very young student at the Slade), exploited the notion of chance formations as a source of imagination and art. How much she was aware of Surrealism as a movement is uncertain, but it seems more than likely that she absorbed some of its atmosphere and, in a completely unforced way, her work has long had a surreal streak. There is naturalness and spontaneity in the notion that things fall where they will. Her work often contains a strange combination of firm intention and chance. (Ill. 44)

Before setting up with Julian Trevelyan in 1949, her paintings were, she believes, 'literal' in the extreme. He had been closely involved with Surrealism in England in the mid-1930s and later often discussed it with his wife. 'Julian thought my pictures were too romantic, old-fashioned, and not very original. He said, "You've got much more to your painting than what you are doing. You are not using your imagination."' He showed her that 'you must use your mind as well as your eye'. He undoubtedly opened doors for her work.

This said, however, her pre-Trevelyan work is actually unlike anyone else's and 'literal' is about the last word one would attach to it.[8] These elaborate paintings are not really much like the seventeenth-century Dutch flower paintings they appear to ape. One collector (who prefers her later work) is tellingly reminded by them of Miss Havisham in Charles Dickens's *Great Expectations*. They are somehow preserved and faded, a bit musty, rather lightless and sad. Fedden herself now dislikes them intensely, but they simply cannot be dismissed as without imagination. One of the paintings Fedden has donated to the Tate – *The Staffordshire Horse* (1948) (Ill. 45) – belongs to this period. If she hates it as much as she claims, she would surely have destroyed it rather than allow it, even unwillingly, to be placed in the Tate for posterity.

She is openly pleased at the suggestion that she can be slightly surreal. Richard Shone has this to say about the English strain of Surrealism: 'English Surrealism was generally concerned with the unavoidable strangeness of the *objet trouvé*, with the juxtaposition of disparate elements to create poetic, disturbing or humorous images and the introduction of unusual or unlikely objects into realistic settings, creating ambiguity in both.'[9] T.S. Eliot described something similar: 'When a poet's mind is perfectly equipped for its work, it is constantly amalgamating disparate experience.'[10] Lewis Carroll and Edward Lear could be adopted as peculiarly English precursors of English Surrealism, but Surrealism had originated across the English Channel in the 1920s and had claimed as a fellow spirit a nineteenth-century writer called Isidore Ducasse, in particular his words describing 'the chance meeting on a dissecting-table of a sewing-machine and an umbrella!'[11]

Mary Fedden's chance meetings of objects generally occur on a dining table, kitchen table, or windowsill and don't strike you as all that odd until you look again. They are hardly disturbing, but they can be quietly ambiguous or improbable. The bold conviction of her brush persuasively suggests at first that you are seeing something perfectly familiar and even ordinary. However, these still lifes are never like a Paul Cézanne or a Jean-Baptiste-Siméon Chardin, with objects physically arranged on a table to be solidly observed and recorded by the artist at his easel. Their juxtapositions and placements take place primarily in her imagination and then on her canvas. In a typically matter-of-fact description of

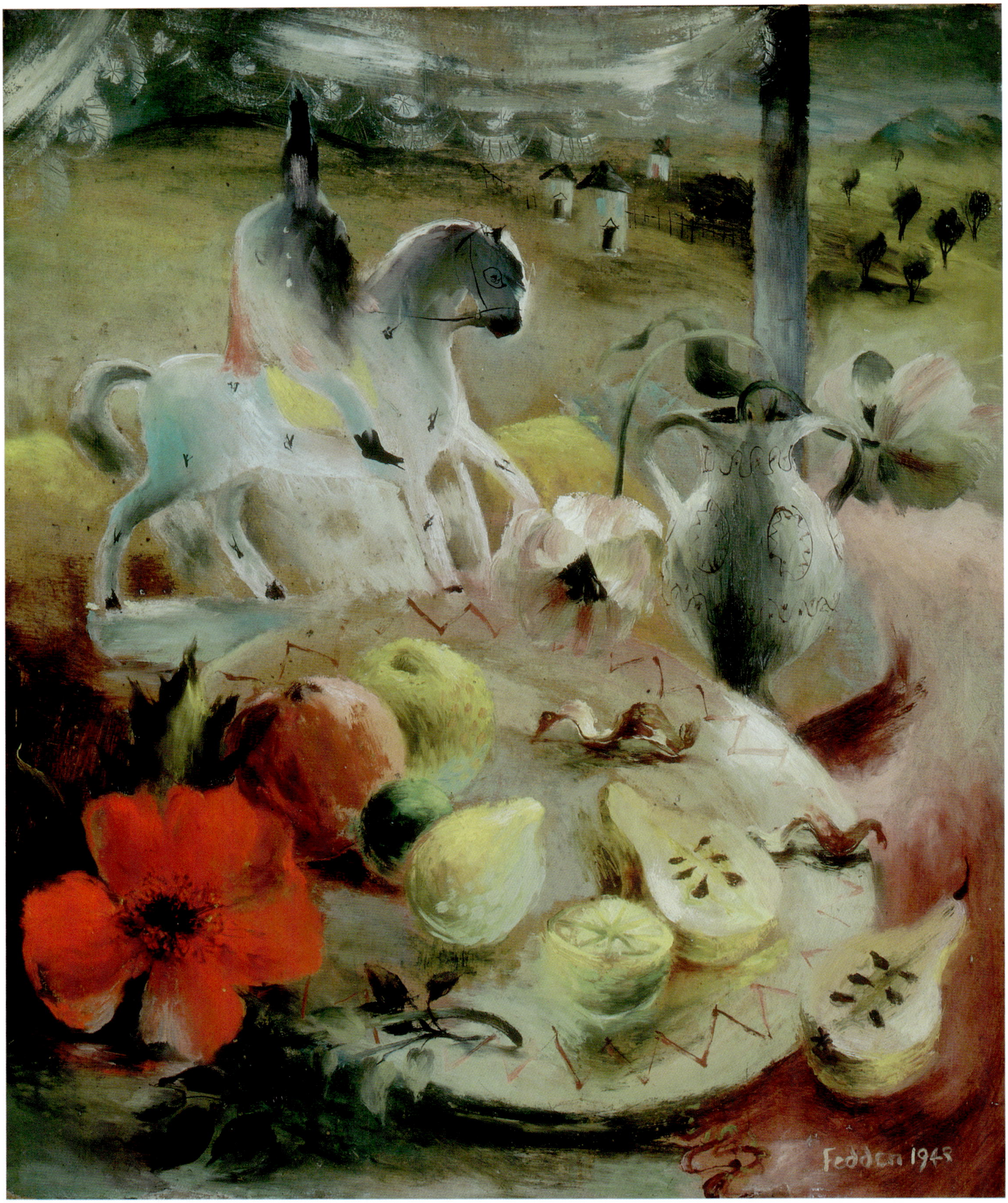
Fedden 1948

her work to an interviewer, Ossian Clark, she said, 'I get hooked onto objects: quinces, volcanoes, quail's eggs, feathers … and sometimes a stripy zebra will show up at a tea party'.[12]

Her matter-of-factness, in her talk as well as her paintings, is disarming – and rather misleading. The unexpected and the strange lurk under the surface. Edward Lear's absurdism is just round the corner. At home in her Thames-side studio, she cooks up an intimate world in her paintings that is as imaginary as it appears to be ordinary and every day. (Ill. 46)

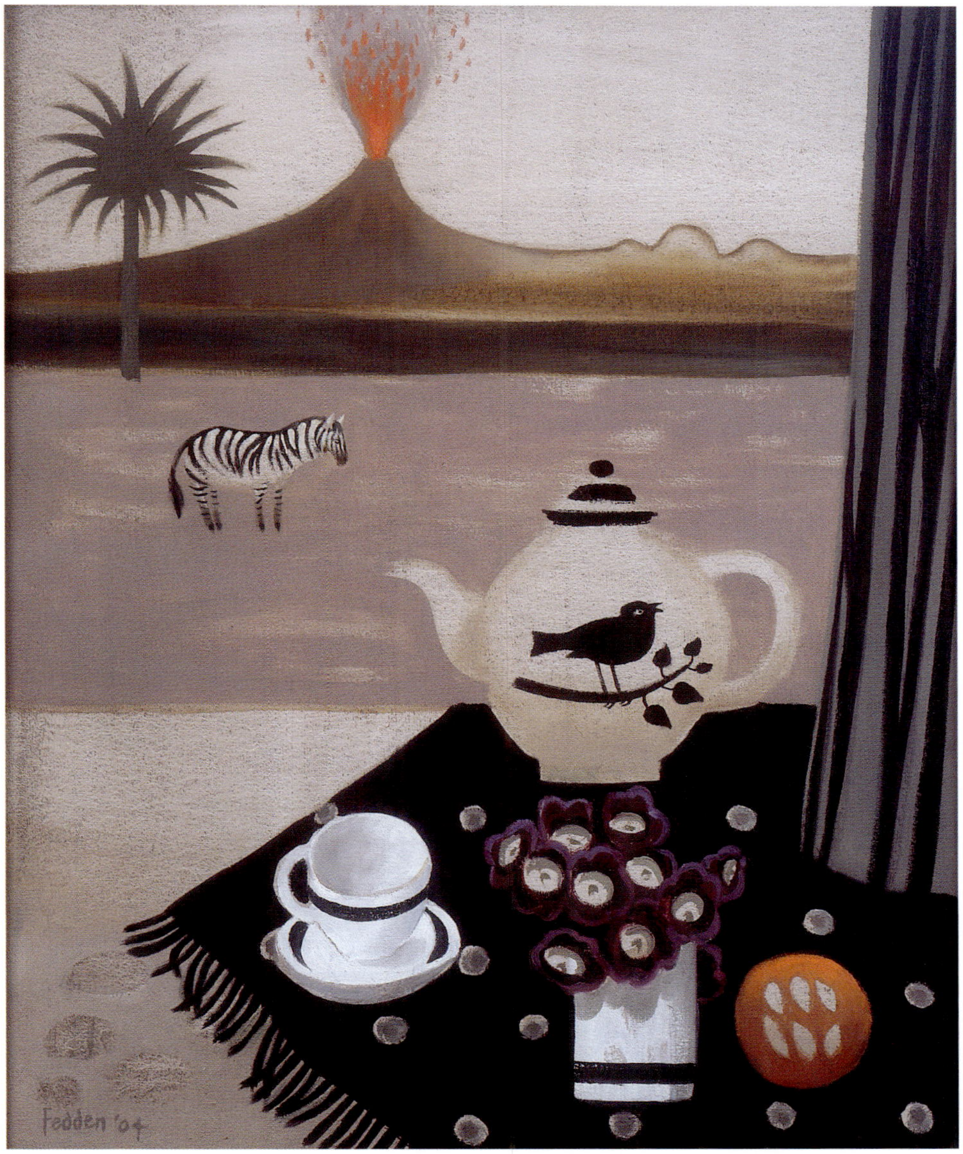

46
Zebra, Volcano and Teapot, 2004
Oil on canvas
59.5 x 49.6 cm (23¼ x 19½ in)
Private collection

Notes

1. I first met Mary Fedden in 2005, although her work was already familiar to me, particularly through Mel Gooding's book *Mary Fedden*, Scolar Press (Aldershot), 1995. Unattributed quotes from the artist come from conversations and correspondence in 2005 and 2006
2. *Selected Poems* by John Keats, Penguin Classics (London), 1999, p.172
3. *Generally Speaking* by G.K. Chesterton, Methuen (London), 1928, p.2
4. *British Romantic Artists* by John Piper, in the 'Britain in Pictures' series published by William Collins (London), 1942, p.7
5. *English Watercolour Painters* by H.J. Paris, in the 'Britain in Pictures' series published by William Collins (London), 1945, p.46
6. *Indigo Days: the Art and Memoirs of Julian Trevelyan*, Ashgate Publishing Company (Aldershot), 1996, p.77
7. 'Mary Fedden: an artist's diary', *Art Review*, March 1995, vol.47, pp 44–5
8. See *Mary Fedden* by Mel Gooding, Scolar Press (Aldershot), 1995, plates 17, 18 and 19
9. *The Century of Change, British Painting since 1900* by Richard Shone, Phaidon (London), 1977, p.25
10. *Selected Essays* by T.S. Eliot, Faber and Faber (London), Third Edition 1951, p.287
11. *Maldoror & The Complete Works of the Comte de Lautréamont* by Isidore Ducasse, trans. Alexis Lykiard, Exact Change (Cambridge), 1994, p.195
12. 'Quite Contrary', *Art Review*, February 2003, vol.54, pp 56–9

45 (opposite)
The Staffordshire Horse, 1948
Oil on board
76.3 x 64.3 cm (30 x 25¼ in)
© Tate, London 2006

CHAPTER ONE

A Gallery of Mary Feddens

This chapter presents some pictures by Mary Fedden in chronological order. The selection is not, however, an attempt to be in the least comprehensive. A *catalogue raisonné* of Fedden's work would run to several volumes. The scope of this book involves no such ambition.

The gallery of works that follows cannot be taken as an infallible guide to the changing character of her work as the years roll. Yet there are marked differences to be noticed at different stages. In the late 1980s and early 1990s, for example, there seems to be evidence of a change towards sourer and sharper colours and fiercer contrasts. There is even (for her) a wilder approach to composition. But then this different mood gives way to a more measured and mellow tendency, even if her paintings now have harder edges and there is a more specific separation of objects in her still lifes than there was in the 1960s and 1970s. Yet occasionally – just to confuse the enemy – Fedden paints pictures in the later 1990s and early 2000s that look either like a deliberate attempt to return to the looser 1960s style or, alternatively, to revive for a moment the astringency of the 'sour' period.

In some of her most recent paintings there appears to be, on the one hand, a quieter mood and also, in other paintings, a touch of neo-Romantic atmosphere resurfacing, with greater contrasts of light and darkness that somewhat soften her so-called 'hard' edges.

It would be simplistic to read too much into 'periods' of Fedden's work; yet while her themes and subject matter do remain remarkably consistent, she always paints them with an eye to seeing something different about them. From her point of view, each painting is a new attempt and a new view. In practice, one painting is separated from another by *days* rather than years. She works firmly in the present, so she doesn't much think about her art having different styles or periods that are years apart from each other. To her, 1999 was not all that different from 1989, or 1962 from 1972. Differences are probably more apparent to an outside observer.

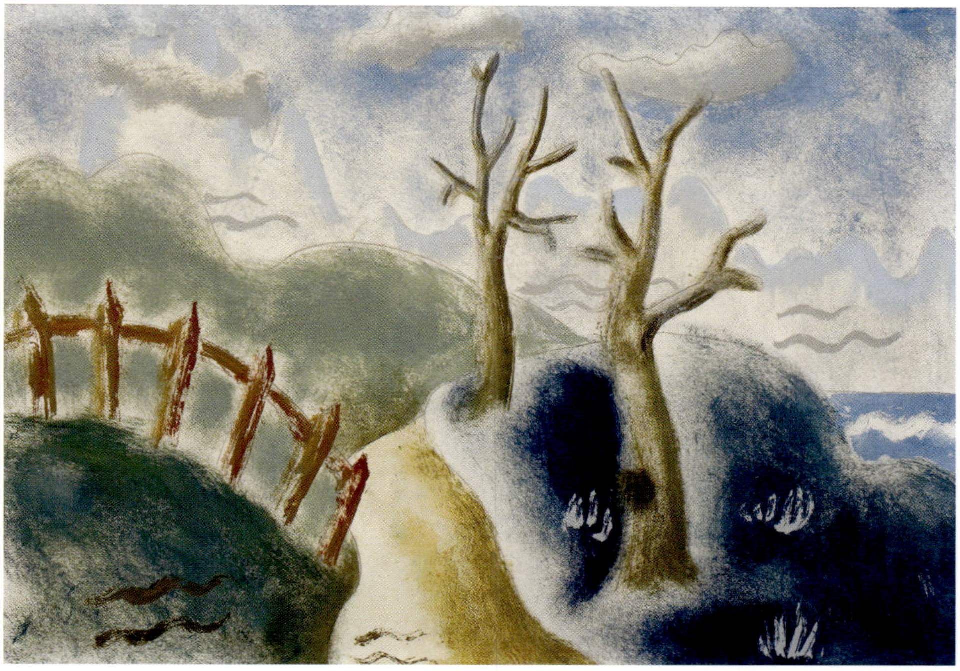

47 (right)
An Abstract Landscape Composition, 1936
Pastel and gouache with pencil outline
20.4 x 25.6 cm (8 x 10 in)
UCL Art Collections, University College London

48 (below)
Shell Still Life on the Sea Shore, 1948
Oil on canvas
40 x 46 cm (15¾ x 18⅛ in)
Private collection

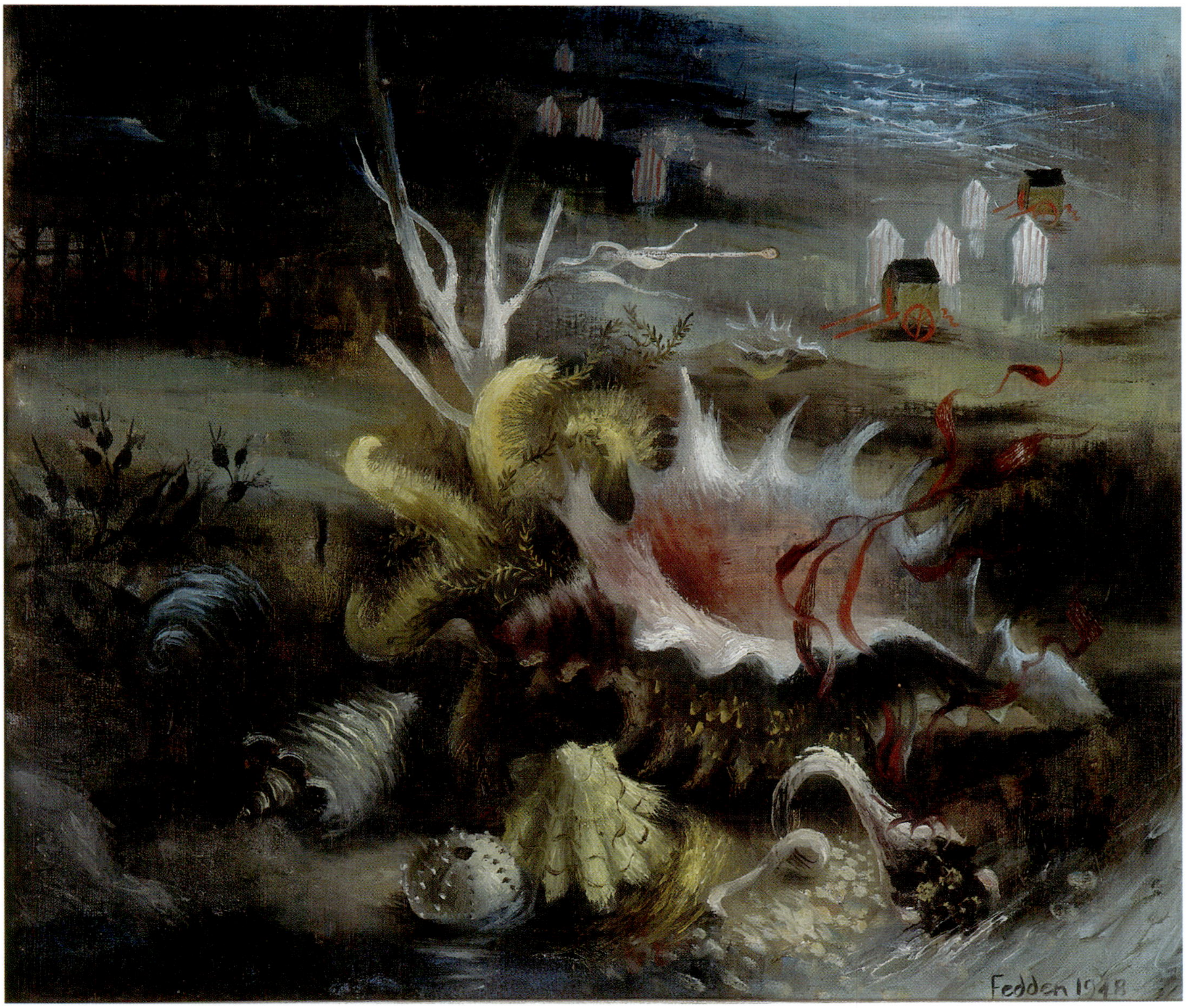

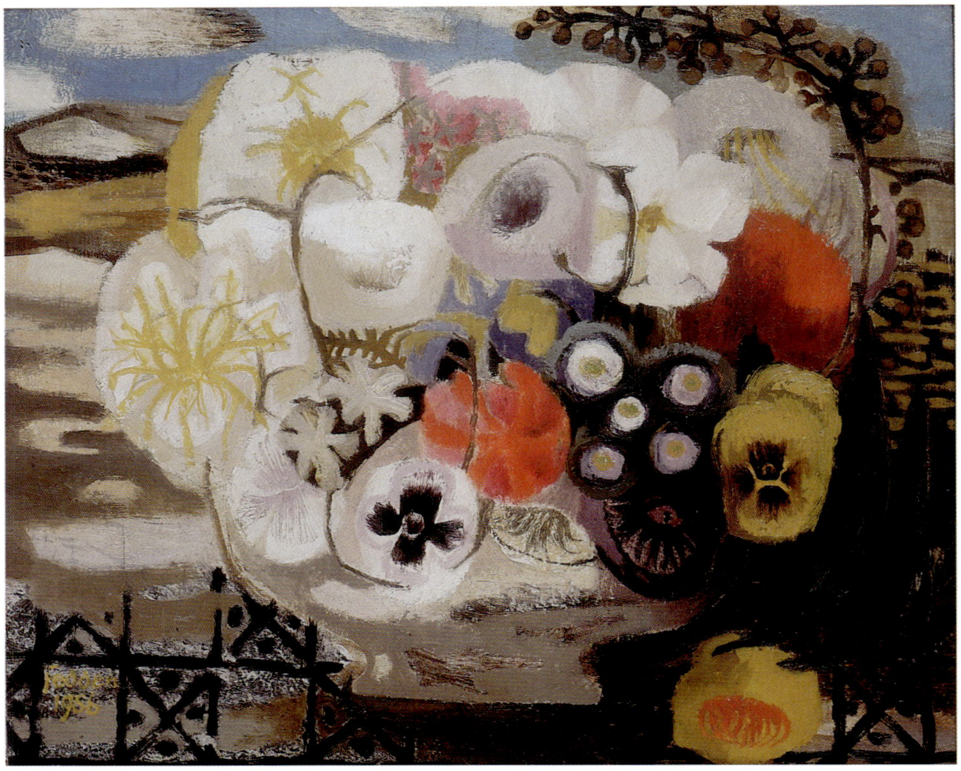

49
Flowers on a Tiled Floor, 1956
Oil on board
39.3 x 49 cm ($15\frac{1}{2}$ x $19\frac{1}{4}$ in)
Private collection

50
A Bowl of Spaghetti, 1960
Oil on canvas
49.4 x 89.8 cm ($19\frac{3}{8}$ x $35\frac{1}{4}$ in)
Private collection

In a letter to the owner of this painting, Fedden wrote: 'I love painting red pictures, & probably everything in it – landscape, flowers, spaghetti & all came out of the top of my head. Except maybe the half red pepper. I guess I had a real one.'

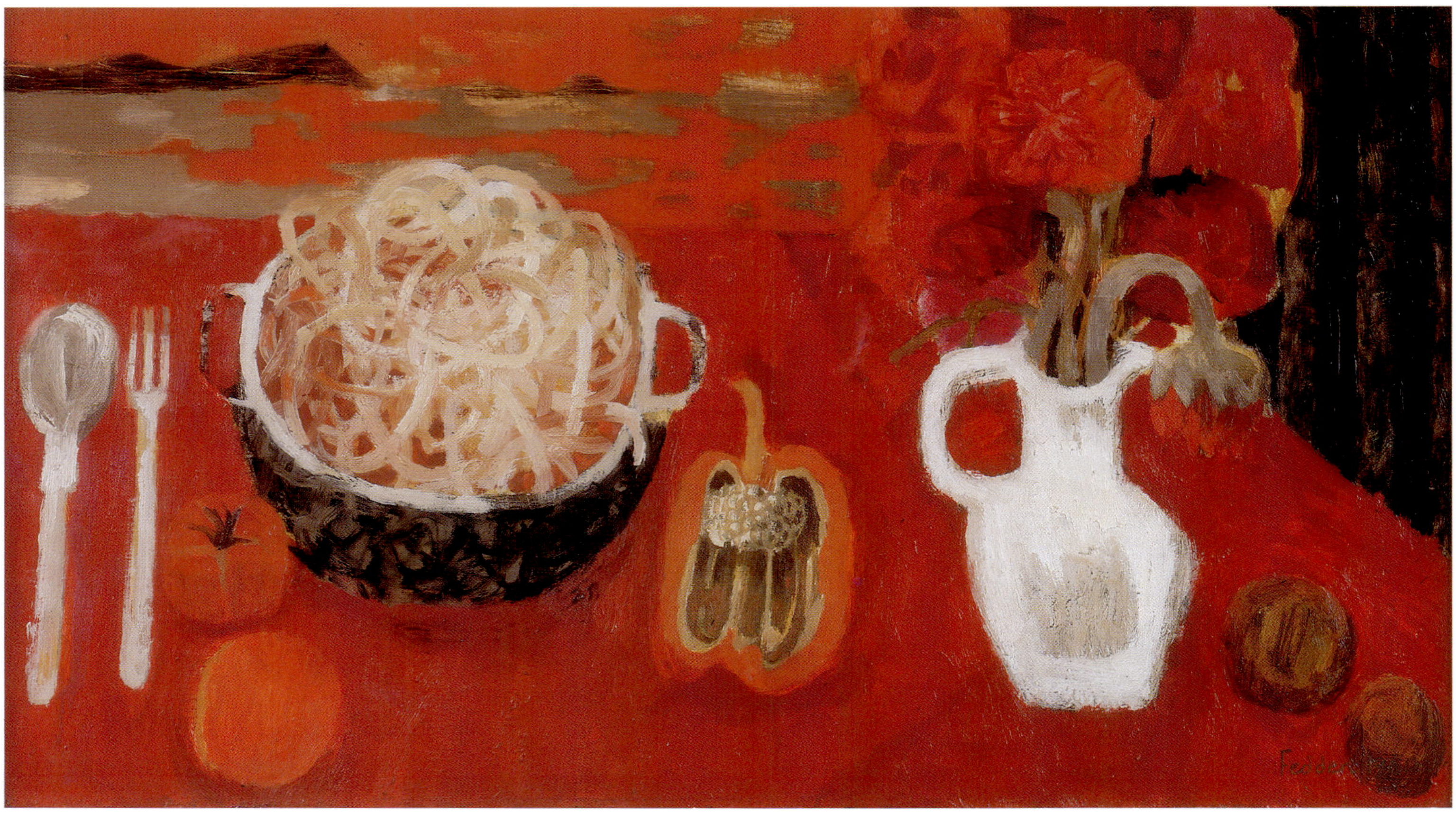

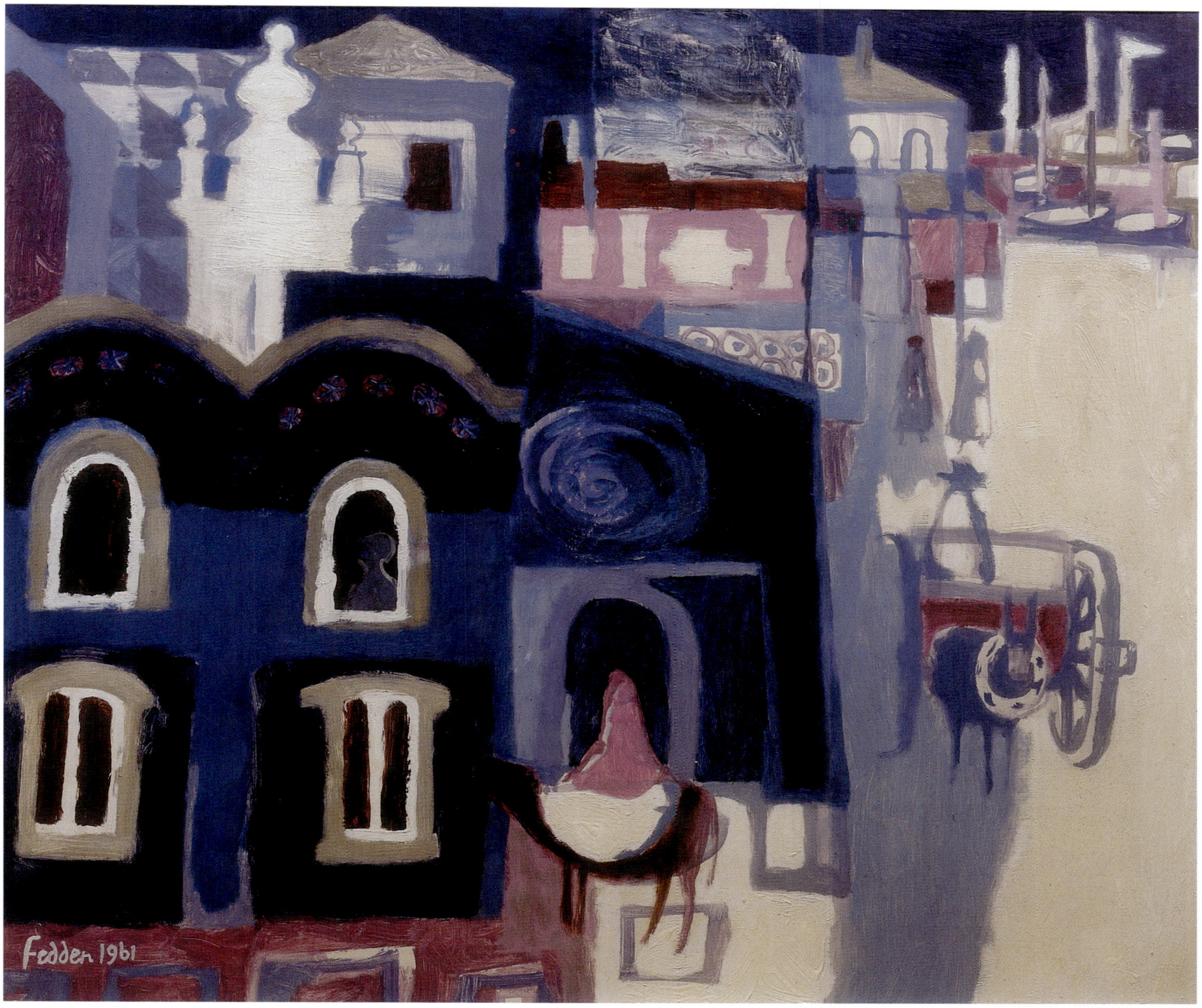

51
Village in Portugal, 1961
Oil on canvas
71.1 x 76.2 cm (28 x 30 in)
Lena Boyle Fine Art, London

52
Cottage in Portugal, 1964
Oil on board
30.6 x 40.8 cm (12 x 16 in)
Private collection

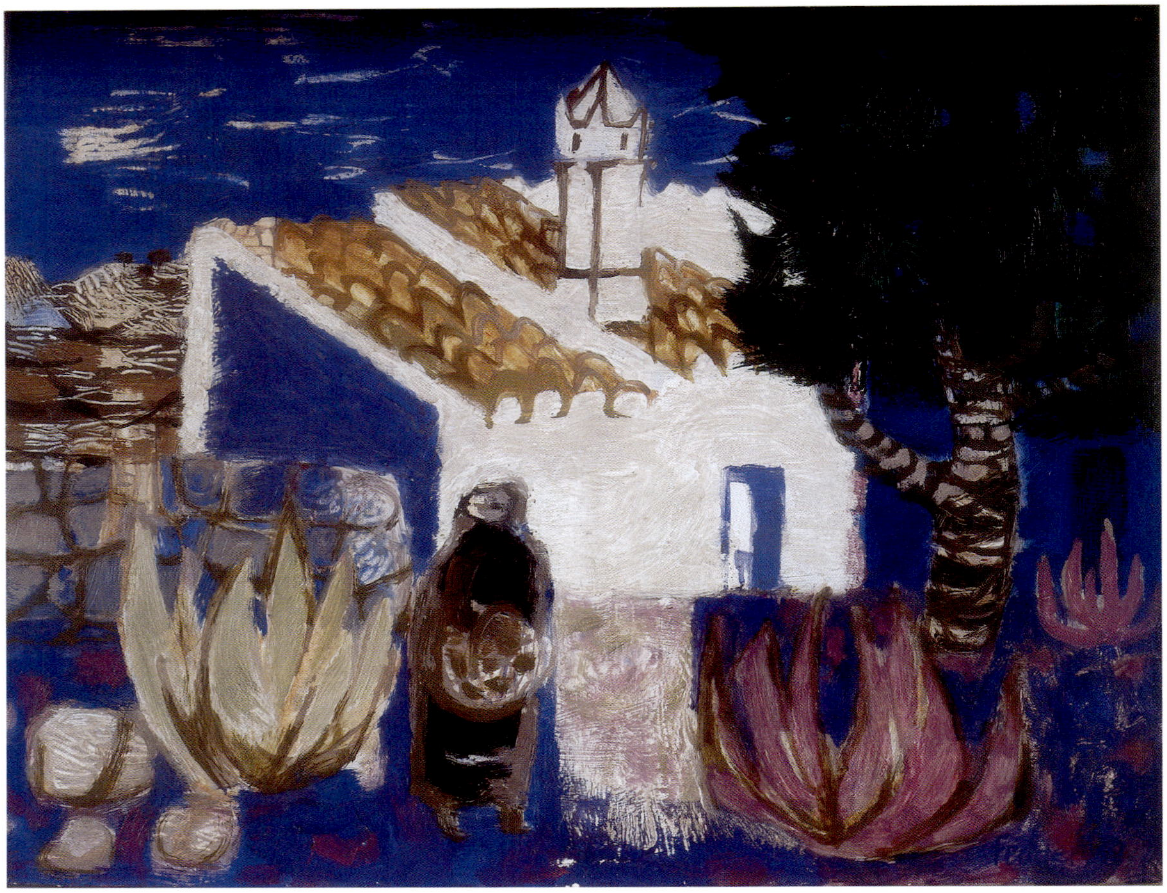

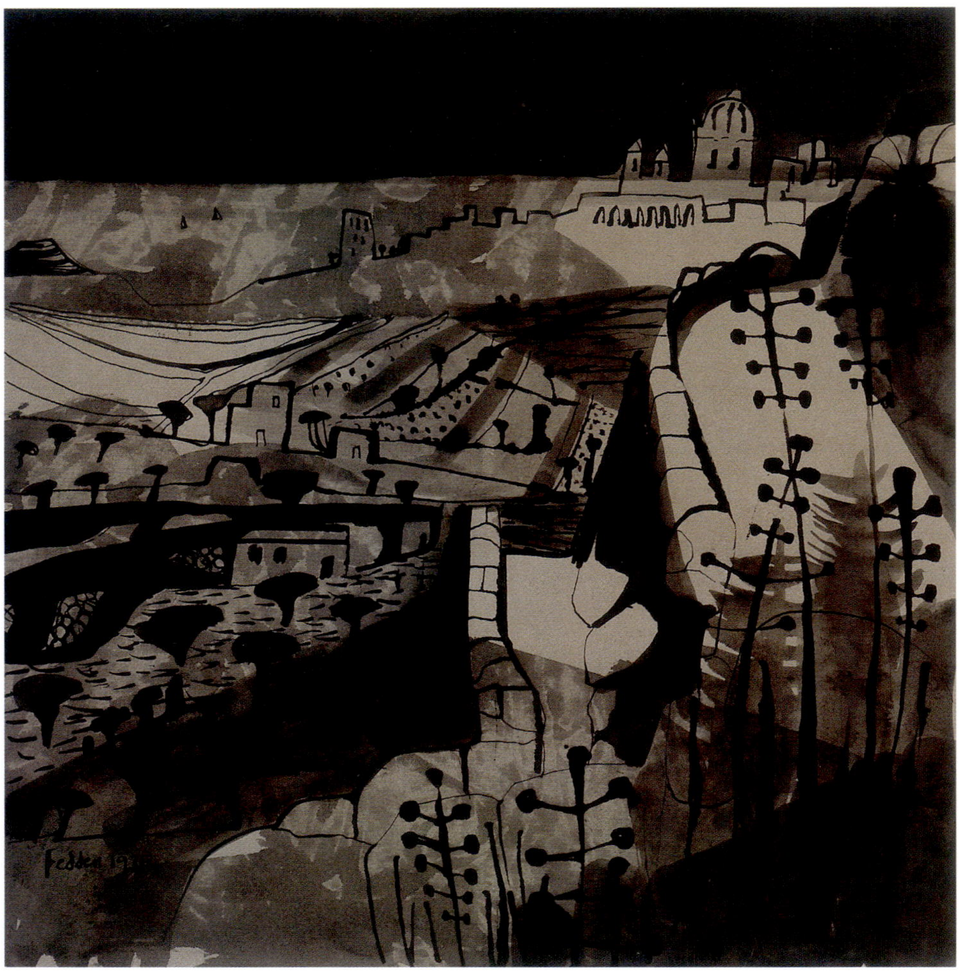

53
Mediterranean Landscape, 1971
Ink
26 x 26 cm (10¼ x 10¼ in)
Private collection

54
Couple in a Landscape, 1972
Gouache
28.5 x 38.7 cm (11¼ x 15¼ in)
Private collection

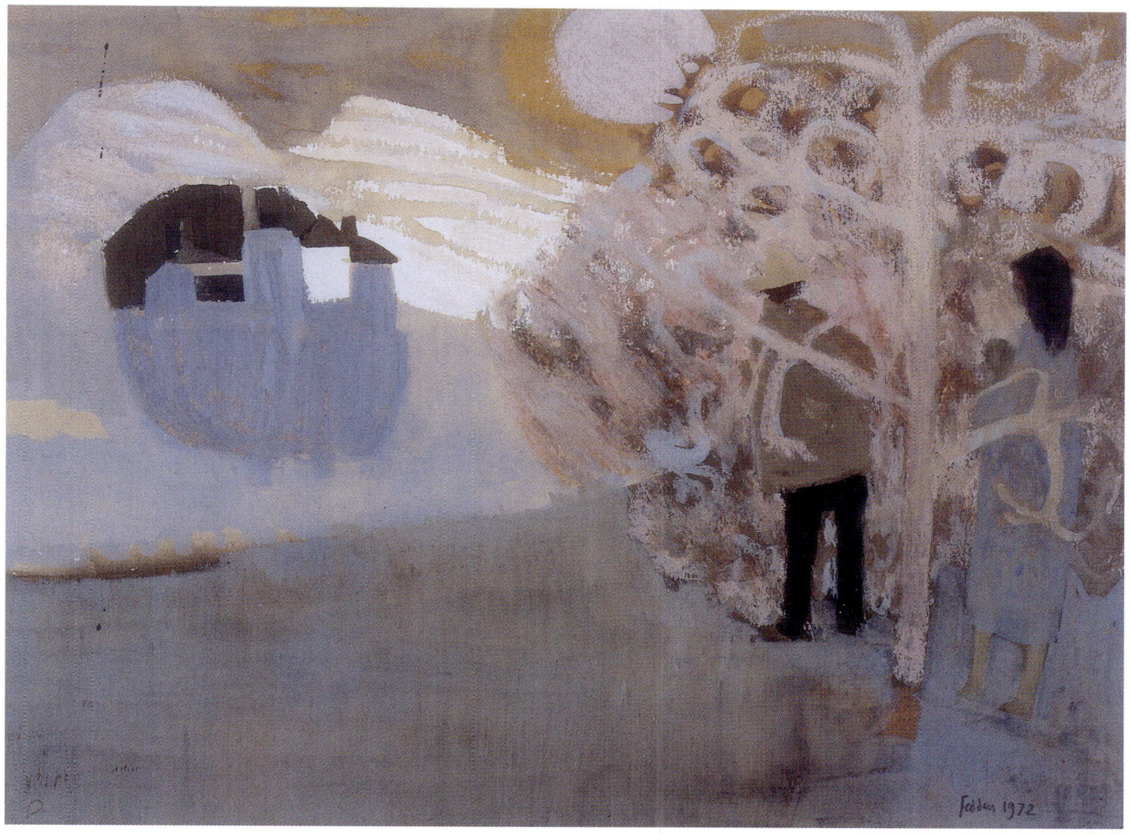

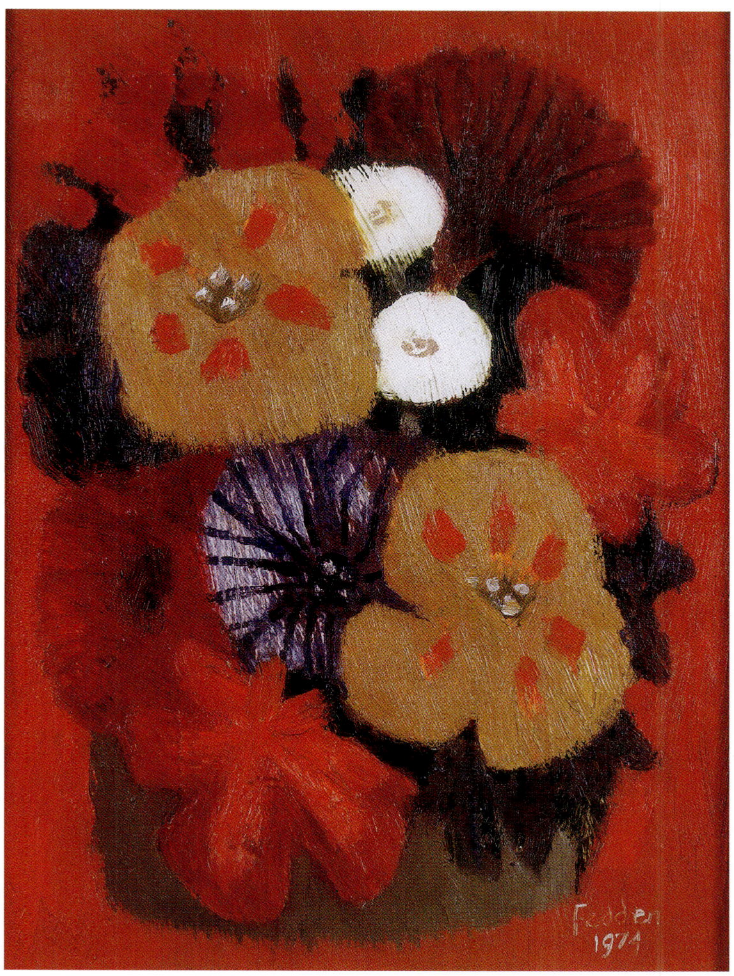

55
Red Still Life, 1974
Oil on board
25.5 x 19.5 cm (10 x 7⅝ in)
Private collection

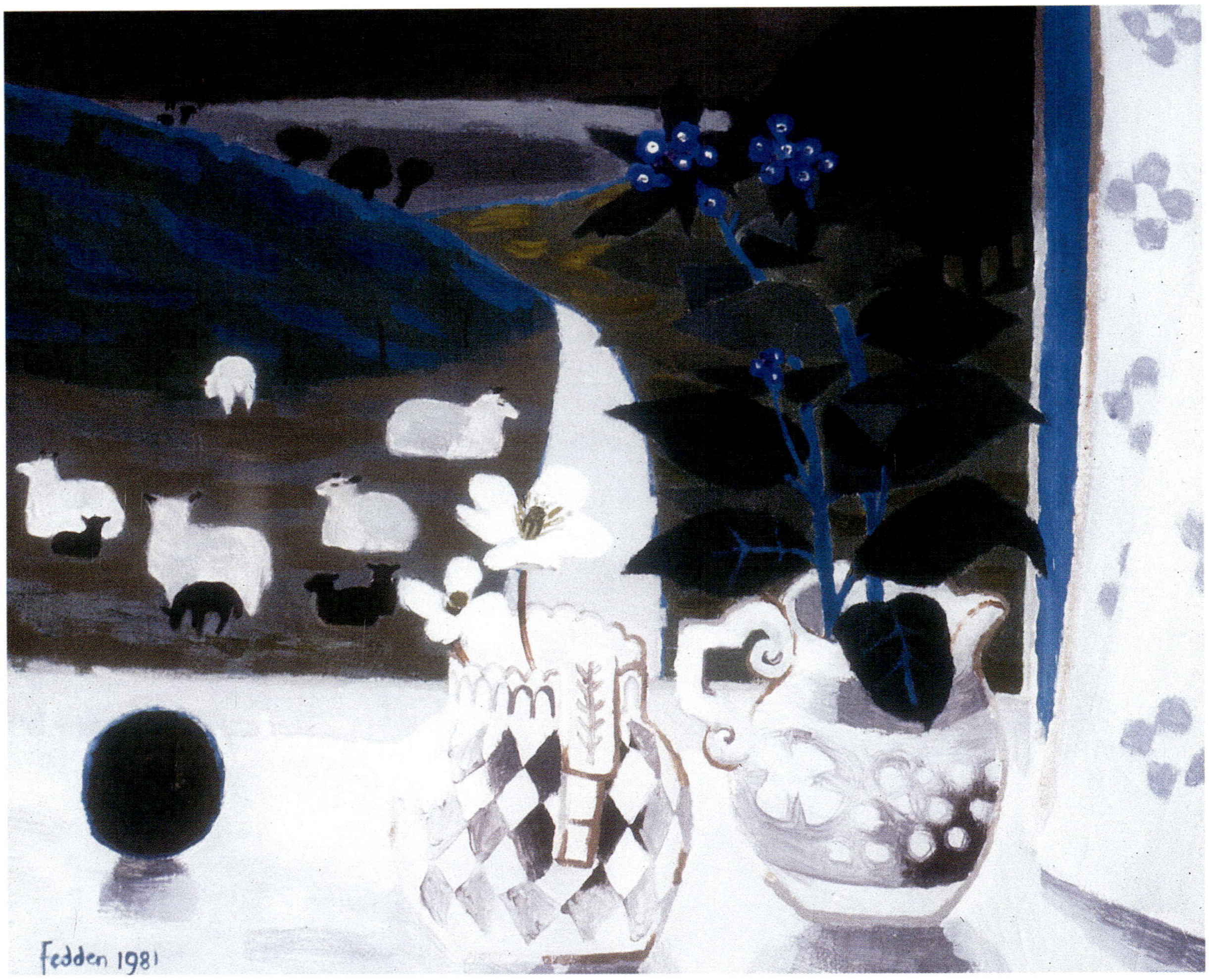

56 (above)
Sheep in Yorkshire, 1981
Oil on canvas
49 x 59 cm (19¼ x 23¼ in)
Trevelyan College, University of Durham

57 (below)
Still Life with Fruit, 1987
Oil on canvas
30.5 x 61 cm (12 x 24 in)
Private collection
Sotheby's Picture Library

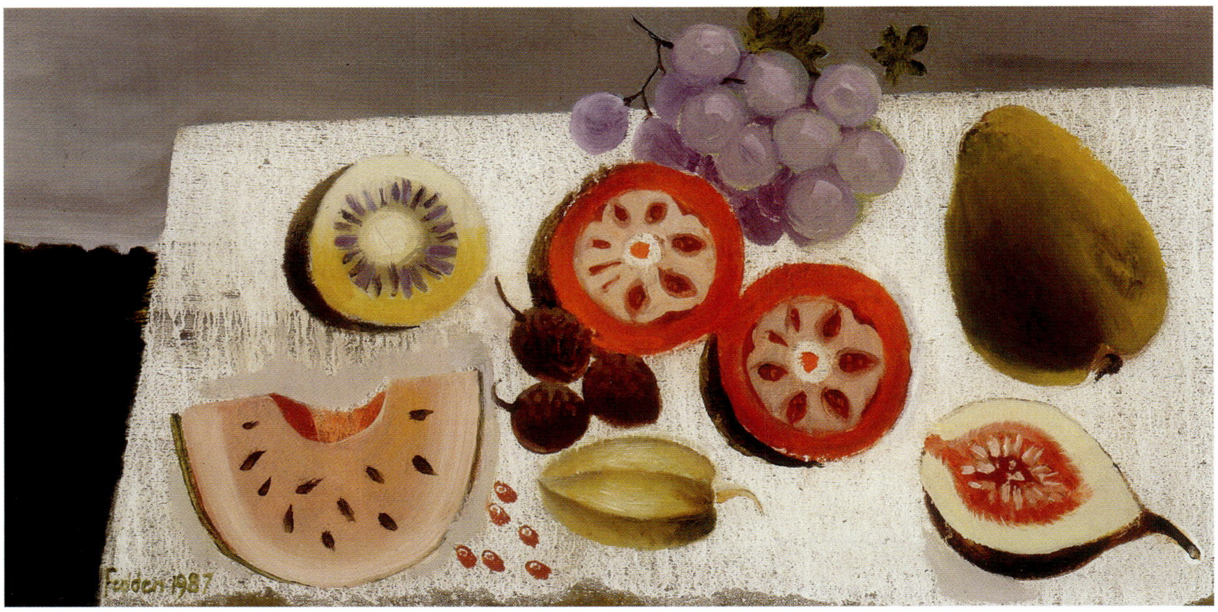

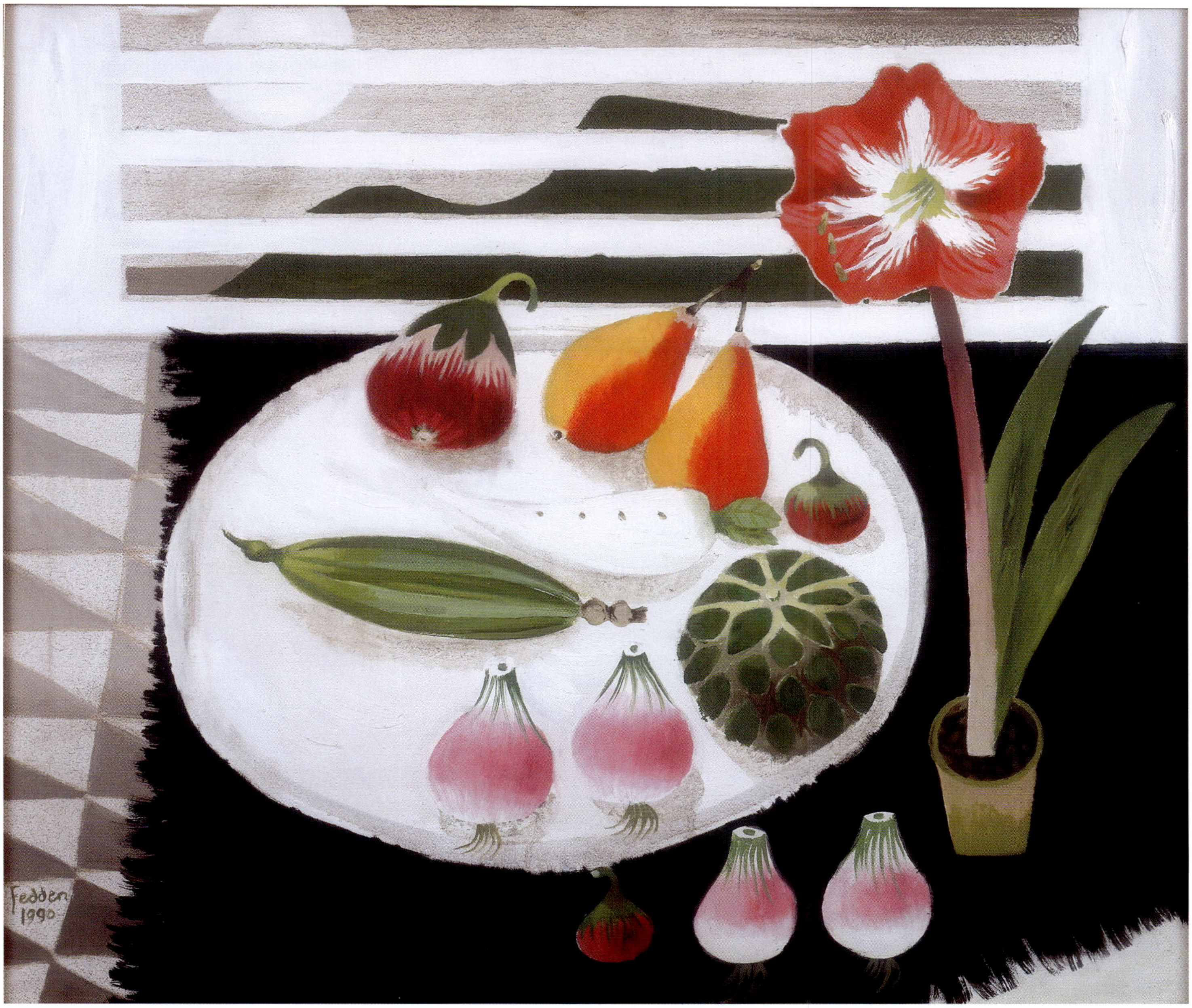

58
Indian Fruit, 1990
Oil on canvas
76 x 91.5 cm (30 x 36 in)
Private collection

Sometimes called 'Michael's Fruit' after the friend who brought them to her from India, these are not real but artificial. Their artificiality clearly gives Fedden an added, intriguing challenge – how to paint them so they don't look genuine.

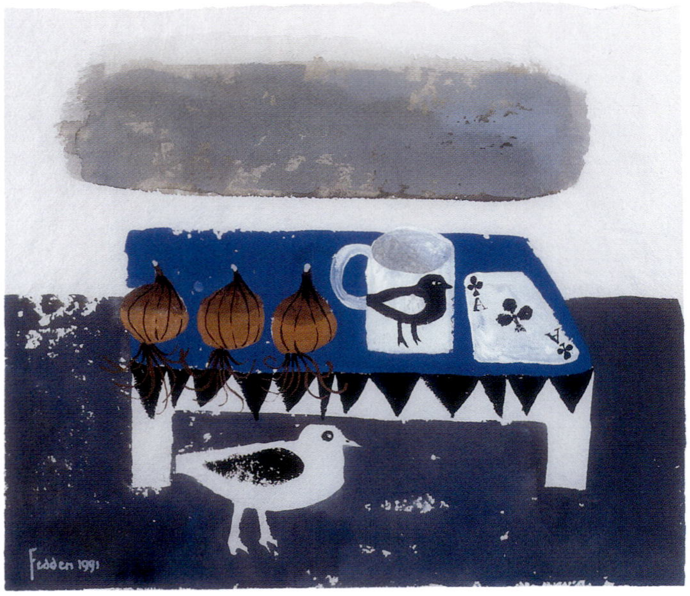

59
Two Birds, 1991
Gouache
23 x 26.5 cm (9 x 10 in)
Private collection

60
Stormy Weather, 1994
Oil on canvas
59.5 x 74.8 cm (23⅜ x 29⅜ in)
Private collection

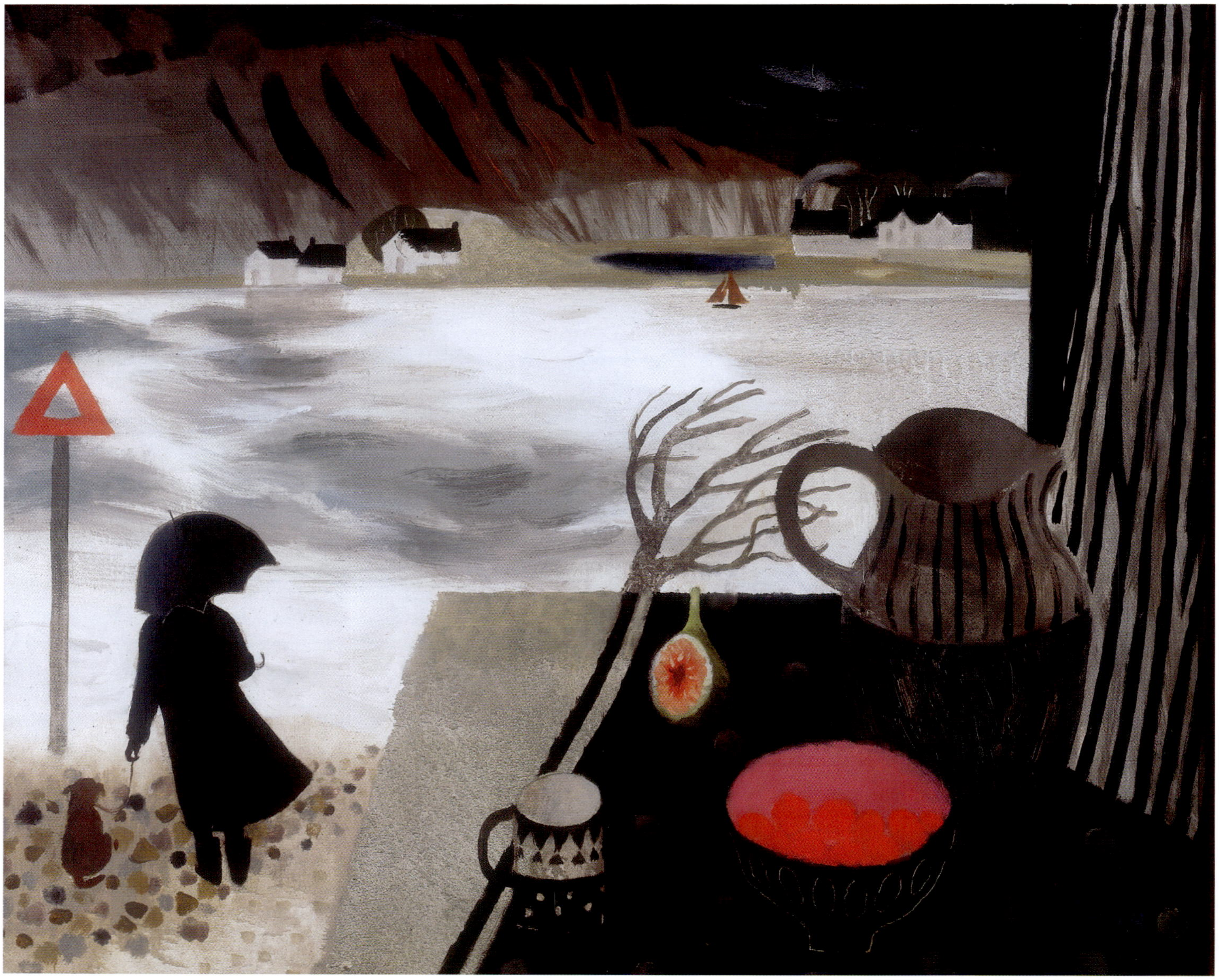

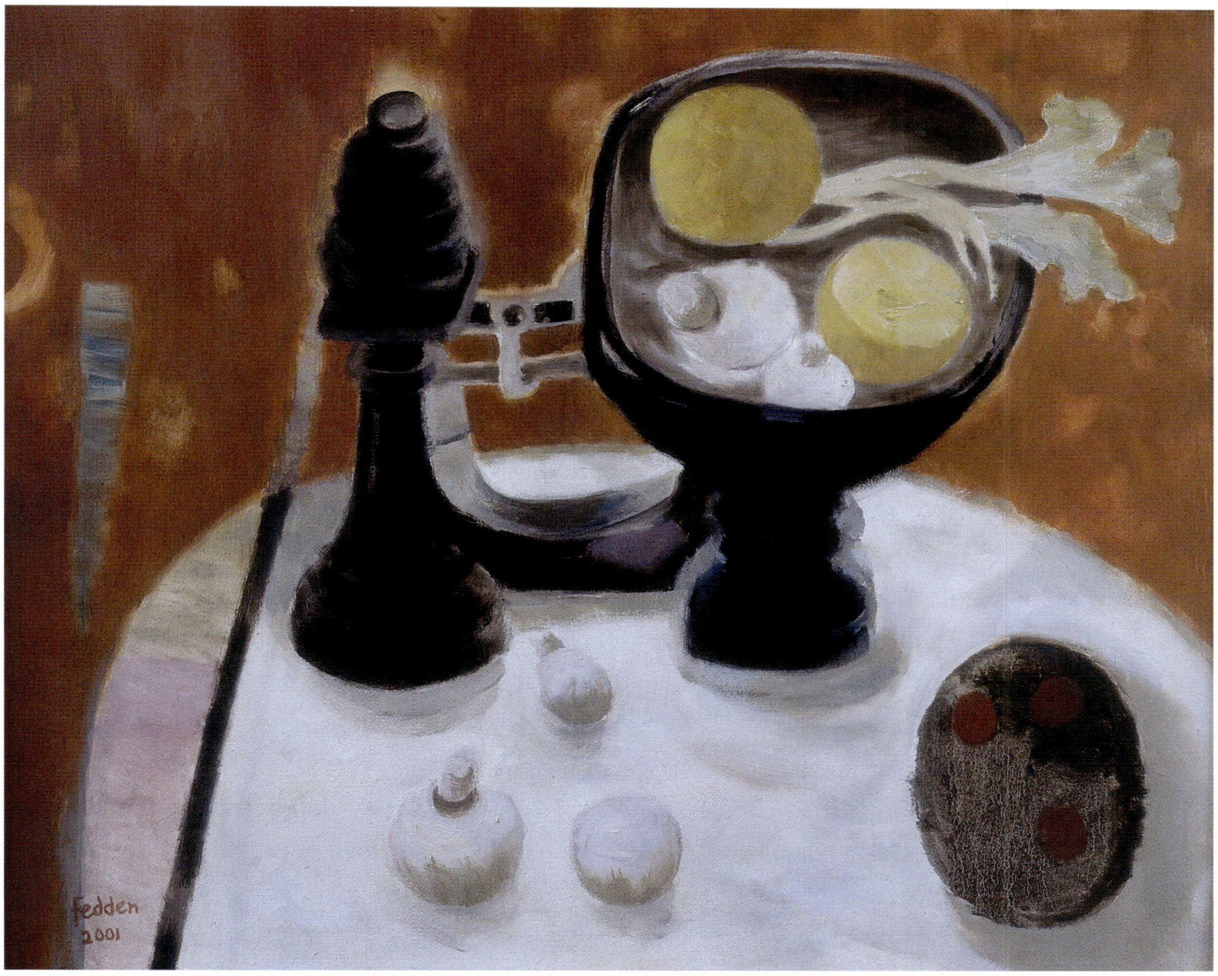

61
The Weighing Machine, 2001
Oil on canvas
60 x 75 cm (23⅝ x 29½ in)
Credit: The Artist

A favourite subject – her mother's Victorian weighing machine. Fedden still uses it in her kitchen today.

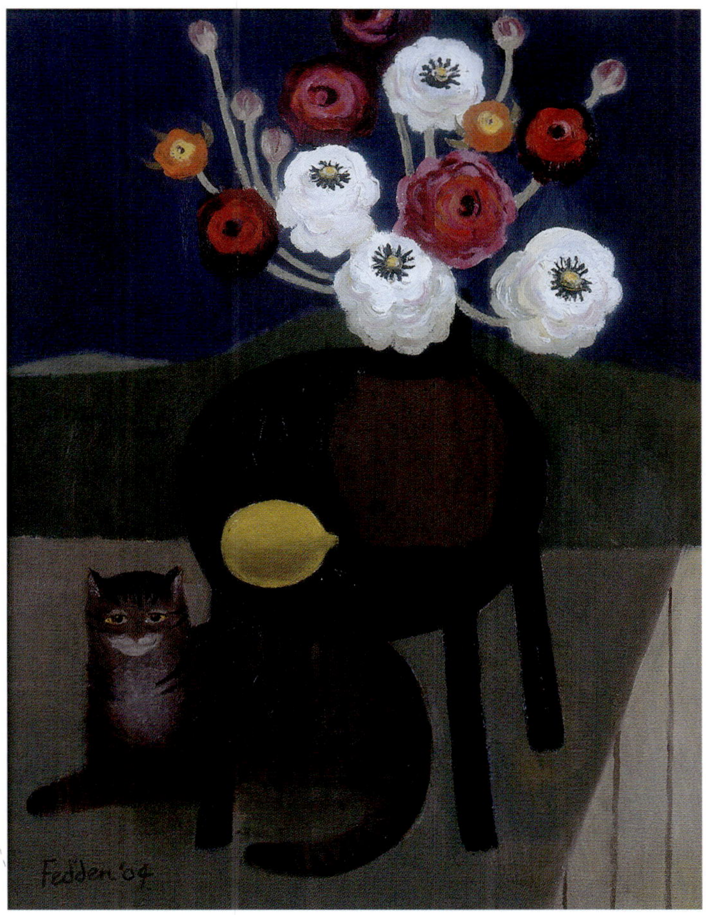

62
Ranunculus and Cat, 2004
Oil on canvas
49.4 x 39.2 cm (19½ x 15½ in)
Credit: The Artist

CHAPTER TWO

Three Beginnings

The development of Mary Fedden's art has taken place over more decades than is the case with most artists. After the promise of her early years, two later significant events strongly changed or influenced her practice as an artist. So she might be said to have experienced *three* beginnings.

Early Days

'I loved drawing and painting when I was very small. I always did,' Mary Fedden remembers.

She was born in Bristol in 1915. Her father was a sugar broker, one of a long line of sugar merchants in the Fedden family, stretching back to the eighteenth century. They were well-to-do; her father was the third person ever to own a car in Bristol. When he proposed to her mother, he drove to her house and she knew for certain who was coming because of the exceedingly rare sound of a car engine.

Mary's first school report, dated 14 December 1920, suggests early recognition of certain talents possessed by this 'bright, sunny, lovable little thing' who was a 'great favourite with everybody'. The school, Gordon Lodge, Stoke Bishop, which she loved, was what in those days was known as a 'Dame School'.

Under 'Writing', the teacher Edith E.G. Preston-Tewart commented, 'Good, at times v. good', while the comment for 'Elocution' for this *five-year-old* was 'Voice production good. Expression v. good & memory work excellent'. Her 'Painting & Crayon Work' was also 'V. good' and her 'Drawing' was 'Excellent'. The concluding comment was: '[Mary] should have a most promising school career'. Today, over 80 years later, Fedden laughs and says, 'All she could think of was a "school" career!'

Mary then went, aged 11, to Bristol's highly academic Badminton School as a day-girl. This all-girl independent boarding school with an impressive reputation wasn't her cup of tea. She hated it. She was not destined for a university career as many of the girls were, but there was one redeeming feature for her in the person of Miss Monica Young, the art teacher, who had been a student at the prestigious London art college, the Slade School of Fine Art. 'She was very nice, wonderful. She made school *just* bearable for me.'

Mary left school at 16 – as soon as she could. She told her parents she wanted to go to art school. Her parents said that was fine, she could go to Bristol Art School, but a provincial art school was not what Monica Young had in mind for her star pupil: she had to go to the Slade in London. 'And she went and saw my parents,' Fedden remembers, 'although she was a very nervous and shy woman, and she told them, "Don't send Mary to Bristol Art School." So they sent me to the Slade. I'm always deeply grateful to her.' As it turned out, Mary won a scholarship at the Slade and was granted free tuition. When she left home for the big city, she was a mere 17 years old.

63
Little Soft Lion
Fabric and thread

Fedden marks the births of the babies of friends or family members by the gift of little soft lions. She reckons she's made hundreds. They are all different. Some would almost be at home in the Phoenician galleries of a museum. 'Here is a lion for your daughter,' she wrote to one family. 'I hope she likes it.'

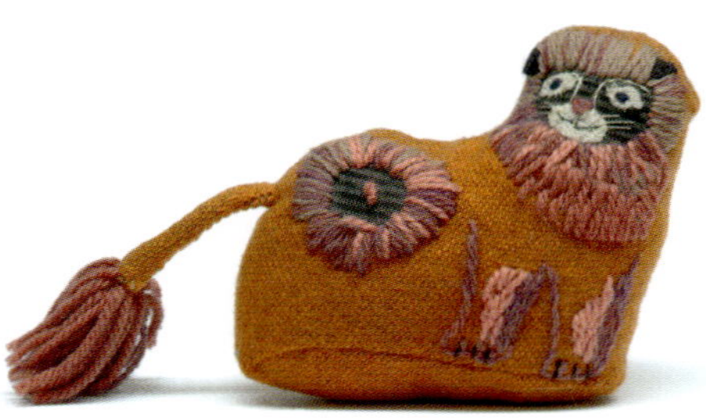

Clearly, as a child, Mary had been precocious in painting and drawing, but today there is nothing left of her childhood efforts – or at least nothing yet discovered – because at some point she decided they were worthless and deliberately destroyed them.

In the course of Mary's childhood, her art teacher had not been the only one to encourage her artistic ambitions and spark her attraction to the notion of being 'Bohemian'. There had also been Uncle Romilly. When she was 12, she had gone to visit this artist uncle in France. A watercolourist, he lived by the Seine north of Paris, near Rouen, in a village called Chantemesle. Mary humorously recounts that Romilly and his wealthy American wife Katharine, a writer, lived a rather luxurious existence with servants and wonderful food. There was wine at lunch every day (and not, as at home in Bristol, just a couple times a year). She decided there and then that if *that's* how painters live, then she was 'going to be a painter'. More seriously, perhaps this 'wonderful food' did contribute to the eventual choice of still life as her central painterly interest, given the traditional connections of this genre with the table.

She loved Uncle Romilly. He was a highly amusing man. He wrote an entertaining book called *Food and Other Frailties*[1] and another on fly-fishing. She says today that his watercolours were 'rather good' but that he was 'very idle', so that there are not many of his paintings around. Some do show up at auction now and then.

On that early visit to her uncle and aunt by the Seine, she recalls three other things not without relevance to her ambitions. On one occasion, she self-consciously confessed to her aunt: 'Aunt Katharine, I've got such a big nose nobody will fall in love with me.' 'My dear child,' her aunt replied with memorable sagacity, 'there has never been a successful or talented woman with a small nose.' She gave this encouraging notion due consideration afterwards, and she seems to have followed her aquiline feature pretty successfully throughout her long career. Nor, more than 20 years after her aunt's remark, when she was 34, did it in the least prevent the love of her life, Julian Trevelyan, from falling for her. She was, after all, a strikingly beautiful young woman with jet black hair and a winning sense of adventure and fun.

Another event that sticks in her mind from her first visit to France was when Uncle Romilly took her one day to peer through a gate on the boundary of a large garden. It was in a place called Giverny. Through that gate she saw a large water-lily pond, weeping willows and perhaps, also, a Japanese bridge, though she is not now sure if she has added this detail in retelling the story over the years. Romilly said: 'A really interesting painter lived here, and he died last year. You'll know about this painter one day.' She asked his name and he replied that it was Claude Monet. 'I'll remember that,' she said, and she did. This happened years before Monet's garden was open to the public. Today, Fedden says that while she respects

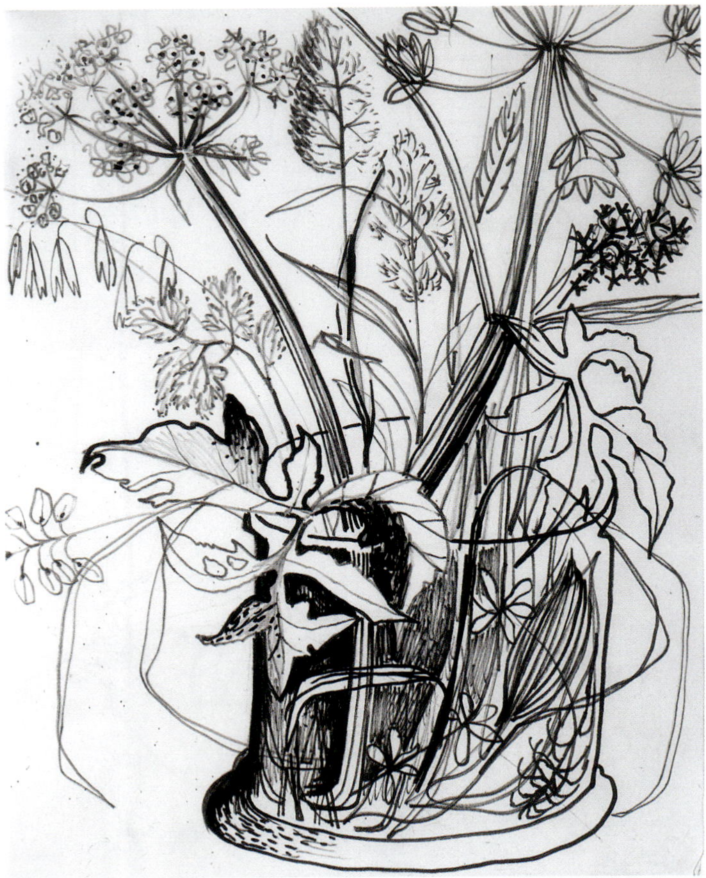

64
Giant Hogweed, date unknown
Pen and ink
Dimensions unknown
Credit: The Artist

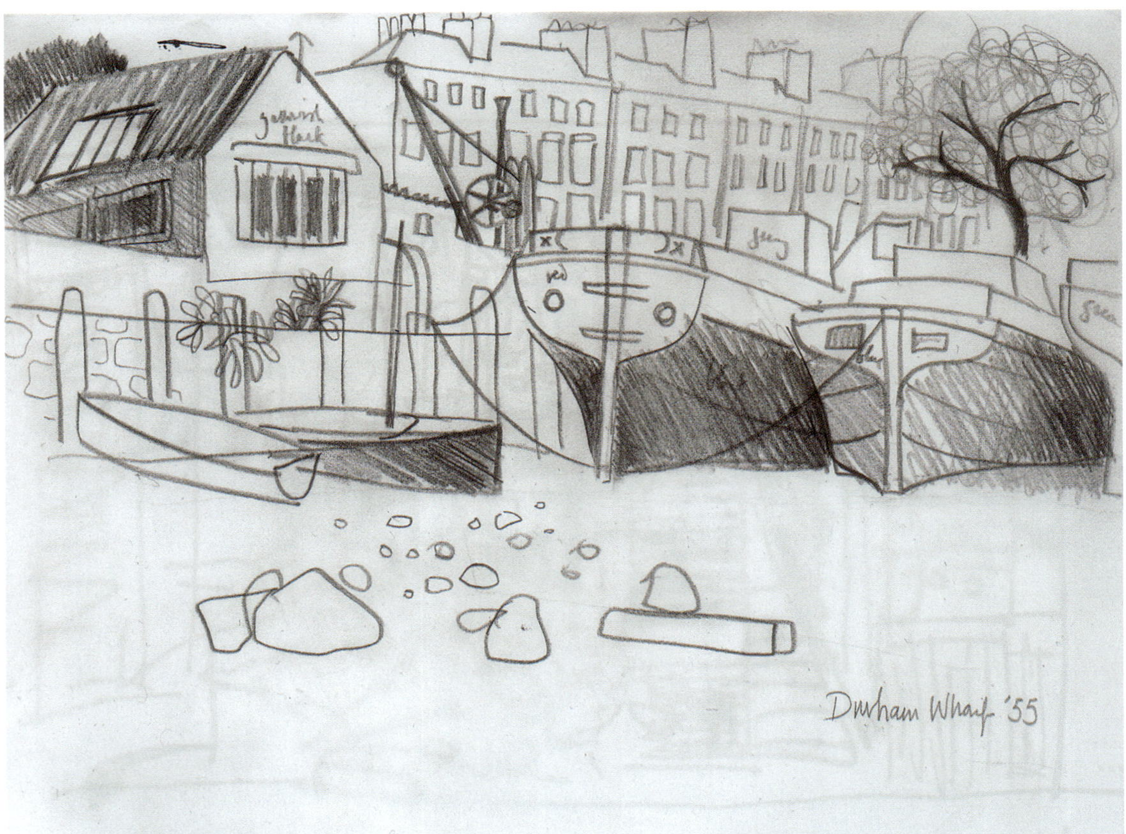

65 (opposite)
Hellebores, 1996
Oil on canvas
Dimensions unknown
Credit: The Artist

66 (left)
Durham Wharf, 1955
Pencil
12.8 x 25.9 cm (5 x 9 in)
Credit: The Artist

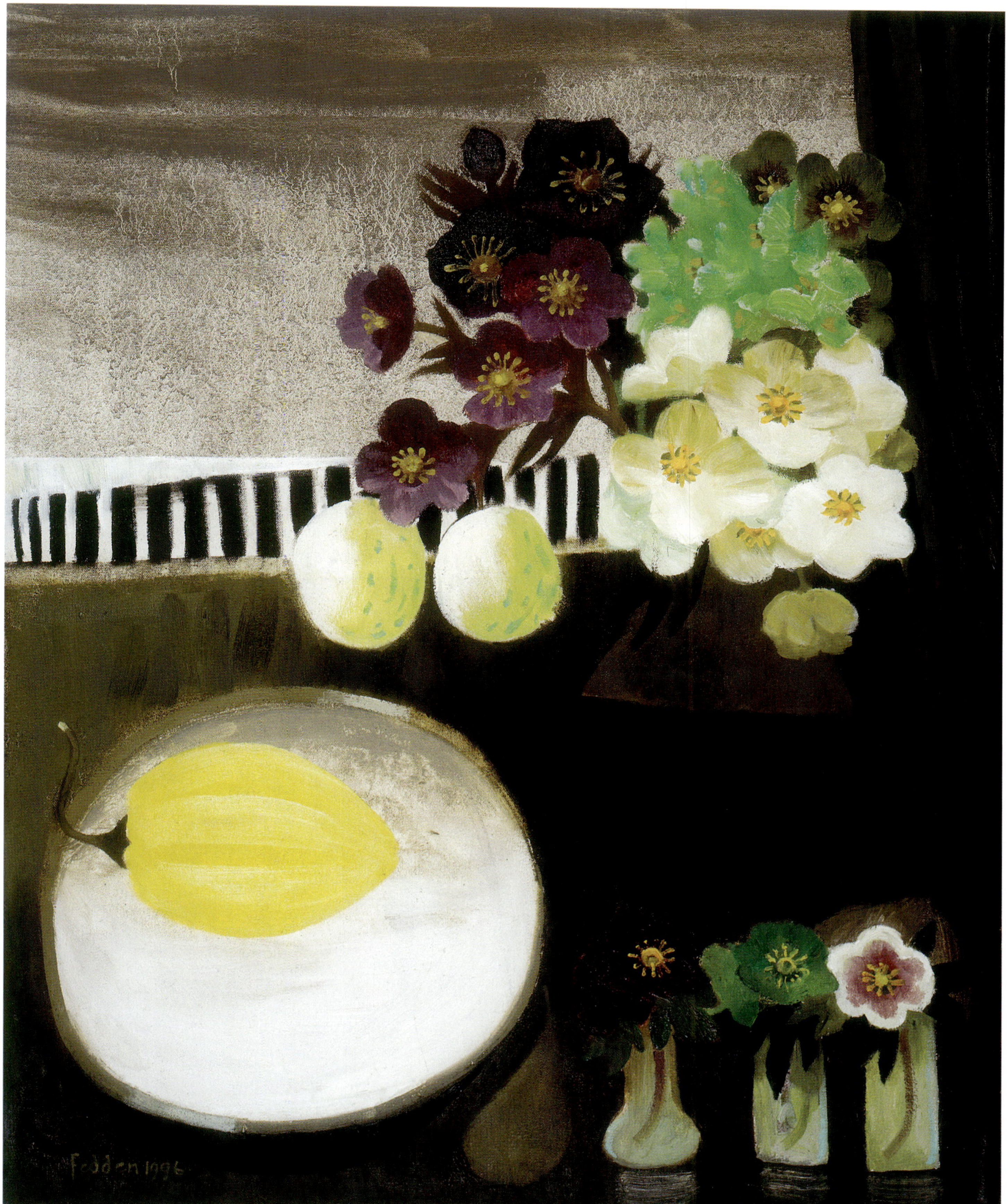

Monet's art, she has never really been *excited* by it, finding it too 'soft'. However, she hasn't forgotten that the appropriateness of artists' surroundings can have strong meaning for them and for posterity.

Durham Wharf by – or very nearly *in* – the Thames at Chiswick and Hammersmith, where she has lived and worked since 1949, has this kind of meaning. Its two converted warehouses open onto a couple of little enclosed gardens (massively stocked with camellias and poppies, giant hogweed (Ill. 64), clematis, catmint and many other cottage-garden plants. All this feeds her art, though the river itself she felt was Julian's beat. Durham Wharf has already become some sort of a mini-Mecca in the imagination of Fedden enthusiasts. (Ill. 66)

Another unforgettable aspect of her French visit at the age of 12 was meeting an artist called Claude Flight (still much honoured for his vigorous Futurist linocuts). He was living in one of the inhabitable Neolithic caves above Chantemesle. A photograph of him in his cave, standing casually with his hands in his pockets, appeared in the *Daily Mail* in 1927 (the year of Mary's visit) with the headline: 'The Cave Man Artist's Home above the Seine'. Flight, along with Mary's cousin Robin Fedden (Romilly and Katharine's only child and later a significant figure in the history of the National Trust), Mary and other local ex-patriots were co-opted to form a cricket team to play in an England versus France match. But what totally fascinated Mary was that 'Flight lived in his cave with his *mistress*. I'd never met anyone before who "lived in sin", as my parents would put it.'

At the Slade School of Fine Art, Fedden remembers above all having a wonderful time: it was her first lengthy taste of freedom away from home. She trained there for four years, until 1936, but this art school's importance to her as

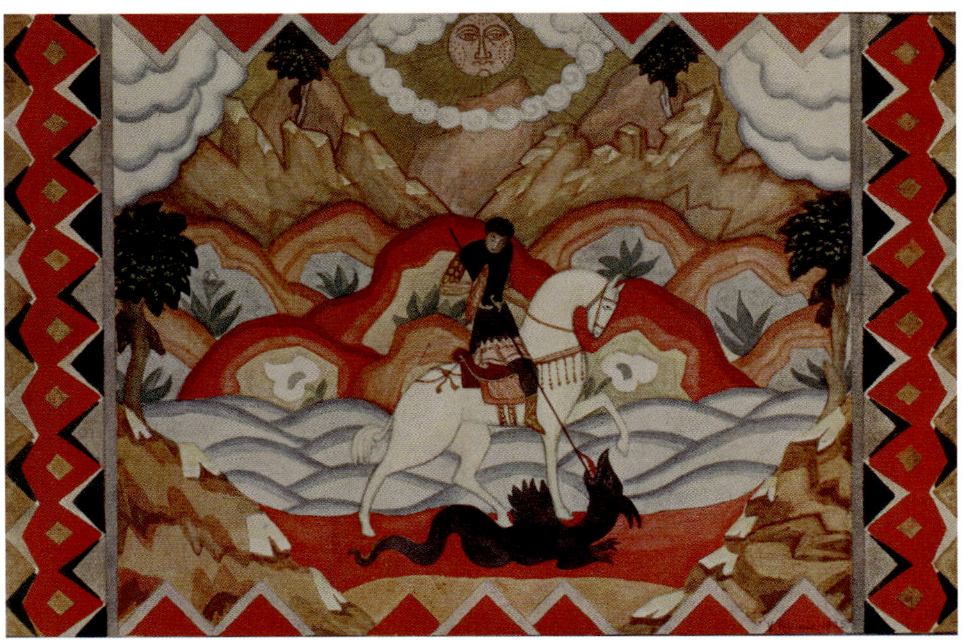

67
Drop curtain design
by Vladimir Polunin
© 2006 Trustees of the National Library of Scotland
By permission of the Polunin Family

'Polunin was the only person at the Slade who really interested me. He was an inspiration,' Mary Fedden remembers. Her later work was to show the effect of Polunin's teaching and paintings in her love of bright colour and compelling patterns – borders and bands of diamond-shapes, for example.

a painter is something she now downplays. A number of notable British artists who were students at the Slade attended either before her time there or after it. Stanley Spencer and Paul Nash had been at the Slade in the 1910s. Roger Hilton was there 1929 to 1931 and Patrick Heron from 1937 to 1939.

Fedden characterises the Slade teachers as 'nice old gents'. The single exception was Vladimir Polunin. He had joined the staff in 1929, introducing stage painting. (He had connections with Sergei Diaghilev, founder of Ballets Russes.) Mary found him very entertaining – 'a sweet man' – and, more to the point, his work inspired her. It involved bold, vivid colour and lively pattern in contrast to the duller chromatics that prevailed (Ill. 67).[2] 'I did think I'd like to take up theatre design when I was at the Slade,' she recalls. She also gave a lot of time to actually painting scenery that was not necessarily of her design. This doubtless helped her later to think large and wide when designing and painting murals. 'But,' she says, 'with theatre design I realised you've got to please everybody, and I really liked working by myself.' Working in a team didn't suit her. 'I like what I put down to be good or bad – but *mine*. If a painting goes wrong, it's entirely my fault.' And she adds: 'I don't like to be interrupted when I'm painting!' (See her Edward Lear parody, Ill. 5)

However, this early foray into theatre design must have influenced the way she came to compose her easel paintings – still lifes, landscapes and the combination of the two which she frequently exploits in paintings such as *Pansies in Provence* (2000) (Ill. 68). The top and sides of her canvas or paper are like a proscenium arch (though often in the guise of a window to look through); a curtain sweeps back to reveal the scene; the still-life elements, carefully directed or choreographed by her, are deployed stage front . . . hills and sky form a distant, lively backdrop. Sometimes she introduces side elements that look exactly like stage flats hiding the wings (see the red 'flat' on the right in *Casey's Bar*, Ill. 23, p.26).

So Polunin's influence was strong. She is still, 60 years later, fascinated by stage design. She returned recently from a rehearsal at Glyndebourne of Handel's *Julius Caesar*, and even after the late-night journey home, she was alight with the excitement of it – particularly the remarkable staging. The sea, forever in motion, was in the distance, as it so frequently is in her paintings such as *Susannah's Mug* (1997) (Ill. 69), with occasional ships passing across it. The whole effect had touched her pictorial imagination.

After the Slade, Fedden had to return home to Bristol, weeping at the prospect. For a while she made an attempt to be a portrait painter, only to discover it was not at all her forte. She taught art at two different local schools. Then war was declared.

In her long career, the war years were the longest period during which she did no painting or even drawing. 'I felt: what a waste of four years,' she has said. 'But that was a purely selfish personal feeling.' First, she became a Land Girl. In her

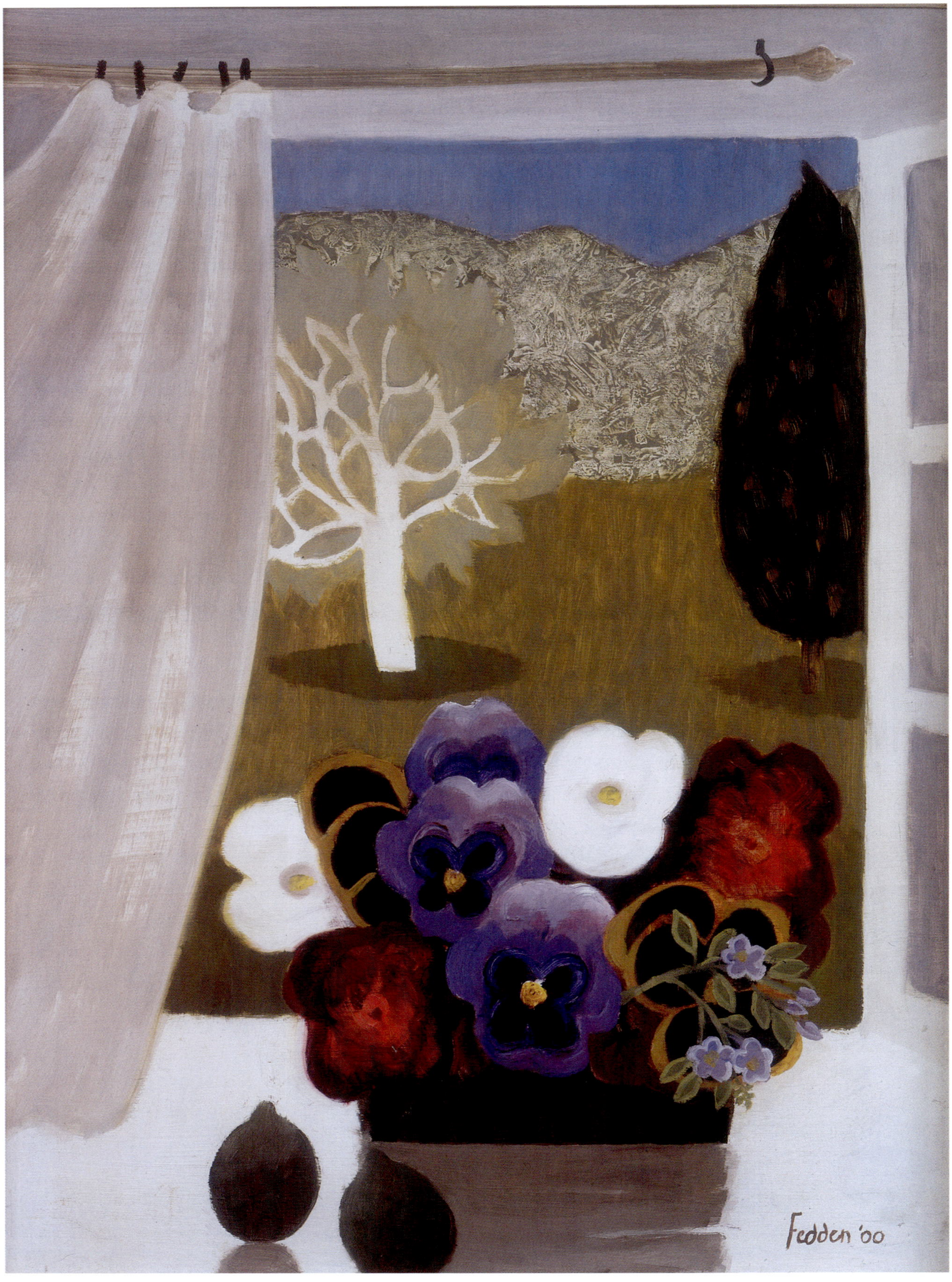
Fedden '00

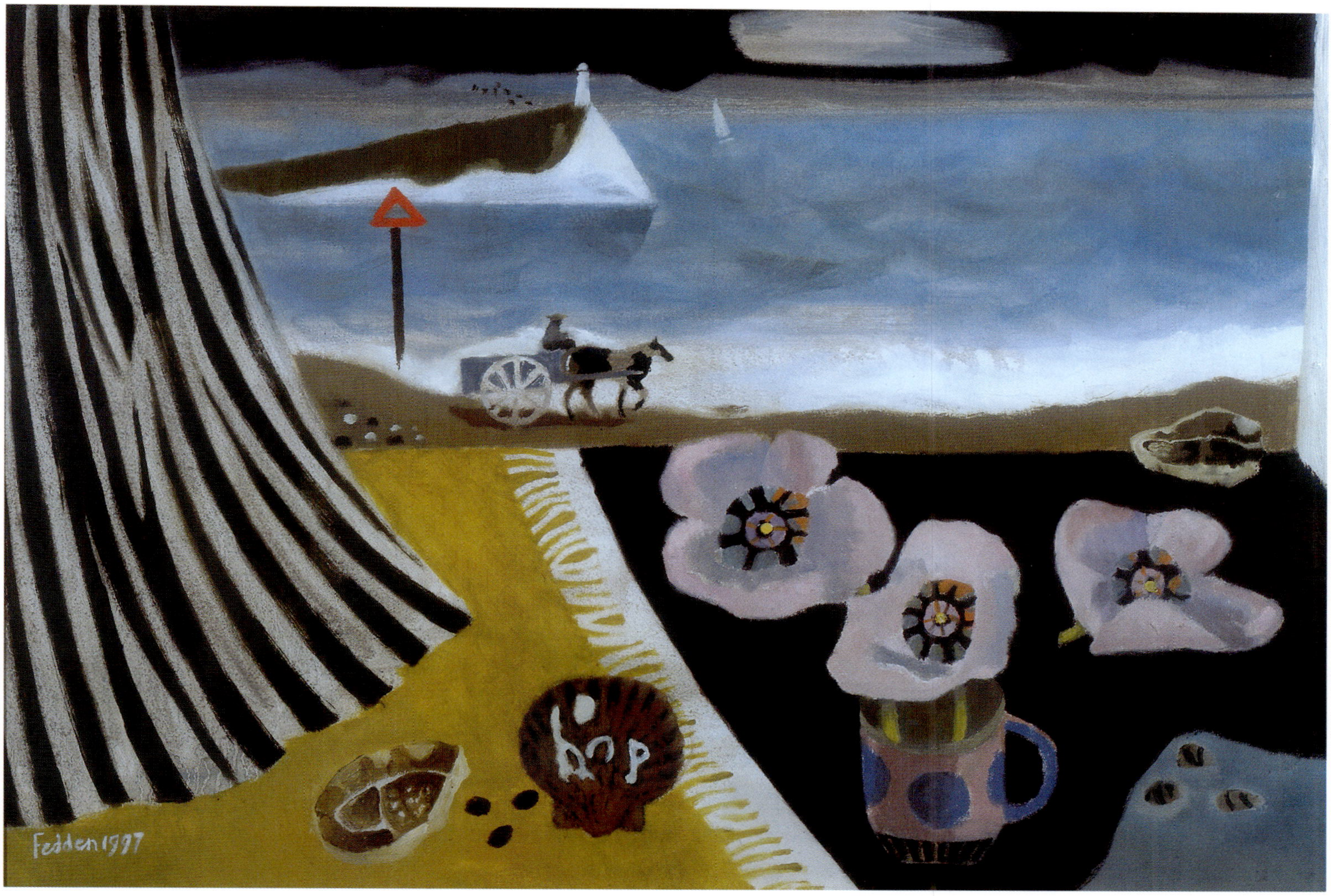

69
Susannah's Mug, 1997
Oil on canvas
48.4 x 73.5 cm (19 x 29 in)
Private collection

68 (opposite)
Pansies in Provence, 2000
Oil on board
59.4 x 44.8 cm (23⅜ x 17⅝ in)
Private collection

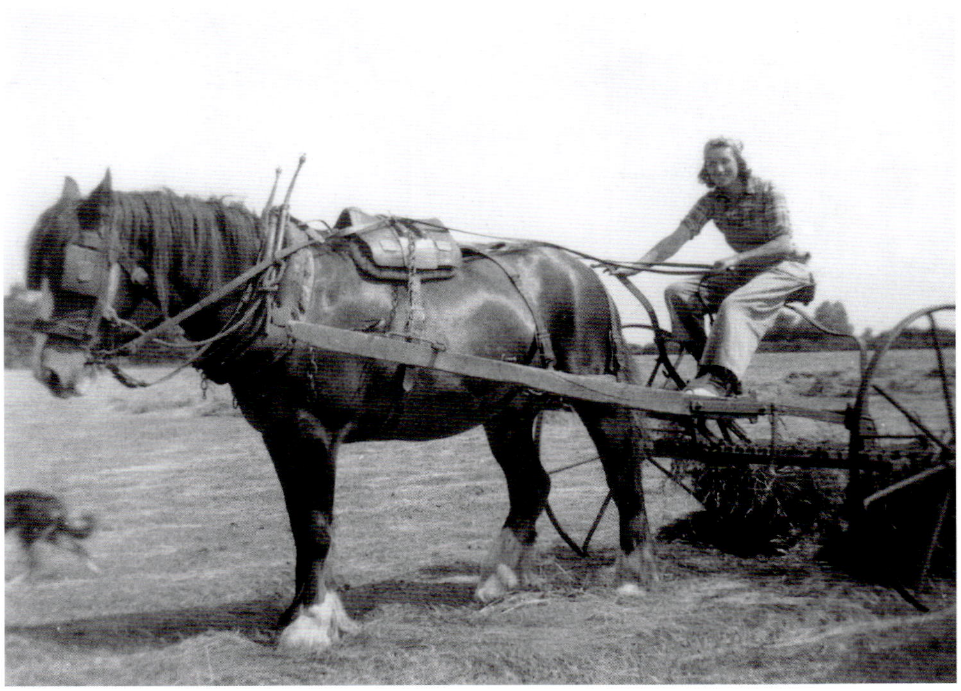

70
Mary Fedden harrowing a field in 1940

contribution to Mavis Nicholson's book *What did you do in the war, Mummy?*,[3] she movingly recounts her wartime experiences (Ill. 70). Employed by a farmer who did not much appreciate mere females (and young ones at that) working for him, she showed a side of her character that has certainly underpinned her career: downright determination. She had to prove to that farmer that she was up to the job, whatever he threw at her. Much of the work was mind-bogglingly dreary. Up and down the fields harrowing or turning hay, she started to recite Keats and Shelley aloud to herself (and the horse), learning a poem the night before so that she could stave off the next day's boredom with it. Her memory for poetry remains quite startling. Start her off with a line or phrase, and she recites like a river in spate.

She had to return home to care for her mother who had suffered a nearly fatal accident. When she did recover, however, Fedden went to London and managed to do some painting there after all: propaganda murals for the Ministry of Information. She also helped a close friend from Slade days, Maisie Meiklejohn, paint scenery for the Arts Theatre. Although this was not the kind of painting she wanted to do, at least she had brushes in her hand (her left hand to be precise), and I suspect such experiences contributed to the quite practical, matter-of-fact approach she still has to her art. She is not one for aesthetic mystique. She is open about the way she paints, even allowing a video to be made of her in the act. Her work cannot be entirely private. Today, she has not painted murals for many years, and avoids commissions like the plague, yet she willingly donates paintings to all sorts of good causes and continues, in her 90s, to paint like a dervish in order to meet the demands, if possible, of the unending line of people wanting to own a Fedden.

At different times, she has also shown a straightforward approach to the need for enterprise in order to make money from her paintings. She proudly tells the story of how, in Sicily, 1949 – on her first trip abroad with Julian Trevelyan – she managed to extend their stay to a couple of months. Julian had money, but as post-war tourists, they were only allowed to take a miniscule amount of it out of Britain. They ran out in no time. But a fortunate and rare snowfall in Taormina prompted her to buy some blank cards, paint the novel scene on them, and sell them at an antique shop.

As it happened, this was not her very first taste of the commercial potential of popularity. Between the war's end and moving in with Julian, she had made ends meet thanks to a commission. This came directly from her first one-person exhibition – in the art gallery of Heal's department store in London. The editor of a magazine called *Woman* engaged her to paint seasonal covers, specifying flowers. This was a purely commercial commission and made no claims to be 'art', but the covers were attractively old-fashioned, elaborate still lifes with landscapes beyond. They served their purpose. Today they are rather faded period pieces.

Julian

Her painting underwent a revolution throughout the 1950s. Julian Trevelyan's influence was dominant for a while. He more or less yanked her into the world of modern art. His criticism helped her find her own contemporary individuality; but for some time she was also strongly influenced by his paintings as well as his words (see Ill. 41, p.42).

A comic event in 1949 illustrates Julian's dominance. He spotted she was using Prussian Blue. He was dramatically outraged and banned it forthwith. During their long drive in his car down to their idyllic sojourn in Sicily, a tube of Prussian Blue was discovered to have unwittingly found its way into the bottom of a picnic basket. Mary has no idea how it got there. Julian pounced on it like a tiger and threw it far out into the larger landscape, beyond all retrieval.

'I've never bought a tube of Prussian Blue since,' Mary says. 'It *isn't* a good colour. There are other such beautiful blues. Winsor Blue is a good colour. Not quite so sharp.' (Ill. 72)

Despite Trevelyan's influence, her own voice is still definitely heard in the newly developed style of her paintings in the early 1950s. Comparisons between her paintings and Julian's at that time immediately show this. She is never his clone. She says that, for one thing, their subjects were different. He only painted a couple of still lifes in his whole career, while it was her main preoccupation all along. And her paintings were always 'much prettier' than his.

71
Little Soft Lion
Fabric and thread

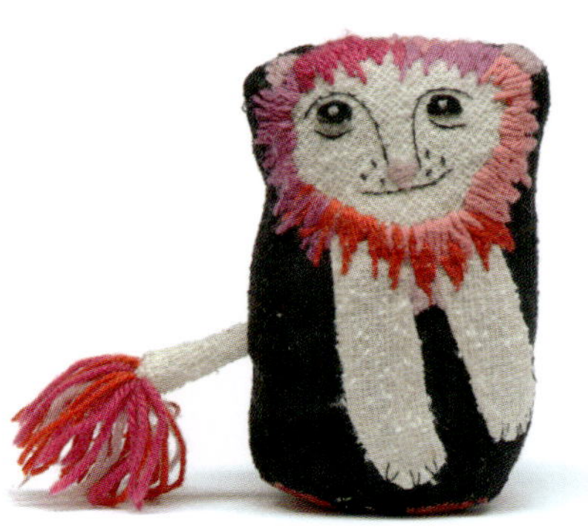

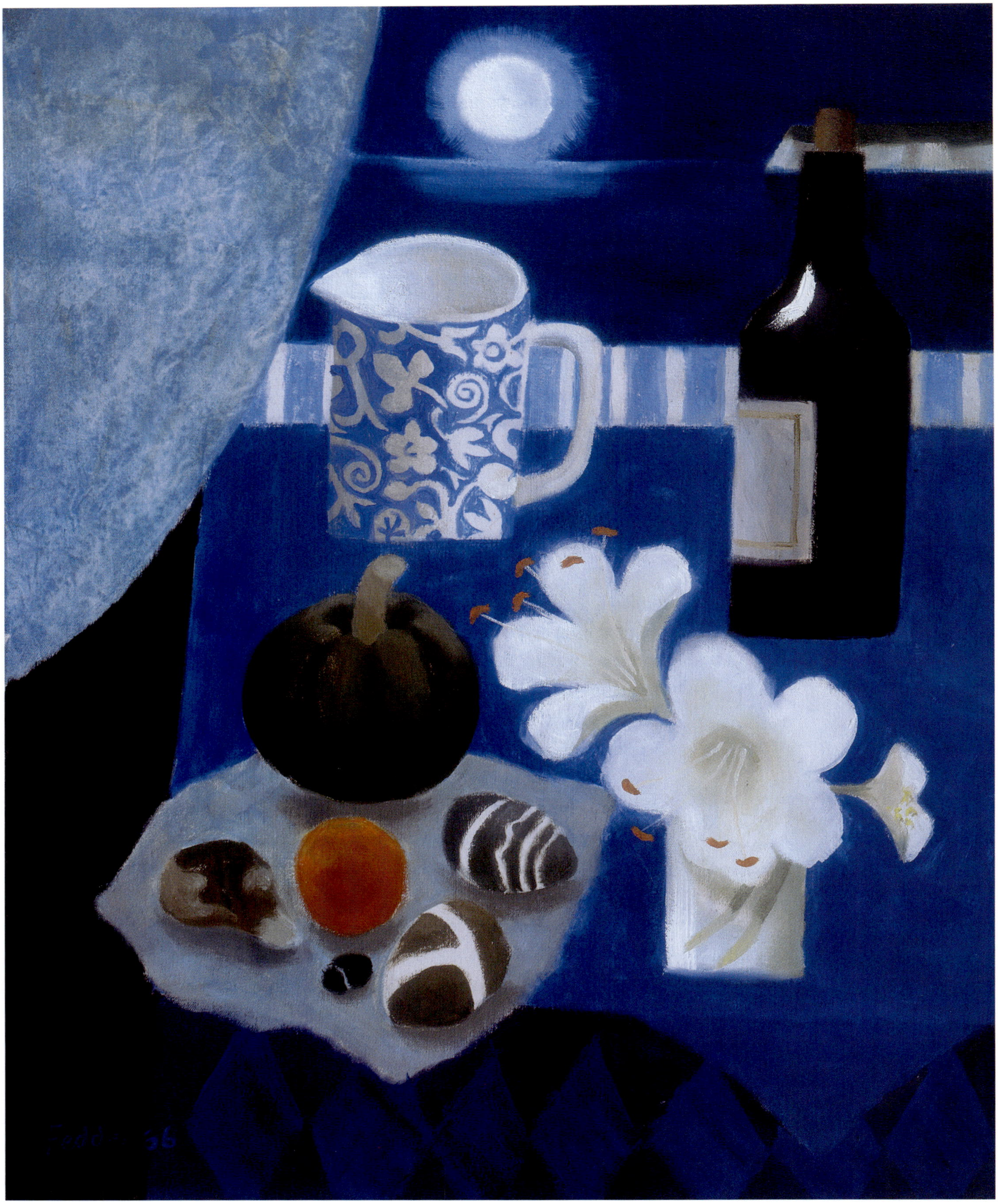

72 (opposite)
The Black Bottle by Moonlight, 2006
Oil on canvas
60 x 50 cm (23⅝ x 19⅝ in)
Private collection

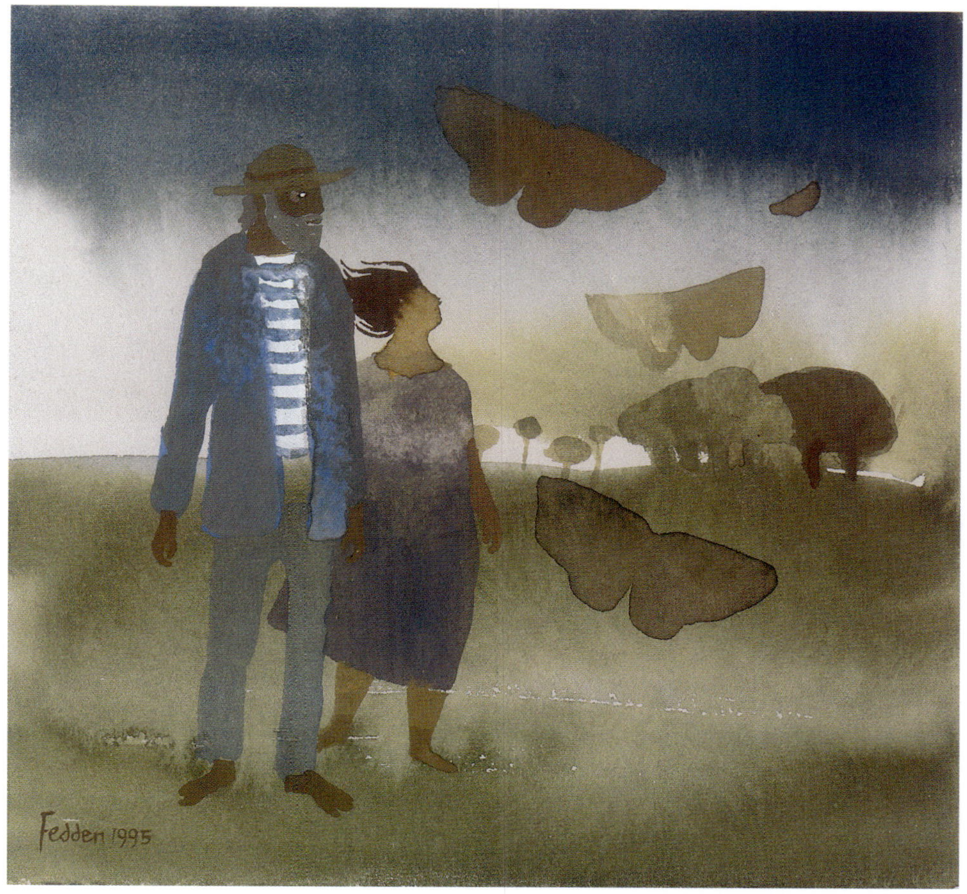

73
Mary and Julian, 1995
Gouache
40.6 x 44.5 cm 16 x 17½ in
Credit: Sotheby's Picture Library

What is undeniable, all the same, is that without Julian's daily input, Fedden's art would have developed quite differently. Her frequently spoken gratitude to him is not just typical modesty. His advent was without doubt a new beginning for her. She perhaps got from him, artistically, something that the Slade teachers (with the exception of Polunin) had failed to provide: he pushed her to find her originality.

Mary and Julian lived, worked, and travelled together for very nearly 40 years (Ill. 73). By any standard, it was a successful marriage … of equals. Tellingly, she records that she would eventually offer criticism of his paintings, the way he had for her in their early days. It was an echo. She would tell him to take out his favourite passage in a painting he was working on; he would refuse and whine: 'That's my favourite part!' But she noticed that he always quietly removed that part later on when she wasn't looking.

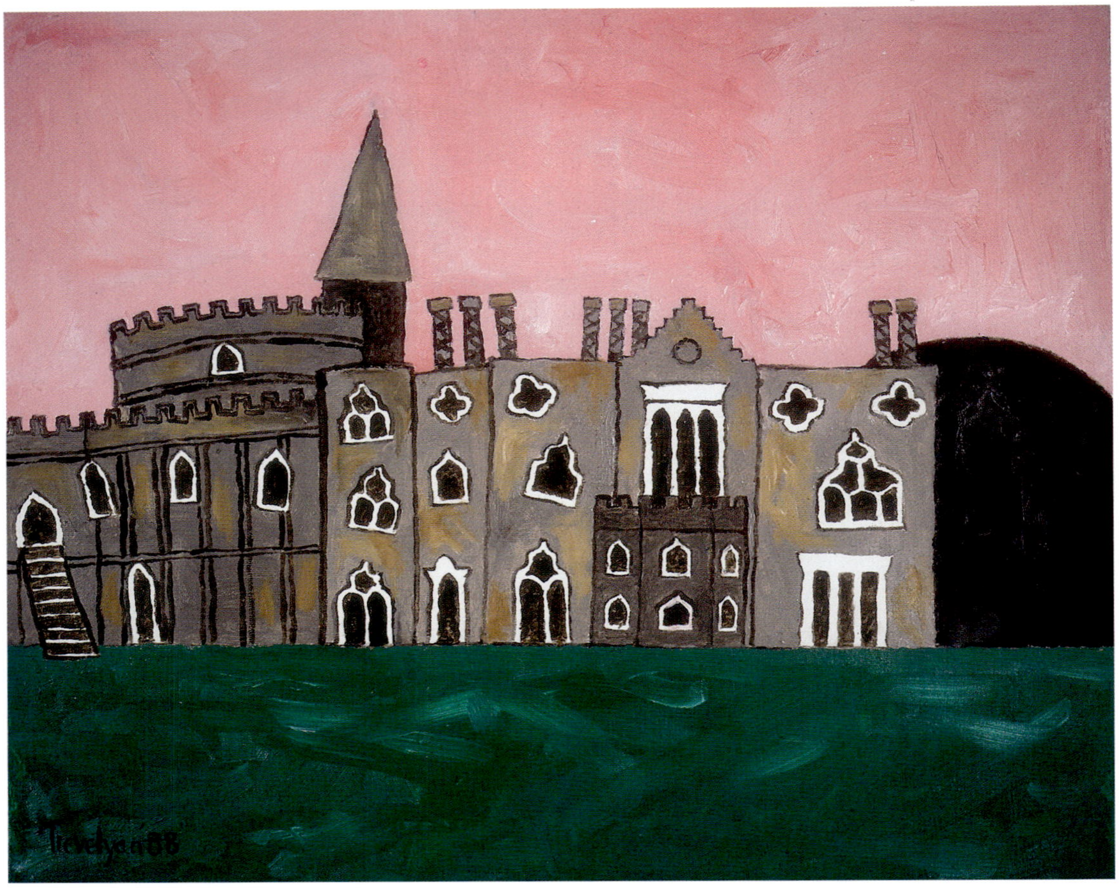

74
Strawberry Hill, 1988
by Julian Trevelyan
Oil on canvas
61 x 77 cm (24 x 30¼ in)
Bohun Gallery, Henley-on-Thames

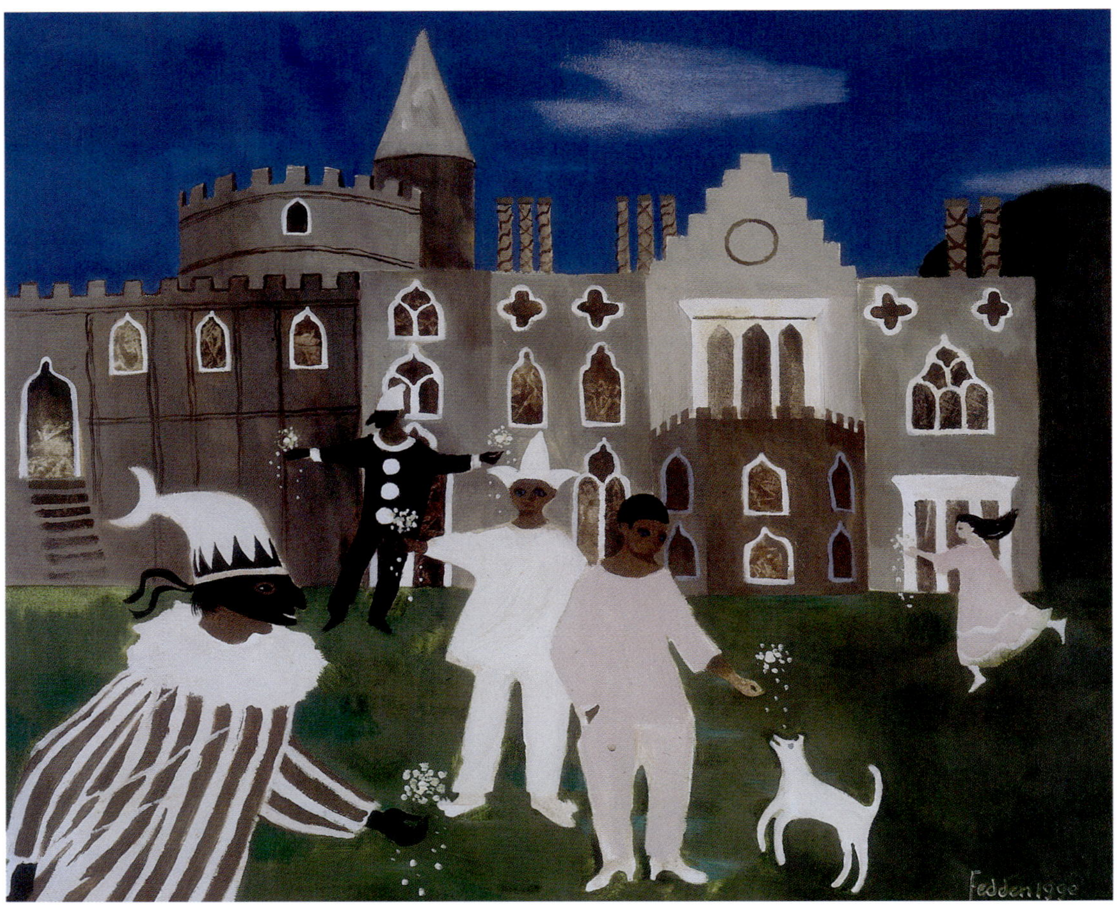

75
Strawberry Hill, 1990
Oil on canvas
61 x 76.2 cm (24 x 30 in)
Private collection

After Julian

Julian Trevelyan died suddenly in 1988. A friend and collector, John Iddon, happened to phone that day to see if Julian had finished a painting for him of Strawberry Hill, Horace Walpole's extraordinary Gothic Revival house in Twickenham where Iddon was working as a teacher (Ill. 74). Julian had finished the painting, but Mary, so soon after Julian's death, could not bring herself to let Iddon buy it. Later, she painted two different versions of the subject, and he bought one of them. (Ill. 75)

Comparing versions of the same subject by these two long-married and close-knit artists is revealing. Julian's version of 'Strawberry Hill' makes great play with the eclectic eccentricity of the architecture, turning it into a topsy-turvy, surreal building with a jaunty life of its own. Mary uses the building as a backdrop for an imaginary *commedia dell'arte* performance – fantastic, amusing, a bit sinister. Perhaps, as Iddon suggests, the architecture's somewhat Venetian appearance may have prompted the invention of Fedden's masquerading characters. On the other hand, they are related to some production or other she'd seen at Glyndebourne. It was Julian who had introduced her to opera. Glyndebourne in particular had become an integral and enjoyable part of her life, borne out in her work. (Ills 76 and 77, overleaf)

Trevelyan's sad departure could hardly be called a beginning, but it wasn't only an ending. He is in many ways still at the centre of her thinking. She constantly refers to him. His printing press (Ill. 78) now inhabits what had been her studio,

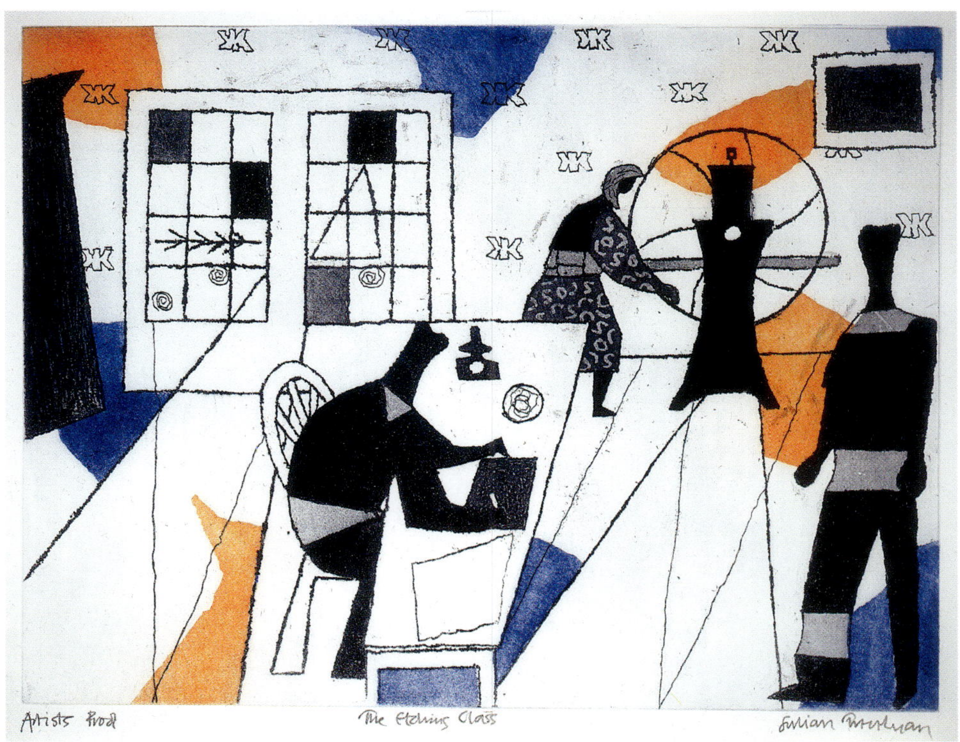

78
The Etching Class, 1973
by Julian Trevelyan
Etching and aquatint
35 x 47.9 cm (13¾ x 18⅞ in)
Bohun Gallery, Henley-on-Thames

The figure in the background operating Trevelyan's press is Mary Fedden. She was her husband's 'clean pair of hands' when he printed his etchings.

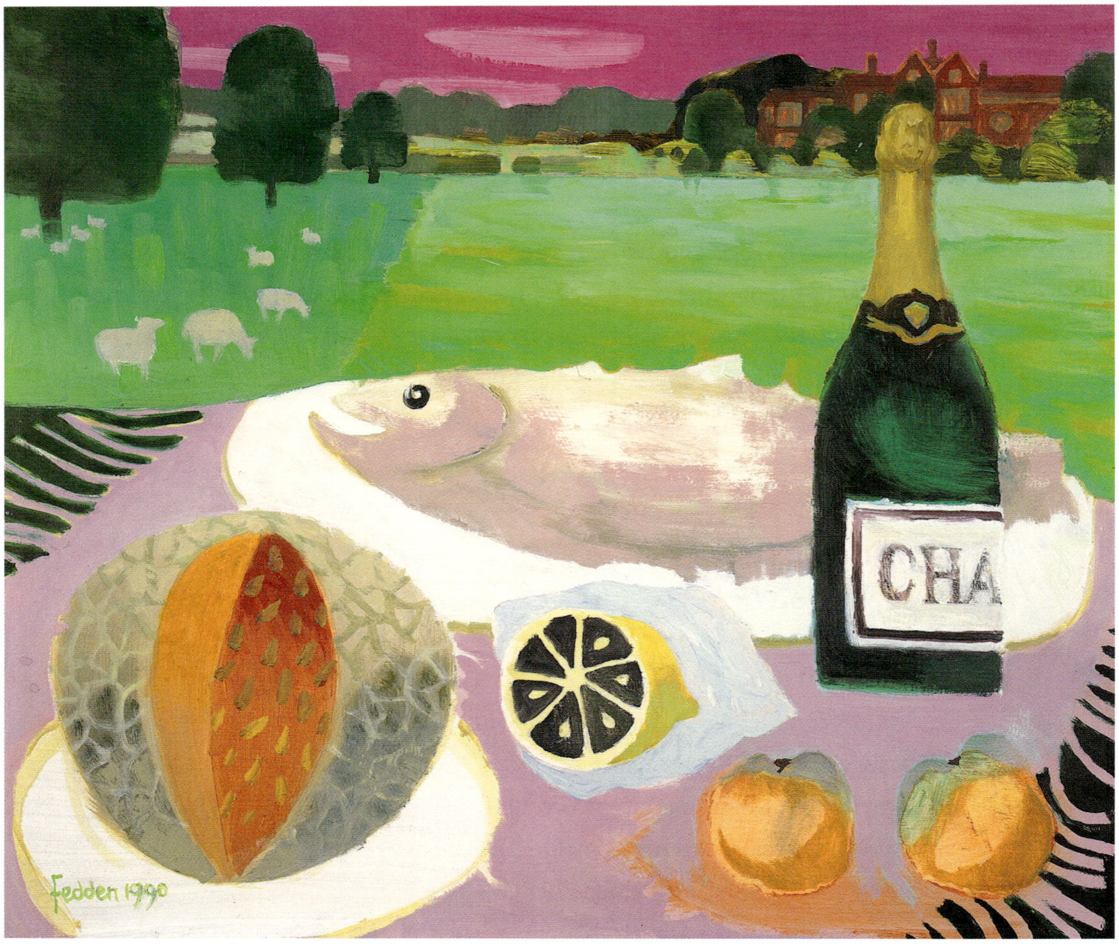

76
Picnic at Glyndebourne, 1990
Oil on board
51.5 x 61 cm (20¼ x 24 in)
Private collection

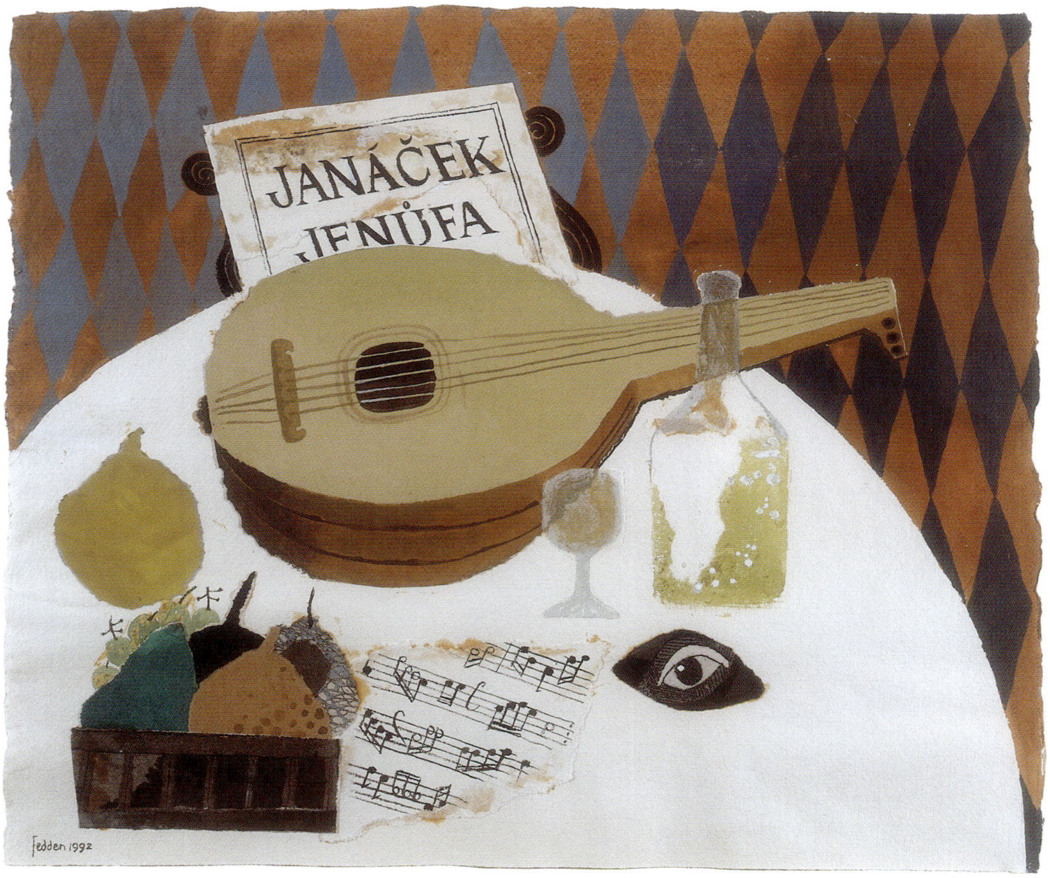

77
Jenufa, 1992
Collage and gouache
46 x 56 cm (18⅛ x 22 in)
Private collection

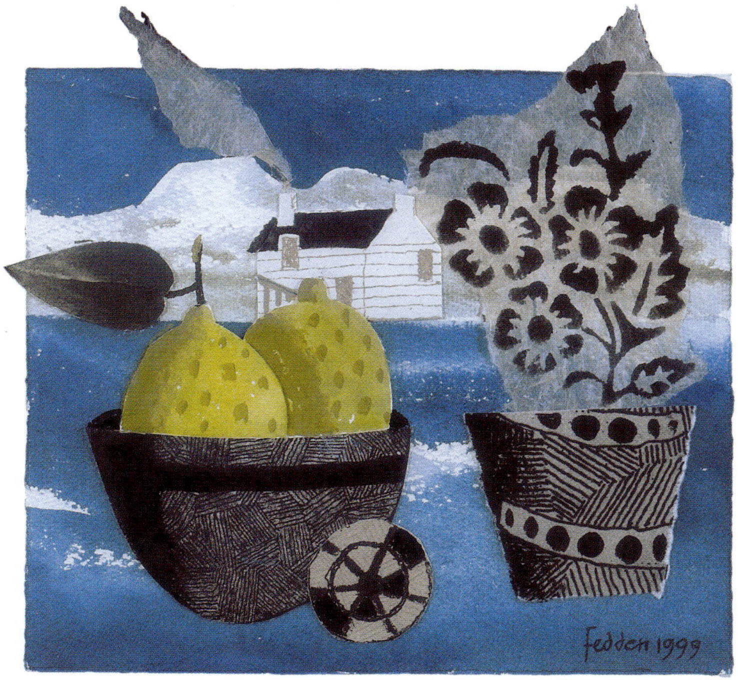

79
Two Lemons, 1999
Collage and gouache
18.5 x 20.2 cm (7¼ x 8 in)
Private collection

while she has moved next door into his. It's larger and airier, and she fills it with her paintings continually.

His press is still used by visiting printmakers, one of whom is gradually completing the editions of Trevelyan's prints, since most were never printed to the full edition in his lifetime. There are always cast-offs from the printing process and Fedden uses them in her collages (Ill. 79). His images of bridges, chimneys, architecture and urban places, his visual wit and the playfulness of his etching needle, still form part of her art just as these things had contributed to their shared interests during their lives together. Mary's collages that incorporate bits of Julian's etchings are, in their own light-hearted way, similar to what Picasso did to the Old Masters, to Velázquez or Delacroix – deconstructing and then reconstructing them on his own terms. In Fedden's case there is a cheeky humour involved, as well as an appreciative homage paid to Trevelyan's work.

Since finding herself alone, Fedden's liberal production of paintings, finished drawings and collages has, if anything, increased. This has coincided with her rise in popularity and, consequently, the prices for her work. However, the relish expressed by her collectors makes it hard to believe that cynical speculation is their sole motive. Perhaps her very profuseness has helped bring on this wave of popularity – or maybe it's the other way round.

Either way, the misfortune of having to continue without Trevelyan may have paradoxically acted as an incentive to work. To that degree, the years since 1988, like the years after 1949 when she started to live with Trevelyan, have proved to be some sort of a third beginning.

Her style has quietly changed in this late period until it is quite different in feel and sinew from her work in the 1950s and 1960s. She is partly unaware of this change. As she paints, day by day, she is not consciously endeavouring to alter her style. She still paints with 'passion', but her paintings have become more 'hard-edged'. This is a relative term, of course, but the incisive drawing that underlies her paintings is revealed in the final pictures as precisely delineated or silhouetted motifs. They exist in a kind of new order and simplicity. Her pictures now depend less on what appears in earlier work, such as *Artichoke Flowers* (1962) (Ill. 81), to be one vigorous rush of execution in which all the elements are almost thrown together by gutsy brushwork and thick applications of paint. Today, her pictures have air and space and order. Objects are separated, the intervals between them becoming as important as the objects themselves in order to make balanced and poised compositions that hold firm. There is more calculation. Objects no longer overlap or confuse each other. Clarity of shape is what matters.

All the same, she still paints boldly – and surprisingly fast. The marks of her brush and sensuous enjoyment of paint itself still brand her work indelibly. There is a sensitive roughness. This is something that fakers cannot duplicate. It's like handwriting – individual, the result of long practice. Fedden says she can immediately recognise a fake because of the brushwork (though it has to be said that some fakes out there in the marketplace are appallingly obvious to others' eyes as well). The apparent simplicity of her paintings is misleading. Even innocent imitators, usually keen to make greetings cards that sell as well as hers, dismally overlook the quality of her paintings.

Ironically, Fedden wishes she could still paint as she did in the 1960s. 'I think I am a rough painter – I hope.' She points to a 1960s' oil she keeps above her bed (Ill. 82). 'That one has very loose outlines to each colour, and I like that. But I find it now incredibly difficult to do.' Turning to *Fruit and Mozart* (2005) (Ill. 83), she continues, 'I get sort of hard-edged, as you can see. And I find it hard to explain to people that I am *led,* rather than me leading. Something makes me paint the way I do, and no matter how hard I try to paint like that one done 30 years ago, with a very rough outline, it comes out with a hard edge … and I don't like being a hard-edge painter.' She points to a new picture. 'That one, you see, – all the edges are quite firm and hard, and I wish they were more … well, that one behind you is a little looser, but not *very*'.

There is a hint in her most recent paintings that this predicament – which, after all, is the kind of unresolved predicament that drives artists to continue painting – could be answered by the re-exploration in her paintings of *light*: moonlight still becomes her. Light is a pervasive, unifying influence. *The Black Bottle by Moonlight* (Ill. 72, p.70) is still perfectly clear and definite in its delineated, spaced objects, but the softness of moonlight is creeping in with a subtle magic.

81 (opposite)
Artichoke Flowers, 1962
Oil on board
120.5 x 89.8 cm (47¼ x 35⅜ in)
Private collection

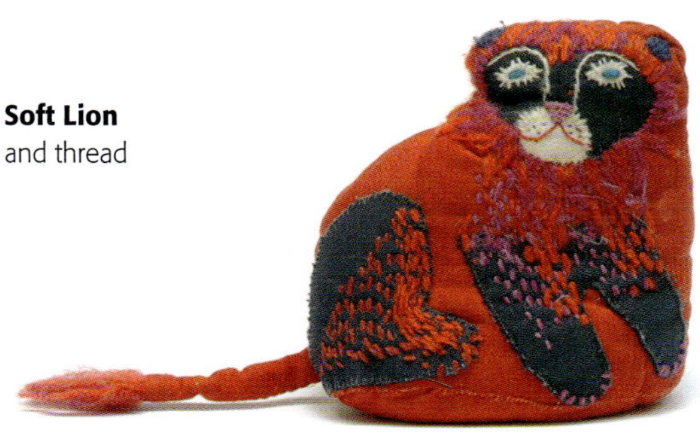

80
Little Soft Lion
Fabric and thread

Notes

1. *Food and Other Frailties* by Romilly Fedden, Seeley Service & Co. Ltd (London), 1948
2. *The Continental Method of Scene Painting* by Vladimir Polunin, C.W. Beaumont (London), 1927, frontispiece
3. *What did you do in the war, Mummy?* by Mavis Nicholson, Chatto & Windus (London), 1995, pp 51–61

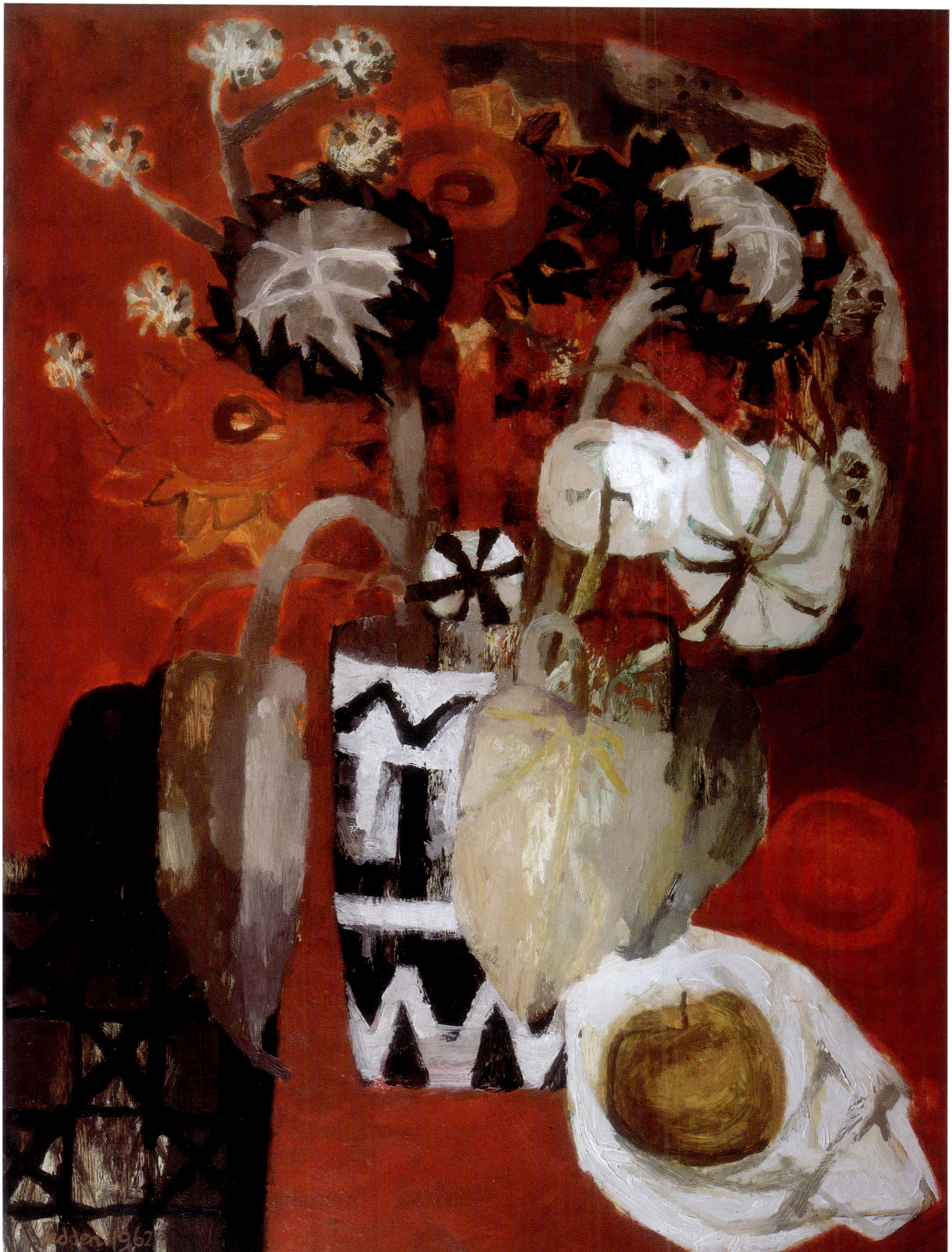

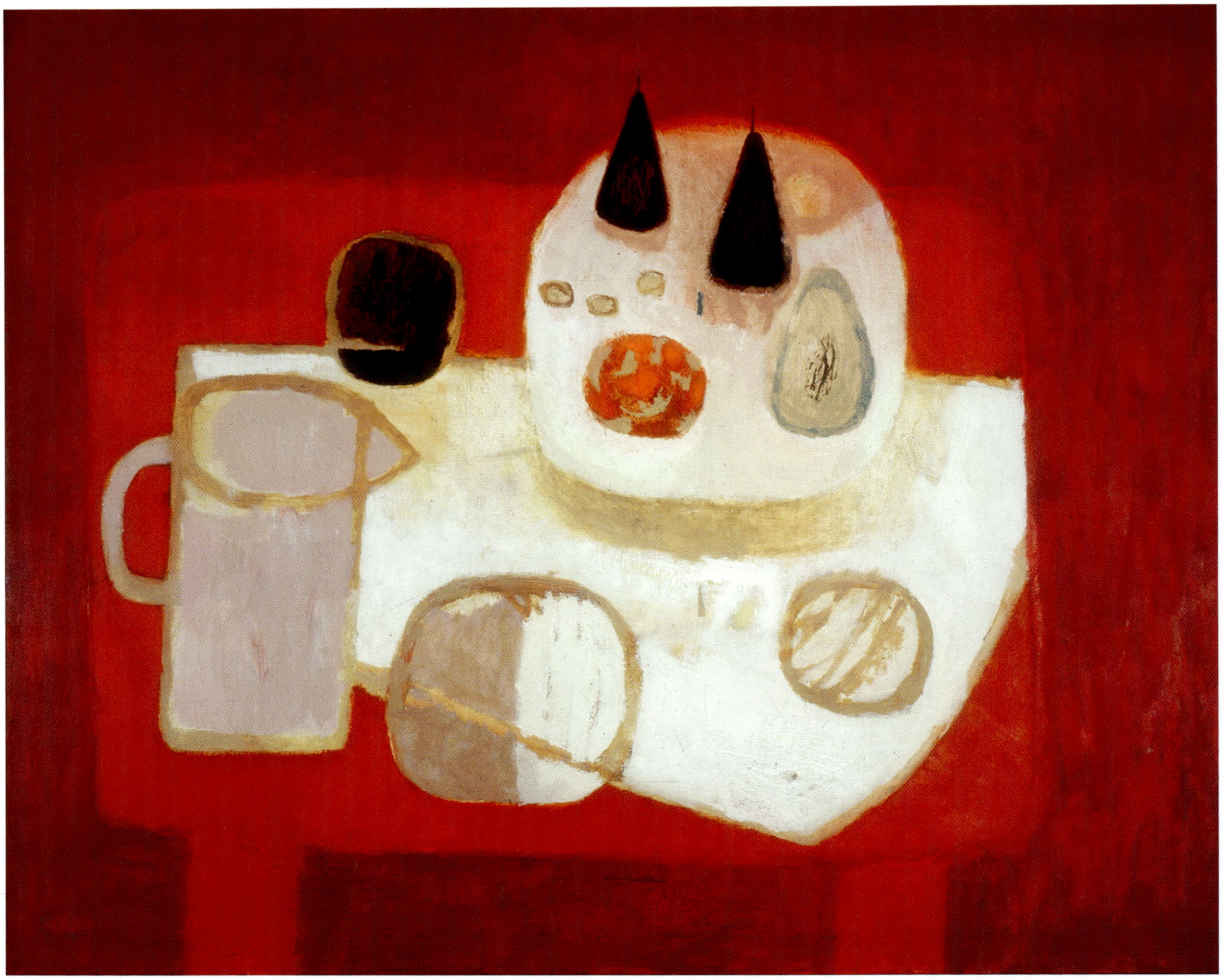

82
Red Still Life, 1967
Oil on canvas
101.9 x 132 cm (40 x 52 in)
Credit: The Artist

This painting from the late 1960s hangs near Mary Fedden's bed. She refers to it often because she wishes she still painted like this today. It has soft edges, which she finds hard or impossible to achieve in her latest paintings.

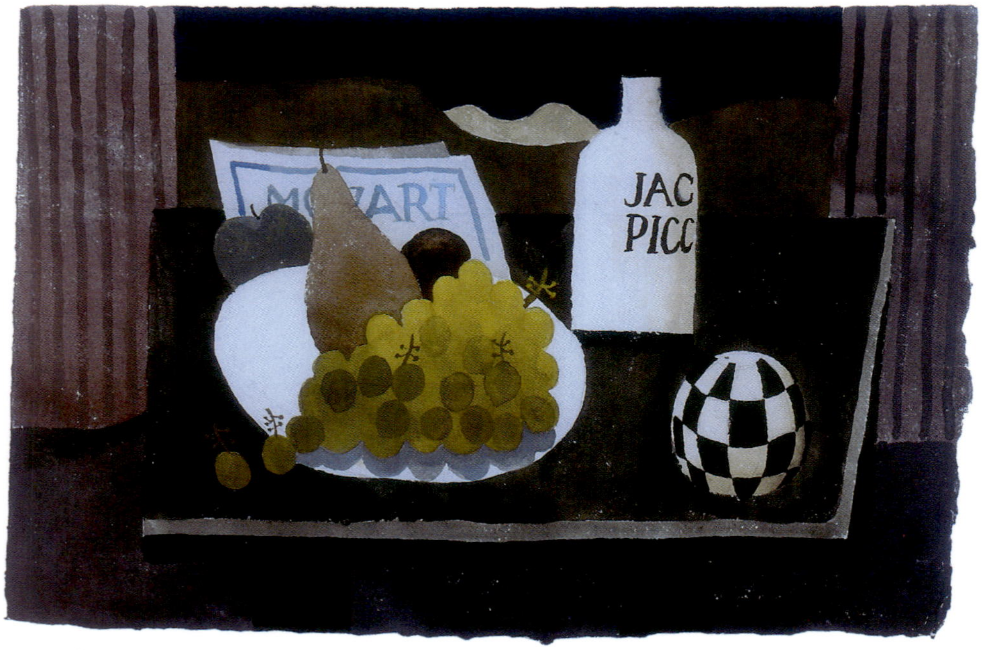

83
Fruit and Mozart, 2005
Gouache
30.6 x 47 cm (12 x 18½ in)
Private collection

A Poetical I·N·T·E·R·L·U·D·E

John Iddon's poem (below) about Mary Fedden is not the only one to be inspired by her work. Hazell Hills and Biddy Selden wrote a dialogue-poem called 'The Fierce Girl (from a painting by Mary Fedden)'. It is a fascinating poem that takes off, in fact, from two Fedden paintings and other sources. Iddon's 'Feddenesque' is directly about her paintings. It has a whimsical tone but an underlying accuracy:

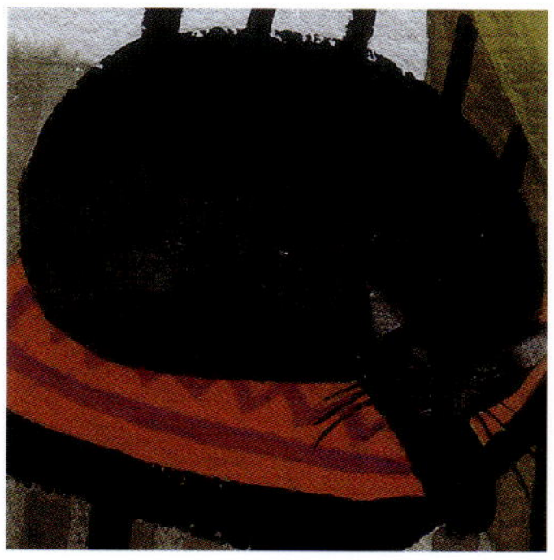

Feddenesque by John Iddon

'You're a Rousseauesque, sort of tea-cosy cat'
Said the girl in the wind, holding on to her hat,
'I'd rate you as high as an Odilon Redon.'
'We agree!' said the diamonded, harlequin mugs,
'We agree!' said the beautiful flat-bottomed jugs,
'One is, when one's painted by Fedden.'

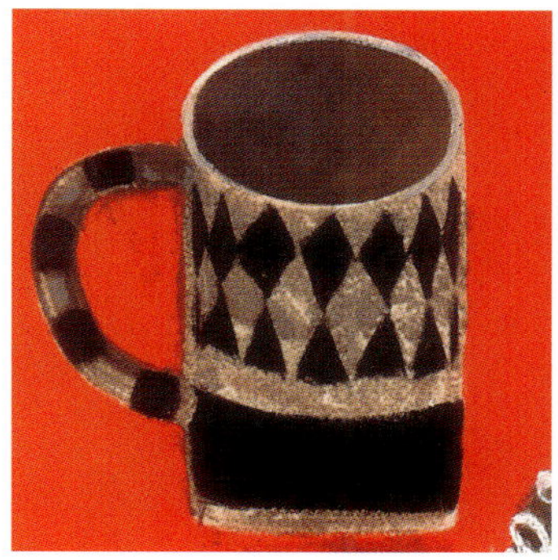

'And you', she said, 'are the most divine,
Surreal, post-Stubbsian, svelte equine:
You make all other horses look leaden.'
'I'm actually a zebra', he nearly said,
But he bit his tongue, he was very well bred,
As one *is*, when one's painted by Fedden.

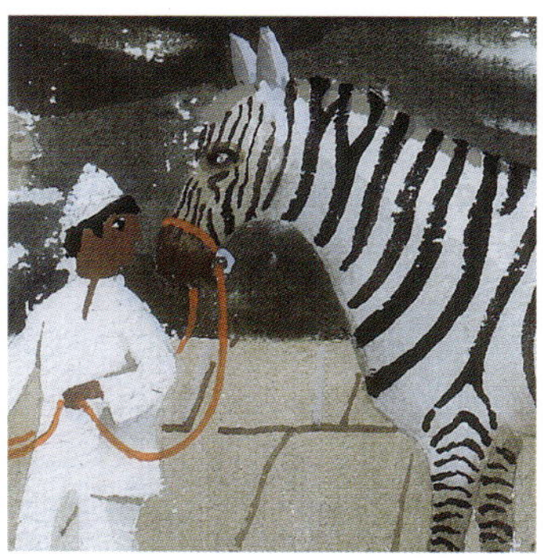

Details from Ills 149, 159 and 168

CHAPTER THREE

Fedden vis-à-vis Other Artists

The artist Ben Nicholson, according to the writer and art critic John Russell, once said that '*Every* alive painter (and sculptor) has influenced me (I hope).'[1] Mary Fedden – whose paintings have been openly influenced by many artists, Ben Nicholson among them[2] – would find the catholicity of Nicholson's statement appealing. Early on, she fell in love with the very idea of being an artist. Is there a better way of discovering what being an artist is all about than by looking intently and excitedly at the work of other artists?

She has been known to say that she has continually, throughout her career, moved from great enthusiasm for one artist to great enthusiasm for another. 'They come in waves,' she says of such enthusiasms. And these waves do not wash over her without leaving behind some valuable deposit that she absorbs into her own vision.

The first and most obvious influence in her career, even today, has been seventeenth-century Dutch still life. It underpins her visual world: it is domestic, accessible, solid, close-up and real. It is tangible. It is not vaporous. It is involved with the familiar. It relishes food and drink – and flowers (Ill. 84). Fedden also admires and enjoys Chardin for similar affinities.

The range of her appreciation is almost startlingly wide, taking in the classic authenticity of George Stubbs, the delicate precision of Eric Ravilious and the sweep and power of J.M.W. Turner's landscapes. She loves Giorgio Morandi's paintings of boxes and bottles with their interplay of objects and the intervals between them. She is clearly fascinated by Giorgio de Chirico's hallucinatory piazzas and has used recurring features from his repertoire, making them her own: a running girl with flying hair (Ill. 85), with a road that charges with a steep 'whoosh' straight up the picture surface.

In her 90s, she still finds art exhibitions stimulating and renewing. She also continues to discover fresh ideas in unlikely places. One recent example is the illustrated letters of Percy Kelly, a Cumbrian painter who had originally been a postal worker.[3] She has already sent various painted letters of her own to people, inveterate letter-writer and painter that she is. She is like a relay runner, eagerly taking the baton and running with it.

Her interests are, however, just as likely to be in a mainstream artist. Henri Matisse is a given. Her increasingly effortless simplification or elimination of fuss, as time goes on, owes plenty to Matisse while still being distinctively her own approach. This was well described by Mel Gooding in 1996 as 'her late style, remarkable for its clarity of address, its formal economy and decorative grace'.[4] Her sense of one particular background colour as a key to the whole painting is Matissean. Her patterning of shapes relates to the French master, too. At the same time, it also connects to Edouard Vuillard.

After the Vuillard exhibition in 2004 (at the Royal Academy), she spent quite some time 'trying *very* hard not to paint like Vuillard'. She even brought the

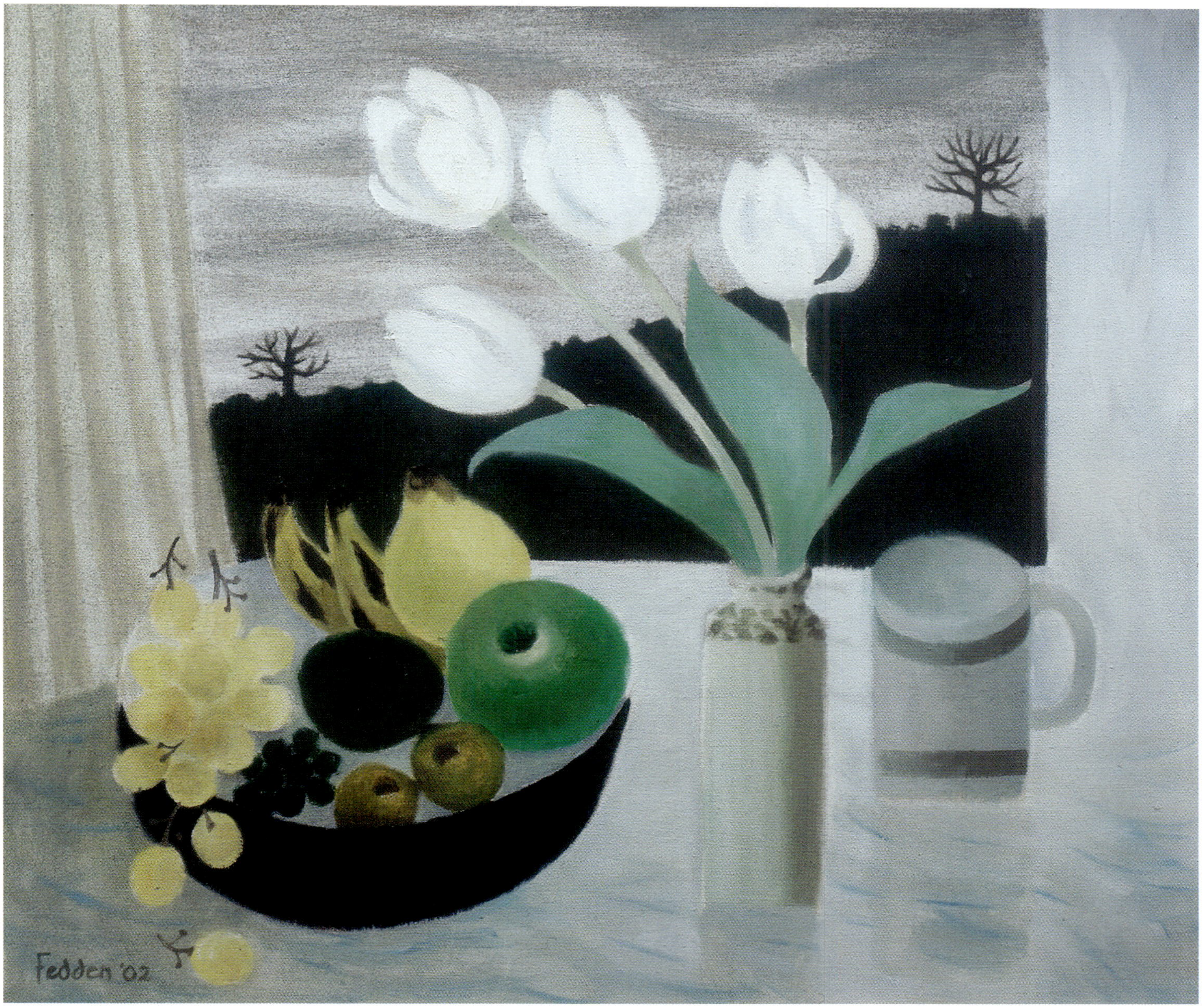

84
White Tulips, 2002
Oil on canvas
50.8 x 61 cm (20 x 24 in)
Private collection

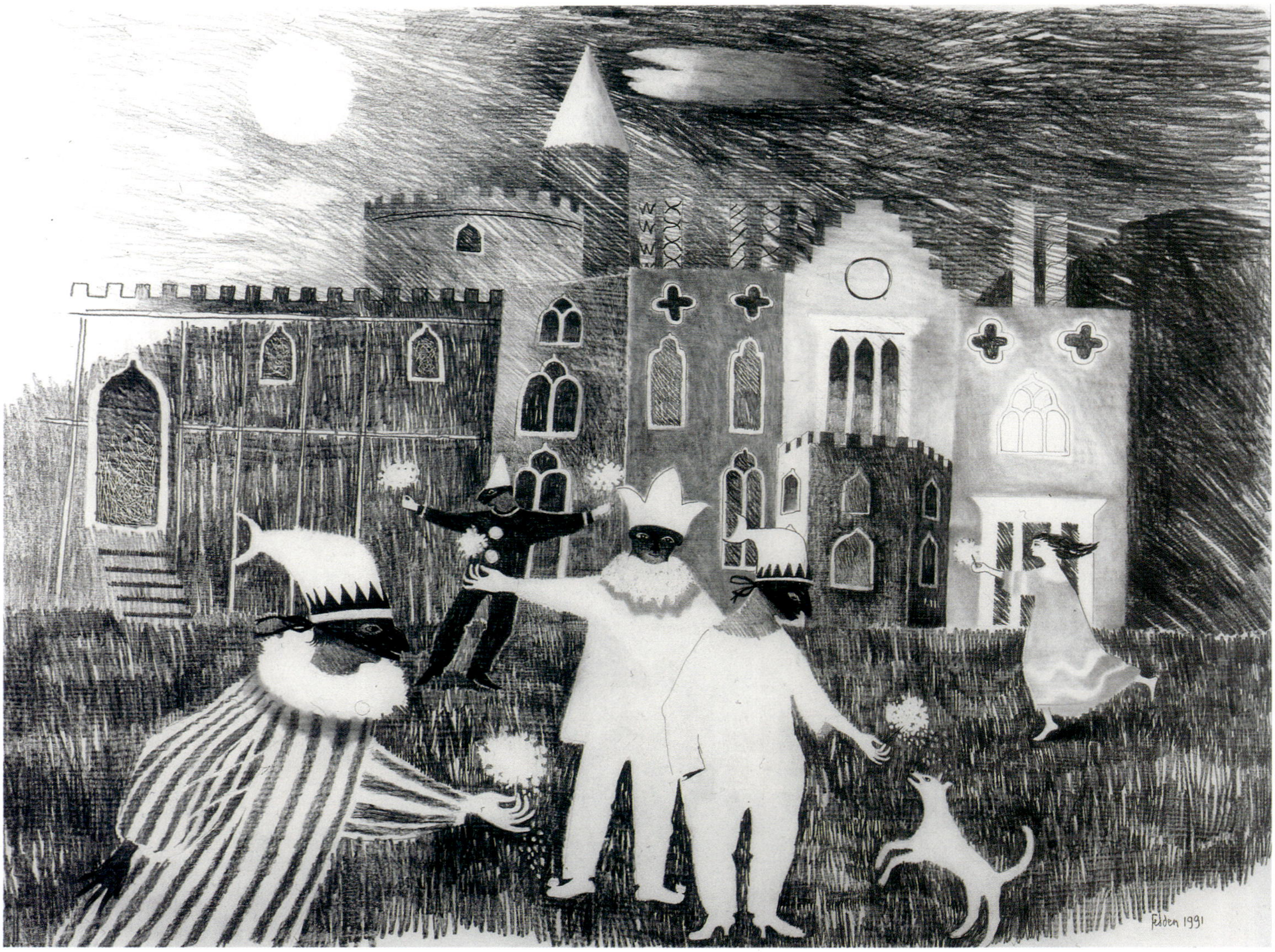

85
Masque at Strawberry Hill, 1991
Pencil
62.9 x 78.8 cm (22¾ x 31 in)
Private collection

massive catalogue home to help her! 'I loved these sort of sombre patterns that he did. He puts patterned surfaces next door to each other where I always used to think that if you had a patterned surface, it would come next to a plain surface.' Of course, when Fedden translates her Vuillard enthusiasm into her own painting, it looks … just like Fedden (Ill. 86). 'I like the ambiguousness of his paintings,' she goes on. 'There's an area of colour, and suddenly you see there's a woman's head at the top there, and then suddenly you see it's a shawl or something over her shoulder. You thought it was just a pattern. I think that's wonderful.' Then she adds, 'I'd like to do that, but I'm not ambiguous enough. I'm too positive!'

It seems to be a necessary incentive to her to 'wish' she painted like some other artist. She told a friend, when they were looking at the colourful, rich work of the English artist Joanna Carrington (1931–2003), whose still lifes have something in common with Feddens but are, perhaps, looser and more painterly in certain

86 (opposite)
Fruit and Flowers, 2004
Oil on canvas
61 x 50.9 cm (24 x 20 in)
Private collection

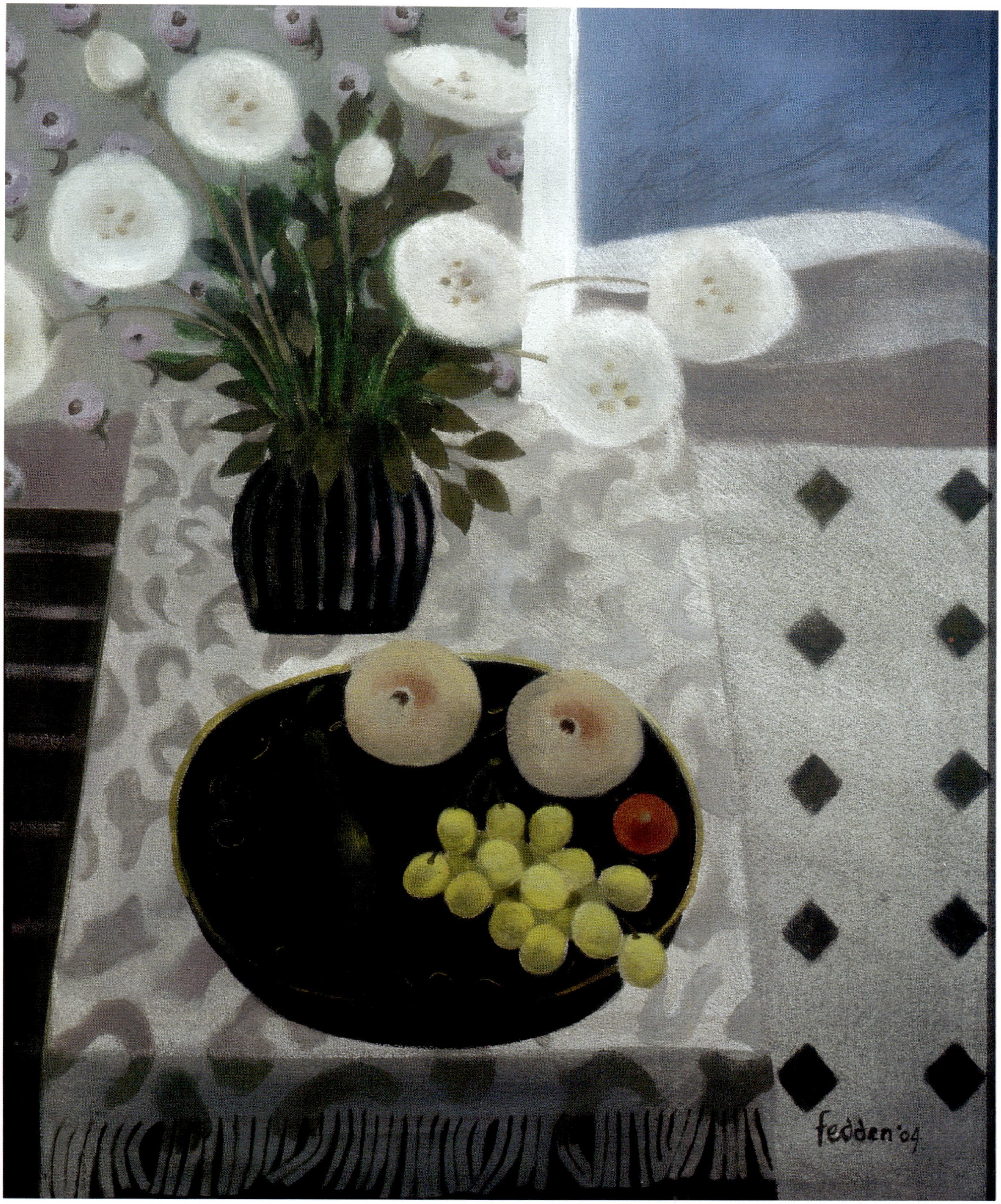
fedden '04

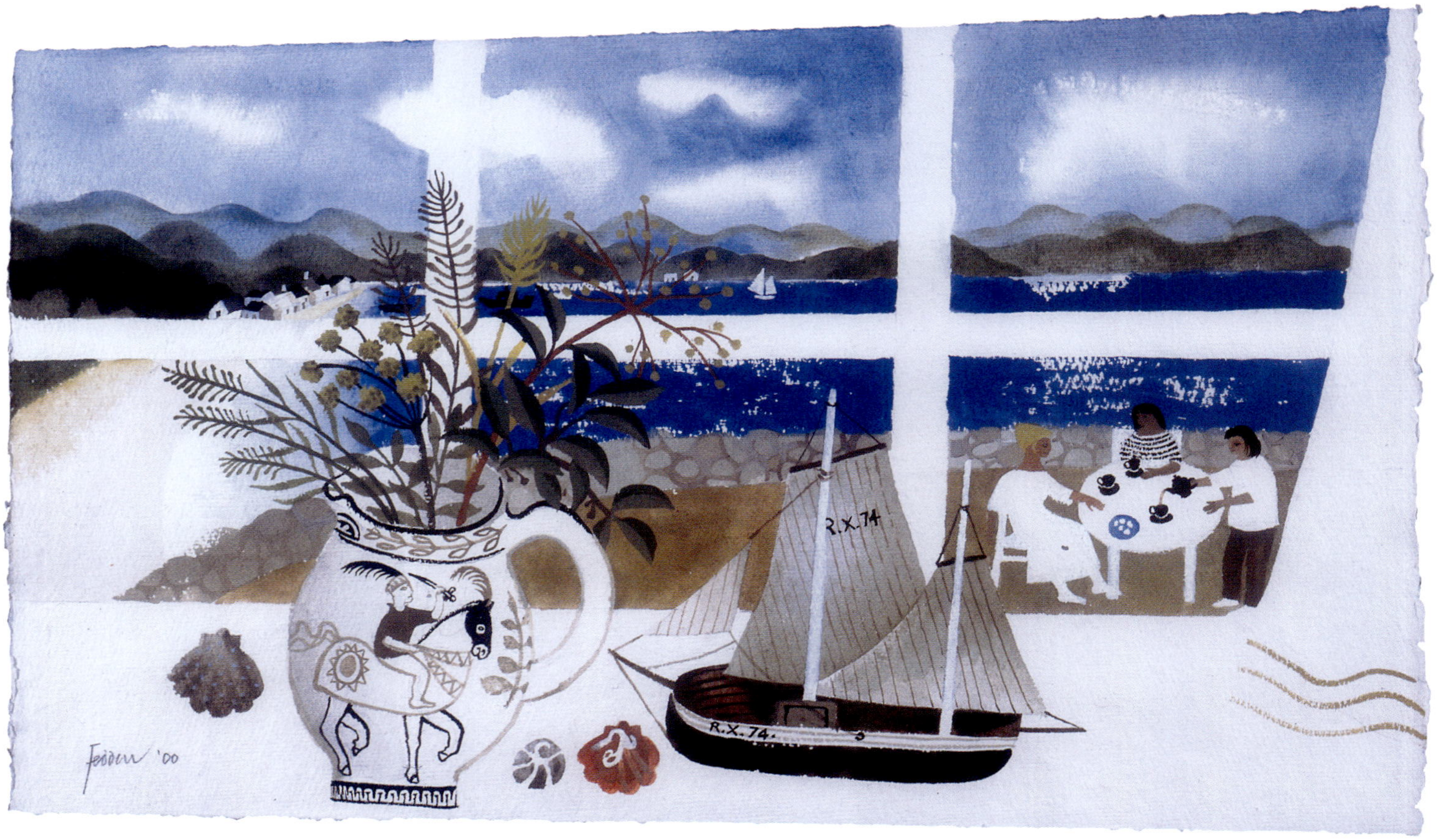

ways, that this is exactly the way she wished she could paint. And talking about Winifred Nicholson, she wished she could paint flowers like her; they are so ethereal. 'I think she painted them with her eyes shut!' (Ill. 87)

She envies Elizabeth Blackadder's cats, wishing she could paint her own cats with such litheness. 'Mine are rather static cats,' she observes. 'Hers are so *languid*.' (Ill. 88) In the past she has had tremendous enthusiasms for the still lifes of Henri Hayden, the Polish-born Parisian Modernist, and the Scottish painter Anne Redpath. The influence of Redpath, with her gestural, painterly, complex paintings, is not easy to see, except, of course, that she was also a woman and painted still life. Fedden finds herself often drawn to paintings by other women.

It is easier to see how Hayden would have appealed to her, particularly in the way he spaces still-life objects on a strongly coloured surface. His landscapes must have also appealed to her, too. Fedden seems less likely to have been affected by his obviously Cubist paintings than his later work. Both she and Hayden bring their table-tops up to the vertical picture plane; the surface on which the still-life

87
View from Knoydart, 2000
Gouache
33 x 58.4 cm (13 x 23 in)
Private collection

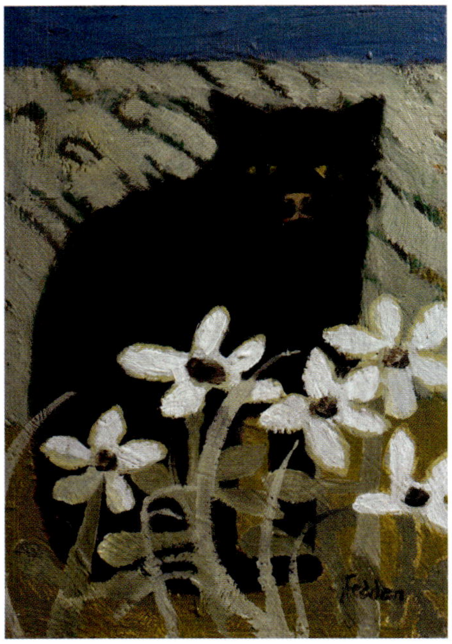

88
Cat in a Flowerbed, date unknown
Oil on board
19 x 13.7 cm (7¾ x 5⅜ in)
Richard Green Gallery, London

objects sit no longer recedes in perspective away from the viewer. This causes the picture surface itself to become virtually a table on which things are ranged without confusion or overlapping. Blackadder does something similar; she often actually paints on a flat table-top. (Fedden uses an easel.) This 'tipped up' table idea – and Fedden by no means *always* uses it – does originate in Cubism, but she has little in common otherwise with that pervasively influential movement of the early twentieth century. She finds those Cubist paintings 'all so much the same'. Nevertheless, she loves that artists' artist Georges Braque and, picking up a postcard in her studio of one of his later still lifes, hands it to me as if to say, 'That explains everything.' It doesn't; but once again Fedden has used Braque to her own ends and has certainly borrowed from him some of her favourite motifs. Her frequent liking for depicting two fish flat on a plate might well have come from Braque in the first place (Ill. 89). Or it might have come from somewhere else: the paintings of William Scott, for example. Fedden, I believe, has carried on a silent dialogue with Scott for years, admiring his simplicity and abstraction, yet never willing to make her own paintings turn abstract to that degree. But she can't ignore him. She pays tribute, while at the same time questioning his reduction of objects to silhouette and mere shape. (Ill. 90)

She isn't, ultimately, fussy about her 'sources'. 'I have a box full of postcards and all sorts of ravishing images,' she says. So when she doesn't know what to paint next, she rummages through it. Knowing her interests, friends send her cards with some of her themes on them. She has, for instance, postcards of paintings with melons in them that have a slice cut out to show the flesh and seeds (Ill. 91). One I have seen is by Jacques le Moynes de Morgues, and another is by a much more obscure nineteenth-century artist, George Brookshaw. 'I get my ideas from photographs, from other painters, from flower catalogues …' And from botanical prints, illustrations in bird books, magazine covers – anything that sets her going is legitimate. 'I have always hoped I've got enough sort of *handwriting* to change things into something that is mine alone …' The individual movements and marks of her brush are as unmistakably hers as her thumb-print or her handwriting.

She has described the stimulus of other artists' work as leading her 'into wonderful new ways of seeing'. What is involved is not plagiarism, or imitation, but an exuberant adaptation of anything that appeals to her. Another artist's work is no less open to her as inspiration, or to suggest a motif, than a pebble on the beach, a seedpod that sounds like a rattle when you shake it, or a sake bottle a student gave her years ago. All this is grist to her mill. Artists have raided each other's larders down the centuries. Rembrandt stole from Raphael, Raphael pinched things from Leonardo and Michelangelo, Manet purloined from Rembrandt, and Van Dyck, and Velázquez, and Coorte, and Boucher, and Goya, and so on.

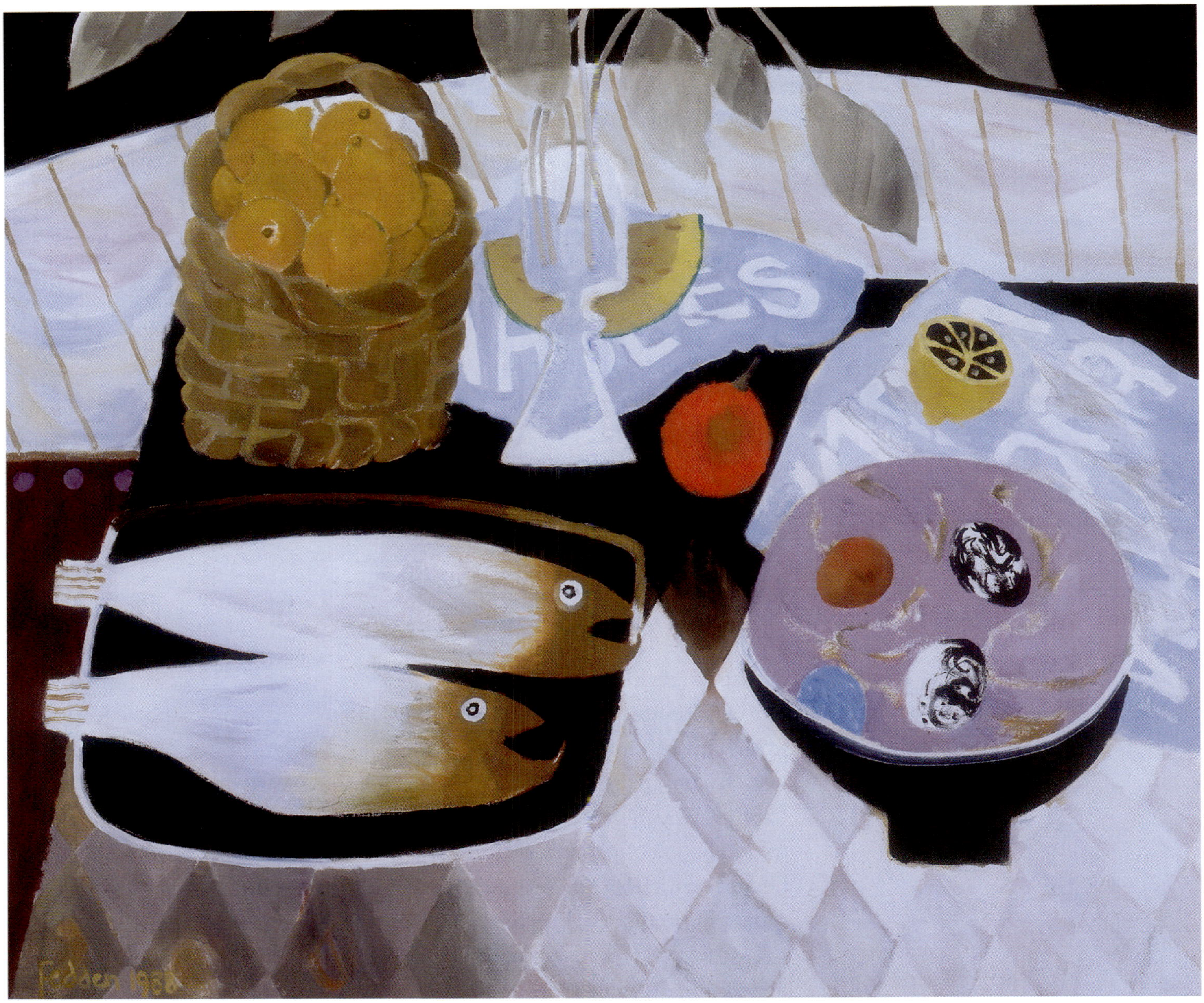

89
Basket of Lemons, 1988
Oil on canvas
74.6 x 90 cm (29⅜ x 35½ in)
Private collection

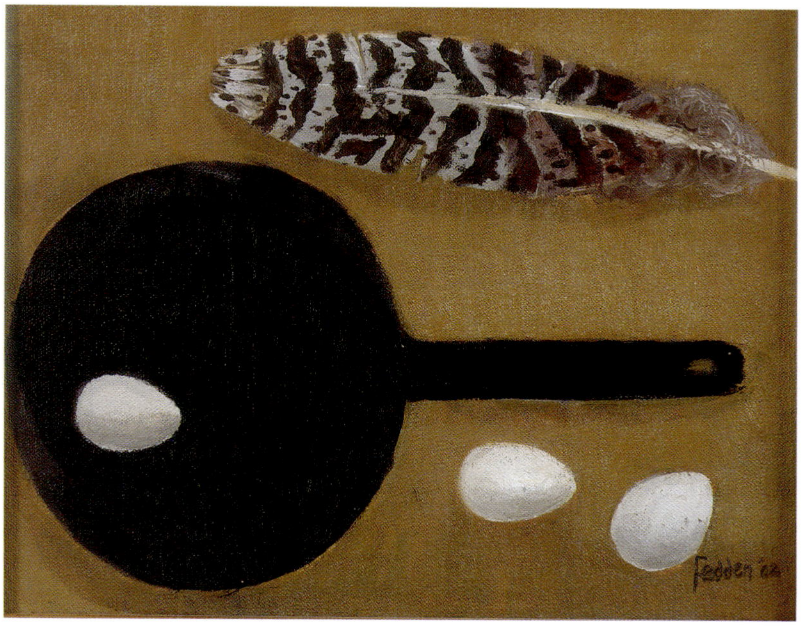

90
Eggs and Frying Pan, 2002
Oil on board
19.2 x 25 cm (7⅝ x 9⅞ in)
Private collection

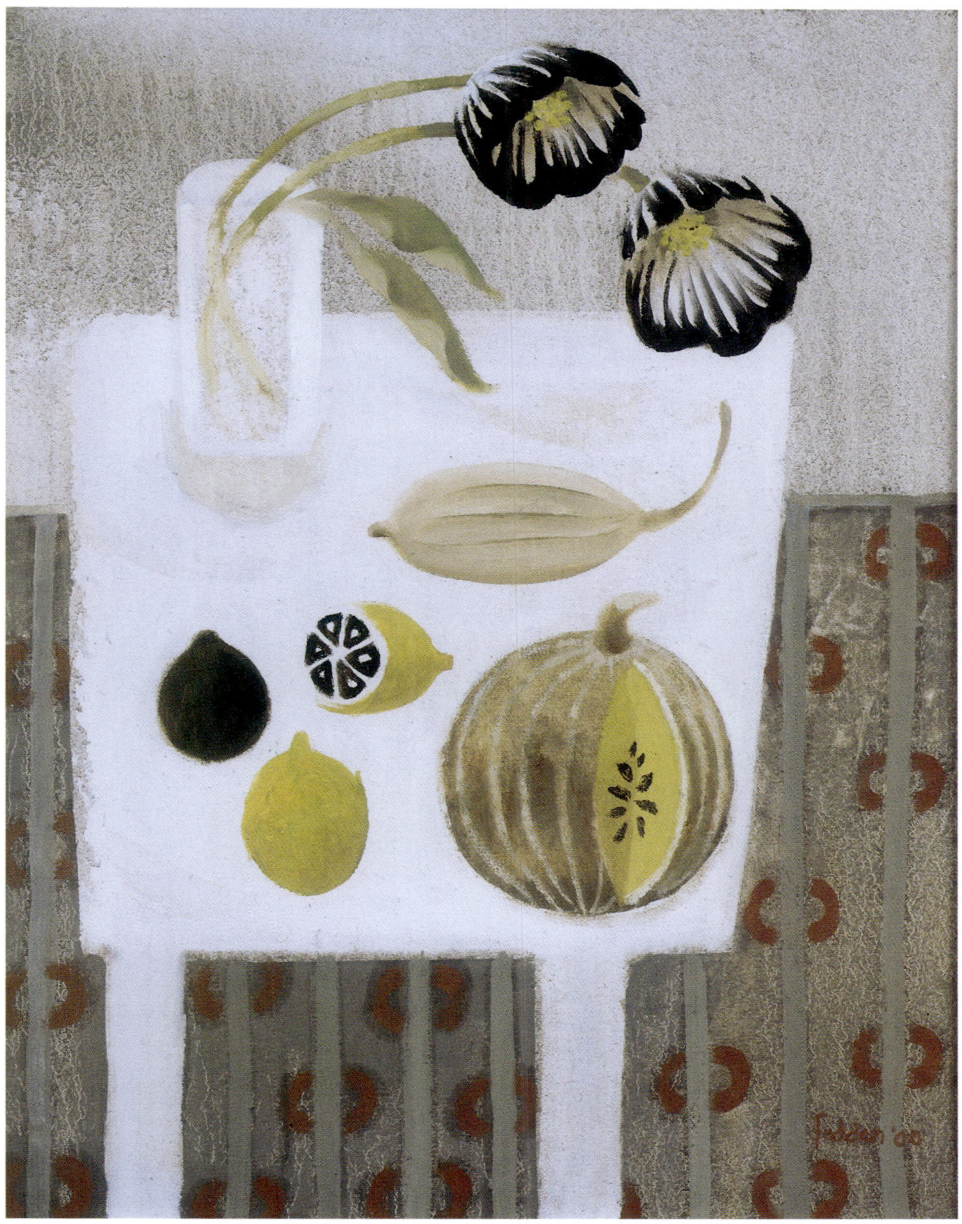

91
A Lemon and a Half, 2000
Oil on canvas
50.5 x 40.5 cm (19⅞ x 15⅞ in)
Private collection

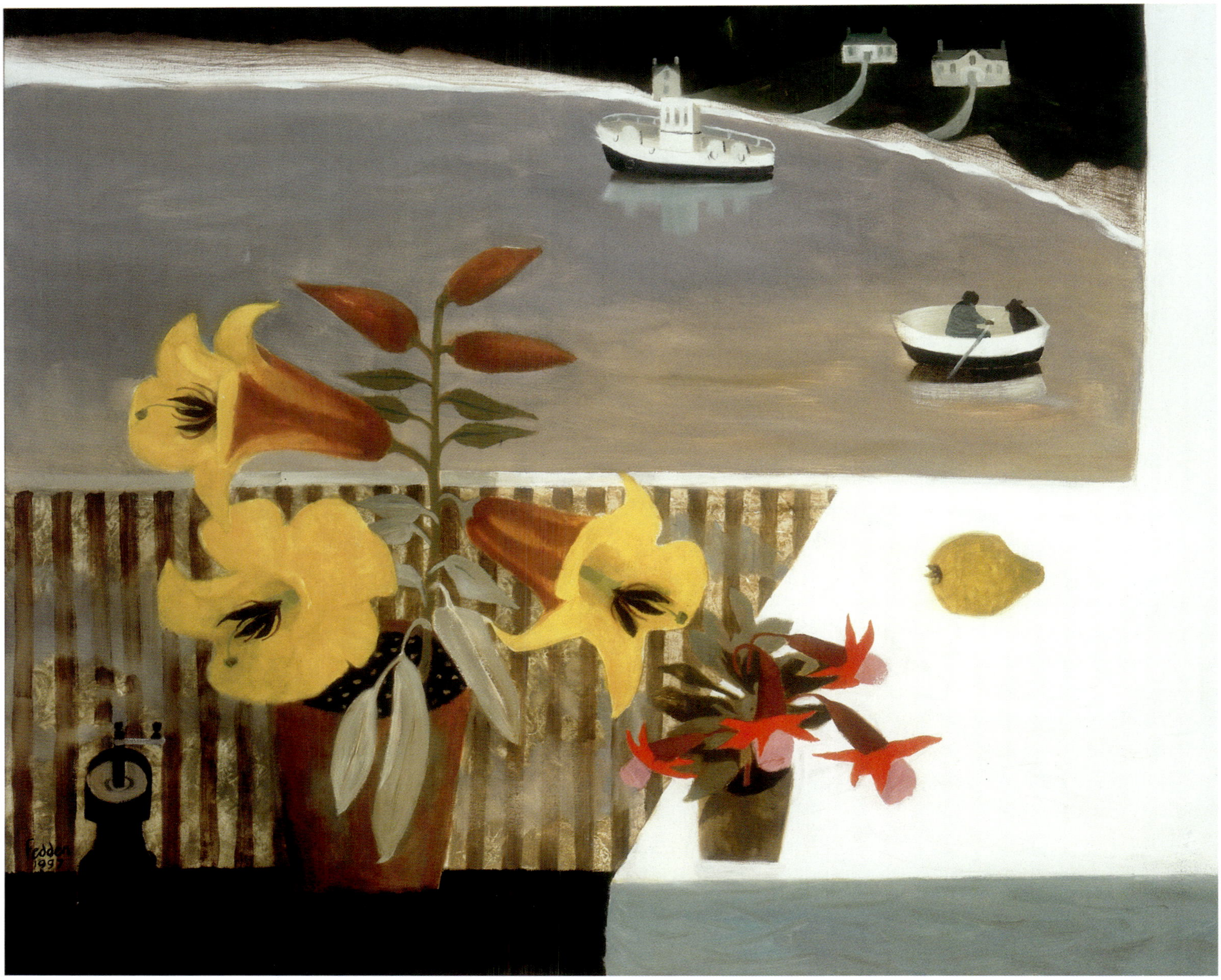

I spotted in the background of one of Fedden's paintings, *Rowing* (1997) (Ill. 92), a small detail of a woman and a dog in a rowing boat. 'Well,' she laughed, 'you know where I got that from!' I did, as it happened. It was from a two-part watercolour by Mary Newcomb called *The rower and the dog: setting out light fading; returning in the dusk* (Ill. 93). 'I cheat all the time,' she says. 'I just love that painting of Mary Newcomb – with one rowing this way, the other coming back. You wonder where the woman and her dog have been. I take out of Mary Newcomb a lot because I love her paintings. It doesn't matter, does it? There aren't enough themes in the world for you to have for your own – are there? It's the way you *interpret* them that matters.'

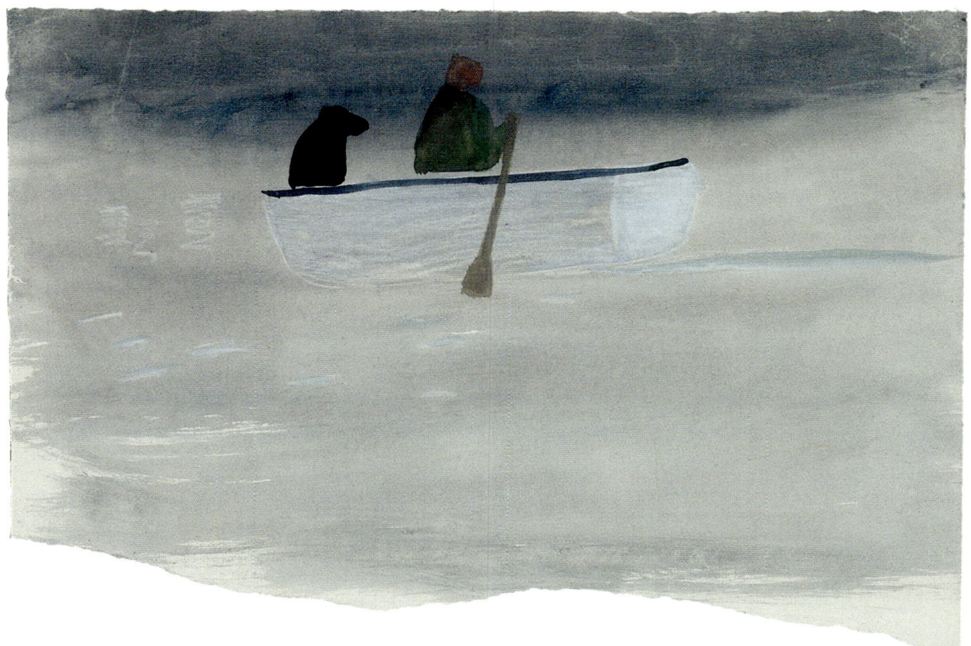

92 (opposite)
Rowing, 1997
Oil on canvas
100.5 x 126 cm (39½ x 49½ in)
© Royal Academy of Arts, London

93 (above)
The rower and the dog: setting out light fading; returning in the dusk
Right half of a diptych by Mary Newcomb
Date unknown
Watercolour
30.3 x 38.3 cm (12 x 15 in)
Credit: Mary Newcomb

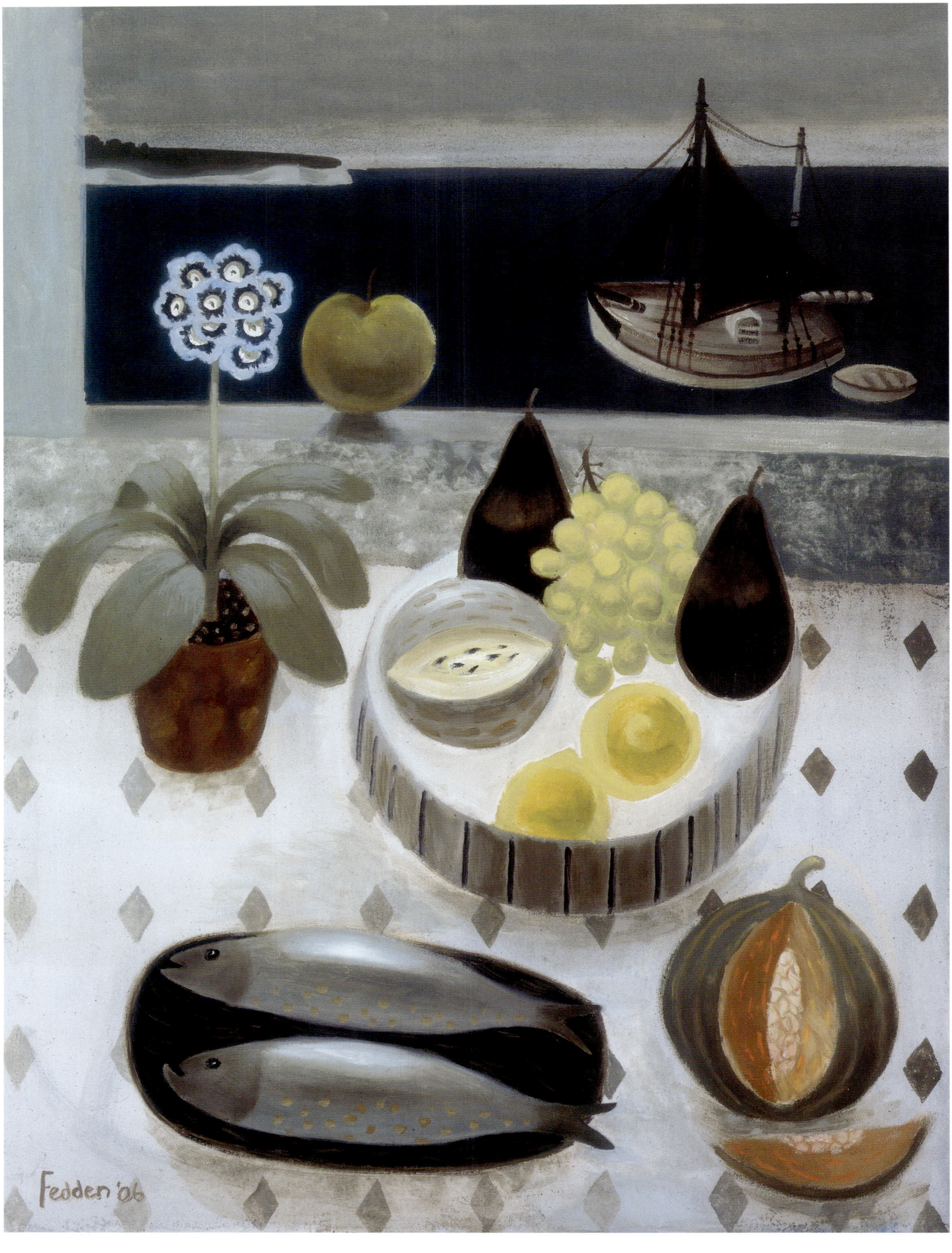
Fedden '06

Sudden inspirations can have her rushing back to the studio to make use of a new idea. This seems to be what happened when she first encountered what might be the earliest of all European still lifes, *Still Life with Quince, Cabbage, Melon and Cucumber, c.*1600, by the Spanish artist Sánchez Cotán. She was obviously entranced by the idea of being able to extend her still-life fruit and vegetables into the upper reaches of the canvas, as Cotán did, by hanging them from strings. Her apples and onions did not have to sit on a table! Some of her apples and pears had long been showing a tendency to perch on the very edge of windowsills (Ill. 103, p.97). They still do sometimes in her very latest work (Ill. 94). They are poised, like alighted birds, so close to the edge of table or windowsill that they could at any moment achieve lift-off. But now the Cotán painting suggested to her that her fruit and vegetables could actually float aloft (Ill. 95). I am sure a link from this to Alexander Calder's mobiles was not lost on Mary – an early Calder mobile having been a lovely airborne feature of her house for years. (She has given it to the Tate but still has a rather good replica of it.)

Sometimes Fedden has been described as having a naïve – or 'childlike' and 'innocent' – side to her art, as if she might have an untrained eye like Le Douanier (Henri) Rousseau (and he has certainly influenced her, too). He also composed his pictures from all kinds of sources. She renewed her acquaintance with him at a major exhibition at the Tate Modern, London (2005) and concluded that he was authentic and wonderful, but probably had no sense of humour about his work.

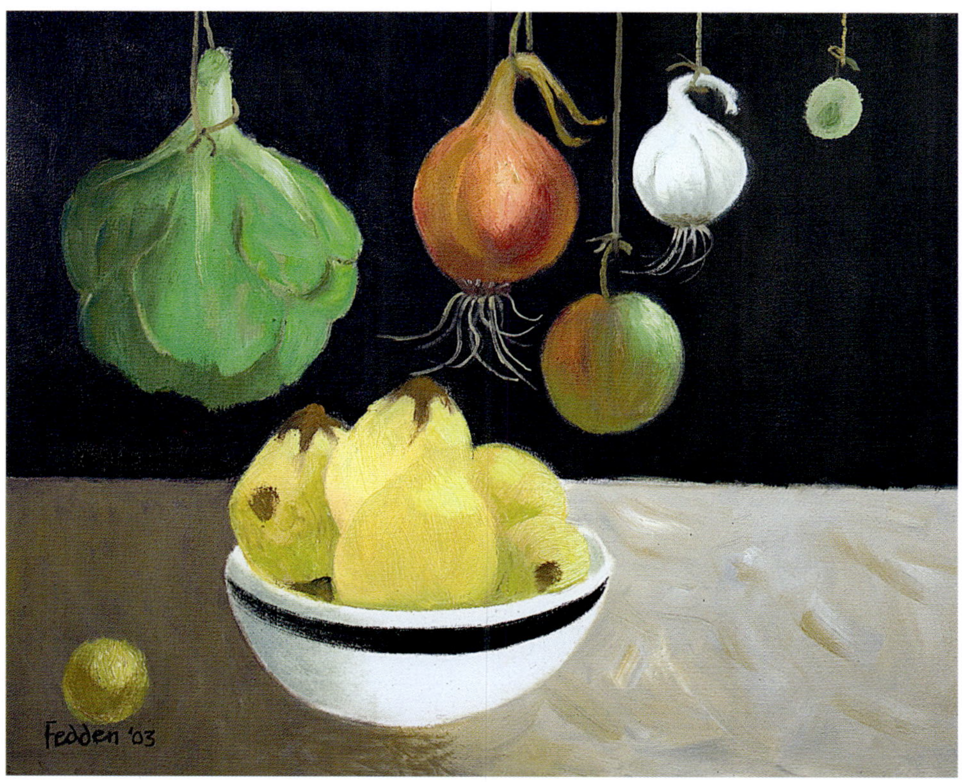

94 (opposite)
Still Life by the Sea, 2006
Oil on canvas
90 x 70 cm (35⅜ x 27½ in)
Credit: The Artist

95 (right)
Quinces and Vegetables, 2003
Oil on canvas
40.6 x 50.8 cm (16 x 20 in)
Credit: Bill Clark

This is a sophisticated observation. Naïve artists do not generally see their art as humorous. Such artists – the Cornish fisherman Alfred Wallis, for instance – often take their paintings very seriously. Wallis painted 'for company' after his wife died. His art was about memory and knowledge of the sea, not about art. Naum and Miriam Gabo sent a floral tribute to Wallis's funeral with a telling inscription: 'In homage to the artist on whom Nature has bestowed the rarest of gifts, not to know that he is one.'

Fedden, for better or worse, knows certainly that she is an artist – through and through. She can be objective and self-critical about her work in a way most naïve artists cannot. Her paintings may have a very direct simplicity, but they are surely not naïve. She has not only taught art, she has been taught it. She remarked to me recently (after she had voiced dissatisfaction with much of her work): 'It's funny; at 90 I'm still trying to teach myself how to paint.' But to treat her art as somehow deliberately naïve is, I believe, to miss the point. Sometimes it is humorous, but intentionally so, as in *The Dotty Dress* (1999) (Ill. 96).

One of the most obvious of all influences on Fedden's work, particularly in the 1950s, has been the work of Christopher Wood (Ill. 97). Not only the St Ives-ian theme of still life on a windowsill, an idea in which Fedden, after decades, continues unabated to find new potential, but also her fondness for boats in harbours, her landscapes of Brittany with gatherings of people, even her love of zebras, can all be related to Wood. (Ills 98, 99 and 100)

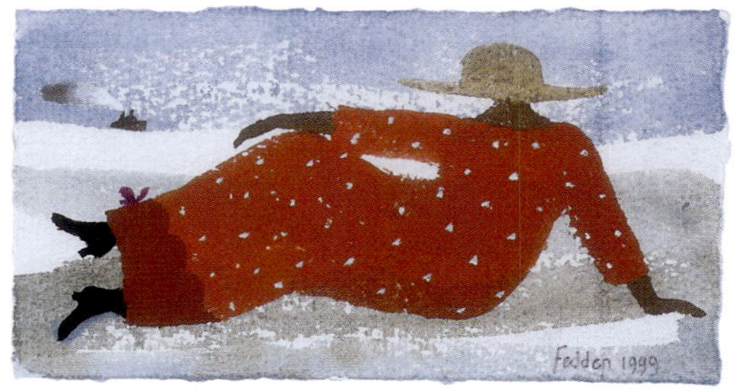

96
The Dotty Dress, 1999
Gouache
8.5 x 16.1 cm (3³/₈ x 6³/₈ in)
Private collection

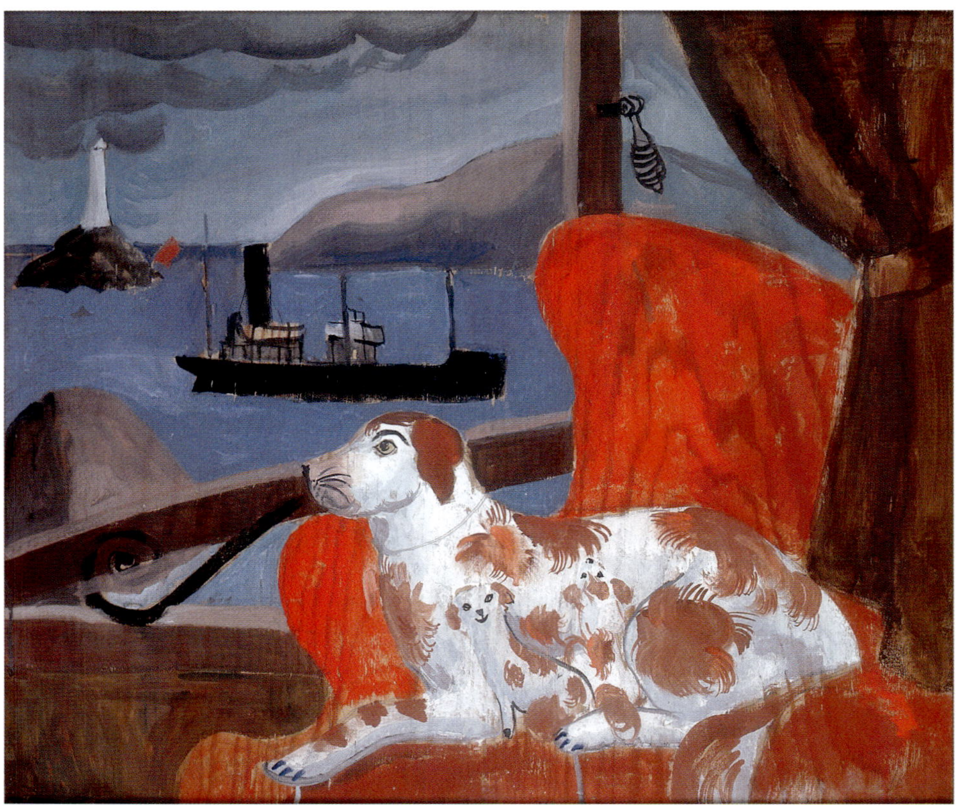

97
China Dogs in a St Ives Window, 1926
by Christopher Wood
Oil on board
63.5 x 76.2 cm (25 x 30 in)
Private collection

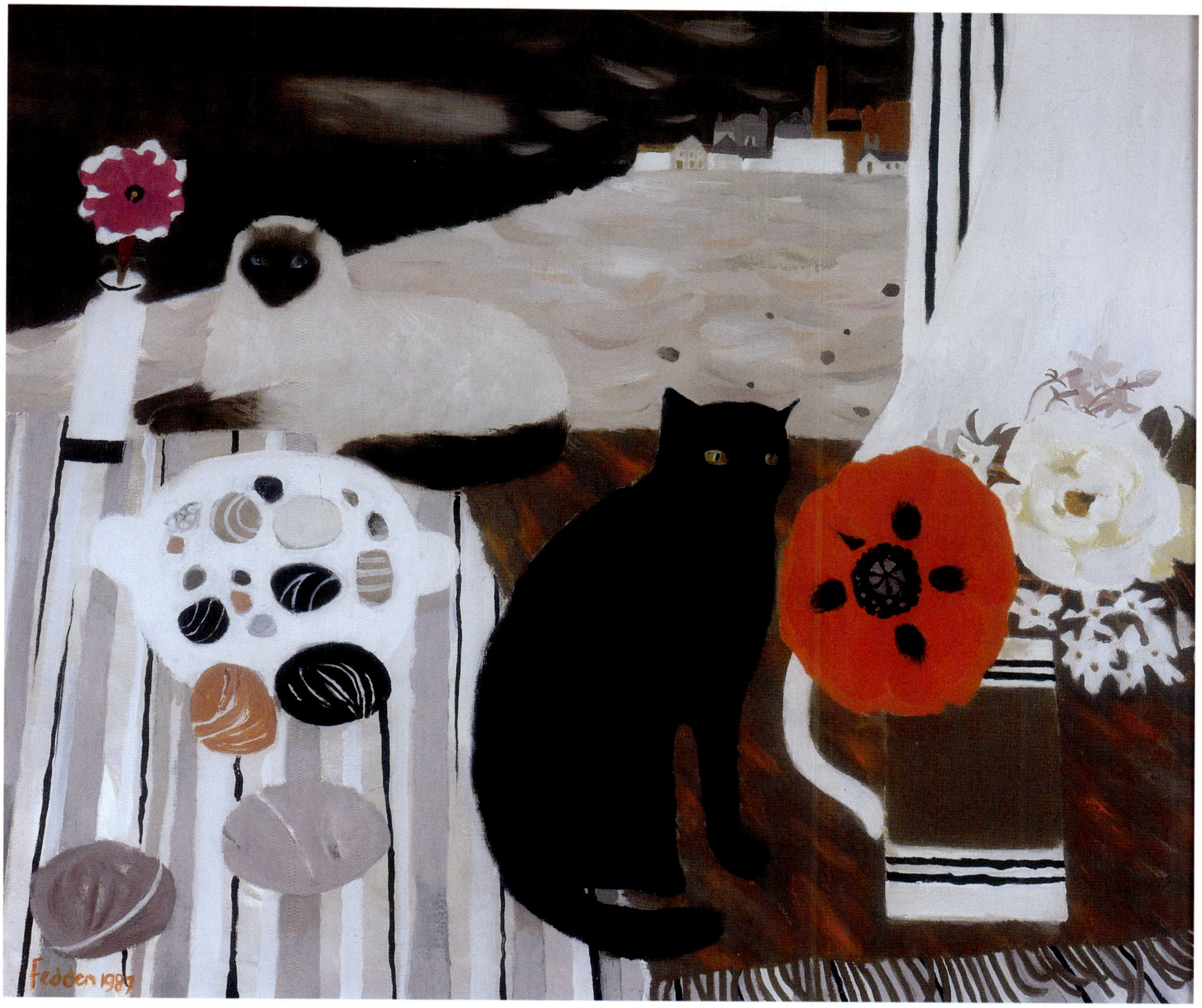

98
Cats by the Sea, 1987
Oil on canvas
76 x 91 cm (30 x 36 in)
Private collection

99
Brittany, 1997
Oil on board
29.3 x 39.4 cm (11½ x 15½ in)
Private collection

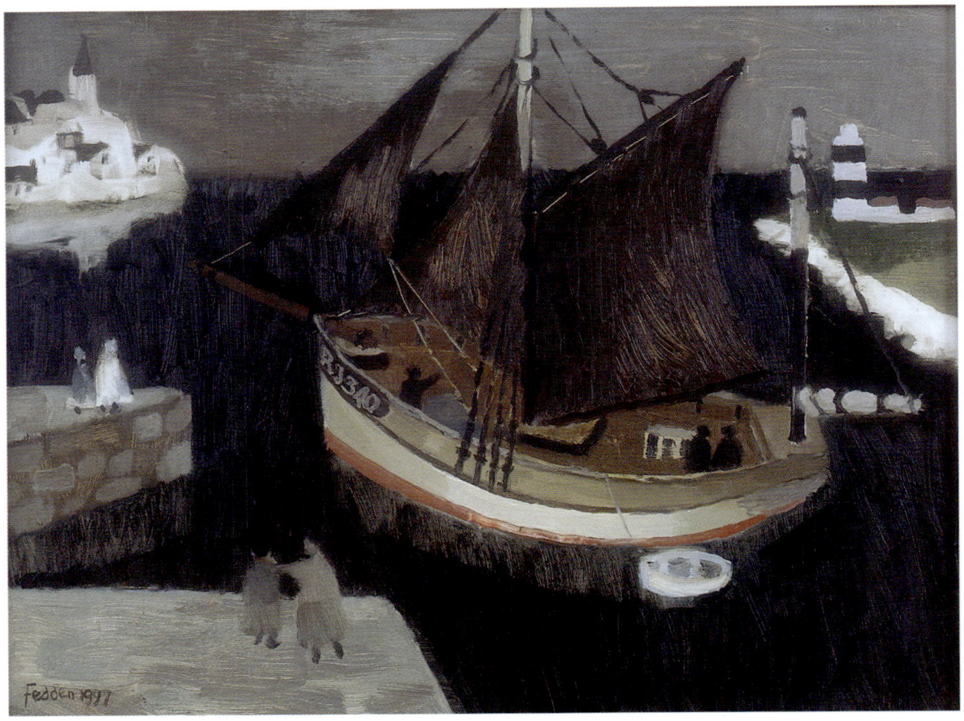

100
Puerta D'Andraix, Majorca, 1951
Oil on board
50.8 x 76.4 cm (20 x 30 in)
Art Consultancy Services

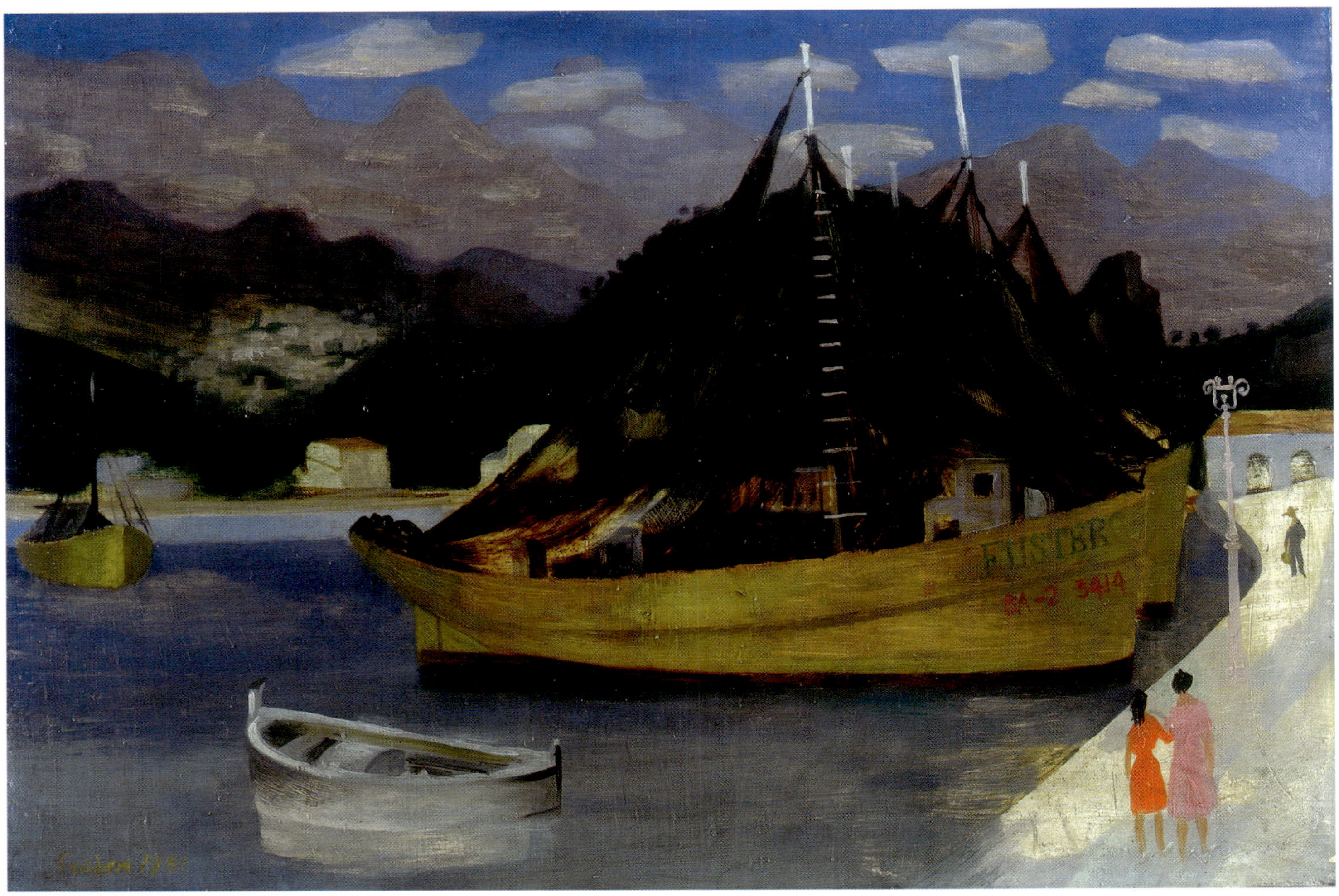

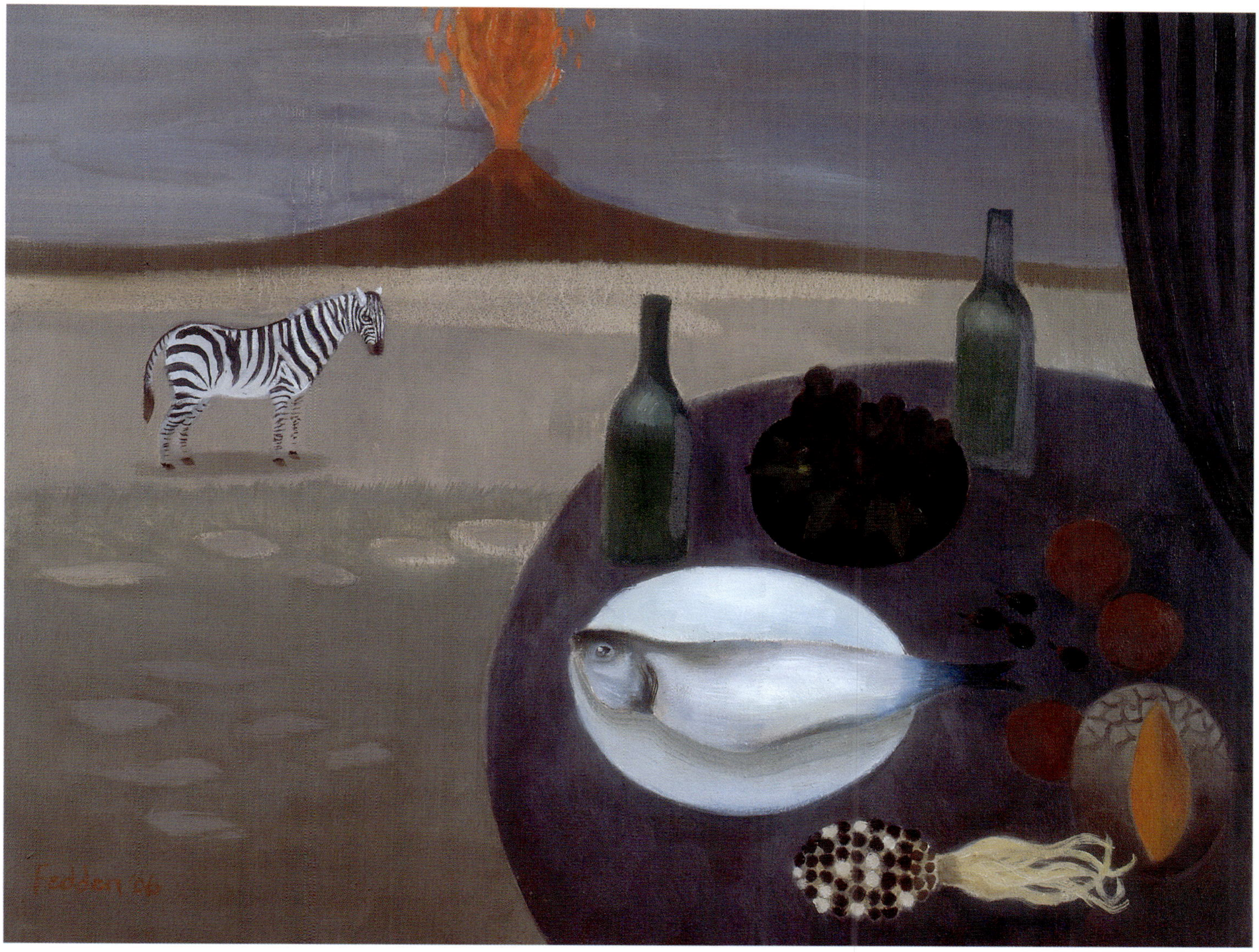

101
The Volcano, 2006
Oil on canvas
60 x 80 cm (23⅝ x 31½ in)
Credit: The Artist

Her love of zebras (Ill. 101), however, has multiple sources. She has a fondness for black and white stripes anyway (in dresses and curtains, for instance), and she also vividly remembers a Mughal miniature of a lone, standing zebra by Ustad Mansur in the Victoria and Albert Museum. Yet she once explained in *Art Review* that when she painted a zebra, it was probably drawn from a memory of a trip to Africa she and Julian took.[5] She is too much of a magpie for a single influence to take her over. Her visual memory is as stocked as her memory for poetry.

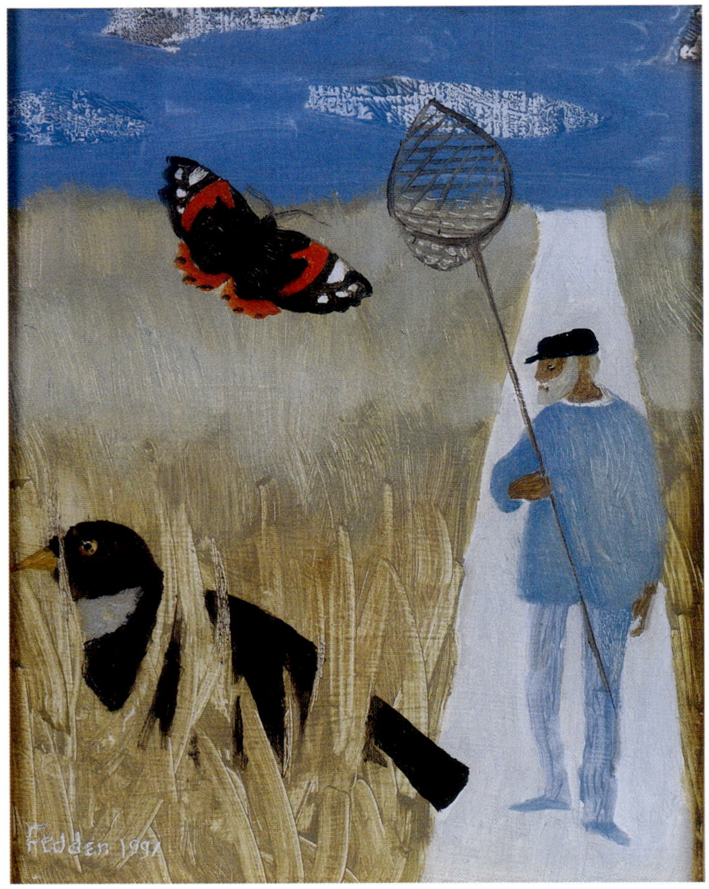

102
The Red Admiral, 1997
Oil on board
23.1 x 18.2 cm (9⅛ x 7⅛ in)
Private collection

At different periods she has taken in prevalent attitudes or styles. Her neo-Romantic strain – something in which she might very well be described as a survivor – derives from knowing such artists as Ceri Richards, Cecil Collins and, above all, John Minton and John Craxton. Some of her drawings, such as *Mediterranean Landscape* (1971) (Ill. 53, p.54), are distinctly Mintonesque. Her love of Samuel Palmer's early sepia drawings and paintings, with their moonlight and deep, rich, varnished shadows, is evident, perhaps seen through the eyes of the neo-Romantics of the 1940s and 1950s. At a British Museum exhibition of Palmer in 2006, she found she was still excited by his work.

Julian Trevelyan's influence on her was the most immediate of all, bringing her into modernity. He encouraged, I believe, a much looser and more painterly approach. His Surrealism was crucial to her, bringing out her own sense of dream and absurdity. He encouraged a less literal and more irrational approach to perspective, for example. Her love of disproportion – of a pansy the size of a mug, a red admiral butterfly as big as an apple (Ills 102 and 103), or a bird bigger than Julian himself (and he was 6 ft-4 in.) – relates to Surrealism, to René Magritte perhaps in particular, though equally to Palmer, or to John Tenniel's *Alice in Wonderland* illustrations (Ill. 185, p.156). This freedom to paint things whatever size she wants or needs them to be, regardless of realism, is so inbred in her now that she doesn't even think about it. About Magritte, she says in a footnote at the end of a letter: 'Yes I do love Magritte. I like to think I have a touch of him?'

Not all of her influences from other artists have been self-evidently stylistic. She says her two favourite paintings of all time are Piero della Francesca's *Resurrection* and Stanley Spencer's extraordinary *Nativity* – his prize-winning final painting at the Slade. The Piero, with its erect central figure in total contrast to the inertia of the sleeping soldiers below, does have something in common with the contrasting zones of her pictures – still life below, tree and landscape above – but essentially it must be the masculine power and compositional certainty of this work that hold her. The Spencer, with its strange mixture of Eros and nature, of figures moving in a landscape of constricted spaces and odd perspectives, and the peculiar baby added in the lower foreground like an after-thought, may well haunt Fedden's imagination. There are a few drawings and paintings by her that could be related to Spencer (Ills 104 and 105), but it seems likely that his intriguing *Nativity* may engage her because it is so complex, inimitable and ambiguous.

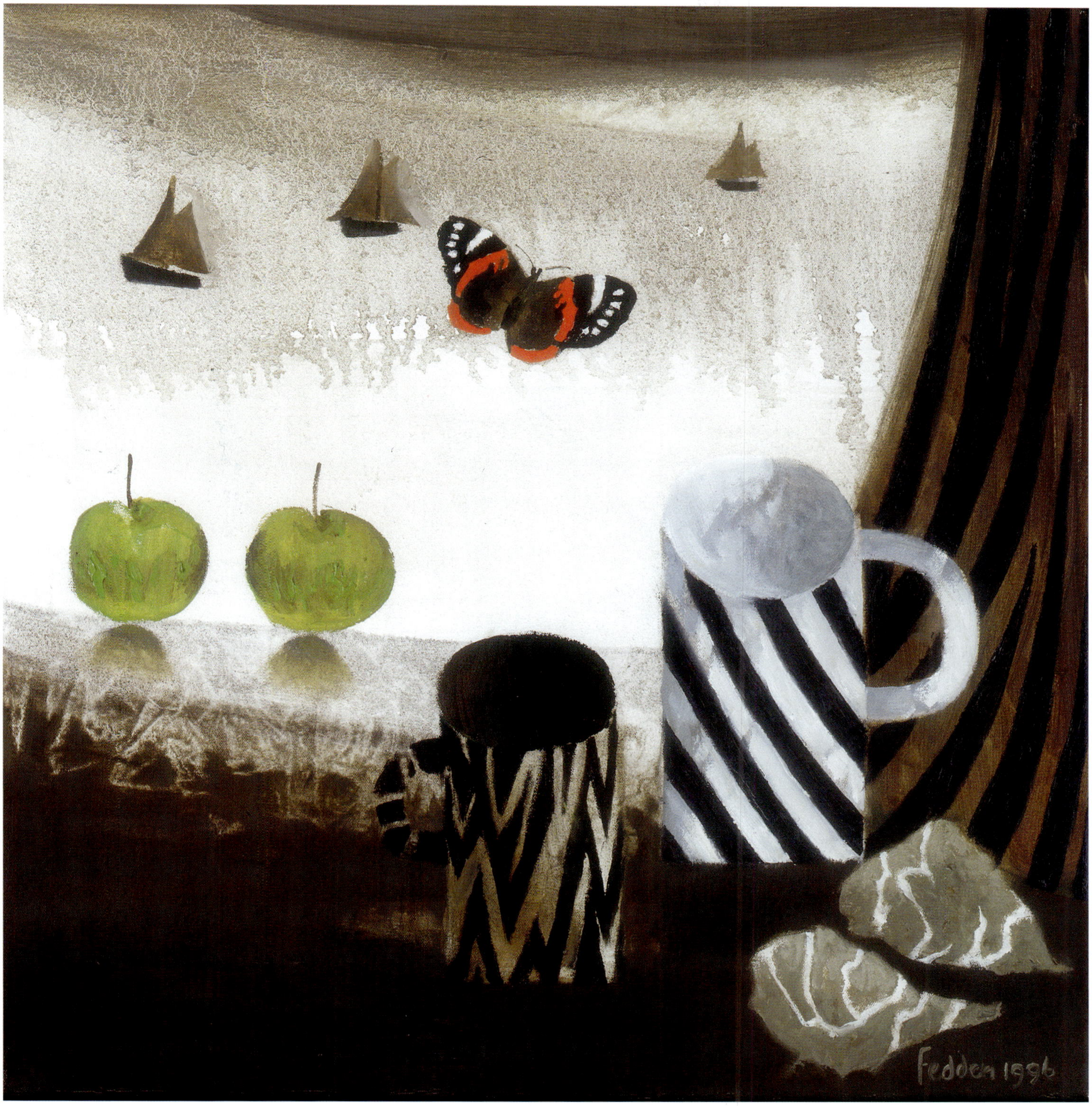

103
Red Admiral, 1996
Oil on canvas
50.5 x 50.5 cm (19⅞ x 19⅞ in)
Private collection

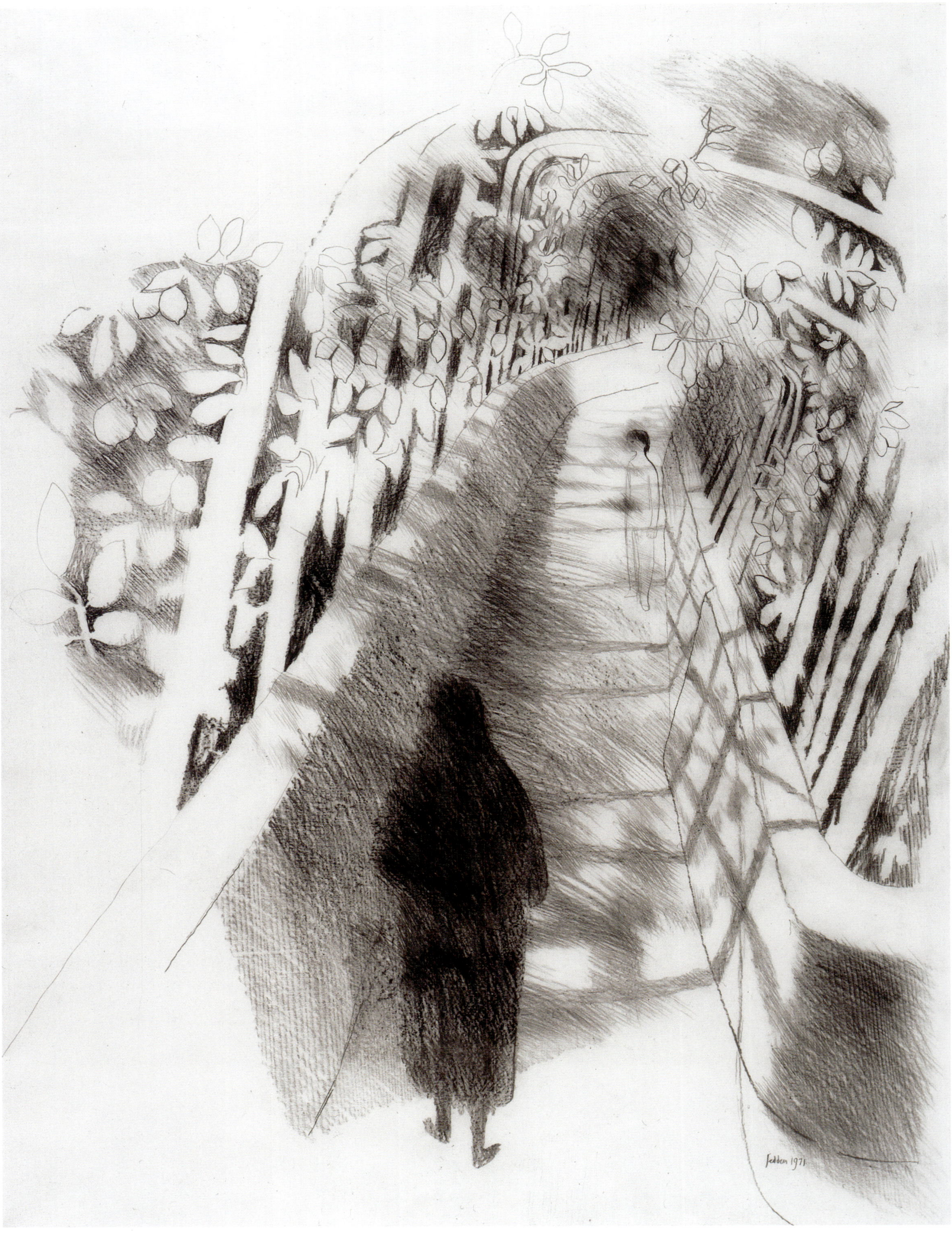
Sedden 1971

104 (opposite)
A Garden Walk, 1971
Pencil
73.5 x 57.5 cm (27¾ x 22⅝ in)
Private collection

105 (right)
The Graveyard, 2003
Oil on canvas
38 x 48 cm (15½ x18¾ in)
Private collection

Fedden is a great admirer of Stanley Spencer, and traces of his influence can be found in a small number of her works.

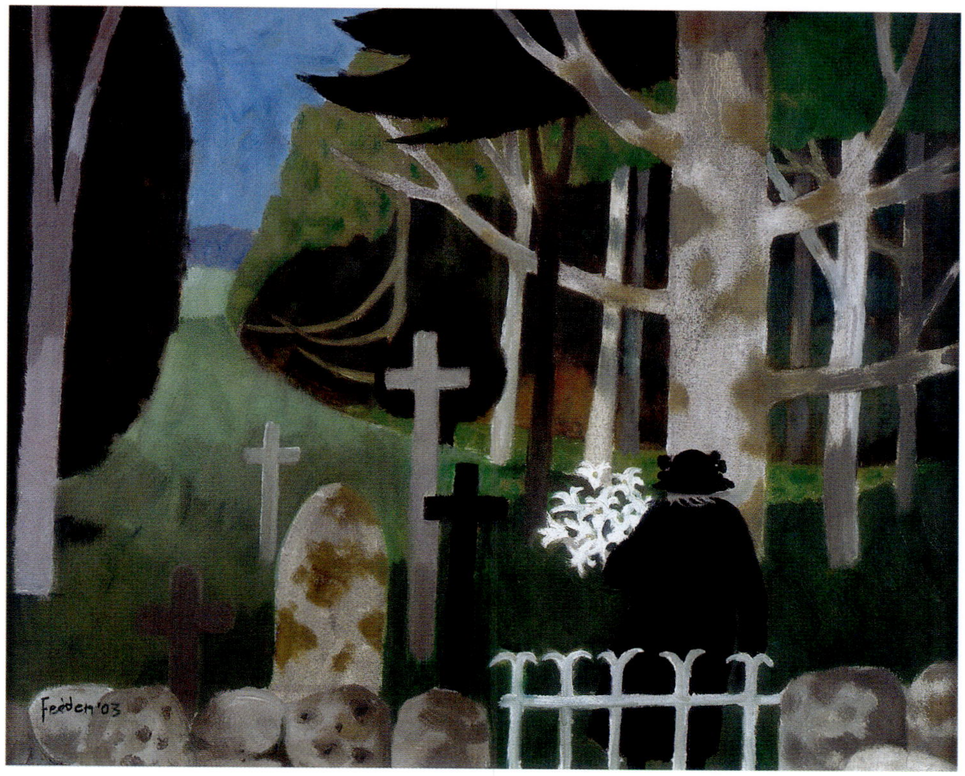

David Hockney's paintings may not have influenced her work, but his character and approach have. Both artists have rather a similar philosophy. As mentioned, he was a student at the Royal College of Art in the early 1960s when she taught painting there. What she got from him was 'something to do with the excitement of painting, I think; he was very deeply thrilled with painting … He is very much a *painter*, and what I like about his work is that he goes through all sorts of phases – he takes photographs, and he paints his little dogs … He doesn't *keep his standard up* – he tries other things, which I think is good, don't you? He is very imaginative and experimental. He's not a boastful man; he's modest in a way.'

Fedden suspects that he may not mind very much what other people think. I suspect Mary Fedden may not, either. 'No, I don't,' she says with emphasis and a deep chuckle. 'If people don't like my paintings, they don't have to look at them. I don't care.' And these days, she says, she feels this more than ever – 'now that I do have a *lot* of people who buy my pictures'. Then she adds, with a touch of irony, 'I don't suffer from lack of appreciation!'

Notes

1. *Ben Nicholson, Drawings, Paintings and Reliefs 1911–1968*, introduction by John Russell, Thames and Hudson (London), 1969, p.28
2. *Mary Fedden* by Mel Gooding, Scolar Press (Aldershot), 1995, plates on pp 80, 84.
3. *The Painted Letters of Percy Kelly* by Chris Wadsworth, Castlegate House Gallery (Cockermouth), 2004
4. *Mary Fedden: A Retrospective*, introduction by Mel Gooding, catalogue, Royal West of England Academy (Bristol), 1996
5. 'Mary Fedden: an artist's diary', *Art Review*, March 1995, vol. 47, pp 44–5

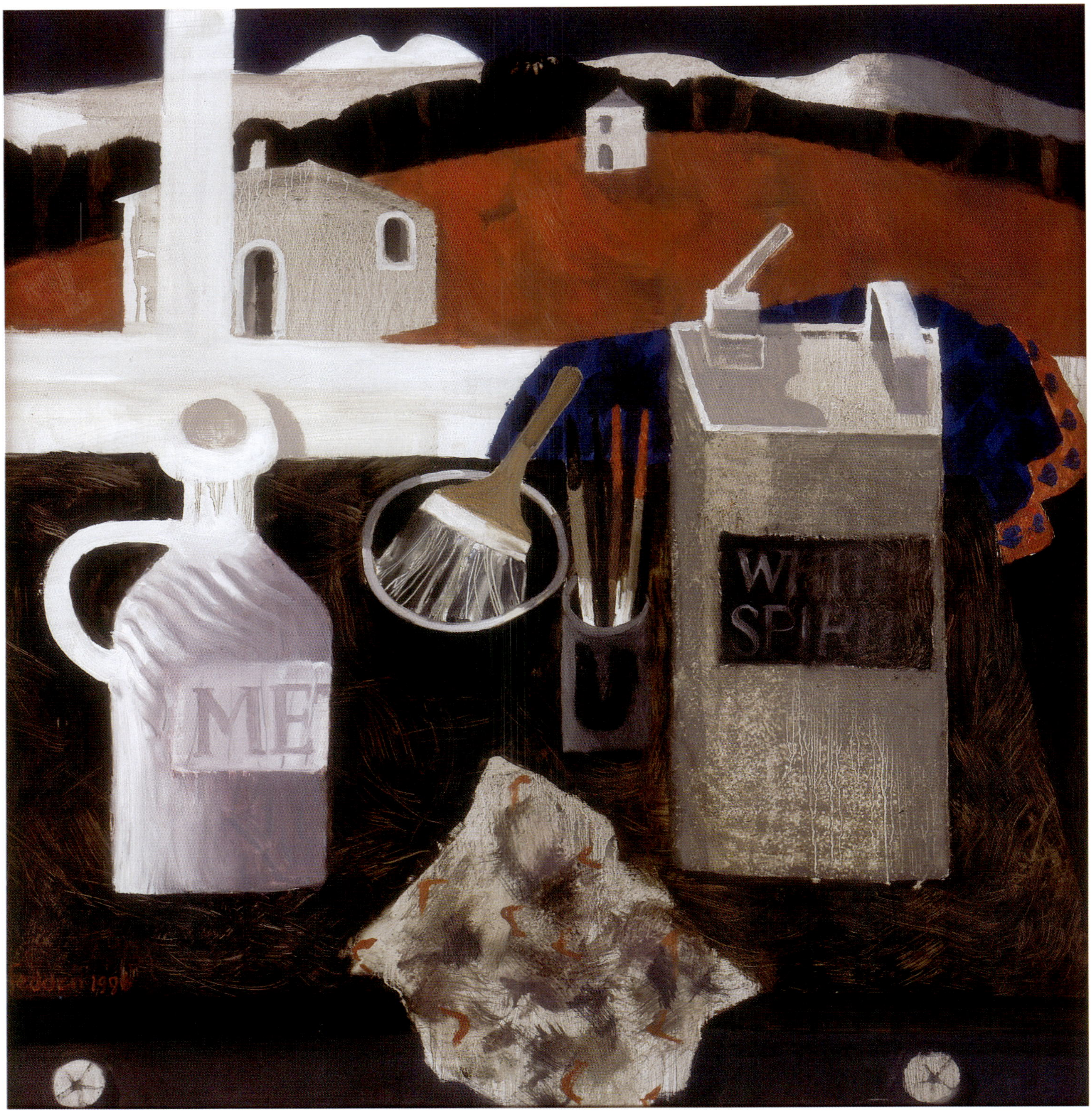

106
The Dirty Rag, 1996
Oil on board
61 x 61 cm (24 x 24 in)
Private collection

CHAPTER FOUR

Painting and Other Media

Mary Fedden's media are conventional for a twentieth-century artist (Ill. 106). She works in five distinct media that are like different compartments: sketchbooks, large finished drawings on single sheets, small gouaches, large and small oil paintings, and collages. Prints are a productive extension of her work, but she does not work directly on these prints – they are not 'hands-on' – and Fedden does not consider herself a printmaker. She is a *painter*.

Clearly, what signifies is not so much the particular medium, but the way in which she uses that medium to her own individual ends. The character of her work is found less in the objects she draws or paints than in the *act* of drawing or painting them, and she does not hide or disguise that act. If anything, she draws attention to it. The viewer is aware of her touch and enjoys a certain intimacy with the process of drawing or painting. This process is quite obviously something she, too, enjoys and explores. It isn't at all laboured.

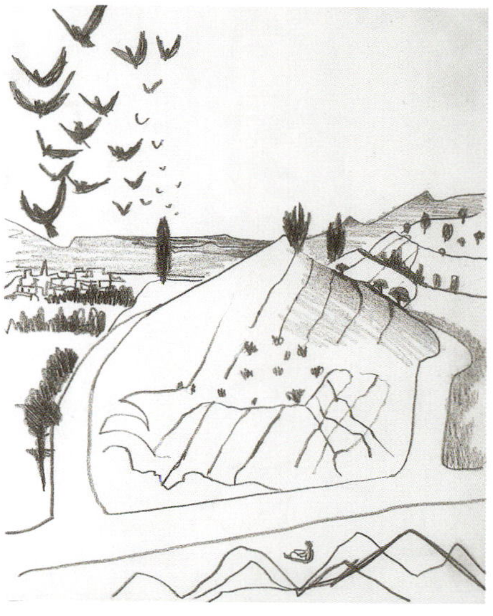

107
Merindol in the Luberon, 1962
Pencil sketch
Dimensions unknown
Credit: The Artist

Sketchbooks

Fedden sketches incessantly when away from home for a weekend, on a longer holiday, or on a long trip (Ill. 107). She sometimes draws in sketchbooks at home, too. Fedden calls her sketchbooks – and there are quantities of them – 'terribly scrappy'. They 'are not meant to be looked at as works of art at all'. Yet they give the privileged viewer a close-up of the way she talks to herself by drawing, and they are also fascinating evidence of her powers of observation. Her line deftly investigates, through contour, the character of a landscape. A few sketchbooks (Japanese in origin) open out like concertinas, fold after fold, and in these she has been able to extend landscapes, right and left, into panoramas.

In fact, her sketchbooks are rather neat – certainly not chaotic. Her drawing in them has the same controlled ease with which she writes letters, though for letter-writing she uses 'an old-fashioned fountain pen, a maroon Parker 51', which she

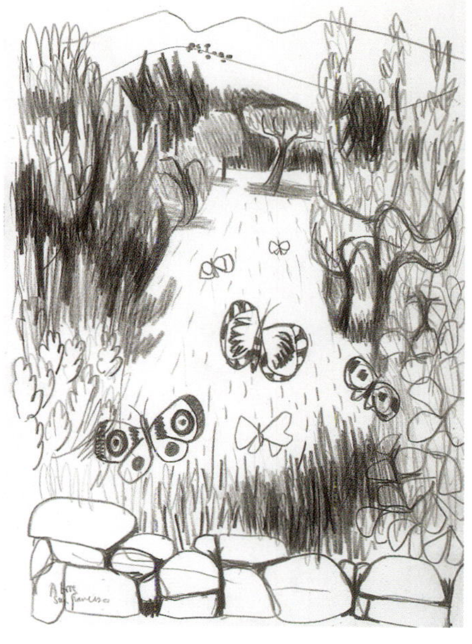

108
Above San Francesco, 1965
Pencil
28 x 21.5 cm (11 x 8½ in)
Credit: The Artist

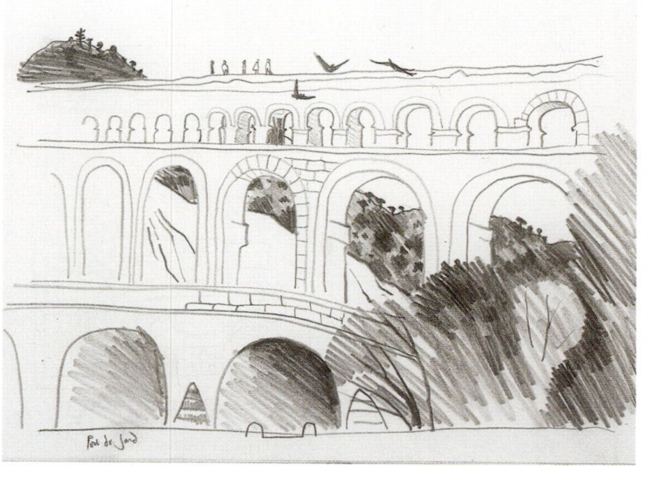

109
Pont du Gard, 1981
Pencil
21.6 x 28 cm (8½ x 11 in)
Credit: The Artist

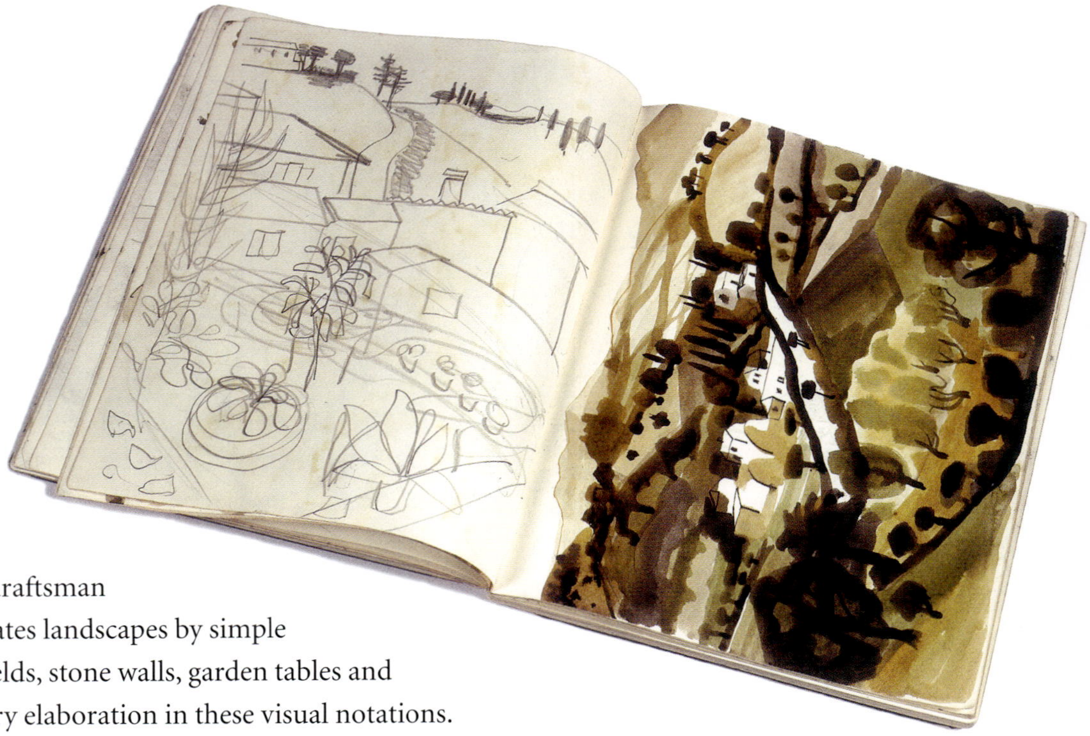

110
Tuscany Sketchbook, 1953
Two pages: pencil, pen and ink/watercolour
28 x 21.5 cm (11 x 8½ in)
Credit: The Artist

fills 'with proper ink'. For sketching, she did use pencil (Ill. 108) but has in recent years switched to a Ball Pentel pen (Ill. 111). Today she never *paints* in her sketchbooks; she does not take paints out of the studio. In the past, though, she did occasionally use paint or ink washes when sketching (Ill. 110).

An economy of line prevails – the mark of a natural and long-experienced draftsman who knows never to overstate. She delineates landscapes by simple contours, tracing the line of hills, trees, fields, stone walls, garden tables and houses. There is no wastage or unnecessary elaboration in these visual notations. They are almost a kind of shorthand, for her eyes only. Why note down anything you won't need? They are *aide-mémoires*, kept in the studio for reference, at hand to recall the essential features of a scene (Ill. 109). They also occasionally prompt new paintings, but not many of them do. 'There might be 20 drawings, and I only use one of them,' she explains. Sometimes they become part of a picture, but not the whole of it. A close-up still life in a painting may call for an escape for the eye into the distance, so Fedden might give it a backdrop … a Tuscan hill, perhaps, with a small church standing on top of it, or an Irish graveyard may serve as the view beyond a windowsill that sports a miscellany of still-life objects, such as in *Irish Lion* (Ill. 44, p.46). The objects and the view have never been anywhere near each other except in Fedden's imagination and pictorial invention.

So her sketches are useful when it comes to the cooking-up of pictures in her studio, but the studio picture is at two removes from the original landscape. There are intervals between the actual landscape and Fedden's economical sketch of it, and then again, between the sketch and the even more simplified image of it in her painting. A kind of fruitful lying takes place. Her paintings are fictions, evolved on their own terms within the confines of the canvas or paper. They are no longer topographical records of a particular place, even when that place means a lot to the artist and when, in her sketchbooks, she has drawn it with accurate care. Memories and observations are now absorbed into a new pictorial order. Picasso ingeniously put it as follows: 'We all know that Art is not truth. Art is a lie that makes us realise truth, at least the truth that is given to us to understand. The artist must know the manner whereby to convince others of the truthfulness of his lies.'[1]

Fedden instinctively grasps, within the relationship of her sketchbook drawings to her studio paintings, this canny business of convincing others of the 'truthfulness' of her images. It's a game of collusion between artist and viewer in which the artist, with charm and conviction, says 'Look how definite and real everything you see in my painting is.' And the viewer, in a willing suspension of disbelief, says: 'It looks utterly real to me. Your painting has persuaded me.'

Fedden's sketching is also a way of 'keeping her hand in' when she is away from the studio. But her sketches are more than useful exercises; she thoroughly enjoys doing them. She has for some years been staying with a friend in Ireland during the summer. Nearby is a subject she persistently returns to – a rather neglected country churchyard (Ill. 111). Showing me a sketch of it, she says: 'I just love it. The sea is here, you see, and the churchyard has got a little ruined chapel. People are still buried there. But the grass is practically waist high. One slab has fallen in, and you can see human bones. But I saw someone putting flowers on a new grave one time. It's beautiful. The first thing I do when I visit my friend – it's about a mile from her house – I go and spend a morning there, drawing ...'

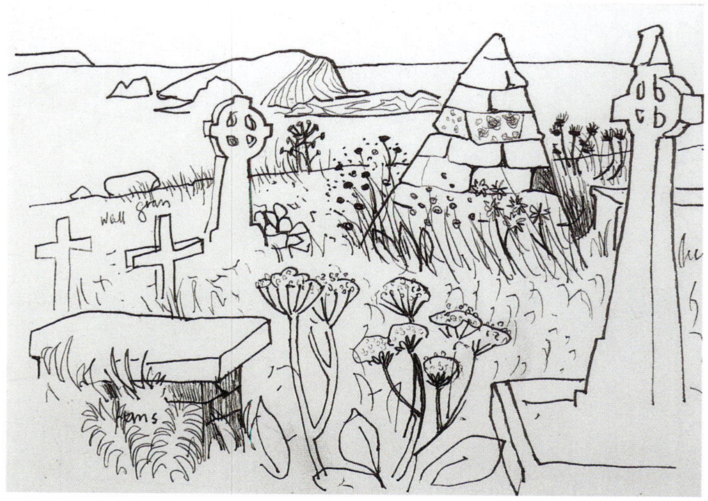

111
Irish Churchyard, 1995
Ball Pentel
12.7 x 22.9 cm (5 x 9 in)
Credit: The Artist

John Iddon writes: 'I've been to Myross graveyard near Skibereen, and it's true you can see bones (and a skull!) in a gap in one of the tombs. The place is solitary and high up above the sea and looks down on a wild empty island spuming with breakers. You feel as though you're on the edge of Synge's western world. No wonder Mary loves it.'[2]

Flipping over the pages of her sketchbooks, she mutters, 'I hate some of my things ... This one is just a scribble ... *That's* not very satisfactory ... Oh, this is from a house in Italy Julian and I used to stay in. It looks across the bay to Istria and Capri ...' Although she is perfectly willing to let me look at her sketchbooks, I have a slight feeling of intruding, all the same, on a conversation she is having with herself.

Large Finished Drawings

If Mary Fedden's sketchbook drawings are private notations, her large finished drawings are just the opposite (Ill. 112). They are for exhibition and sale. They are, she says, 'the drawings I do as an end in themselves'.

They are striking and exquisite. In one drawing, fine, superbly controlled lines, sometimes so fine they are on the edge of visibility, may be in strong contrast with rich black areas of cross-hatching or intense, bold lines. These drawings are not, as most of her sketches are, just linear. They have a much more varied range of texture and substance. She sometimes smudges or rubs the graphite to make subtle intermediary tones, as in *One Tomato* (1997) (Ill. 113). Her furiously energetic (left-handed) cross-hatching may end sharply, apparently stopped in its tracks by an area of white paper. She does this by simply placing a small sheet of card on the surface, drawing over its edge and then taking it away. She makes dark

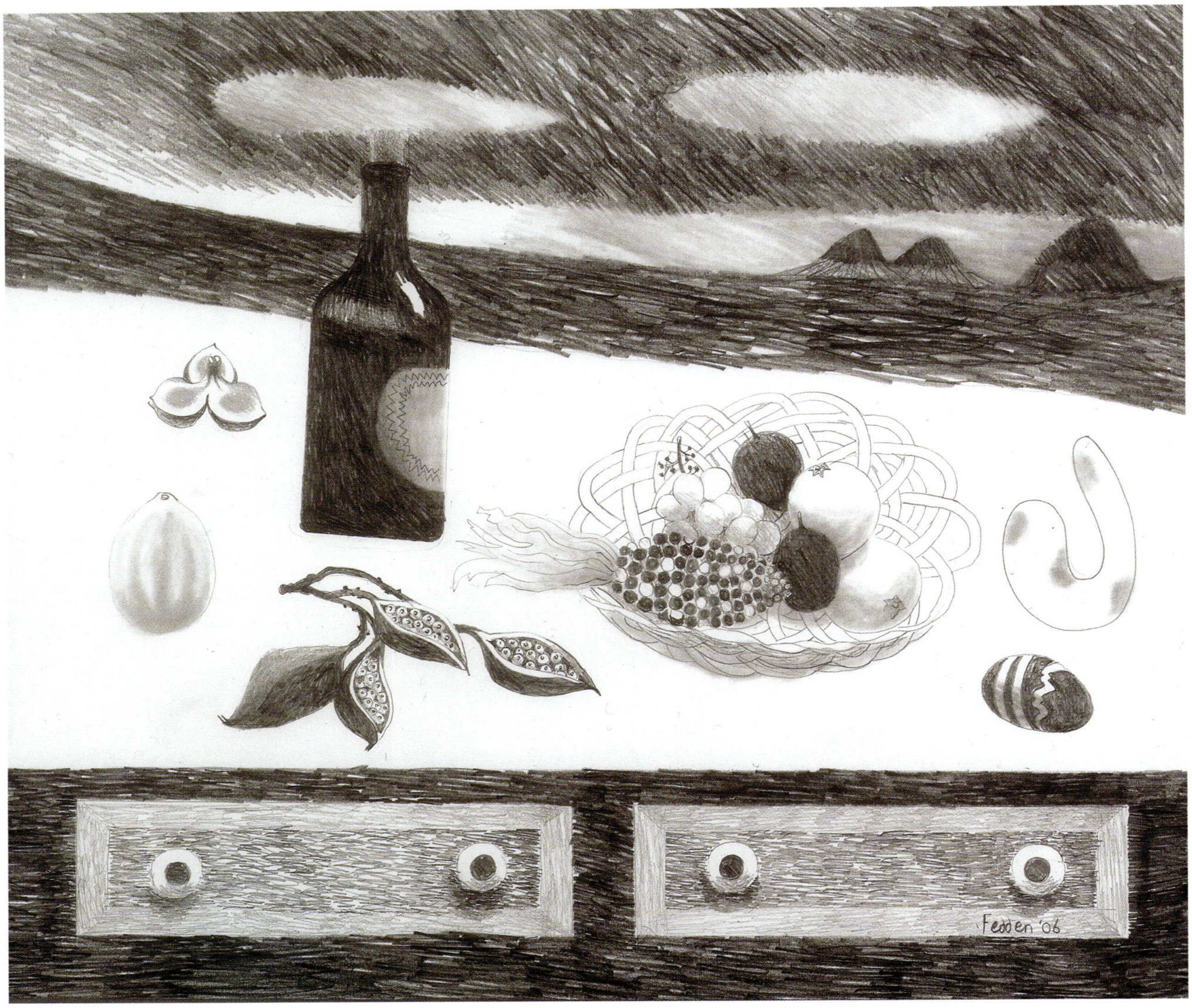
Fessen '06

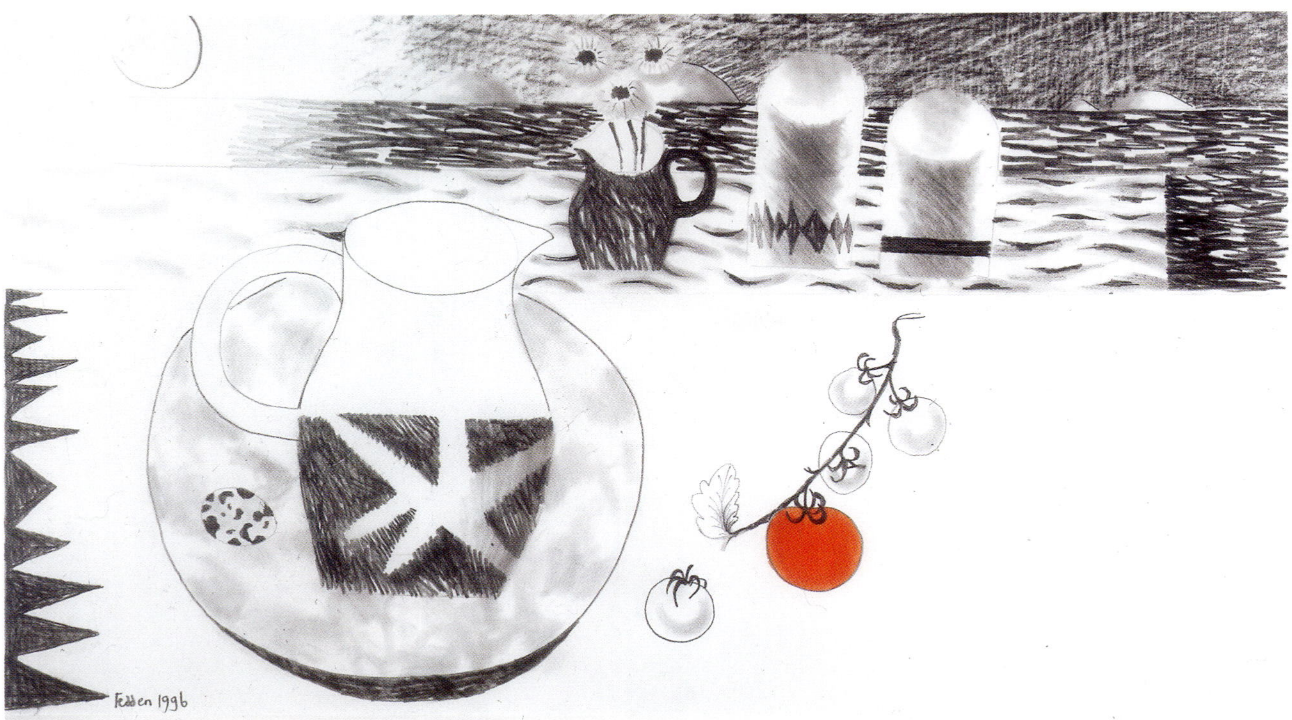
Fessen 1996

112 (opposite top)
Sweet Corn, 2006
Pencil
50 x 60 cm (19¾ x 23⅝ in)
Credit: The Artist

113 (opposite bottom)
One Tomato, 1997
Pencil and gouache
30.5 x 55.8 cm (12 x 22 in)
Private collection

114 (right)
The Checked Mug, 1994
Pencil
56.8 x 42.8 cm (22⅜ x 16⅞ in)
Private collection

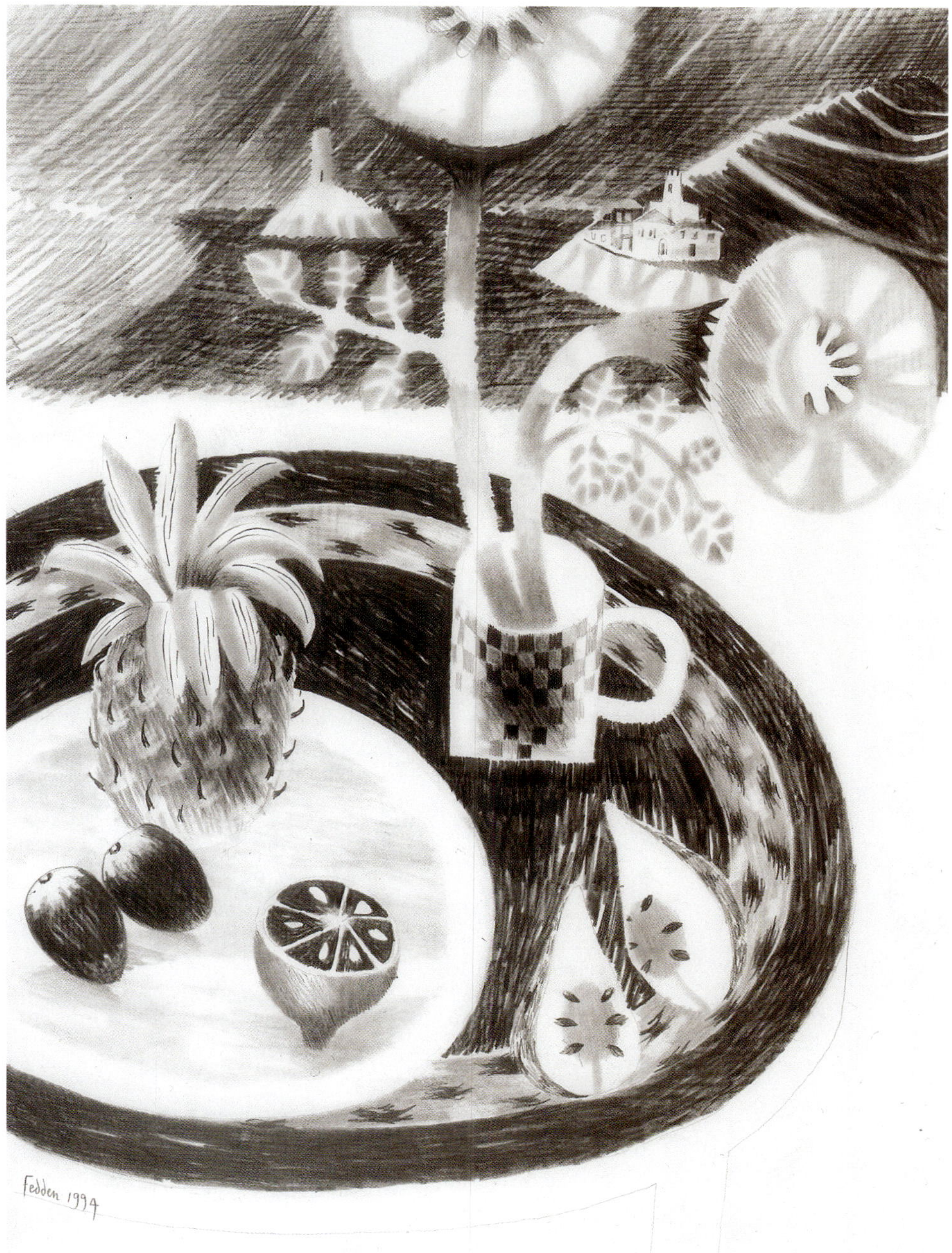

striated passages by moving her softest pencil vigorously over a rough surface placed under the paper. The effect is akin to brass-rubbing, or Max Ernst's 'frottages'. An old drawing board that has seen a lot of use comes into service for such texturings, giving them a residual wood graining. (Ill. 114)

The contrasts that characterise these finished drawings are like fortissimo and pianissimo in a piece of music. A highly sensitive balance is achieved between loud and quiet, mass and line, solidity and airy spaces (Ill. 115). Fedden uses different grades of pencil, from very hard to very soft. She does not use ink or charcoal. Charcoal she finds smudgy: 'You don't get a clear line with charcoal.

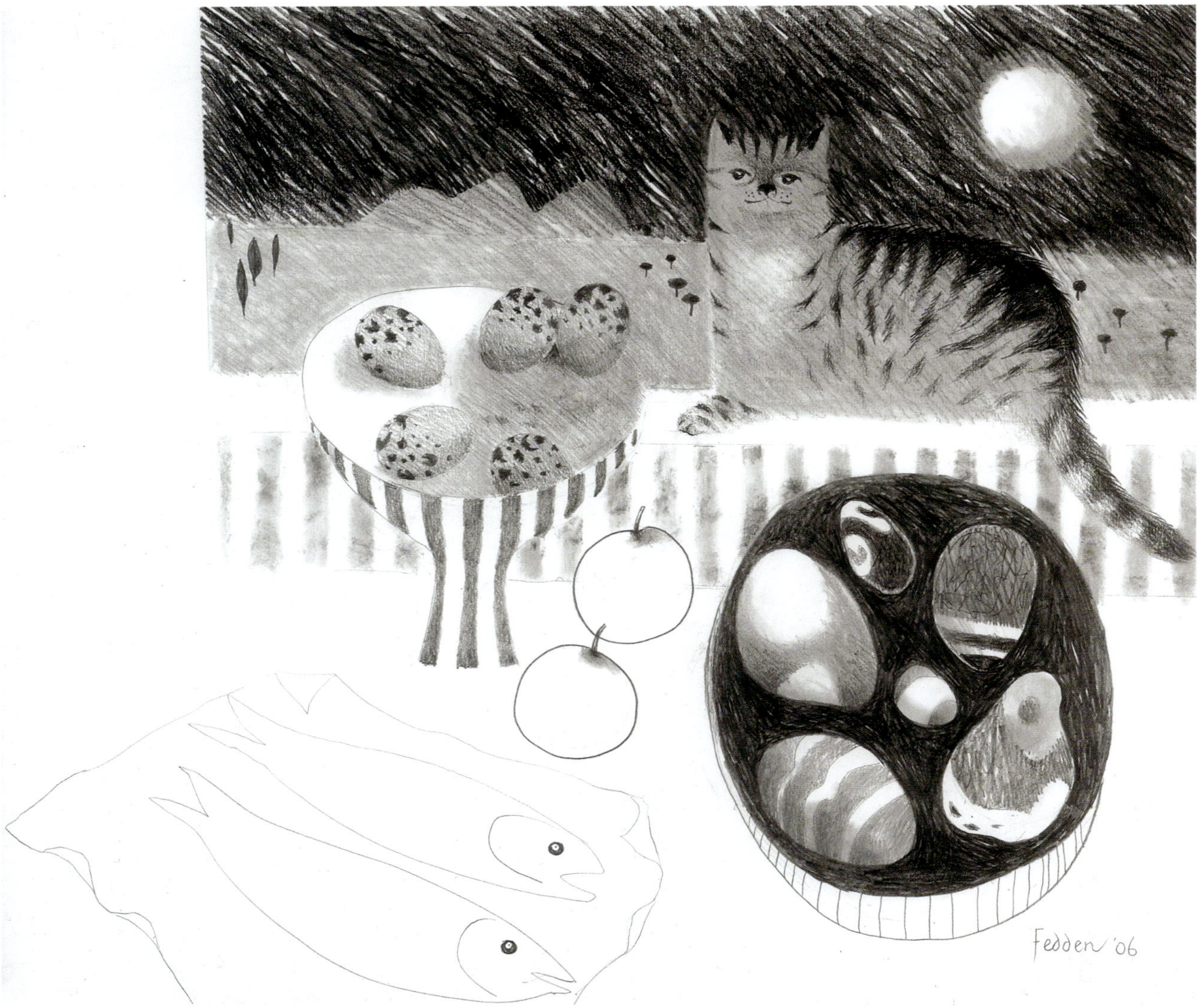

115
Cat and Eggs, 2006
Pencil
50 x 60 cm (19¾ x 23⅝ in)
Credit: The Artist

But even with a soft pencil, you can get something definite.' And the *definite* is integral to Fedden's art.

Many of her finished drawings are made *after* her oil paintings, such as *Three Red Poppies* (Ill. 193, p.161). It is as if she wants to investigate another possible way of presenting the same or a similar image in another medium. Since she confines herself to monochrome, she (as she puts it) 'tries to express the colour *in* the pencil'. The quality of a black can suggest a potent hue. She loves black-and-white photographs; in these, too, colour can only be imagined. Now and then, however, as in *The Lemon* (1976) (Ill. 116), she accentuates a single feature (it might be a lemon or a sun in other drawings) with a single, apt colour. As in *One Tomato* (Ill. 113), this emphasises the fact that the viewer is looking first and foremost at a work of art, a drawing in an artist's hand, and secondly at its subject. Is that a tomato? Or is it really just a splendidly sudden circle of red?

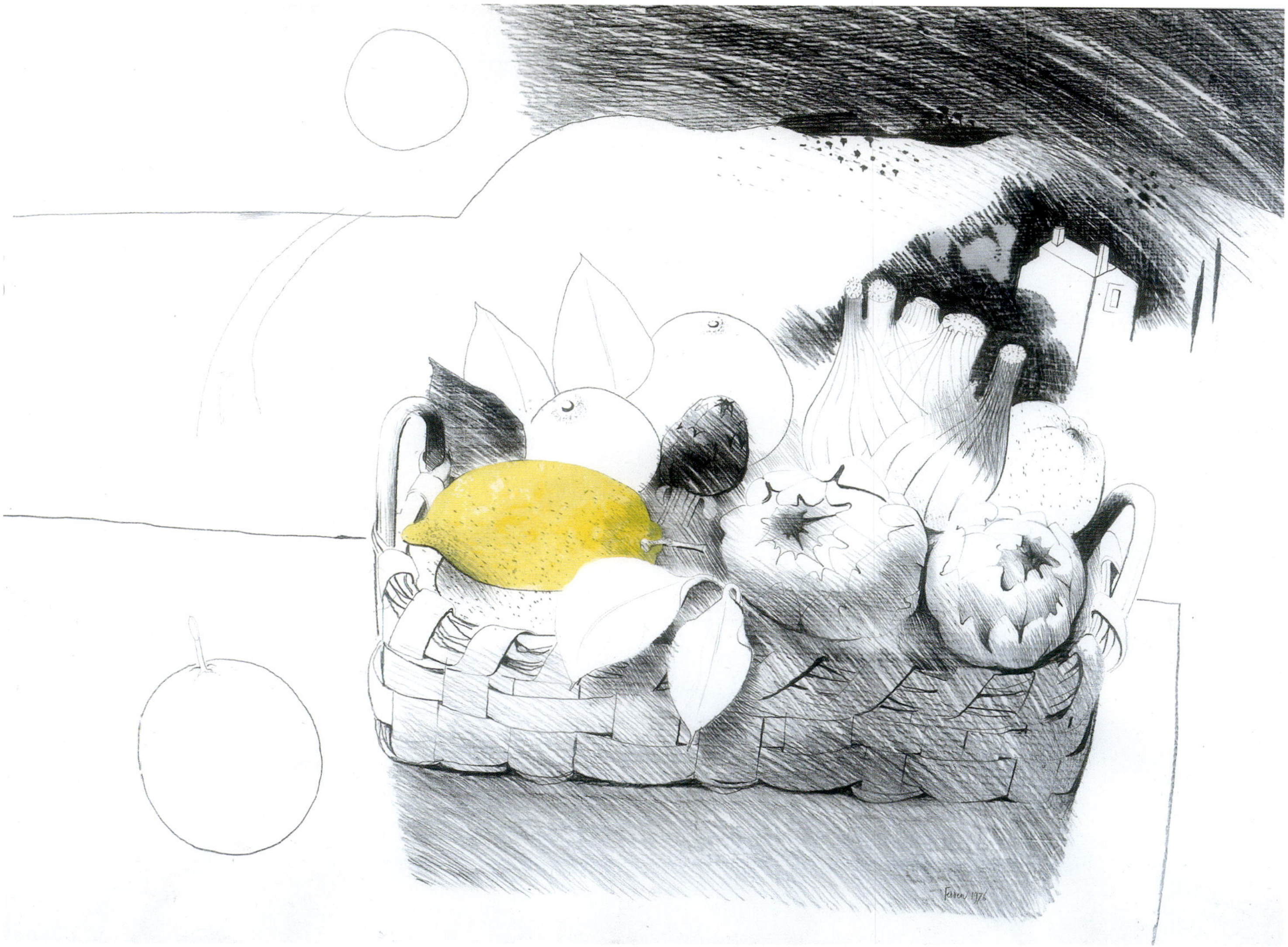

116
The Lemon, 1976
Pencil and gouache
53.7 x 74 cm (21⅛ x 29⅛ in)
Private collection

In *Cat and Eggs* (2006) (Ill. 115), is that really an imperious cat, staring at us with Egyptian majesty up there, apparently guarding a bowl of eggs? Or aren't both the cat and the eggs just parts of one terrific drawing?

Gouaches

Drawing underpins Mary Fedden's paintings. It does not set them in a rigid mould; it is more that when she uses a brush, she *draws* with it. Areas of paint, however freely applied, have their directions, rhythms, boundaries and edges. How strict these edges are depends, in her gouaches, on the wetness of the paper and the liquidity of the paint on the brush, as well as her sure hand, of course. Although she sometimes uses a surprisingly large and loaded brush for quite small passages, the area to be painted is very carefully known and adhered to. Finer brushes describe the finest details.

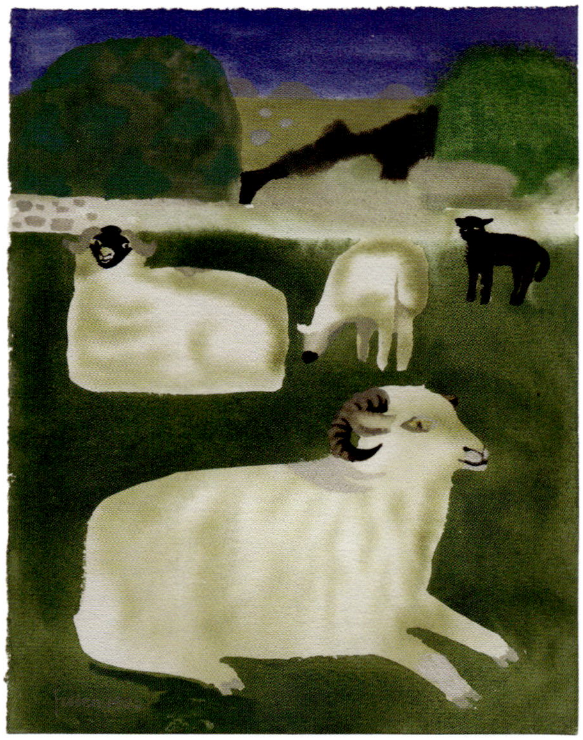

117
Sheep, 1982
Gouache
29 x 23 cm (11½ x 9 in)
Private collection

Gouache is water-based but, being opaque, it is not exactly the same as watercolour. With it, Fedden feels she has the best of both worlds: with gouache she can paint thickly, and even overpaint, as she can with oil paint, but she can also use thin gouache to make washes as fluid and translucent as watercolour (Ill. 117). Gouache used to be known as body colour. It has more body than watercolour, and white, in particular, can be painted on to the paper and can hide other colours, while in a watercolour the white of the paper has to be left bare when white is needed (Ill. 118). Having said this, Fedden's gouaches, often on a heavy Indian rag paper with wonderfully free edges, make considerable play with the white sparkling texture of the paper showing through the paint. (Ill. 119).

On the whole, her gouaches are small. She has a range of subjects and themes she only paints in gouache. Perhaps the more intimate scale allows for experiment and a degree of fantasy, dreaming or poetry, as in the recent *The Woods are Lovely, Dark and Deep* (2006) (Ill. 120). Her gouaches can be quite free, suggestive and atmospheric – though they can be clearly defined when she chooses.

In terms of her development, she had never used oil paint before going to art school in the early 1930s. Once she discovered oil paint, she found herself unable to do watercolours for some years. This may explain why, when she was finally able to paint on paper again, she chose the kind of water-based paint that comes closest to oil. Today, she paints in both media, gouache and oil, with full relish.

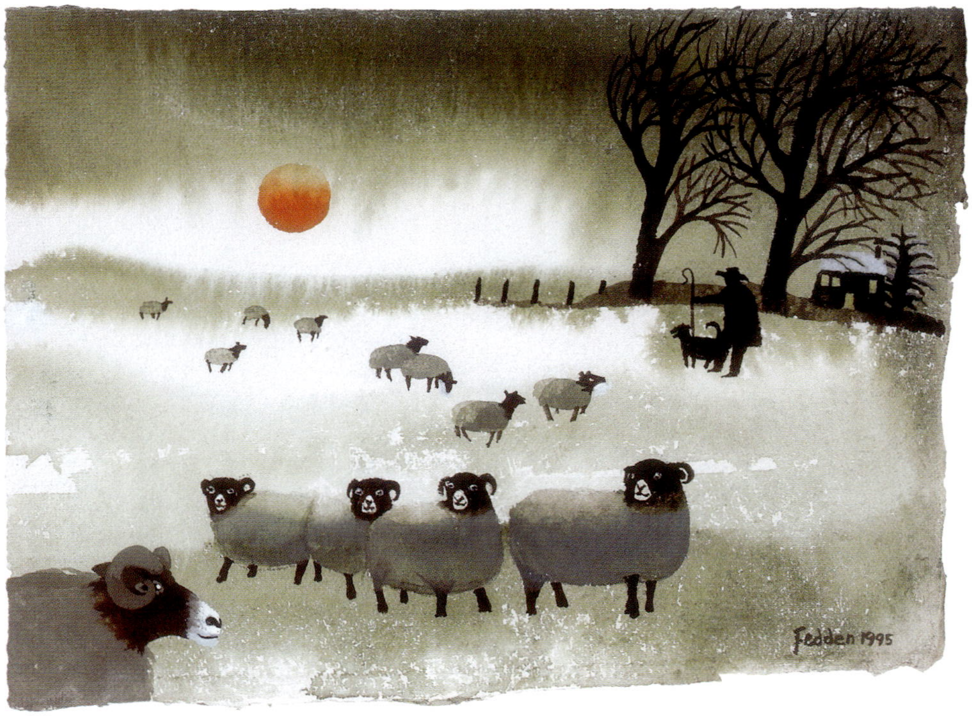

118
Winter, 1995
Gouache
20 x 27.7 cm (7⅞ x 10⅞ in)
Private collection

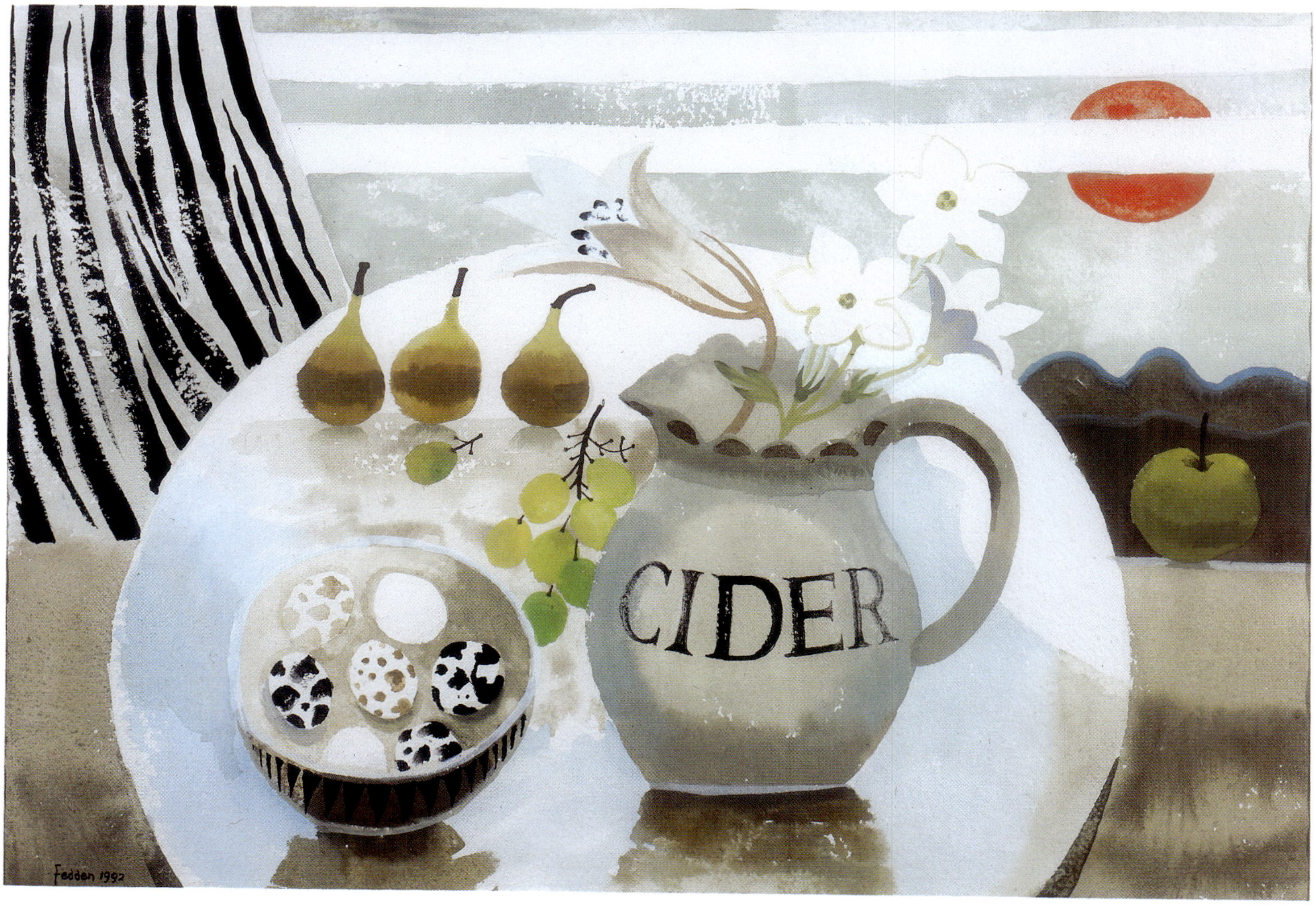

119
Cider Jug, 1992
Gouache
37.2 x 54.7 cm (14⅝ x 21½ in)
Private collection

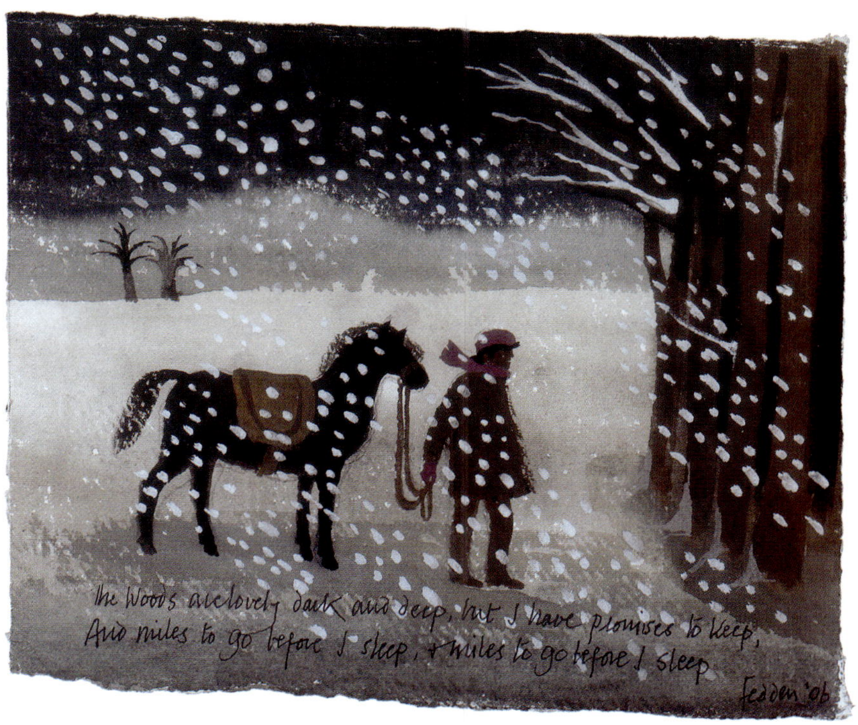

120
The Woods are Lovely, Dark and Deep, 2006
Gouache
19 x 24 cm (7½ x 9½ in)
Private collection

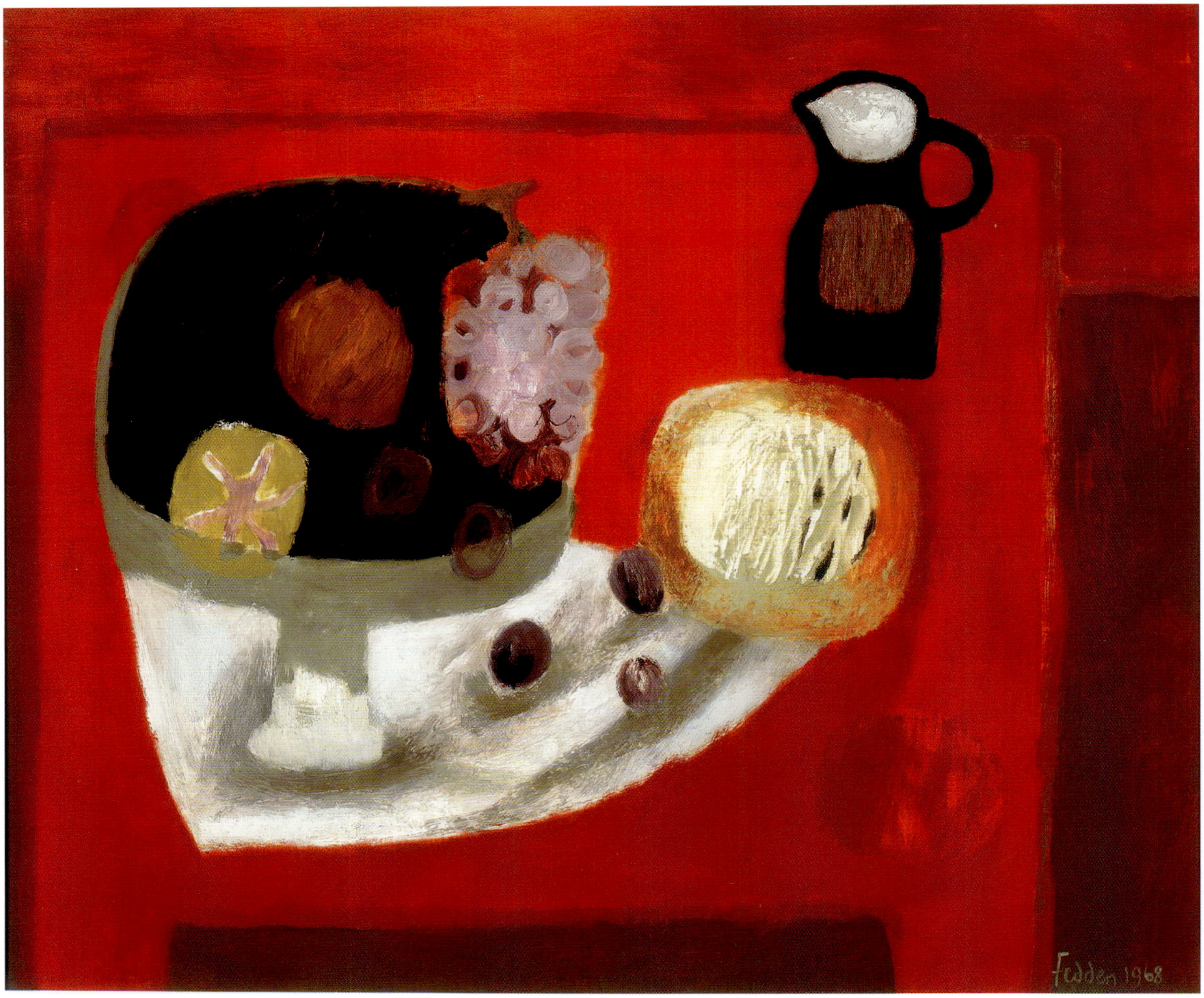

121
Red Table, 1968
Oil on canvas
76.2 x 91.5 cm (30 x 36 in)
Private collection

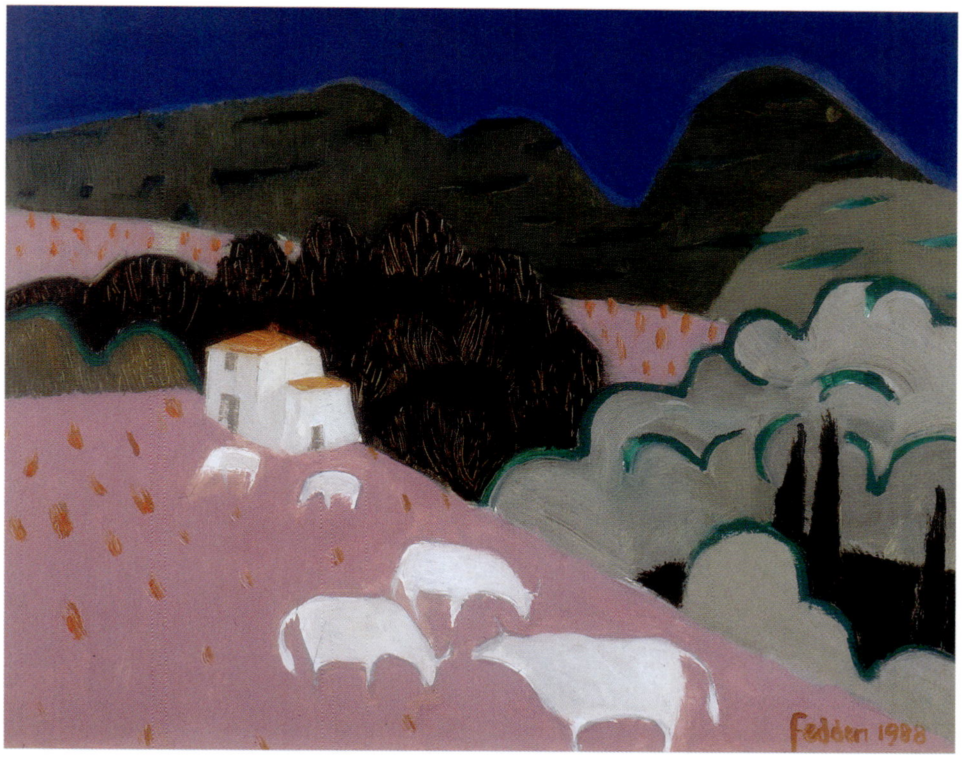

122
Near San Antimo, 1988
Oil on board
29.5 x 39 cm (11⅝ x 15¼ in)
Private collection

Oil Paintings

Most of Mary Fedden's oil paintings are on canvas. Some are on board. She uses oil for her larger works, but she does also make small oil paintings. She often applies oil with a full brush, enjoying the paint's buttery consistency. On the other hand, she went through a phase – there are examples of this in the early 1990s – of mixing sand with her oil paint, exploring a new texture and dryness.[3]

For a painter who believes herself to be unambiguous, and who is indeed very direct and straightforward, oil paint offers firm, bold statement (Ill. 121). Oil paints do not run into each other. Silhouettes and contours can be strong and unmistakeable in oil paint. A form, as in 1988's *Near San Antimo* (Ill. 122), can be substantial and tactile. Yet Fedden sometimes uses turpentine to make her oil paint as washy as watercolour. Runny oil paint has its uses (Ills 123 and 124). She sometimes goes in for 'tonking', where a rag is pressed onto a painted area of wet oil paint, leaving behind it an effect like crinkled paper. She also uses another kind of wet texturing that involves streaks running down the canvas like rain down a windowpane. Generally, however, she is not keen on tricks, and her oil paint is applied with a firm and bold brush, straight from the maelstrom of her palette onto the canvas. (Ill. 125)

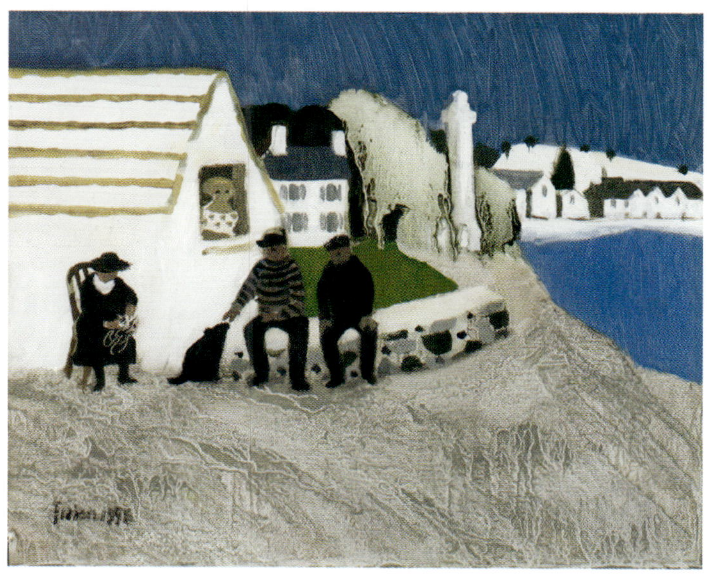

123
Fishermen on a Sea Wall, 1996
Oil on board
20 x 25 cm (8 x 9¾ in)
Richard Green Gallery, London

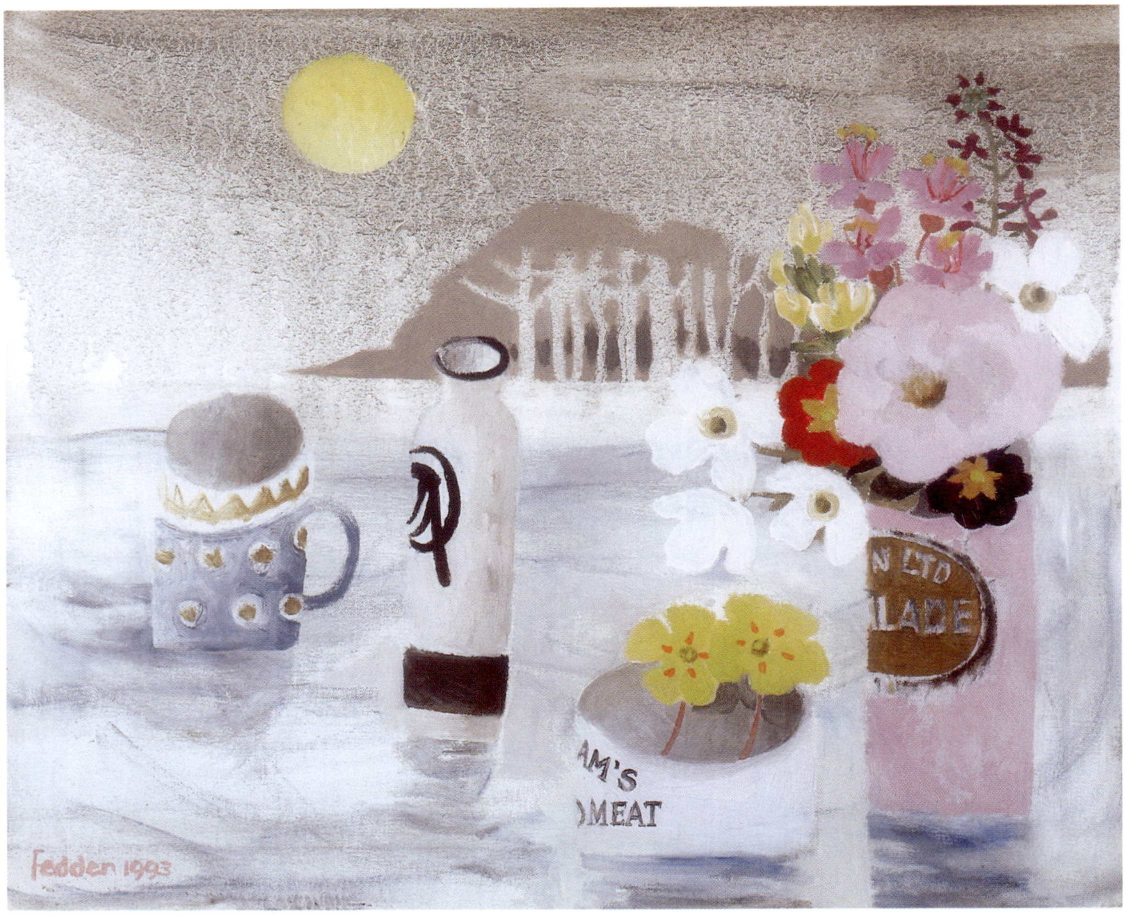

124
Distant Islands, 1993
Oil on canvas
39.6 x 49.8 cm (15⅝ x 19⅝ in)
Private collection

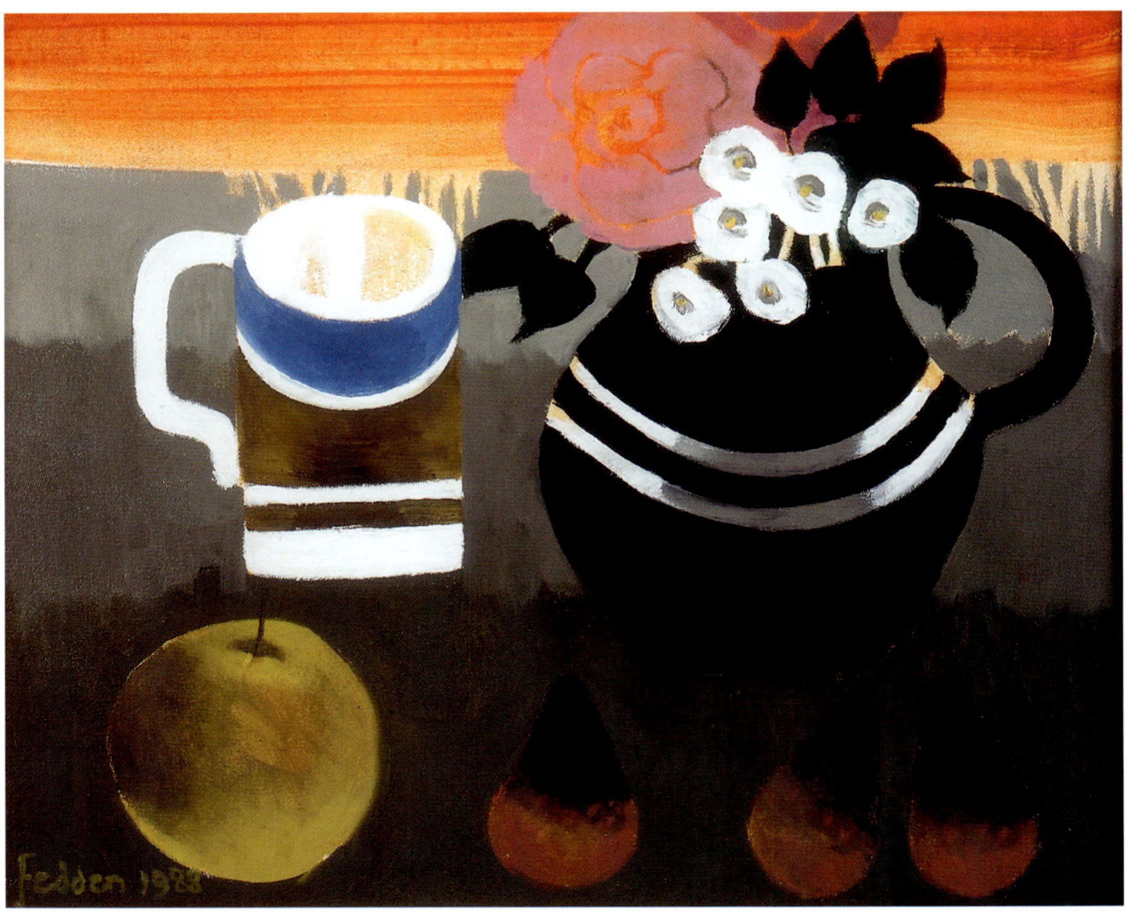

125
Mocha Jug, 1988
Oil on canvas
40.6 x 50.8 cm (16 x 20 in)
Manya Igel Fine Arts, London

Fedden's oil paintings can have much coarser surfaces than reproductions of them suggest. She strives, in spite of a tendency to delineate everything clearly in a painting, to soften her edges and paint with a greater looseness. She looks back at her oils in the 1960s, half wishing she could still paint in the same organic, and at times almost roughshod, way. In any case, she is an artist who knows oil paint very well.

Collages

Though perhaps her least conventional medium, collage (Ill. 126) is now almost a century old as a way of making pictures. Sticking cut-out or torn fragments to the paper surface, which has a background of gouache washed over it, gives full play to her visual wit and compositional ingenuity (Ill. 127). Her Surrealist side comes out, unexpectedly juxtaposing objects, textures and even different styles in a mix of knowing design and happy chance. (Ill. 128)

It was during his lifetime that she began the process of making use of cast-off fragments from Julian Trevelyan's rejected prints in her collages. He liked the result and its touch of mischief. She has continued this fascinating practice ever since in works such as *Fruit* (2000) (Ill. 129). She described the process to John Russell Taylor in *The Times* in 1995.[4] He had spotted 'a basket in the studio full of dismembered prints'. She said, 'You might think that that is my wastepaper

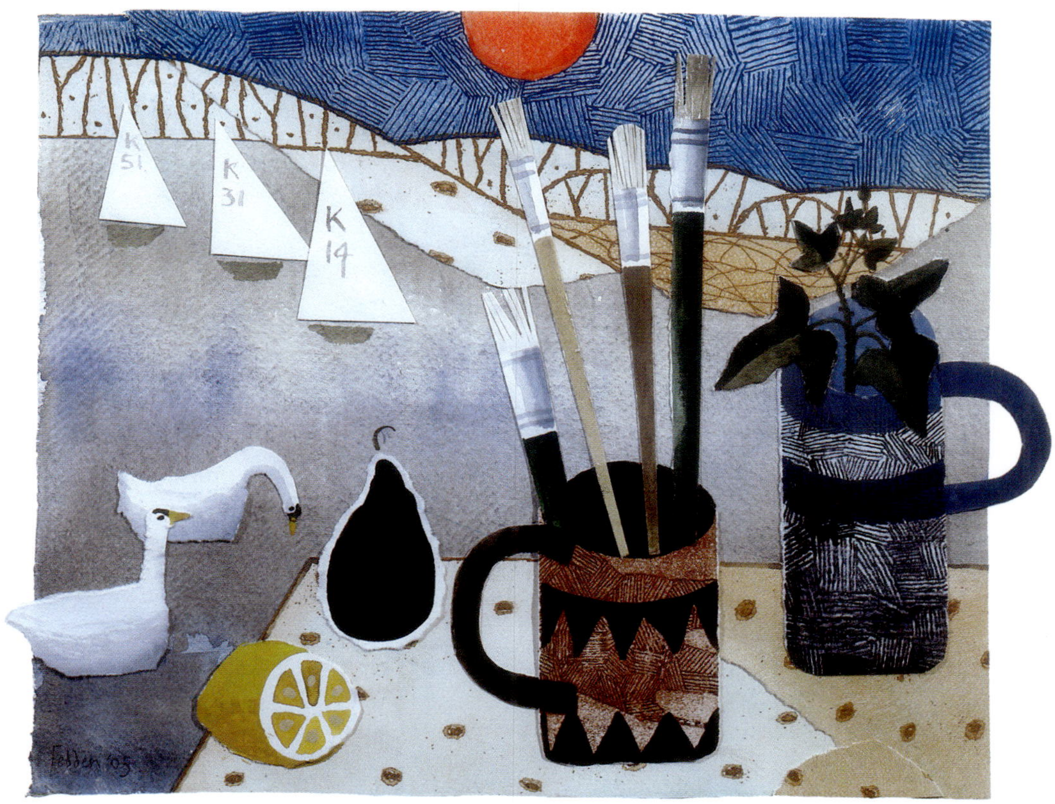

126
Paint Brushes, 2005
Collage and gouache
27 x 34.5 cm (10½ x 13½ in)
Lena Boyle Fine Art, London

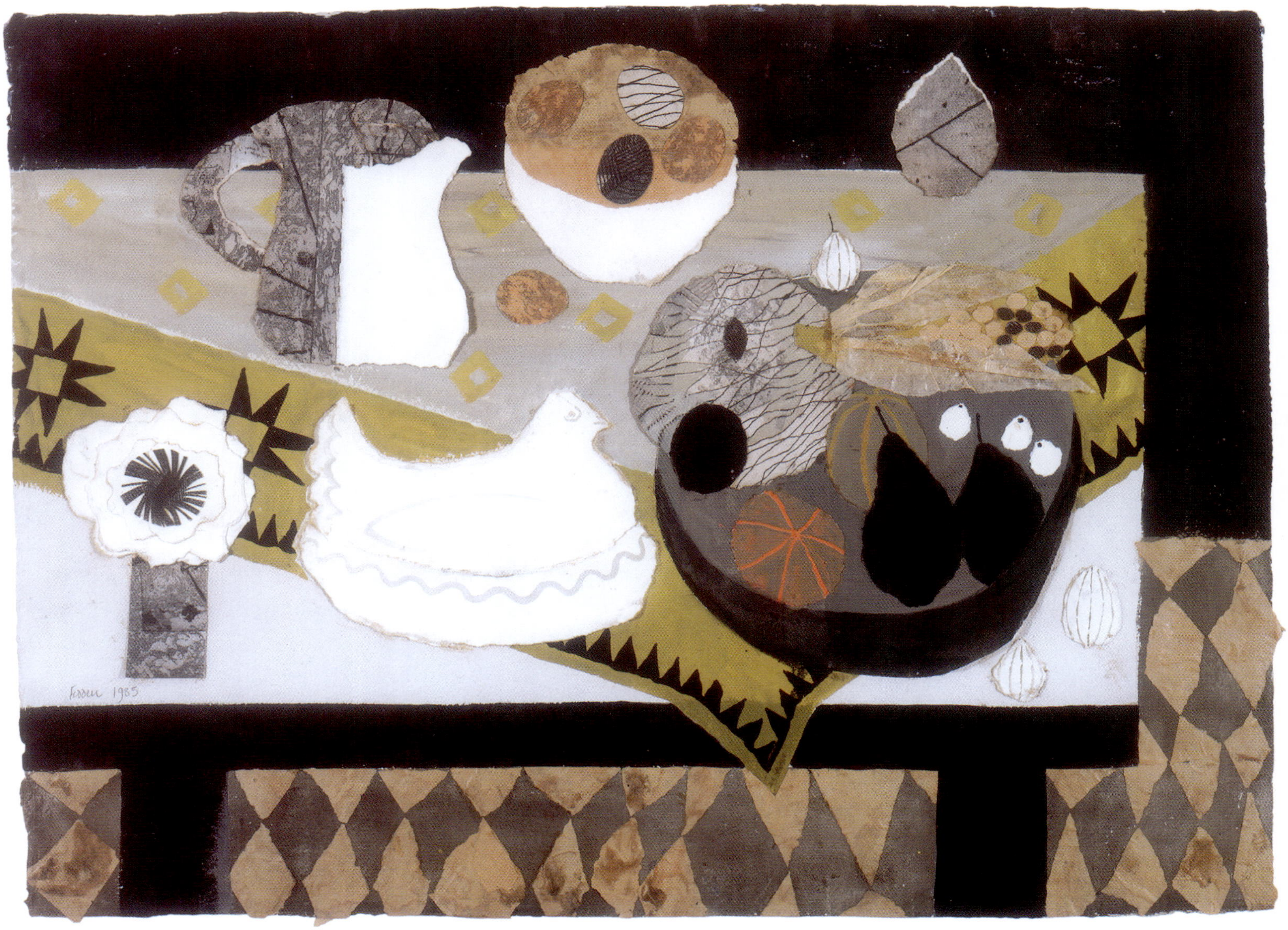

127
China Hen, 1985
Collage and gouache
56.3 x 78 cm (22⅛ x 30¾ in)
Private collection

128
The Harbour, 1996
Collage and gouache
36.8 x 37.9 cm (14.5 x 15 in)
Private collection

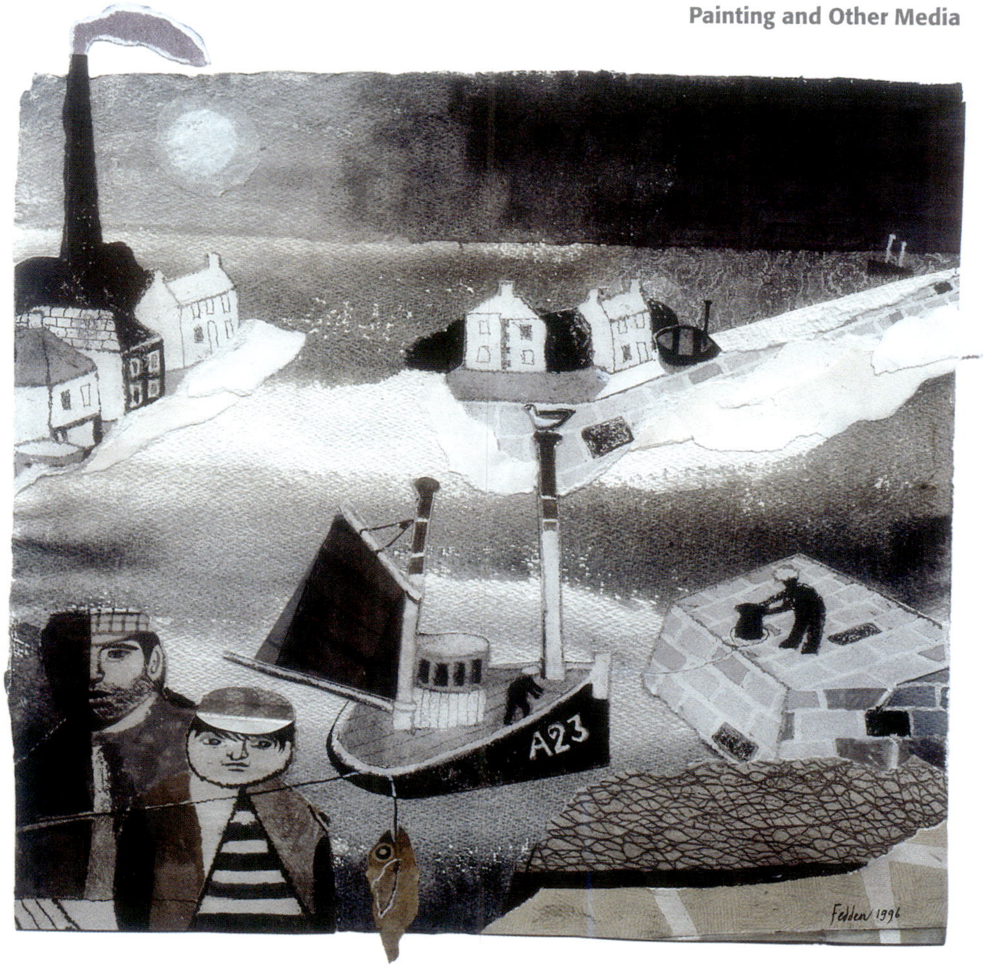

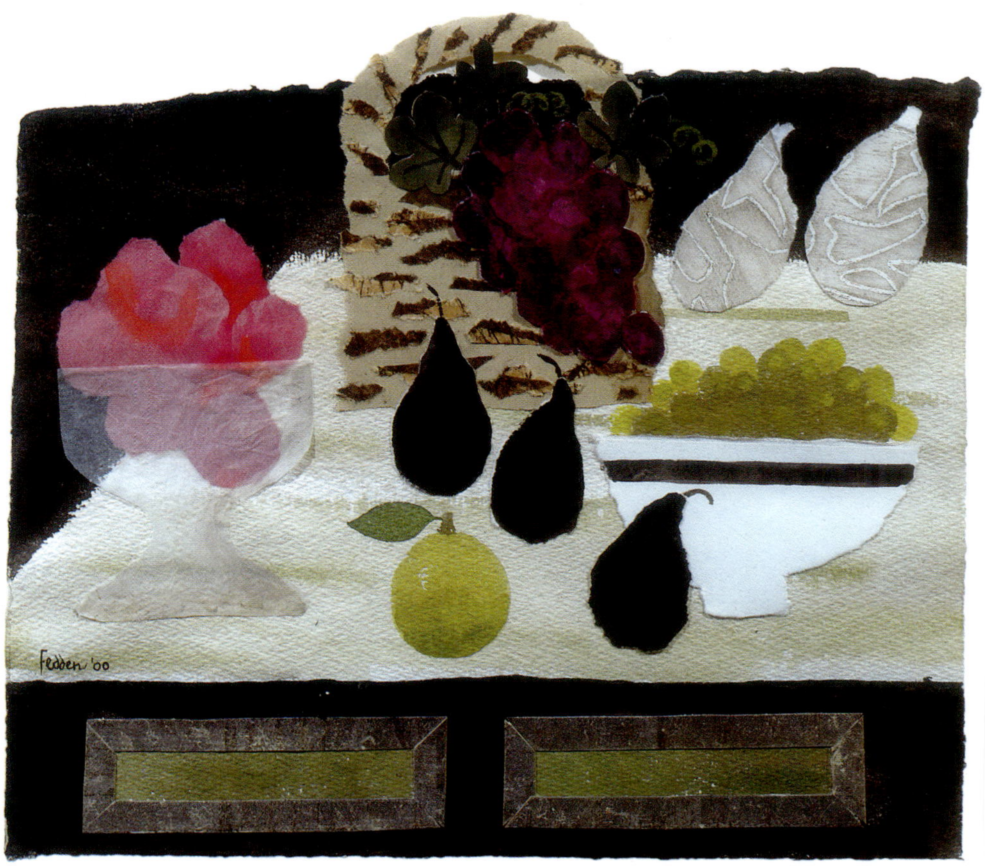

129
Fruit, 2000
Collage and gouache
31.5 x 36 cm (12⅜ x 14⅛ in)
Private collection

basket. Actually, it's my collage basket. Julian was always tinkering with prints, discarding trial proofs. I use them to give textural interest to my collage paintings, just cutting my own shapes out of his: the pattern on the chair in that picture, for instance, comes from a group of skyscrapers in the background of that etching.' The range of textures, patterns and motifs Trevelyan explored in his soft-ground etchings have provided her with a fresh visual language, turning the girders of a bridge into a boat, or the wheels of a vehicle in a sliced half lemon. It's a sort of aesthetic recycling. No wastage. (Ills 130, 131 and 132)

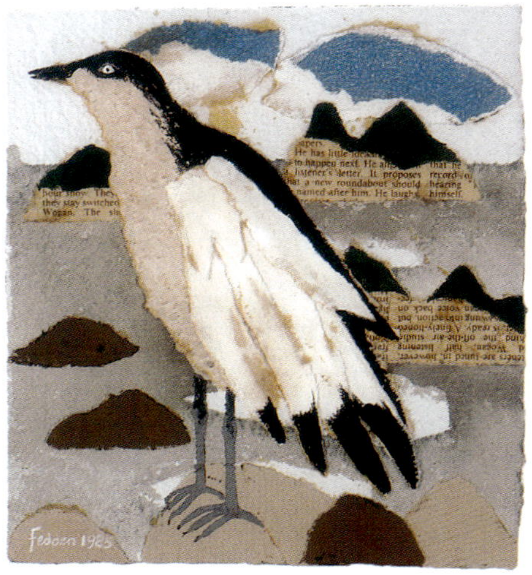

130
Bird, 1985
Gouache and collage
17 x 16 cm (6¾ x 6¼ in)
Sotheby's Picture Library

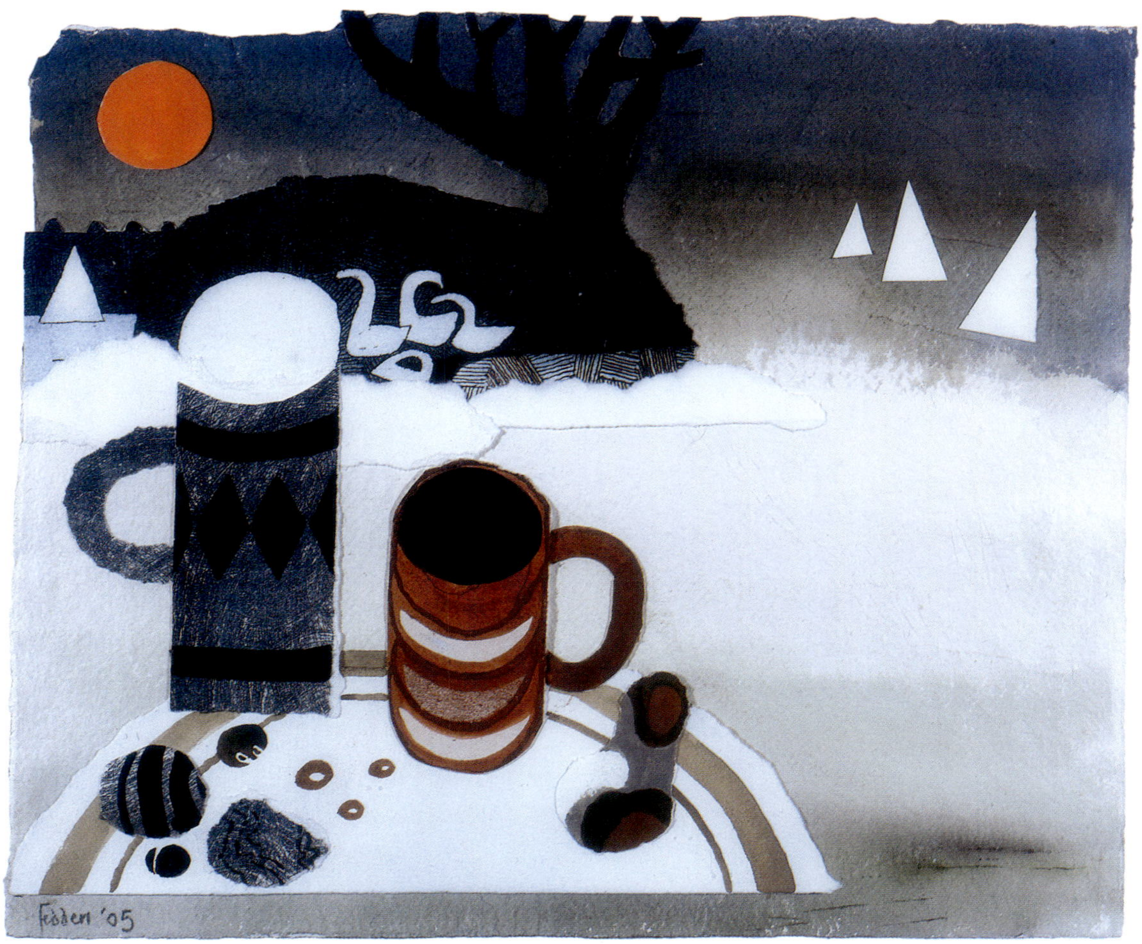

131
Swans and Mugs, 2005
Collage and gouache
31.9 x 39 cm (12½ x 15¼ in)
Private collection

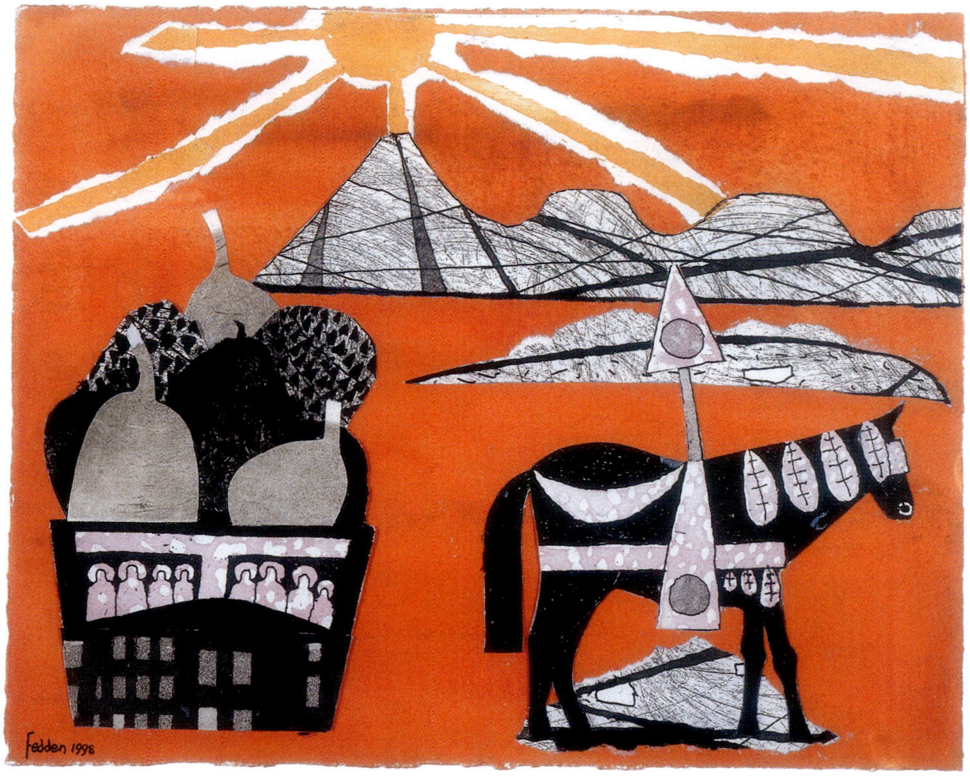

132
Sunset, 1998
Collage and gouache
28 x 35.5 cm (11 x 14 in)
Credit: The Artist

Although Mary Fedden's diverse media are theoretically in compartments, they also cross over their boundaries and suggest possibilities to each other. After all, they are methods or techniques used by the same artist. Drawing, as was drummed into her at the Slade, is the foundation, the skeleton, of everything else. Her sketchbooks are pure drawing. In making collages, she is, as it were, 'drawing' by cutting or tearing edges. She is defining shapes. In her finished drawings, she works to re-create the fluency, tone and colour range of painting, while when she is painting in oils, she also makes the paints produce watercolour effects. Then, when she is painting in gouache, she can be as bold as she is in oil and as atmospheric as she is in watercolour.

In all her media, the clear description of things – of the isolated identity and outline of objects – is itself very like collage. A teapot seems cut out of the tablecloth on which it sits; the undulating line of the hills seems cut out of the sky. Two distinct oranges kiss each other on a white napkin behind a white teacup, standing near a striped mug containing purple-and-white auriculas. Auriculas are the most exact of flowers – their petals and markings like paper cut-outs – and each of the other objects, even the two touching oranges, is just as exact and clear. It could be argued that all her works, in whatever medium, contain an element of collage.

Notes

1. *Picasso on Art, a Selection of Views*, edited by Dore Ashton, Thames and Hudson Ltd (London), 1972, p.21
2. John Iddon, email to the author, 27 August 2006
3. Such as *Ben's Flowers*. See *Mary Fedden* by Mel Gooding, Scolar Press (Aldershot), 1995, p.84
4. 'Still lifes still glowing with life' by John Russell Taylor, *The Times* arts supplement, 21 February 1995, p.1

CHAPTER FIVE

Still Life

'I come back from holiday with sketchbooks full of landscapes,' Fedden says. She does 'perhaps two' landscape paintings from them in her studio – 'and then I'm back to still life. It's my real love'. (Ill. 133)

The words 'still life' – or what the French more morosely term '*nature morte*' (dead nature) – summon up a traditional image of fruit, vegetables, game and a great variety of objects probably connected with the preparation or consumption of food on a table. Fedden operates in that realm: meals are celebrated in paint. (Ills 134, 135 and 136)

Still life is about as unpretentious as art can be, and yet it has enormous sticking power and fascination as a genre. The objects are arranged, rather as they might be in real life, waiting for the diners to arrive. Or sometimes Old Master still-life painters depicted the *remains* of a meal.

So indelibly is still life part of the history of art that a modern painter can take a lot for granted about it and assume that a viewer will accept the convention. And then the convention is free to be played with. Mary Fedden's still-life paintings do just that; they play with the convention. Using familiar tokens and motifs such as fish on a plate, apples, pears, baskets of eggs, bottles of wine, various containers and bunches of grapes, she has taken possession of them and then added other objects that are her unique 'cabinet of curiosities'. (Ill. 137)

One recurrent image is the melon with a slice out of it (Ill. 20, p.23). It clearly appeals to her greatly, with its contrast of hard, fibrously patterned skin and soft interior flesh. And the way in which this warm orange flesh glows in contrast to surrounding ochres, cool greys and muted browns strikes a sensuous colour note in her still lifes over and over again. She never grows tired of ringing the changes

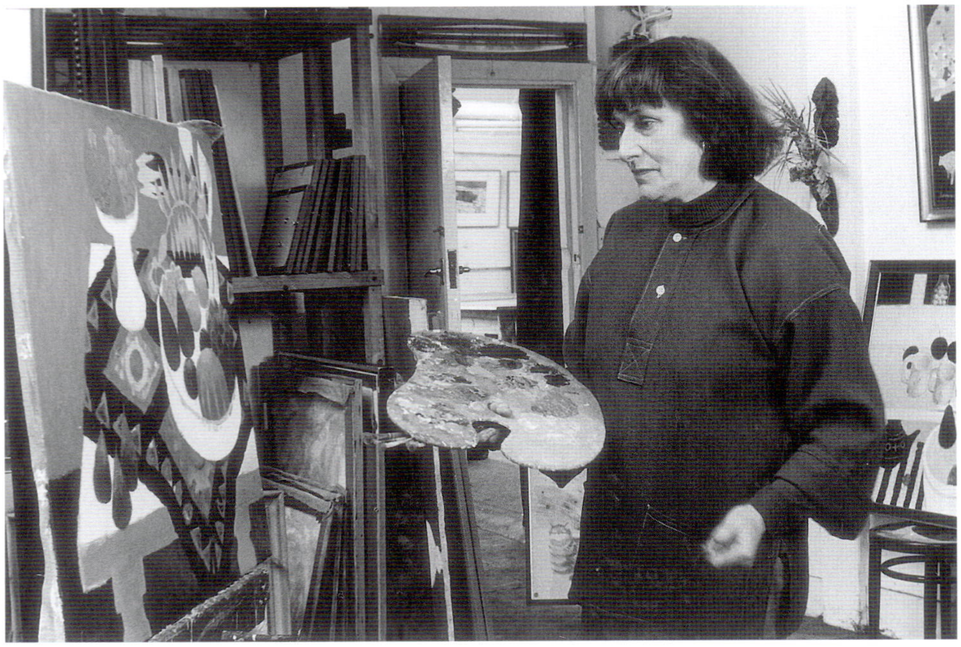

133
Mary Fedden at her easel, c.1960s photograph

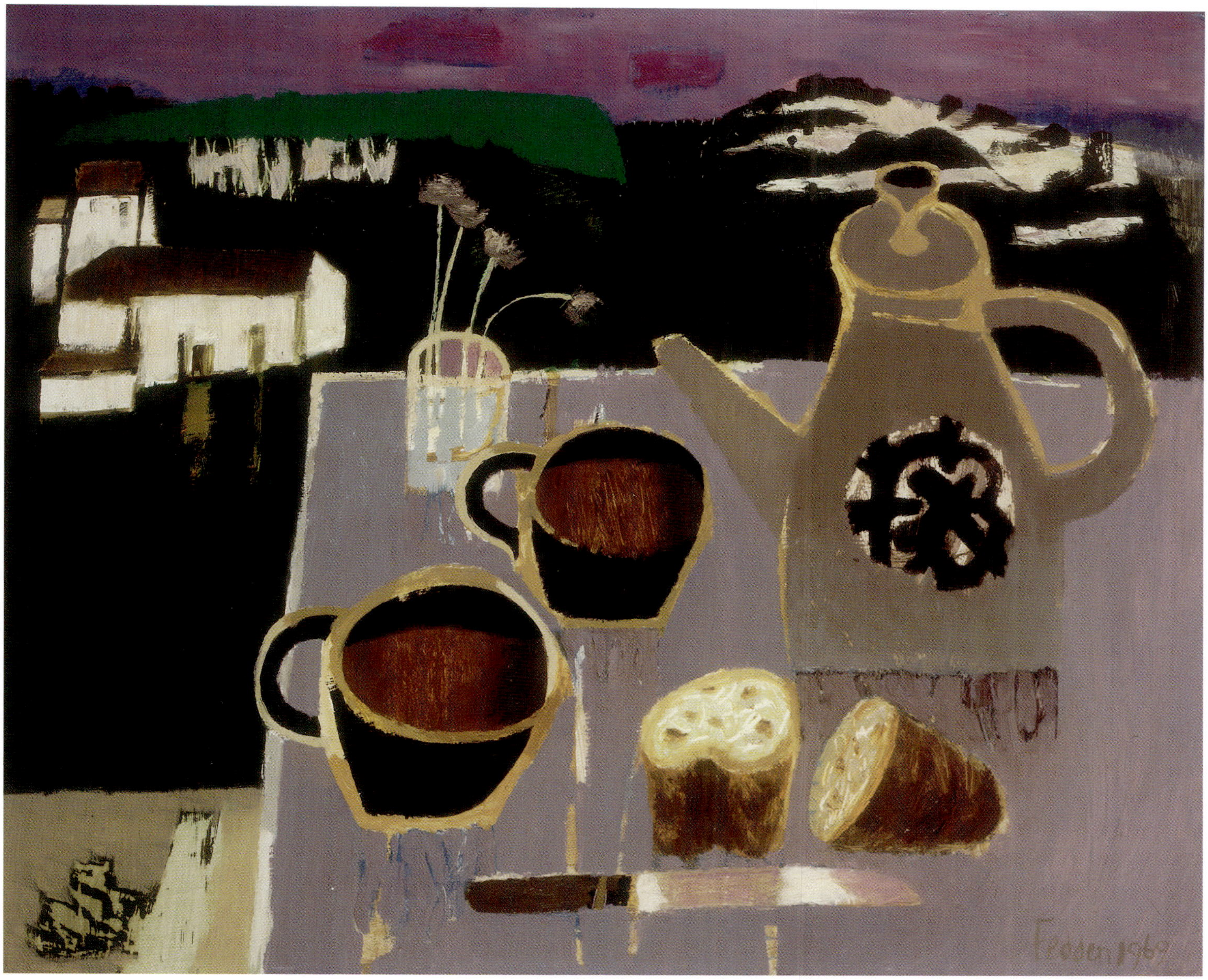

134
Breakfast, 1969
Oil on canvas on board
61 x 76.2 cm (24 x 30 in)
Credit: Miss Sarah Hue-Williams

of this theme. It is not, tellingly, her invention. Many other still-life painters, back in history, have found it irresistible.

Fedden is emphatic that her still-life motifs have no symbolic or emblematic associations or significance. I am sure she means this, but I think that when it comes to the responses of her viewers, it is a battle she may have lost. People will read into her still lifes whatever they are inclined to see or feel, and her art is hardly dictatorial or proscriptive.

On the other hand, the apparently casual way in which she orders her objects on the table-top of the canvas does nothing to suggest an intention much beyond her own pleasure in form, colour and interval, or beyond her affection for the things she paints. Her paintings can be uncomplicatedly enjoyed for what they are. 'What they are' is, however, not always as simple a matter as it might seem. A back-and-forth takes place, for example, between two or more ways of seeing the yellow shape on the left against the violet background in *Fritillaries* (1968) (Ill. 138). It is recognisably a cut lemon. It is alternatively a three-dimensional form moving into or out from the background. Or it is a flat shape cut out of the background. Or it is pigment and paint. Or it is a soft-focus resonant colour. It is all or any of these.

Fedden's still lifes are not always as abstracted as *Fritillaries*, but even in a more realistic still life like *The Avocado* (1992) (Ill. 139), where you take for granted that all the fruit and vegetables are sitting on the shelves, many of the objects are actually free-floating. They are figments in a painting, and a painter is only constrained by the limits of what can be done in a painting. This is the painter's reality. Mary Fedden's comment (it may be a motto) is: 'You can do what you like, can't you?!' There are no laws of gravity in a painting. And a still life can be full of life, and – to borrow a joke from Cedric Morris, a painter for whom Mary has fellow-feeling – it can be decidedly 'unstill'.[1]

135 (below)
Spoon, Fork and Fish on Table, 2000
Gouache
22.5 x 19.1 cm (8⅞ x 7½ in)
Private collection

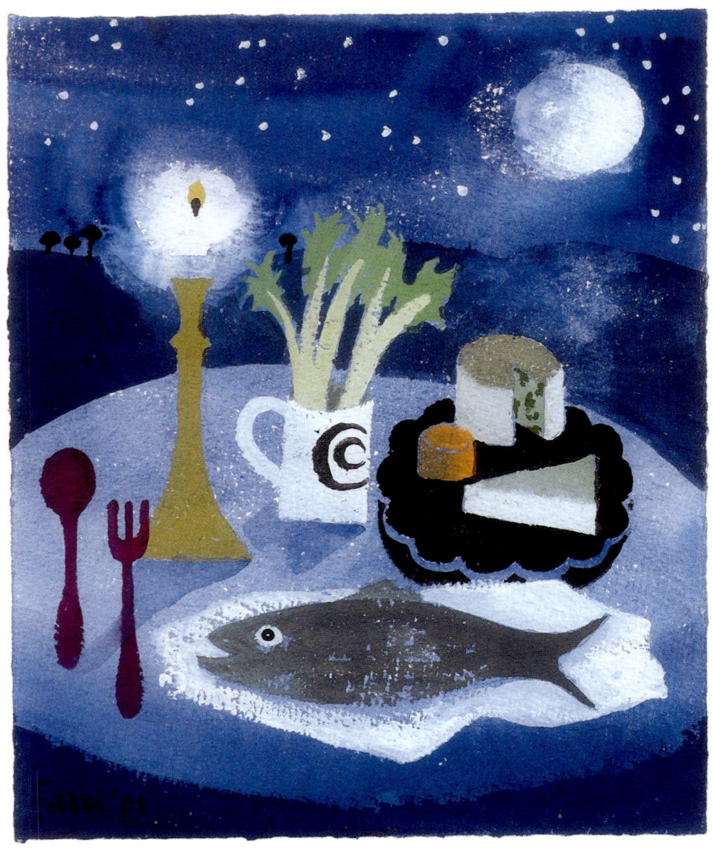

Note
1. *Cedric Morris* by Richard Morphet, Tate Gallery exhibition catalogue, 1984, pp 83, 116

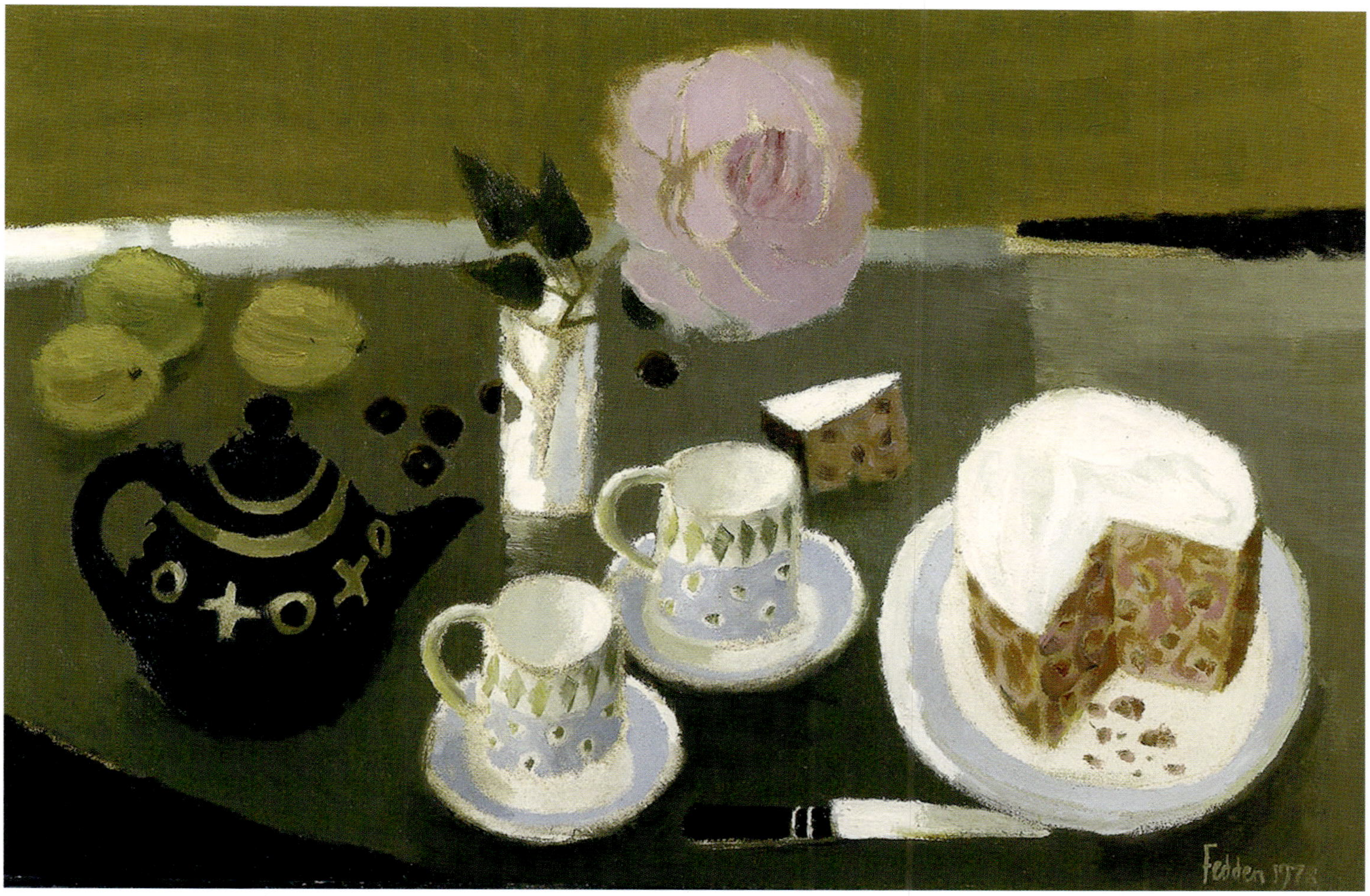

136
The Cake, 1978
Oil on canvas
50.8 x 76.2 cm (20 x 30 in)
Richard Green Gallery, London

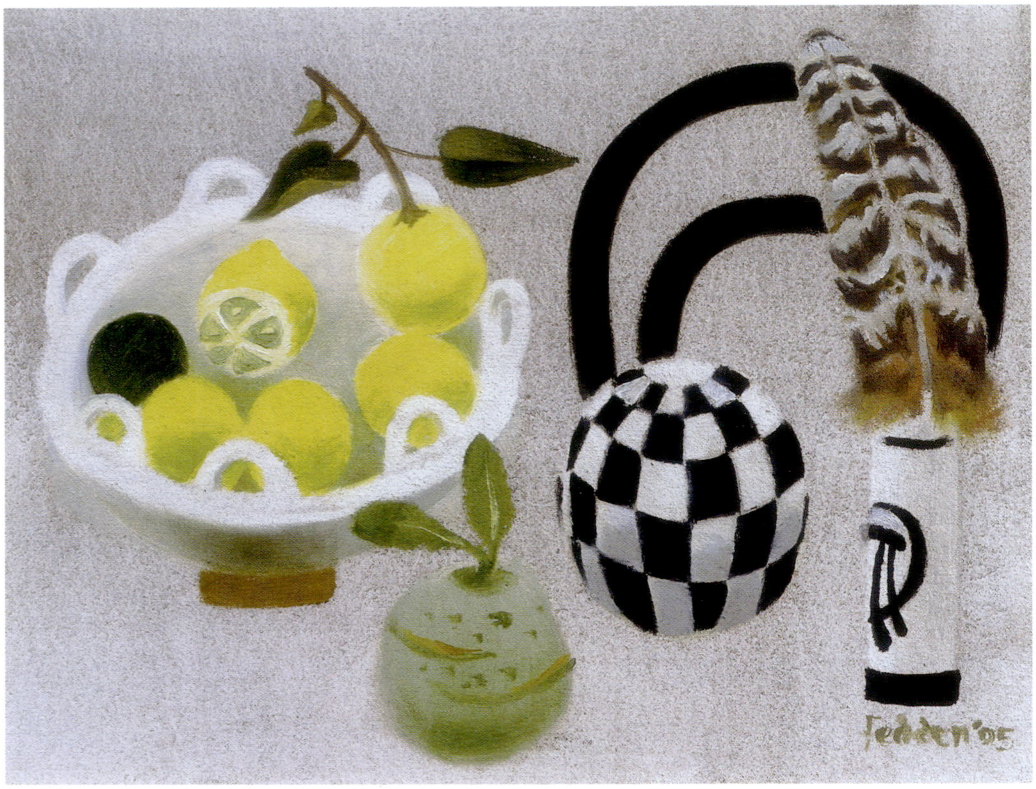

137
Boxing Day, 2005
Oil on canvas
29.1 x 38 cm (11½ x 15¼ in)
Lena Boyle Fine Art, London

Mary Fedden introduces objects into her still lifes that have become part of her 'cabinet of curiosities'. This painting includes several. The sake bottle was given her in the 1960s by a student at the Royal College of Art, Jonathan Kingdon. The black and white bone sphere was a much more recent gift from Tom West. He overheard two ladies at the Royal Academy discussing a larger version of this painting, wondering why it was called *Boxing Day*. He explained: 'Because it is full of presents she has been given.'

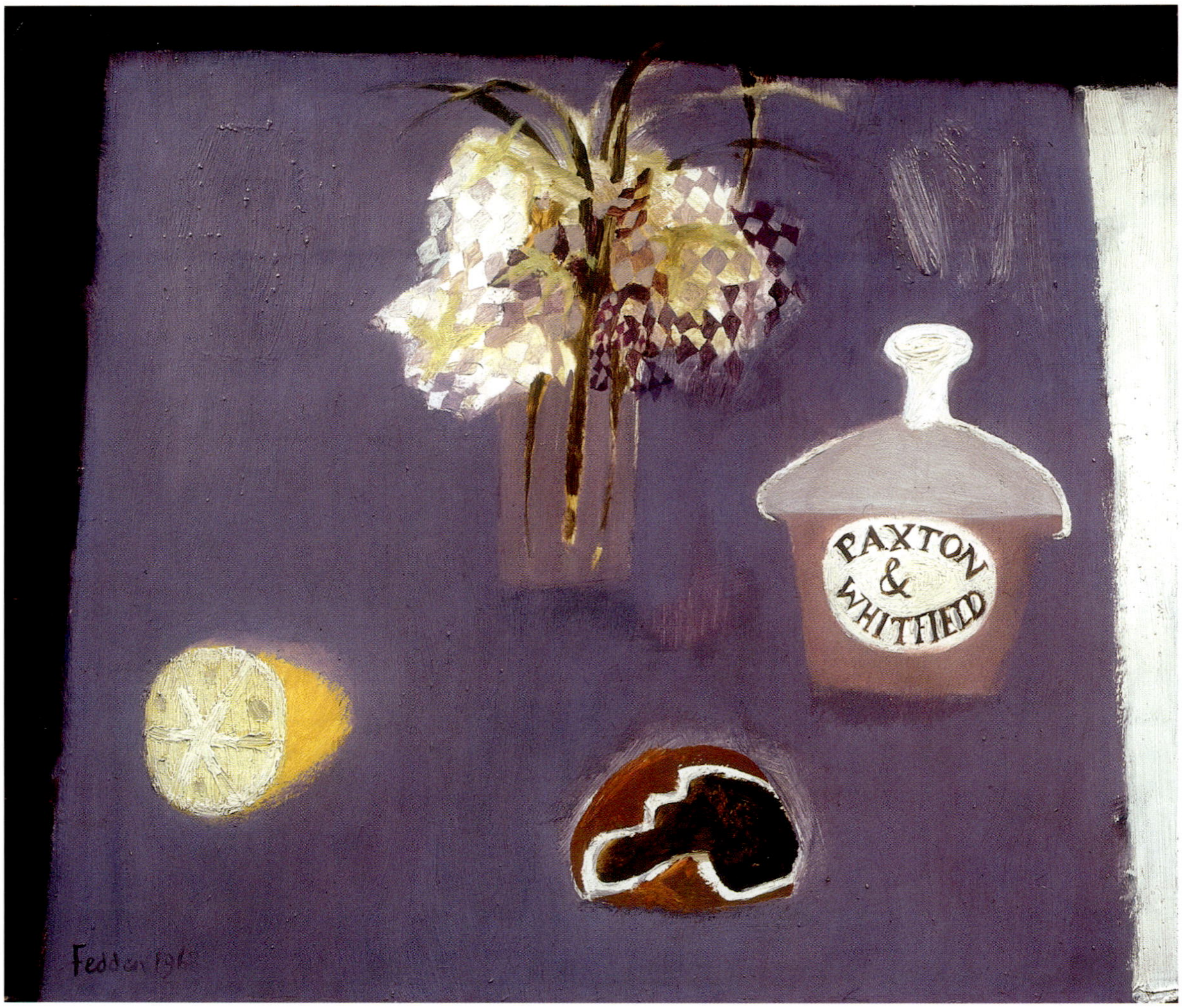

138
Fritillaries, 1968
Oil on board
51 x 61 cm (20 x 24 in)
Messum's, London

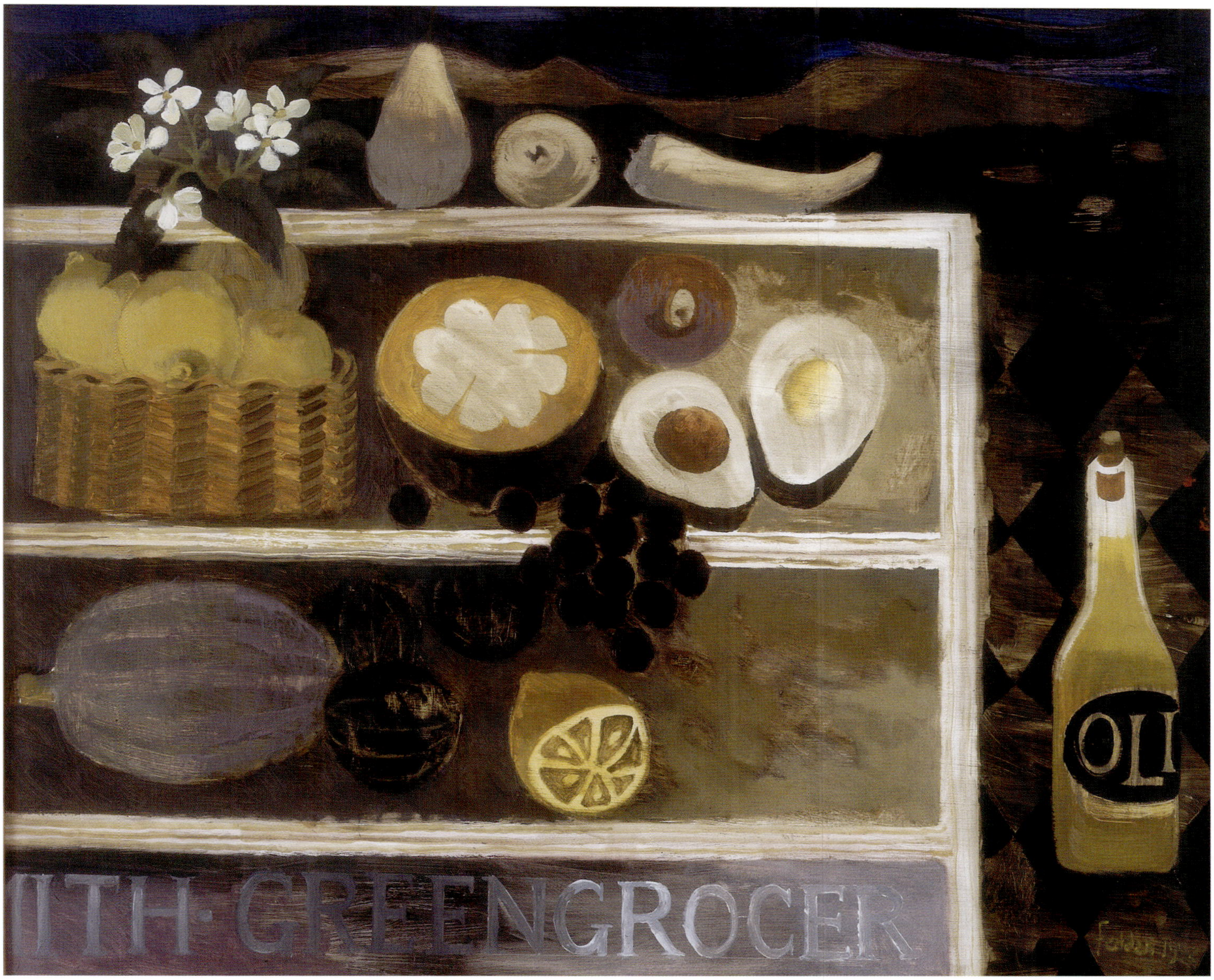

139
The Avocado, 1992
Oil on board
59.6 x 75 cm (23½ x 29½ in)
Private collection

I·N·T·E·R·L·U·D·E

Flowers and Cats

Mary Fedden's still lifes, such as *Nancy's Pot* (2003) (Ill. 140), *The Lighthouse* (2002) (Ill. 141), and *Basket of Fruit* (2004) (Ill. 142), often provide an escape for the eye into a distant landscape or seascape. Yet they also spill over into other forms of life, specifically cats and flowers. She has been a cat lover from early childhood. She knows their uncanny ways. In her paintings her cats are often statuesque and commanding, almost frozen as if they are pretending to be *part* of the still life. Eyeing the viewer, they nevertheless do not condescend to divulge their mysterious musings. *Pussy on the Sofa* (2003) (Ill. 143) and *The White Cat* (1985) (Ill. 144) keep their counsel. Her flowers are also bold, and like the flower paintings of Cedric Morris, they are not too pretty or sentimental. Painted with delicacy and an obvious pleasure in their form, colour and markings, Fedden's flowers also have a convincing tactility and weight (Ills 145–148).

Sometimes, as in *Poppy and Compass* (2005) (Ill. 149), cats and flowers appear on stage together in a painting – together yet apart, each dreaming its own dreams, indifferent to the other's presence, yet brought together in the lively stillness of Fedden's appreciative gaze.

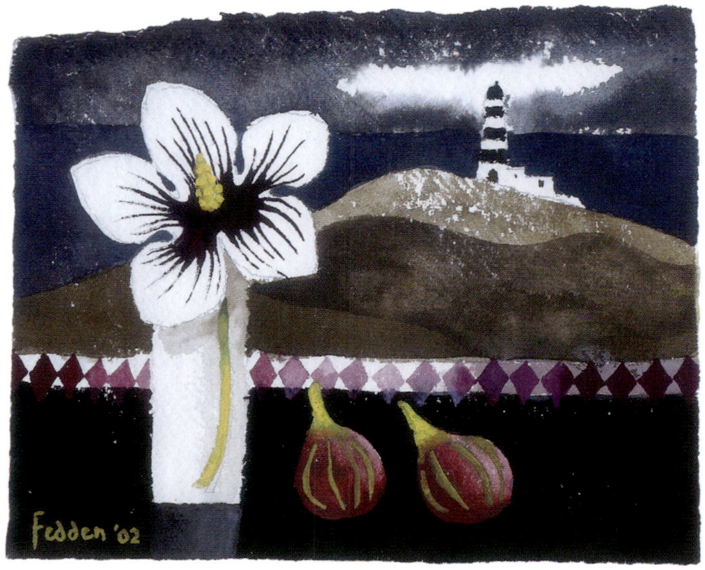

141
The Lighthouse, 2002
Gouache
15.5 x 20 cm (6 x 7⅞ in)
Private collection

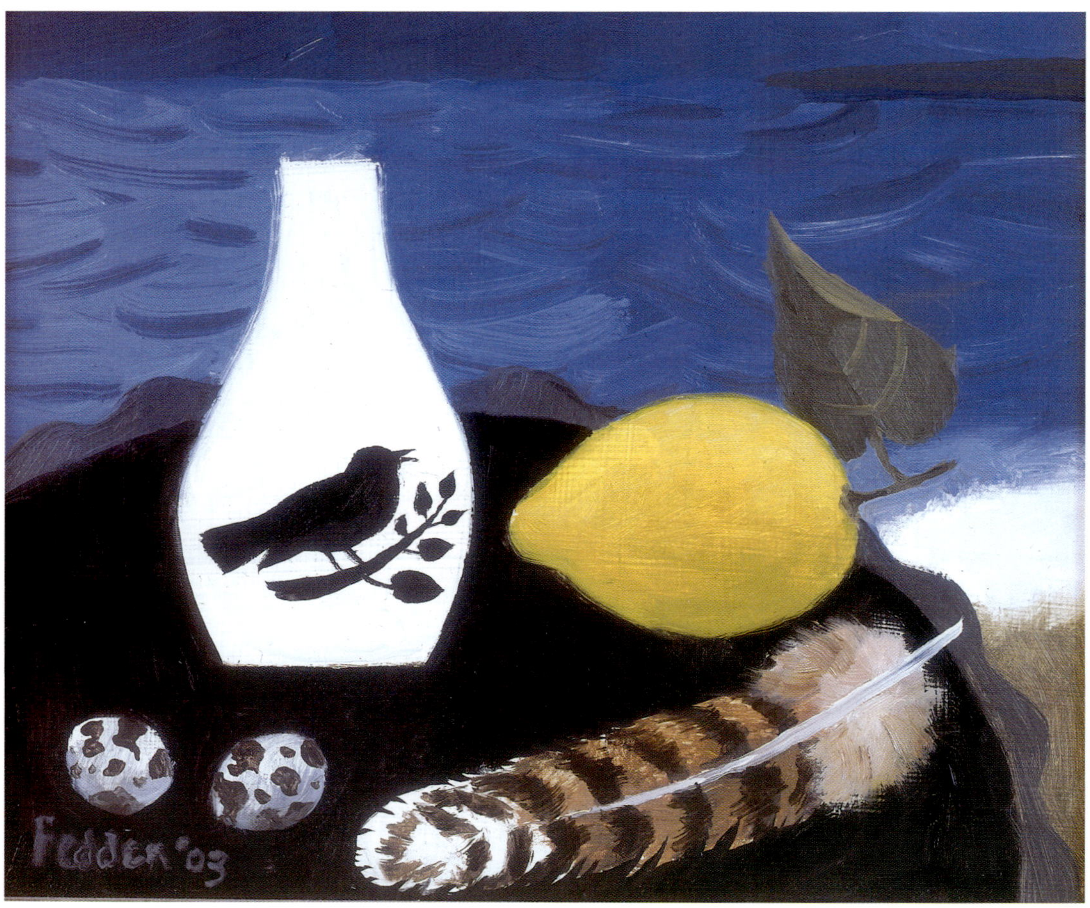

140
Nancy's Pot, 2003
Oil on board
23 x 19 cm (9¼ x 7½ in)
Private collection

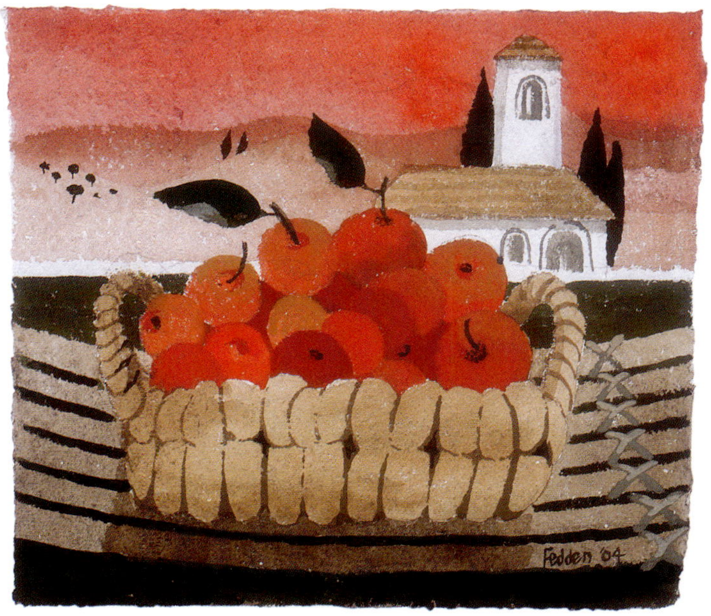

142 (above)
Basket of Fruit, 2004
Gouache
15.5 x 17.8 cm (6¾ x 7 in)
Private collection

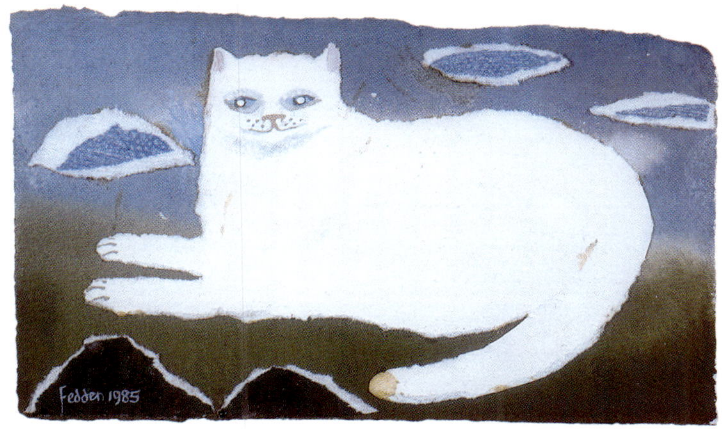

144 (above)
The White Cat, 1985
Collage and gouache
14.7 x 21 cm (5¾ x 8¼ in)
Private collection

143 (below)
Pussy on the Sofa, 2003
Oil on canvas
89.5 x 120 cm (35¼ x 48⅛ in)
Private collection

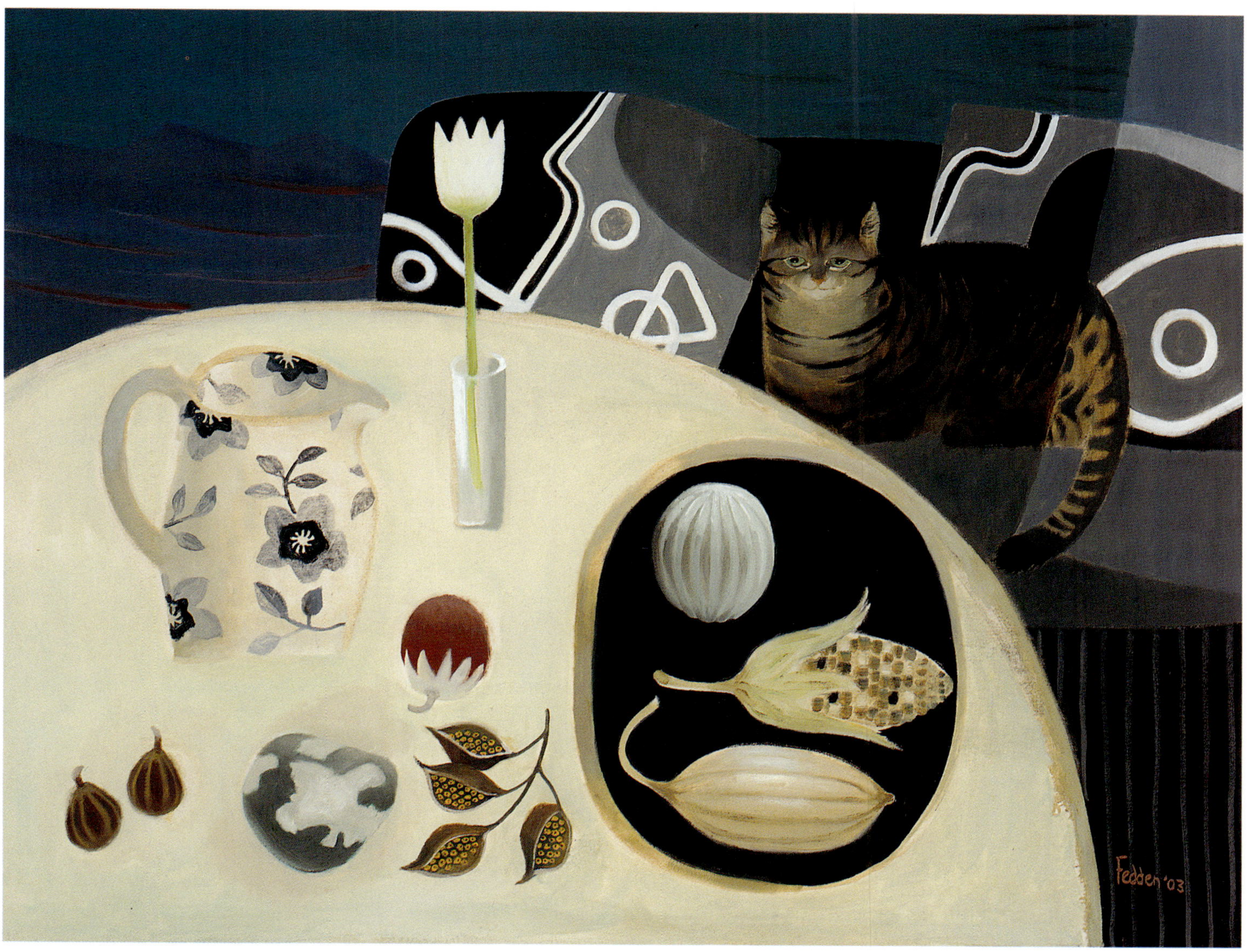

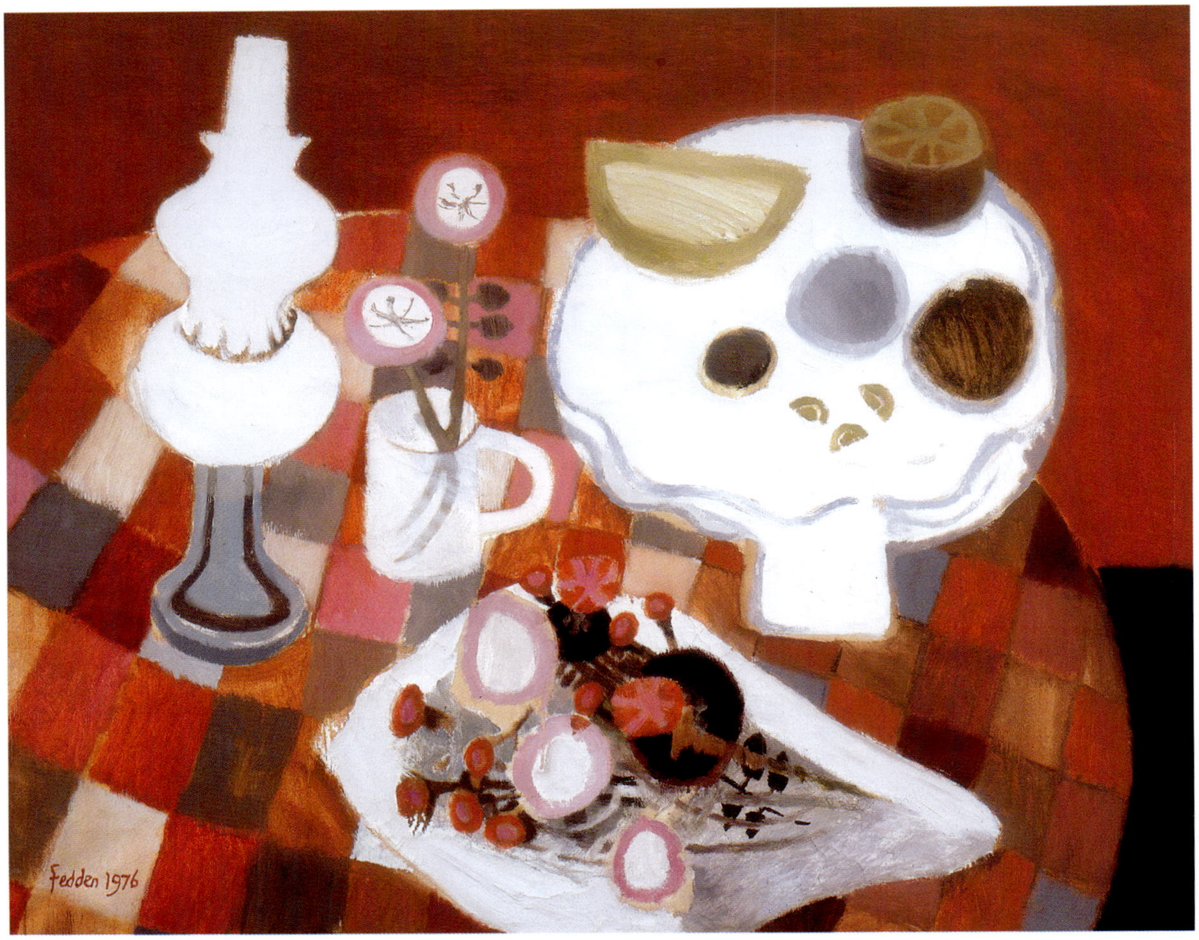

145
Lamp, 1976
Oil on canvas
90 x 115.4 cm ($35\frac{3}{8}$ x 45 in)
Private collection

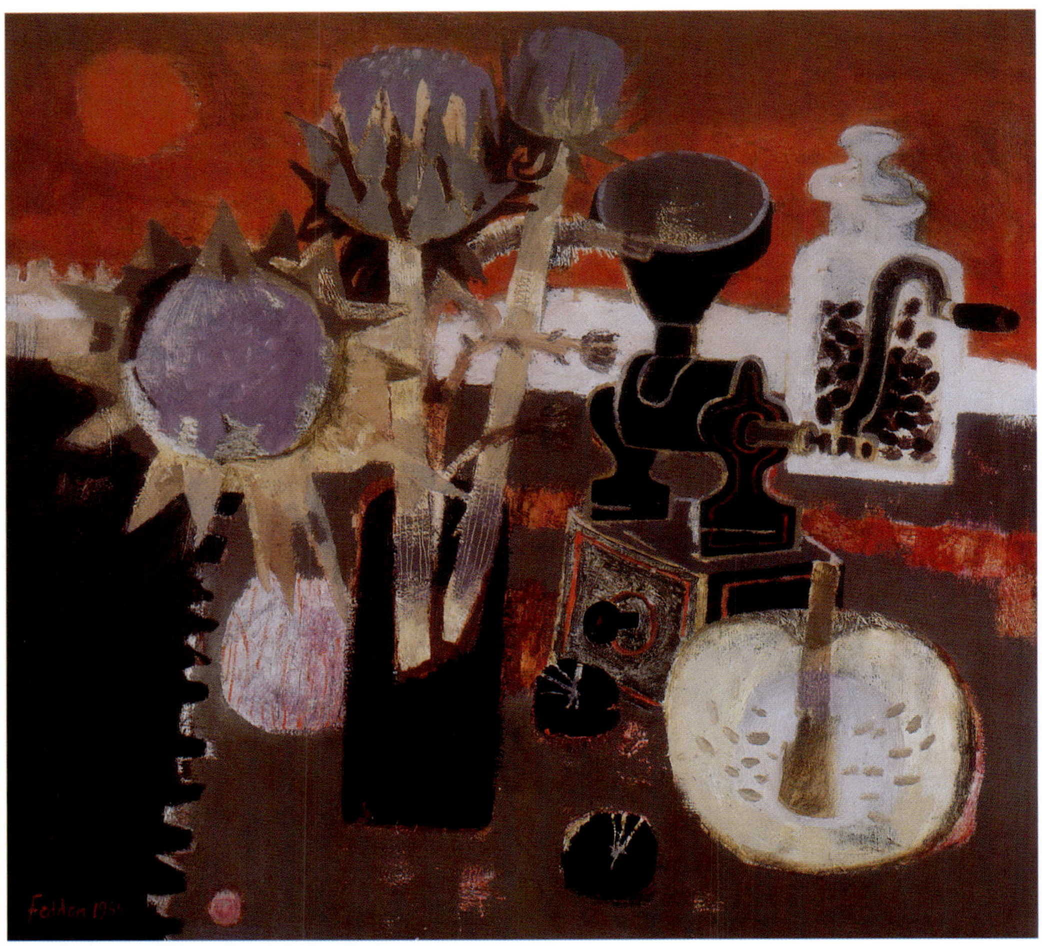

146
Artichokes and Coffee Grinder, 1965
Oil on canvas
91 x 101 cm ($35\frac{3}{4}$ x $39\frac{5}{8}$ in)
Private collection

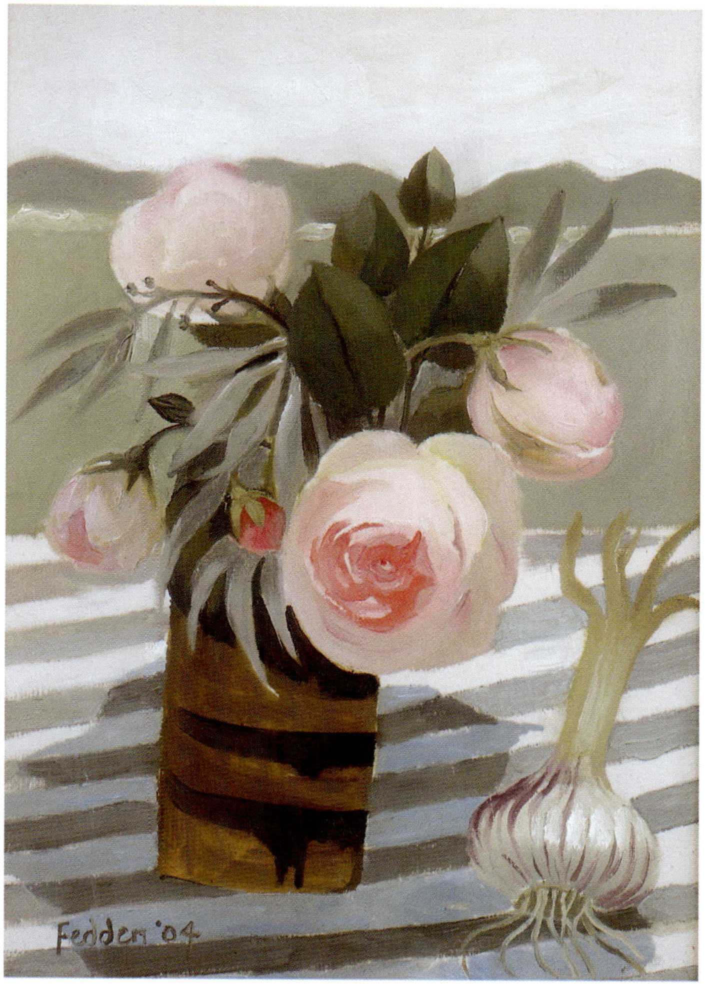

147
Roses and Garlic, 2004
Oil on canvas
40 x 30 cm (15¾ x 11¾ in)
Private collection

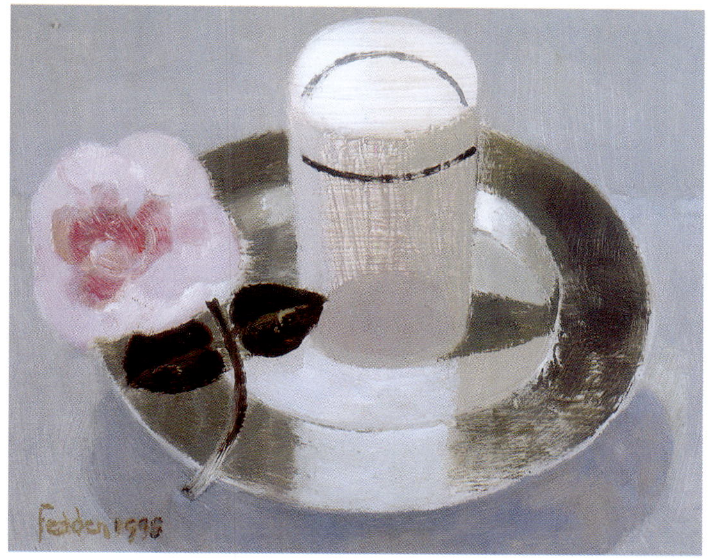

148
The Pink Rose, 1998
Oil on board
20 x 25 cm (7⅞ x 10 in)
Private collection

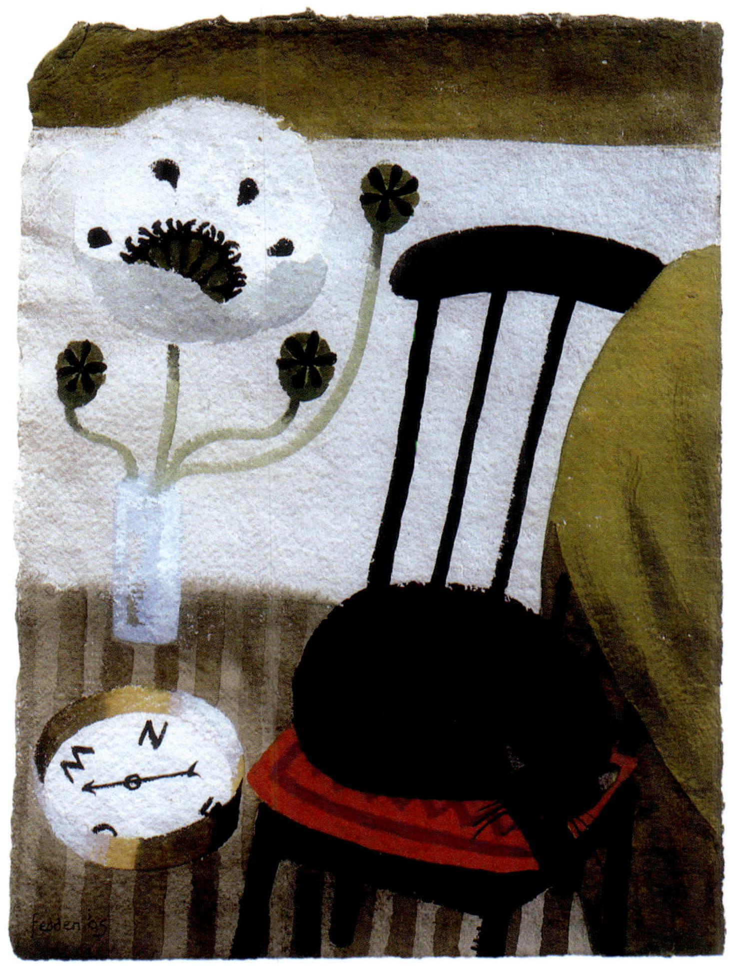

149
Poppy and Compass, 2005
Gouache
28 x 21.5 cm (11 x 8½ in)
Lena Boyle Fine Art, London

CHAPTER SIX

Figures – Memory, Imagination and Fantasy

One figure repeatedly appears in Mary Fedden's paintings – in her small gouache paintings, that is. (Figures rarely, if ever, appear in her still lifes.) This ubiquitous figure is the 6 ft-4 in. form of Julian Trevelyan, her husband. She says disarmingly: 'Well, he's easy to do, with his white hair and beard. And he was very tall. Unmistakable. When I can't think of anything else to paint, I do some pictures of him.'

Her Julian pictures – striking, reminiscent, fond, slightly haunting – are not portraits. They are as much about her imagination as they are about him. From her first glimpse of him (when she was a student at the Slade), she was smitten. It is clear that he epitomised her romantic vision of the ideal man. Her love for him persists today and her art still includes him in more ways than one. In her small gouaches, he strides through the landscapes of her mind. Often, he stands in the foreground of a beach scene. The origin of this favourite image, repeated with all sorts of variations, she cannot explain. Julian is holding a shrimping net, while in the distance a little girl in an Edwardian sailor dress, her hair streaming in the salty wind, waves another long-handled net, as if signalling by semaphore. Sometimes the child is a boy, in a sailor suit. In the example here, *Night Shrimping* (1995) (Ill. 151), a steamship is almost an ocean speck below a big moon. The large man and tiny child are linked but also unnervingly separated by distance. Who is this remote child? Is she out of reach? Walking away? Is she real? Julian had a son by his first marriage and no children with Mary. Is the beach scene a dream? It certainly does not belong in the present tense. A memory, then? It is difficult to imagine what else it might be. Mary herself, as a child, may well have worn a sailor dress like this girl. Julian, with his hat ribbons flying, seems almost a period figure; and he was, after all, really born in the Edwardian era – just.

Maybe the picture is an enigma, but Fedden's preoccupation with this theme seems unlikely to be mere whimsicality. Her apparently off-hand way of mentioning these gouaches, as if they do not matter very much, is misleading. 'Perhaps I thought they weren't important enough,' she says modestly. She admits that actually she rather likes them. She certainly does enjoy the idea that, as one collector puts it, they are open to lots of different interpretations. Yet to jump to conclusions about their 'meaning' might well go too far the other way in an attempt to 'explain' what obviously does not completely explain itself.

Many of Fedden's small, rather meditative gouaches inhabit a world where memory, imagination and fantasy have no definite boundaries between them. They might be stories half forgotten or fleeting moments not entirely recaptured. An atmosphere of vague regret or of unfulfilled wishing, of transience certainly, hovers around some of them.

Departure, so linked to beach and sea, is sometimes more overtly their theme. When she saw Luchino Visconti's film of Thomas Mann's *Death in Venice*, it rang bells for her, and some touching, small gouaches – again distinctly Edwardian

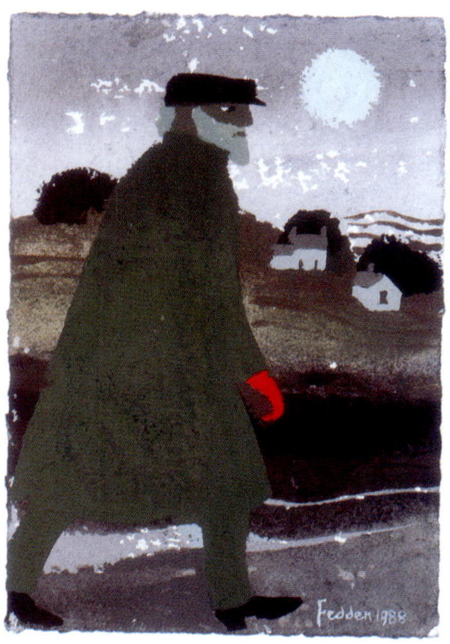

150
Julian Walking, 1988
Gouache
13.7 x 9.6 cm (5$\frac{3}{8}$ x 3$\frac{3}{4}$ in)
Private collection

151
Night Shrimping, 1995
Gouache
29.6 x 21.6 cm (11⅝ x 8½ in)
Private collection

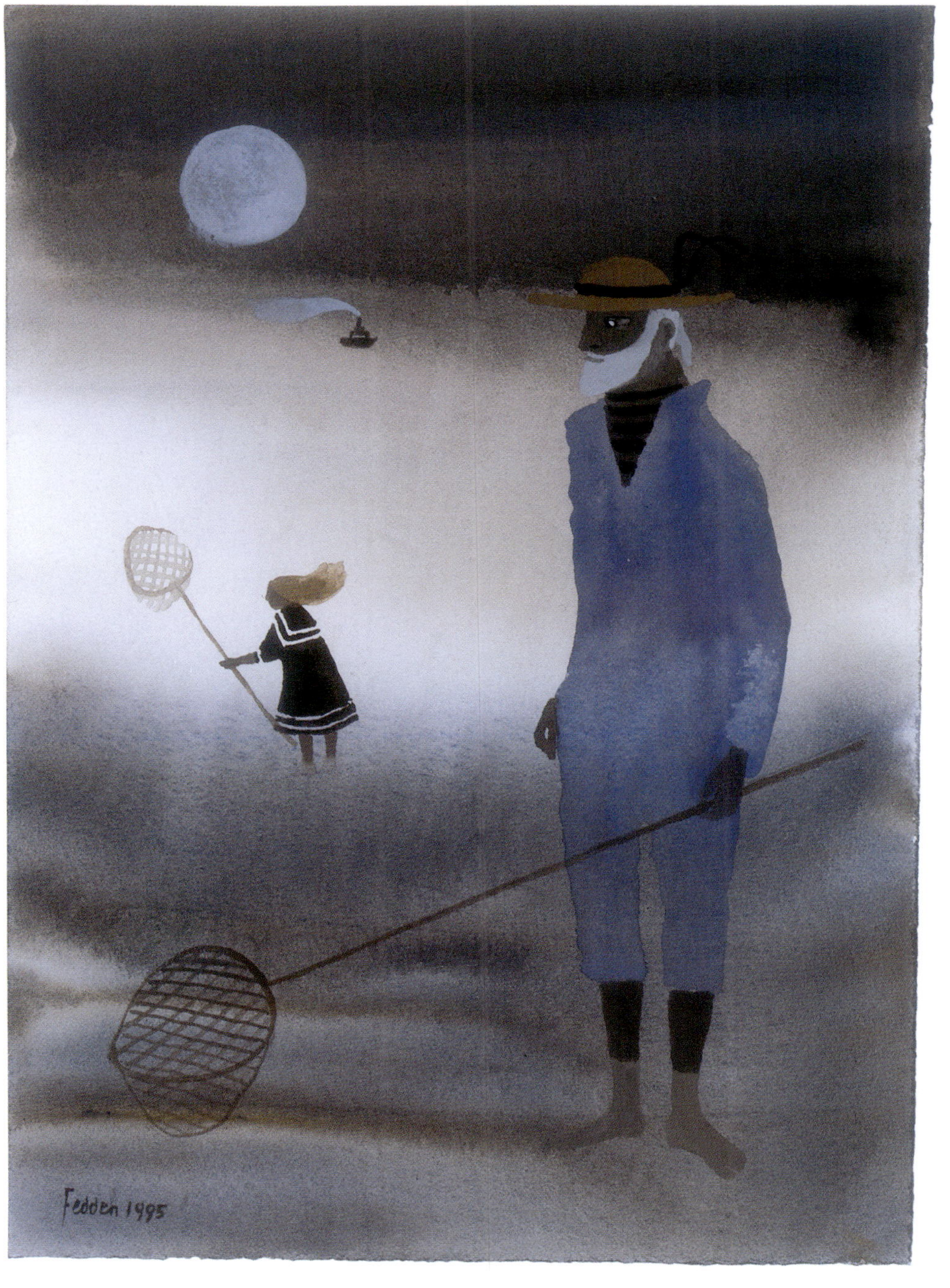

in flavour – developed out of it (Ill. 8, p.13). She scrupulously avoids merely illustrating the story, however.

Clearly there is an imaginative space in this artist's inner visual world that is a departure from the still lifes on which her reputation mainly rests. There is an element of escape. This side of her suits a modest and absolutely unpretentious expression. Nevertheless, a full assessment of her work must include these works that are so full of ideas.

On some occasions Fedden paints herself with Trevelyan. *On the Shore, Brittany* (Ill. 152), though painted in 1995, is quite like a straightforward holiday snapshot

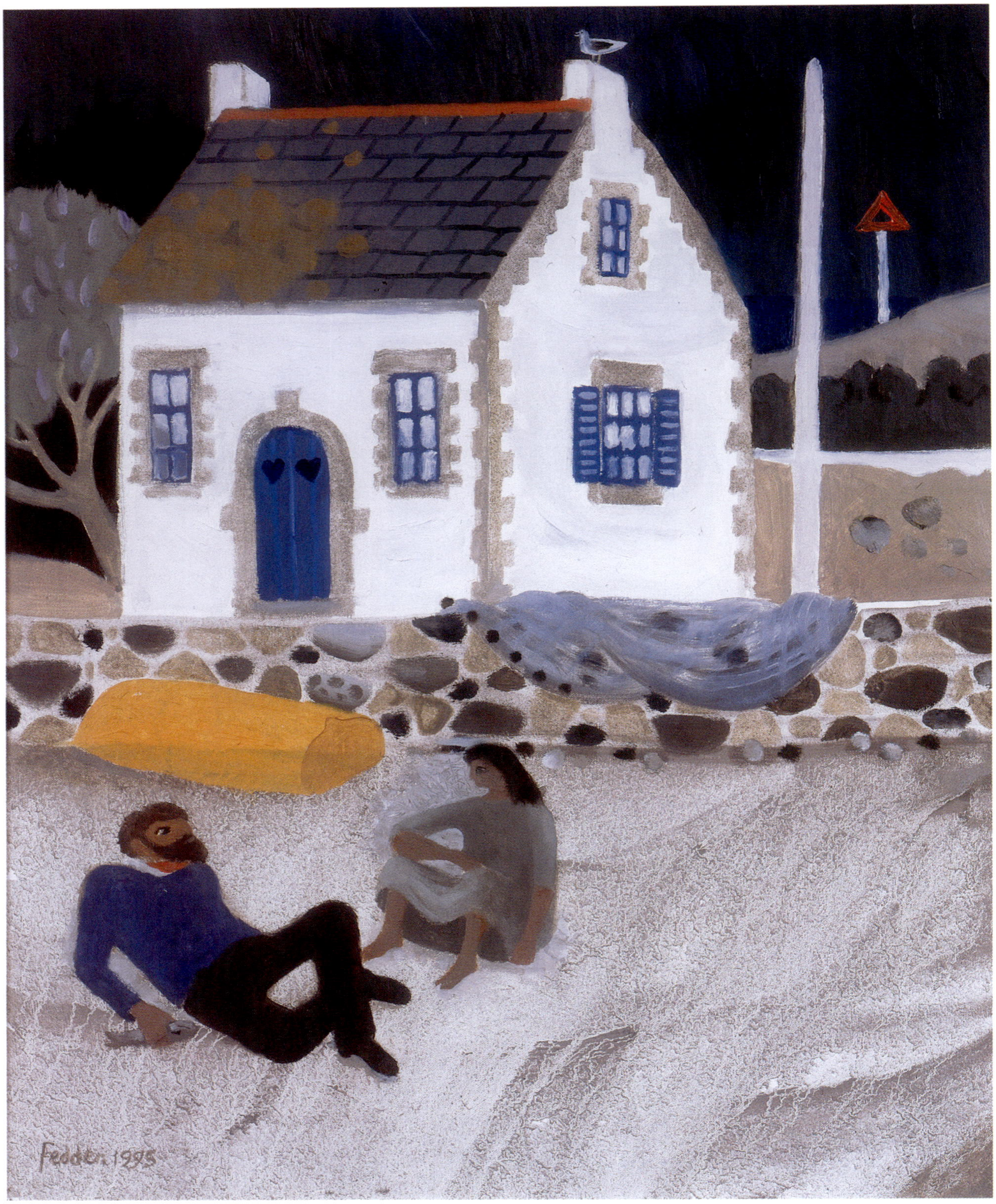

152
On the Shore, Brittany, 1995
Oil on canvas
59.5 x 49.4 cm (23⅜ x 19½ in)
Private collection

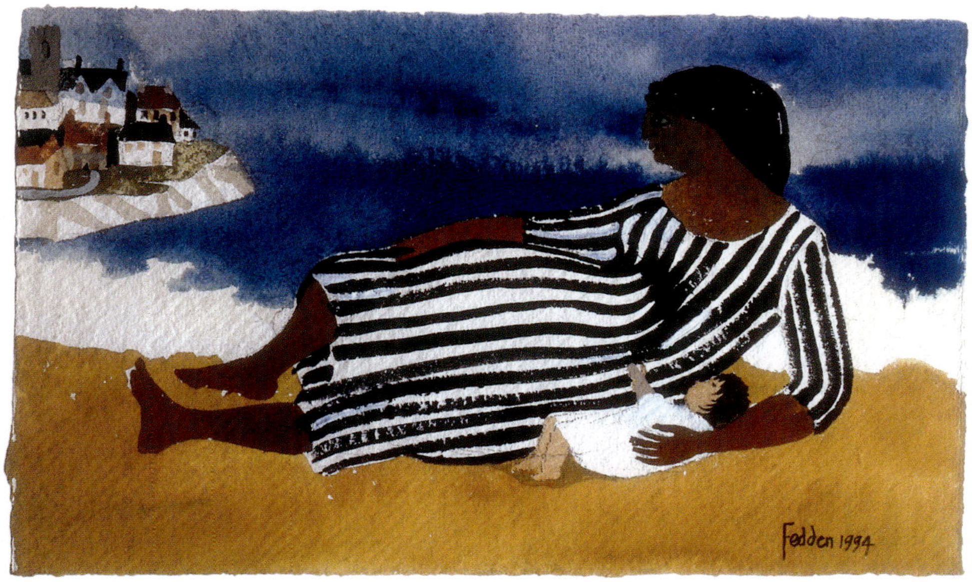

153
Mother and Child, 1994
Gouache
Dimensions unknown
© Royal Academy of Arts, London

of this inseparable couple sitting and lounging on the beach – it's photo album stuff. Julian is playing 'the reclining figure', a subject Fedden frequently paints. Her interest in it has less solemnity than Henry Moore's sculptural obsession with the type and less claim to high art, but again her exploration of the theme cannot just be dismissed as somehow frivolous. More than once, her reclining figures take the form of a rather sculptural, classical woman with a baby (Ill. 153). This foray into an ancient subject is strong, serious and tender. Rather different is her enchanting little painting of a dark-haired, nude girl, seen from behind, romantically, if ineffectually, trying to catch butterflies (Ill. 154). It has a touch of mischievous humour, perhaps, but again it is a Feddenish take on an old symbol – of youthful evanescence. (Thomas Gainsborough painted his daughters chasing butterflies.)

Reclining figures also appear in some of her larger oil paintings – landscapes, not still lifes. *Boy Asleep* (1999) (Ill. 155) and *Sleeping Poet* (2004) (Ill. 156) are indelibly romantic images, once more in a tradition she is certainly familiar with. In Powis Castle, Wales, can be found a seventeenth-century miniature by Isaac Oliver of *Lord Herbert of Cherbury*. This poet reclines on a grassy bank, an archetypal figure of literary contemplation under the trees. Fedden's omnivorous visual memory bank has apparently stored this image, or a similar image derived from it, and its possibilities have now fed her own fantasy. It certainly is her *own* fantasy, however. What inspires her never overwhelms her.

154
Nude with Butterflies, 1983
Gouache
16 x 22 cm (6¼ x 8⅝ in)
Private collection

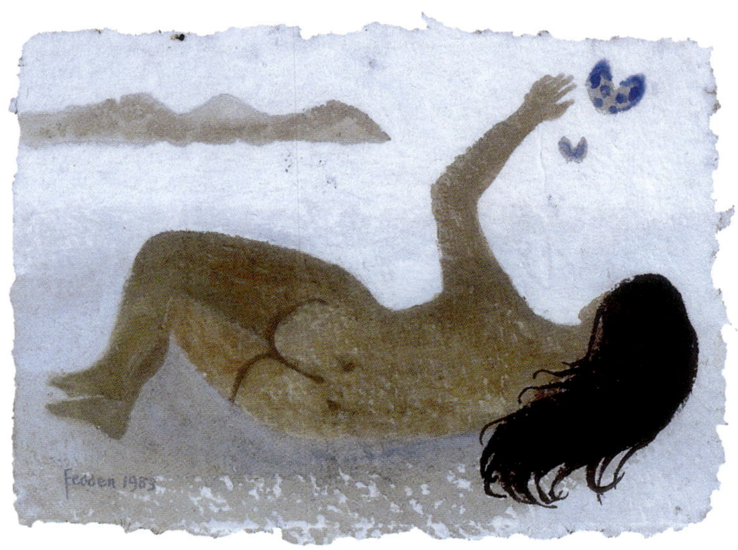

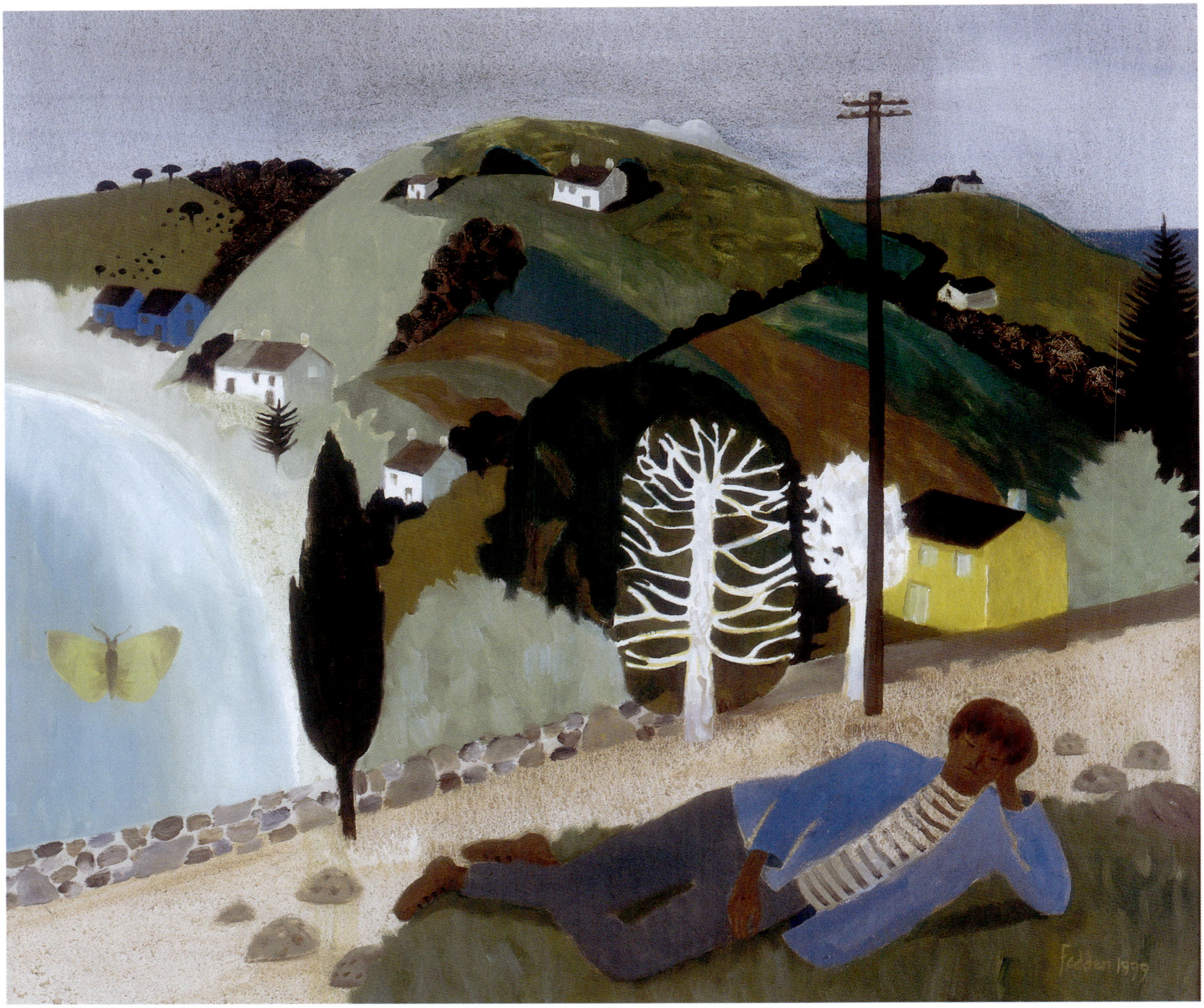

155
Boy Asleep, 1999
Oil on canvas
75.5 x 90 cm (29¾ x 35½ in)
Private collection

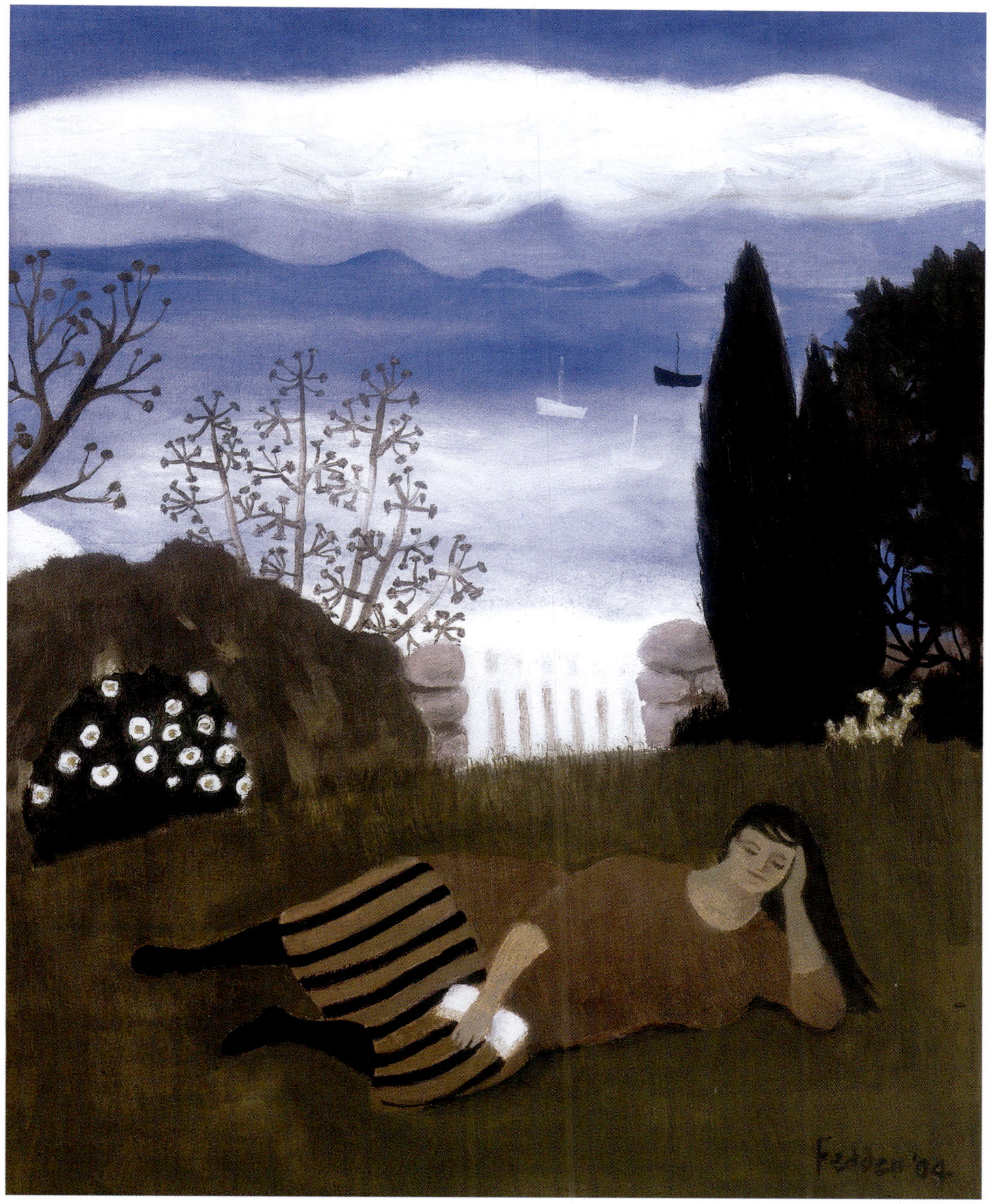

156
Sleeping Poet, 2004
Oil on canvas
60 x 50 cm (23⅝ x 19¾ in)
Private collection

Another theme to appear in her imaginative gouaches involves circus folk, particularly clowns, often with horses or zebras. The circus has appealed to other artists, but Fedden's take on the subject, a kind of cross between folk art and dream, has a strangeness and sentiment completely unlike the clowns of Marc Chagall or Georges Rouault or Picasso's 'Rose Period' acrobats.

Fedden's clown pictures can at times be dramatic. *Girl with Horse and Clown* (1987) (Ill. 157) is a three-way drama, an apparent confrontation between wild and tame, passion and restraint. The girl (in common with some other wild girls in Fedden's gouaches) might almost be out of *Wuthering Heights*. The horse's mane and the girl's hair and white dress are caught in a fierce and desperate wind that is more than mere weather. The clown, timid and dismayed, is apparently trying to calm the animal. The girl may be temporarily beyond calming. But of course one thing is certain: Fedden will read this 'interpretation' of her small picture with disbelief! She will disavow any such story … All she painted was a girl, a horse and a clown. All the same, she is a natural story teller.

The *Bird Men* (1995) (Ill. 158) are related to the clowns, but they are balletic and theatrical. Balancing birds on their fingertips, they have almost turned into

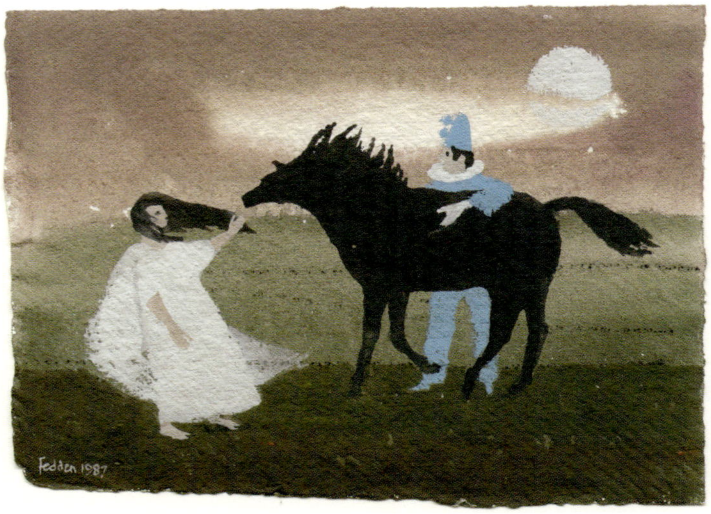

157
Girl with Horse and Clown, 1987
Gouache
14 x 20 cm (5½ x 7¾ in)
Richard Green Gallery, London

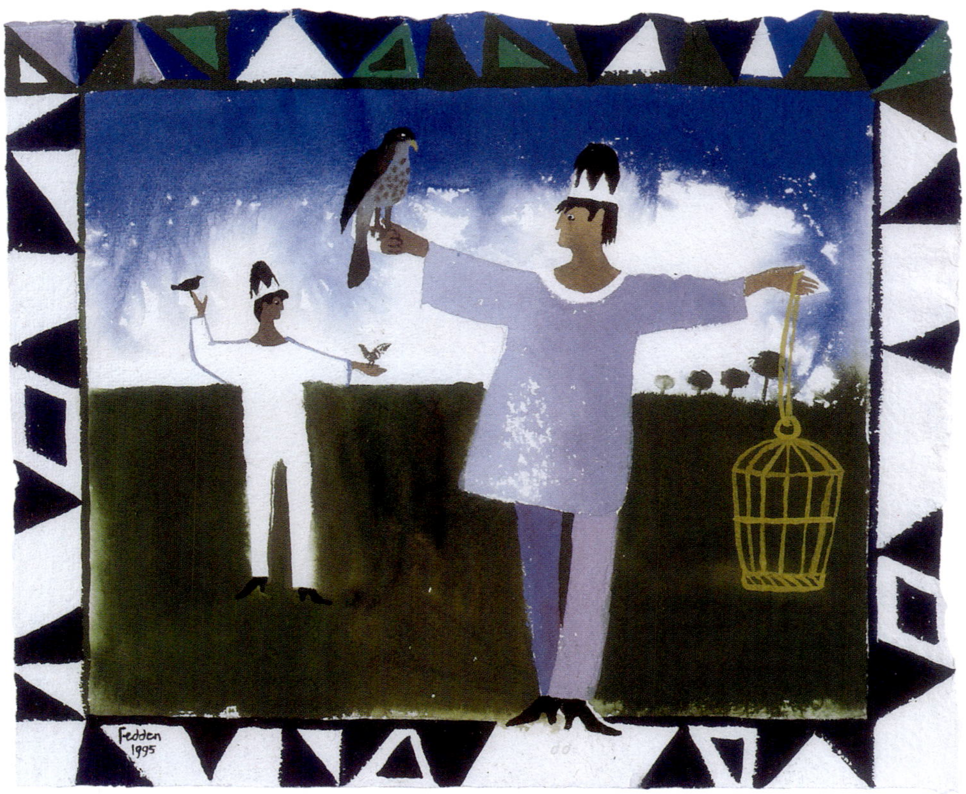

158
Bird Men, 1995
Gouache
22 x 27 cm (8⅝ x 10⅝ in)
Private collection

159
Zebra, 2001
Gouache
21.6 x 28 cm (8½ x 11 in)
Private collection

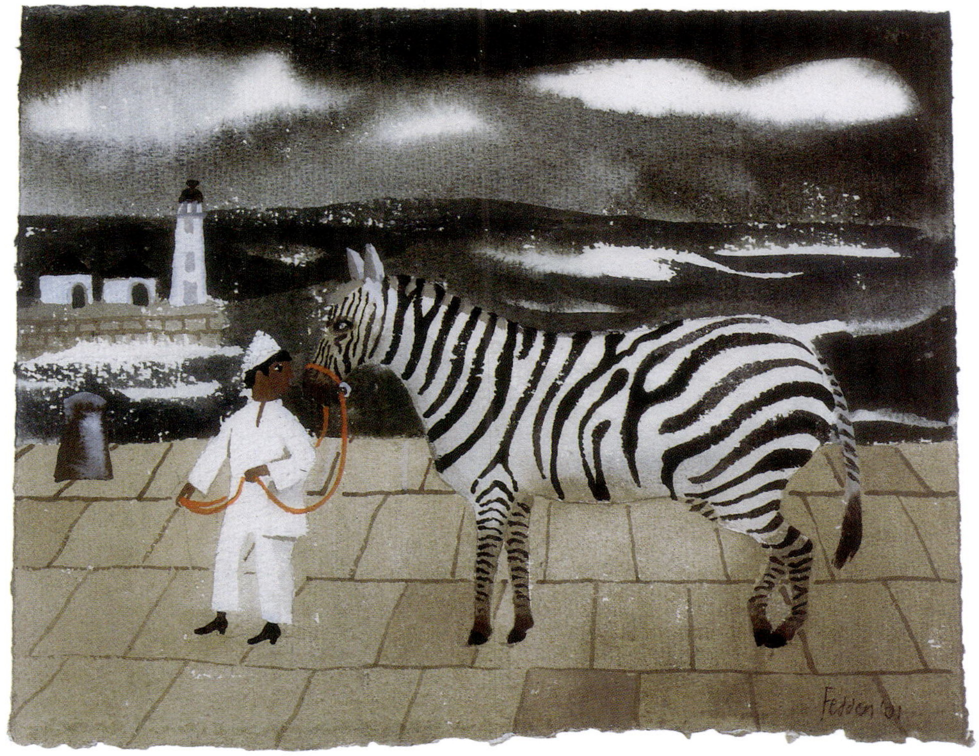

birds themselves, their wings spread, their feet scarcely in touch with the ground. Perhaps, with its patterned border, this is a card for a child or a drop curtain design for *The Magic Flute*.

The enigmatic side of Mary Fedden is given rein in her small figure paintings such as *Zebra* (2001) (Ill. 159). It's as if she feels freer to allow the intimate, the unspoken or simply the light-hearted to come out in them, perhaps because they *are* small or perhaps because she thinks people may not take them too seriously or think them too significant. They are not intended for the Royal Academy Summer Exhibition. Arguably, they are all the better for that. They have charm, but they have much more.

Fedden does not have any obvious similarities to Paul Klee, but in her fantasy pictures, she shares two things with him: a modest scale and a knack for making what initially seems amusing, nostalgic or quirky reveal unexpectedly serious undertones, a surprising poetry, an understated tenderness or a turbulent passion – or even something quite *bizarre*.

A Bizarre I·N·T·E·R·L·U·D·E

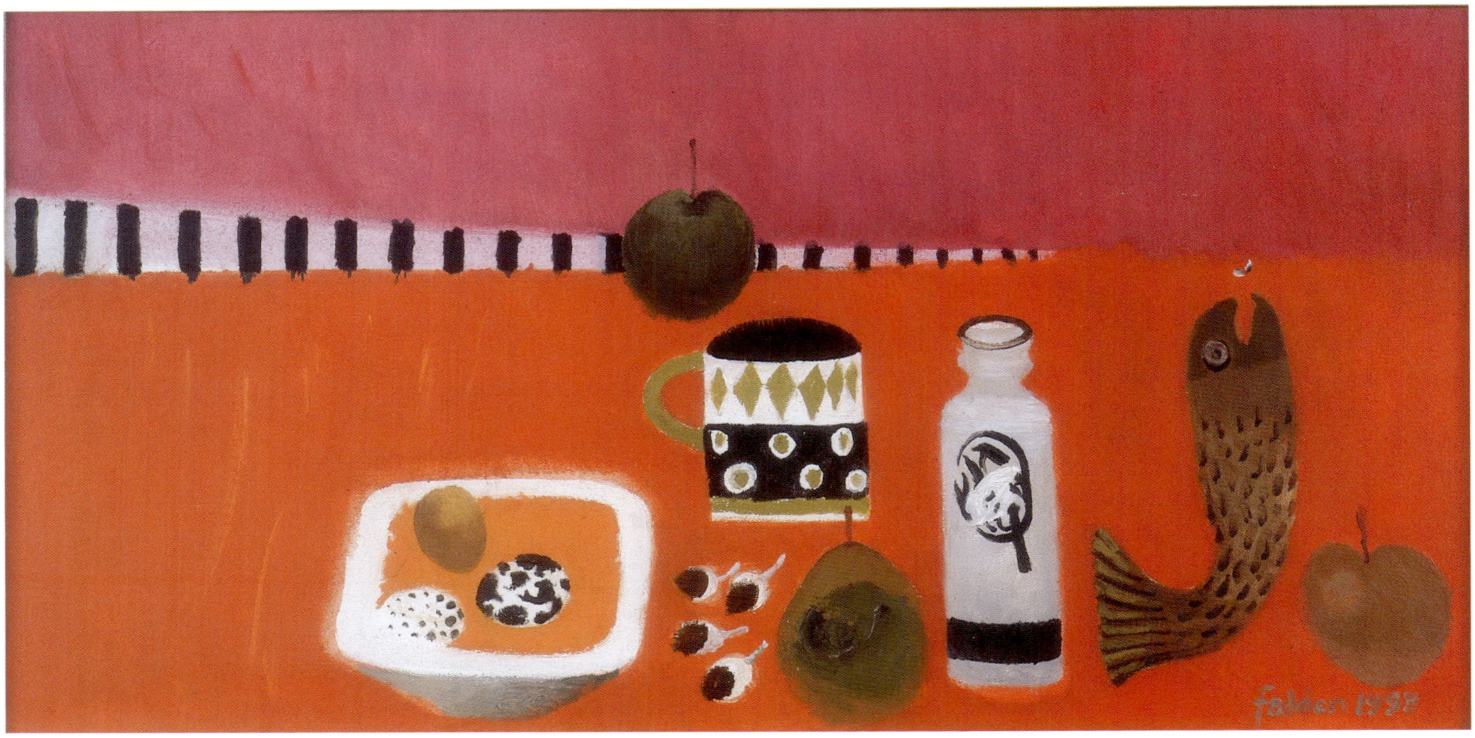

160
The Sake Bottle, 1993
Oil on canvas
30.5 x 61 cm (12 x 24 in)
Private collection

Looking through photographs of her past works, Mary Fedden is highly self-critical, particularly when she finds a picture 'boring'. But then she stops suddenly and says: 'I rather like that one. It's a bit *bizarre*. Quite funny, isn't it?'

In the long painting called *The Sake Bottle* (1993) (Ill. 160), there is a *bizarrerie*. Usually the fish in Fedden's still lifes are inanimately ready to be eaten, though they often have a knowing look. Here, in what looks like a sudden whim as she painted it, her fish rears up rebelliously in an attempt to catch a fly. It is splendidly nonsensical. Perhaps the artist had a sudden sympathy for the poor fish, or she felt the fish might have recalled the misfortunate act that brought it to the table. Mary's Uncle Romilly wrote a book about fly-fishing[1] in which he wrote a truism worthy of Isaac Walton: 'When dressing dry-flies, we must always keep in mind the fish's point of view rather than our own.' Perhaps his niece inherited a similar viewpoint as a *painter* of fish.

Sometimes Fedden has needed to alter a subject very little to arrive at a bizarre image: *Valhalla* (2003) (Ill. 161), for example. Invited by its owners, Robert and Lucy Dorrien Smith, to the island of Tresco in the Scilly Isles off the Cornish coast, Mary made a great many drawings to be turned into paintings later in her studio. Many of the paintings, including this one, are now displayed in buildings on Tresco. *Valhalla* is a slightly spooky depiction of a display in a Tresco museum of ships' figureheads and is evidently true to life. Who else would have thought of a line of three agapanthus plants as foreground to these strange and ghostly figures? Yet this all comes from observation rather than imagination.

Where the idea for the odd little collage, *A Lily for the Bride* (2001) (Ill. 162), comes from, even Mary Fedden quite simply has no idea.

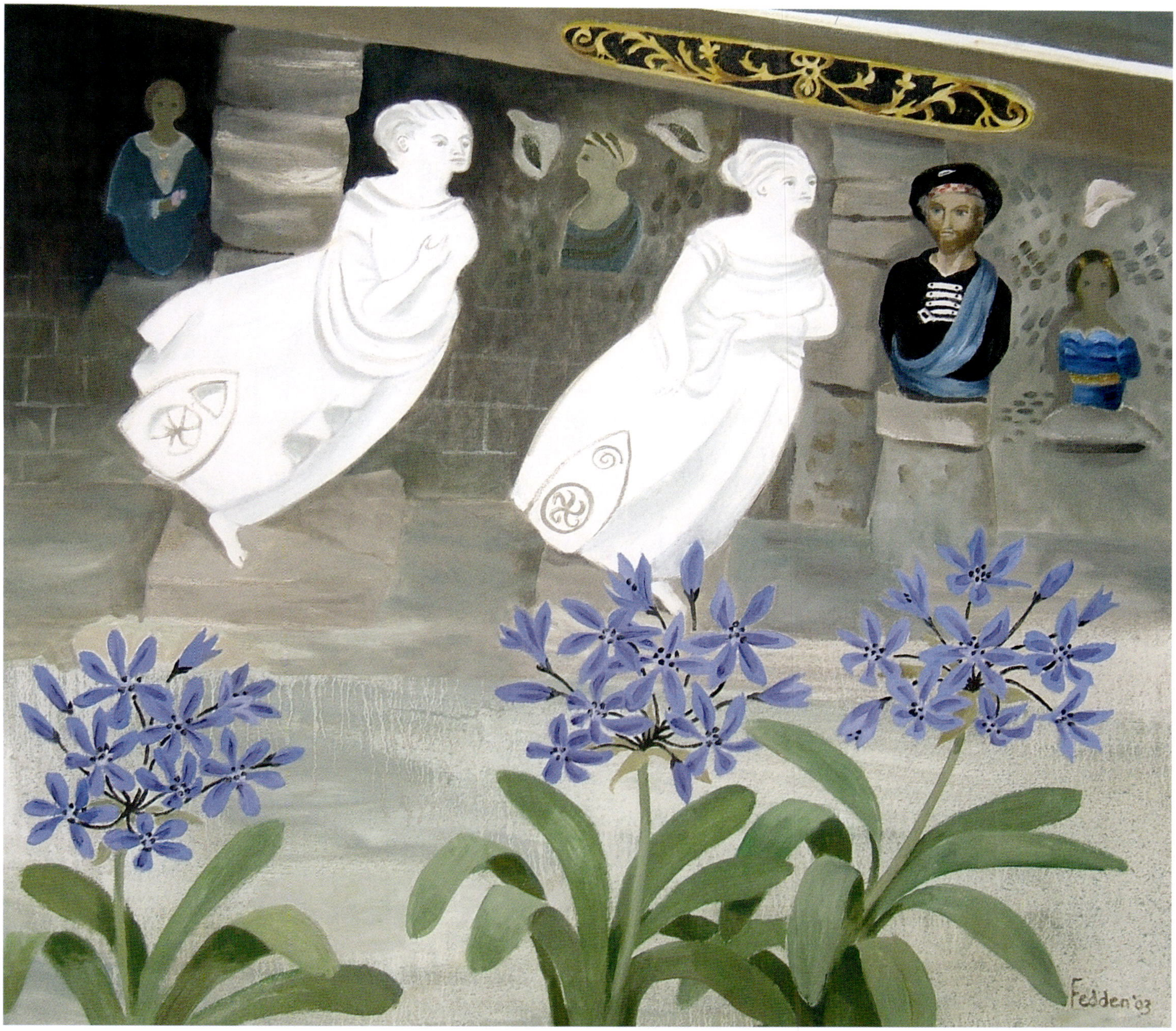

161 (above)
Valhalla, 2003
Oil on canvas
70 x 80 cm (27½ x 31½ in)
Courtesy of The Tresco Estate

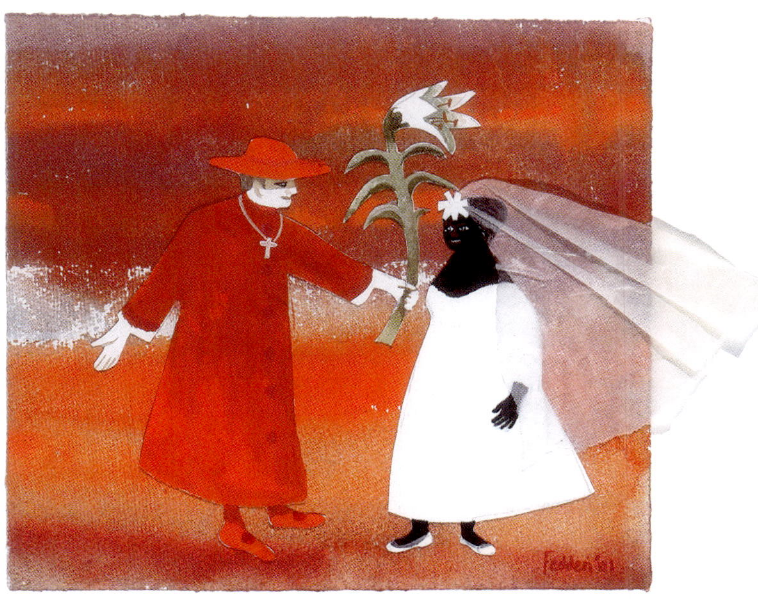

162
A Lily for the Bride, 2001
Collage and gouache
22.8 x 26 cm (8⅞ x 10⅛ in)
Private collection

Note

1. *Golden Days: from the fishing-log of a painter in Brittany* by Romilly Fedden, A & C Black Ltd (London), 1919, p.193

CHAPTER SEVEN

Pattern, Composition, Colour

A critical comment sometimes levelled at Mary Fedden's work is that it is 'decorative' or too much concerned with pattern. It is not entirely clear why this is a criticism. She is in good company, if the allegation is accurate. Such different artists as Gustav Klimt and Edouard Vuillard were preoccupied with patterning. And Henri Matisse, who during his developing career was sometimes dismissed for the same 'fault', in his final period devoted himself almost exclusively to the decorative as the essence of his art.

At any rate, Fedden's undoubted fascination for repetitive patterns (she loves stripes and harlequin diamonds for example) never becomes the *exclusive* feature in a painting. It is part of its character but does not become so insistent that she can be accused of making wallpaper designs rather than paintings. From the earliest painting reproduced in this book, *An Abstract Landscape Composition* (1936) (Ill. 47, p.51), to a comparatively recent one such as *Red Table with Grapefruit* (1994) (Ill. 163), she has given her pictures decorative rhythms and rhymes of a playful nature. Echoes and repetitions are part of her sense of composition-making and involve colours as well as shapes. An analogy might be found in rhyming verse and poetry. If end-of-line rhymes become the only insistent effect, then the verse becomes at least monotonous and at worst meaningless. But poetry into which rhymes are so subtly insinuated, *within* the lines as well as at their tail ends, that rhyming is a structuring presence without drawing unnecessary attention to itself, then such poetry can combine free expressiveness with intelligible design. Fedden's paintings at their best use pattern – visual rhyming – in this way. *The Pink Dish* (1980) (Ill. 164) epitomises this balance.

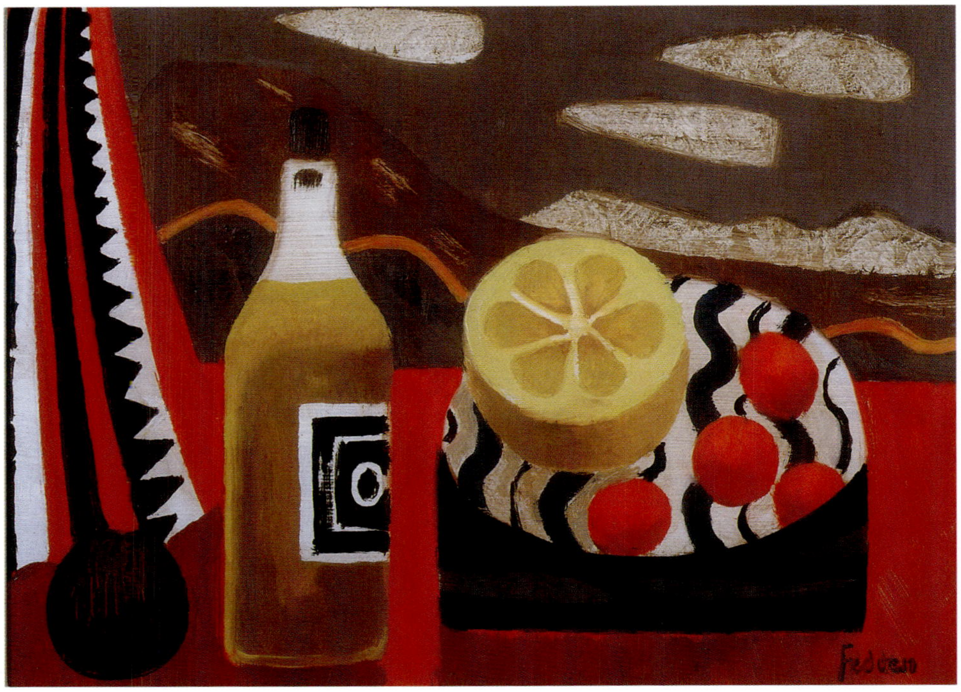

163
Red Table with Grapefruit, 1994
Oil on board
27.8 x 39.6 cm (11⅞ x 15½ in)
Private collection

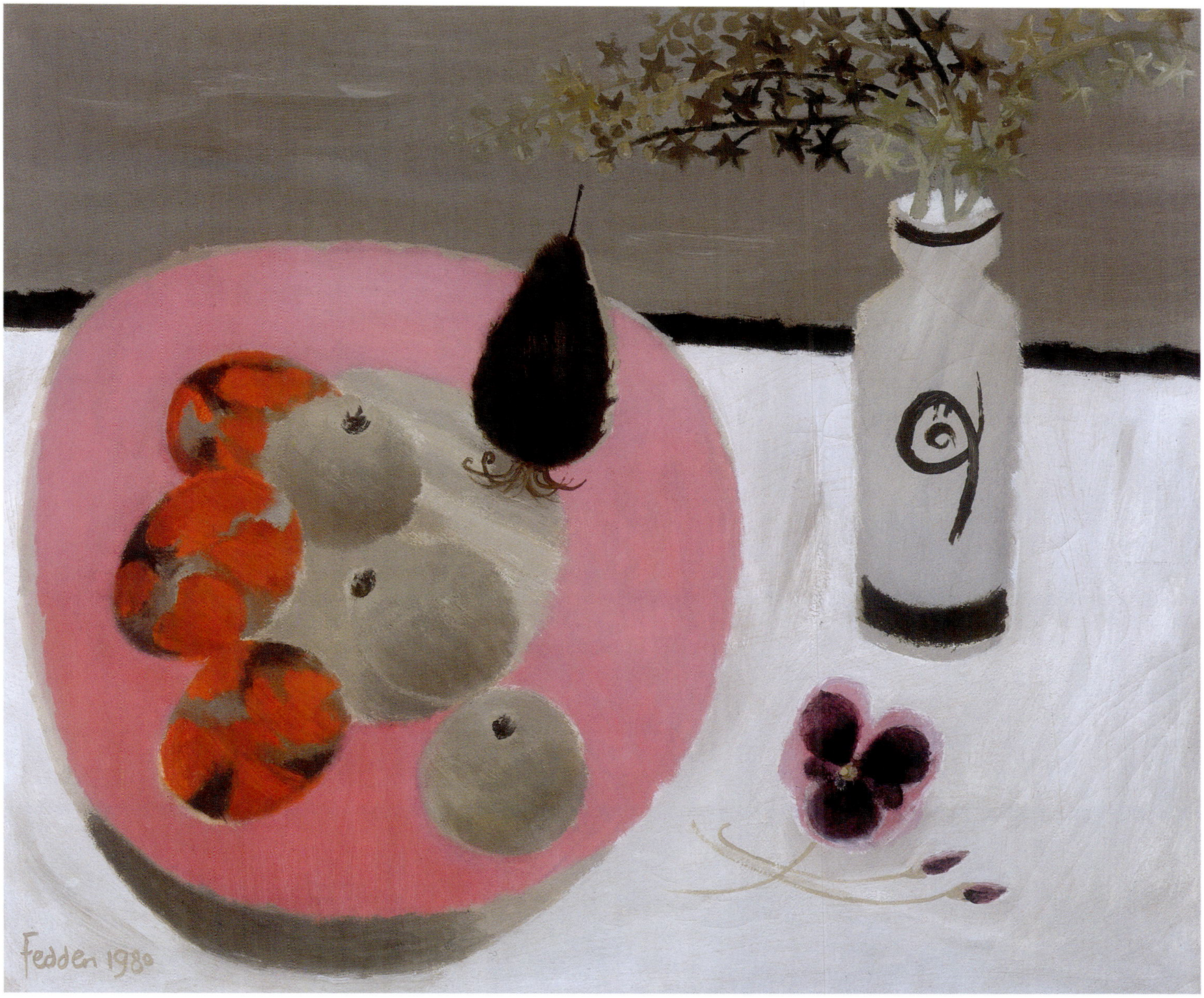

164
The Pink Dish, 1980
Oil on linen
50.5 x 60.5 cm (19⅞ x 23¾ in)
Private collection

In her ideal picture world, pattern, composition and colour go hand in hand. Once in our conversations her habitual modesty quite suddenly took a back seat. 'If there is one thing I am *really very good at*,' she said very firmly indeed, 'it is *composition*.'

With her, composition – the sensitive organisation and balance of picture surface and picture space – is a matter of intuitive satisfaction. It is intuitive, but it is also surely the result of years of practice and finding ways of rearranging the elements of her pictures. A small line sketch on a scrap of paper may be her first idea for a composition. Then she sets out a composition, a shadowy structure, on her canvas broadly with a brush. Forms, shapes and colours follow, and adjustments made. Only very occasionally does she make painted studies for works.

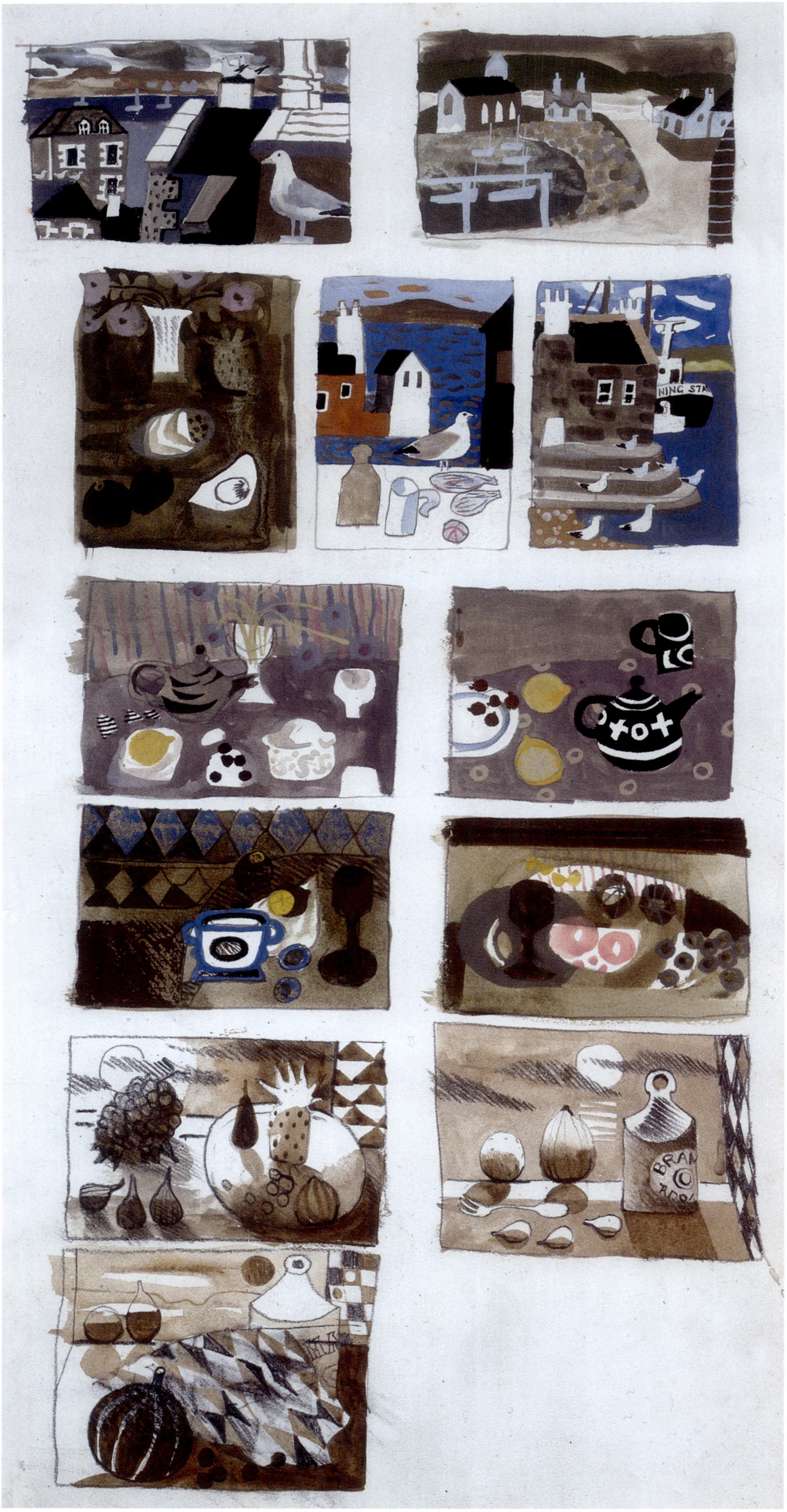

165
A Page of Ideas, undated
Gouache
57 x 30.2 cm (22½ x 11⅞ in)
Credit: The Artist

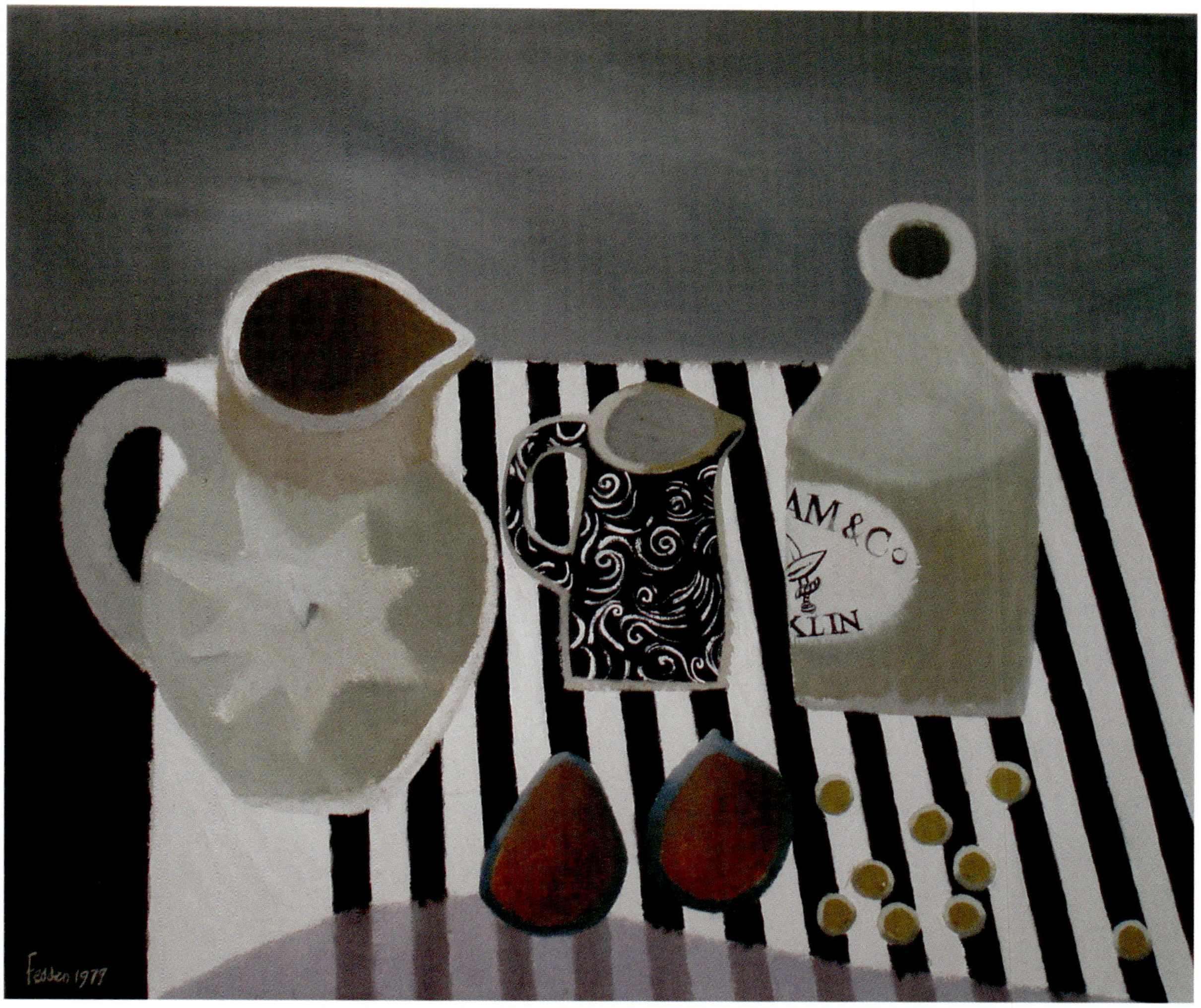

166
Jugs, 1979
Oil on canvas
79.2 x 91.5 cm
(30 x 36 in)
Private collection

It is not her method. However, once, at least, she painted a page full of tiny studies for compositions, a dozen at a trot, all different, all wonderfully placed and positioned inside their framing rectangles (Ill. 165). They provide a glimpse of her spontaneity and easy but remarkable inventiveness. They are each like a window or a compartment. This page of ideas has something in common, though miniature, with the way she composed murals. (Ill. 181. p.153)

Confusion is not a trait of Fedden's art, as *Jugs* of 1979 (Ill. 166) strongly shows. On the other hand, some gutsy paintings of the 1970s also explore the idea of a melee in which, for example, figures in a landscape seem lost in a tangle of foliage and branches. In the main, however, her compositions are a model of what de Chirico once revealingly described as 'an astronomy of things … established by the perfect knowledge of the space an object should occupy in a picture, and the space that separates one object from another …'[1]

Her compositional balancing of solid and space, of air and object (Ill. 167), allows for a rich play of colour, but her colour, too, is ordered and balanced. She often says how much she dislikes too many colours in a painting. She prefers one dominant colour – red, blue, black or grey – like a key in a piece of music. Everything else must harmonise with this dominant colour, which is a kind of surround. But then some small part of the painting might punctuate this main colour with a vividly contrasting hue. 'Punctuate' is the right word.

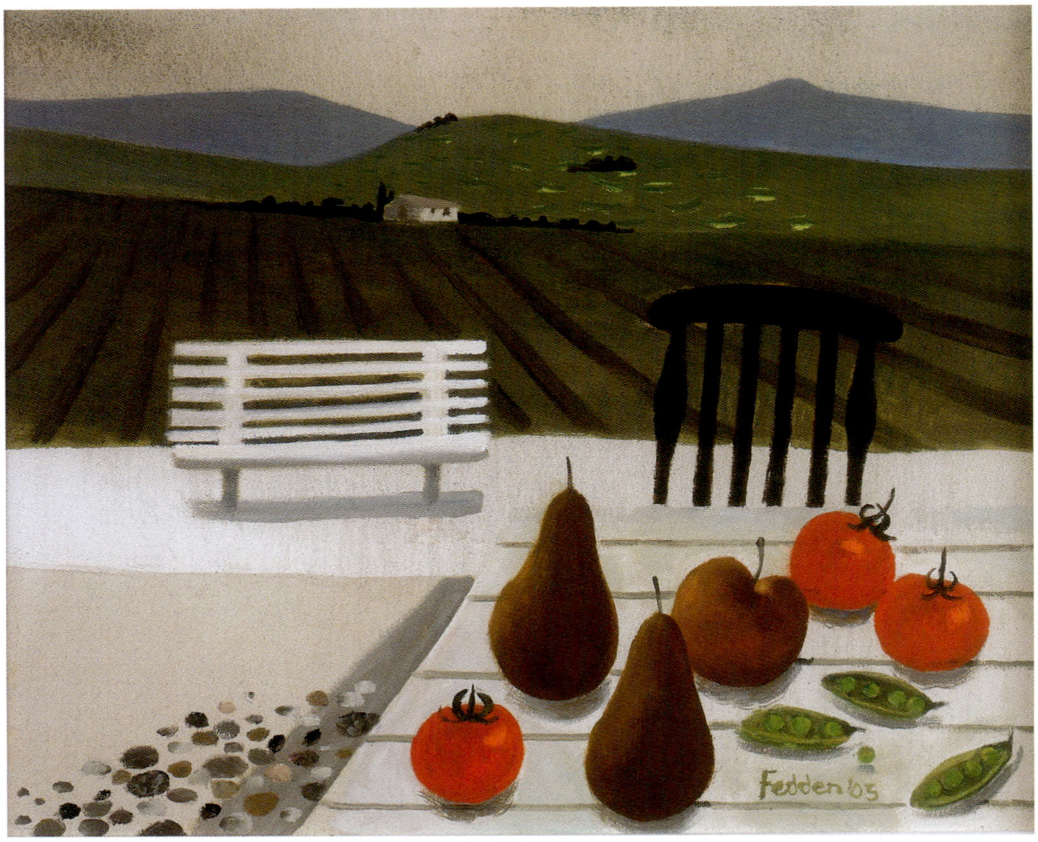

167
Tuscan Fruit, 2005
Oil on canvas
39 x 49 cm (15⅜ x 19¼ in)
Private collection

168 (below)
Playing Cards, 2002
Oil on canvas
40 x 50 cm (15¾ x 19¾ in)
Bohun Gallery, Henley-on-Thames

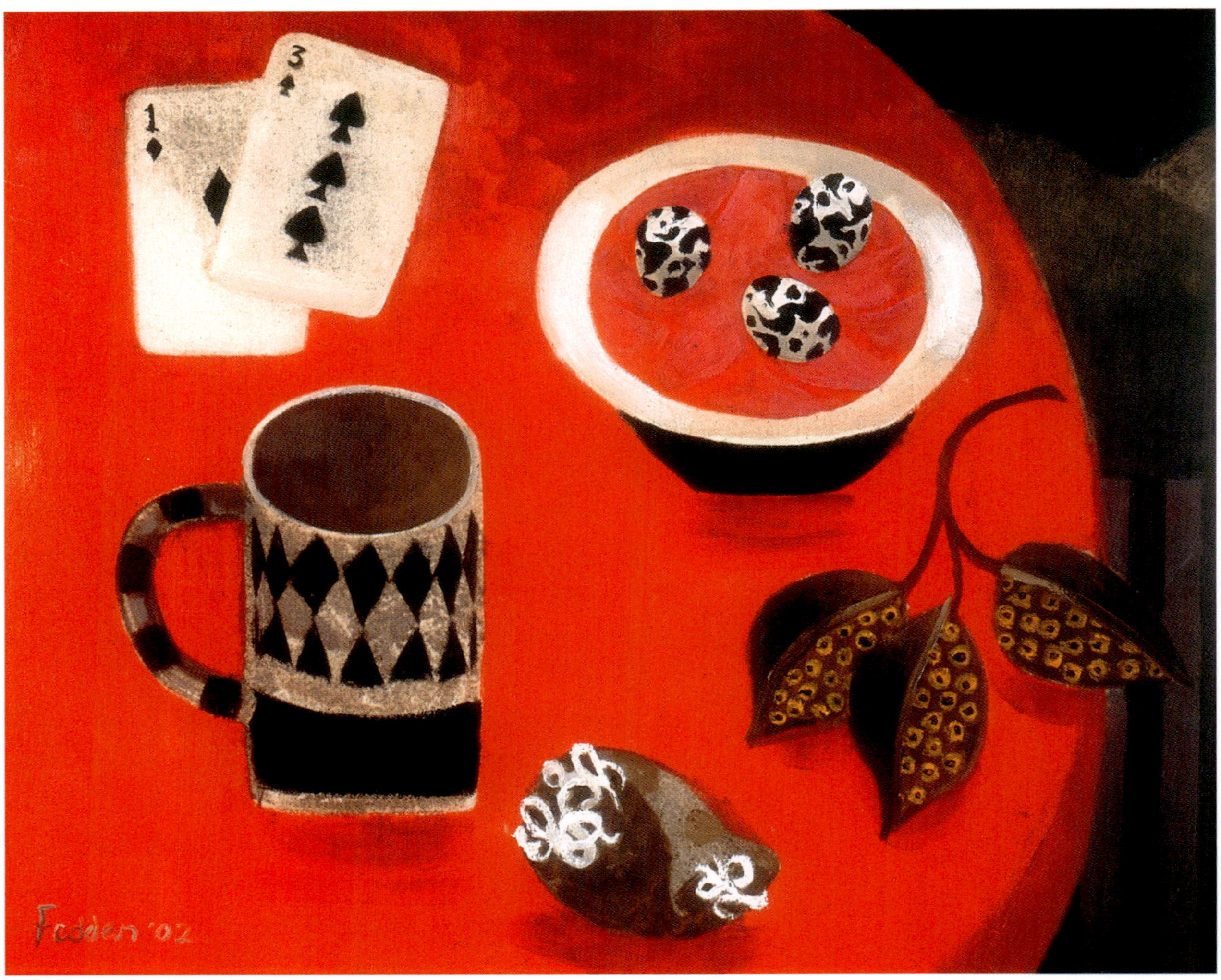

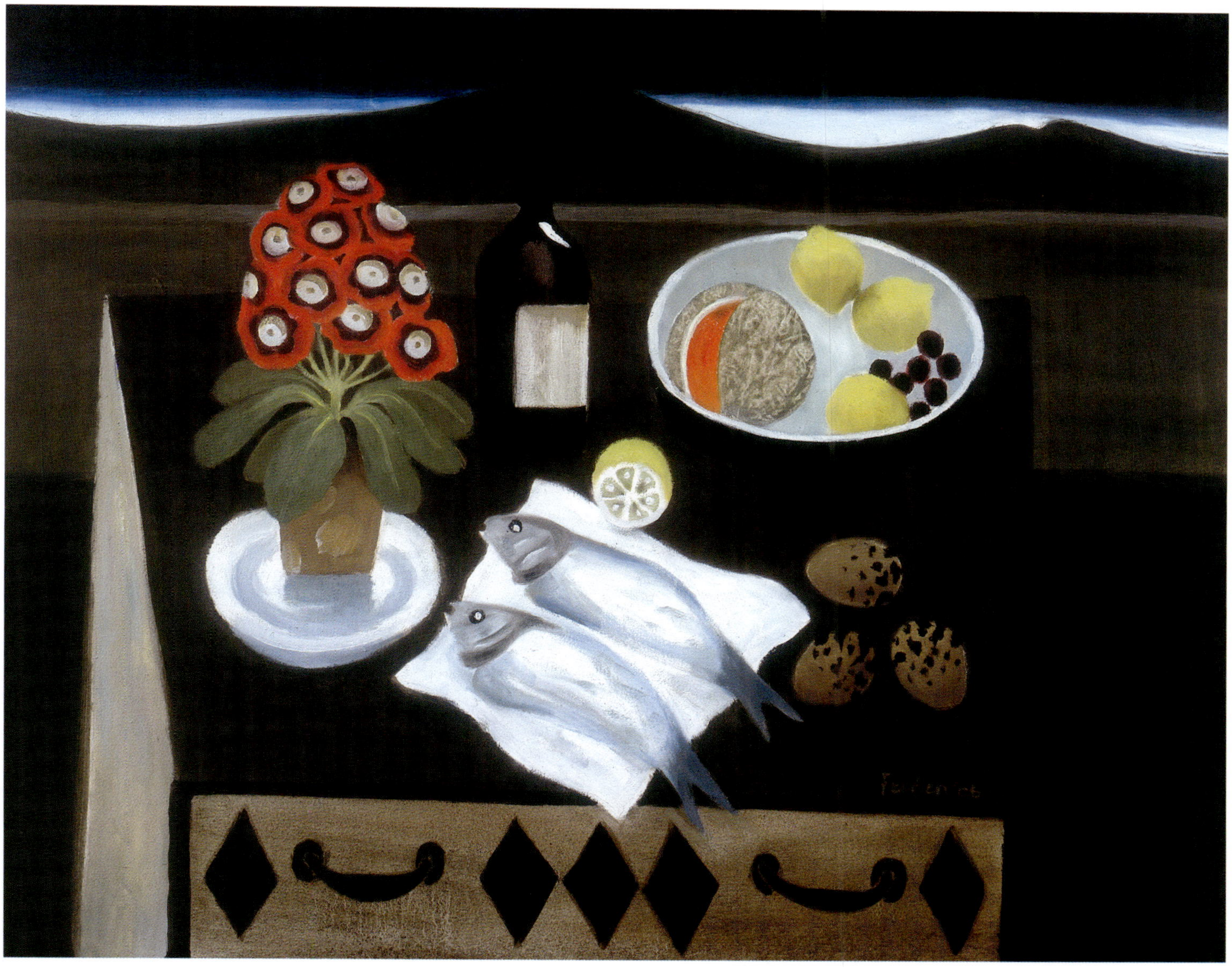

169
Chest of Drawers, 2006
Oil on canvas
70 x 90 cm (27½ x 35⅜ in)
Credit: The Artist

Fedden is not afraid of strong, bright, rich colours; in fact, she loves them. Yet she knows the value of placing muted or even muddy colours near them so that her vivid reds, oranges, greens, or yellows can sing out (Ills 168 and 169). It is, however, in the refreshing, telling ways she uses those two ultimate colours, white and black, that she excels. 'I think black is a wonderful colour,' she enthuses. To her it is not gloomy at all. 'Think of the blacks in Manet's paintings. That young man in a black velvet jacket. Wonderful.'

I suspect Fedden thinks of Edouard Manet quite a lot (without in any way aping him), finding sympathy with his direct, apparently very simple statements in paint, his blacks and greys and whites, his vases of roses or baskets of pears, his sensuous interest in the life of objects – and his lemons. Like him, Fedden knows the value of lemons, their rind and segmented flesh. They appear in her paintings frequently. Lemons whole, cut, or half-peeled. Their form, their acidity, their feel. You can almost smell her lemons, virtually taste the juice. Above all, they are *colour*. It is the *yellow* of Fedden's lemons – a sharp accent of pure, sour colour – that proves irresistible.

Note

1. *Estatica Metafisica,* Valoro Plastici (Rome), April/May 1919. Quoted in English in *Morandi's Legacy, Influences on British Art* by Paul Coldwell, Philip Wilson (London), 2006, pp 31, 48

CHAPTER EIGHT

Travels

Sometimes appearances and meaning do not quite tally. During a flight in India, Mary copied a sign she noticed. It intrigued her by its intricate beauty. Hindi, Urdu – she didn't know. Later, at home in her studio, she thought it would look good in a painting, decoratively inscribed on the wall of a temple. An Indian visitor spotted it. 'That is a strange thing to see on the side of a temple,' he said. 'It means, "Fasten your Seat Belts".'

Mary and Julian – particularly in the long holidays when they taught at the Royal College of Art – never seemed to tire of fastening their seat belts and heading off to numerous corners of the globe: India, Africa (Ill. 171), Turkey, Morocco, Russia, America, Portugal, France, Italy and, indeed, just about everywhere on the Mediterranean.

She had not travelled much before she and Julian were together. Their love was cemented initially on a trip to Sicily – a trip she still describes with humour and relish – and from then on the two of them travelled frequently. I speculate that the appearance in her paintings of a volcano, inactively smoking or sometimes spouting oddly benevolent orange fire, must go back to that Sicily 'honeymoon' (though they actually married in 1951). All Fedden will say about this painted image is that she likes volcanoes, and that she was disappointed that Etna did not erupt when they were in Sicily.

Since Julian's death in 1988, she has continued to travel several times a year – to Jordan, to Spain, and habitually to stay with friends in France, Tuscany, Scotland and Ireland (Ill. 172). She visits Yorkshire where her stepson and family live and she goes to the Aldeburgh Festival in East Anglia. That coastline has also become a favourite subject (Ills 173 and 174). In the same way that she has worked out a balance between working alone in her studio and a rich and hospitable social life, Fedden has achieved a balance between being at home for long periods and being away.

Wherever she goes she takes sketchbook and pen. Paintings back home in the studio follow, but not always immediately. Travel is a persistent ingredient of her painting. Even her still lifes have an atmosphere that is not entirely English – they have an alfresco feel, like meals in a hot country. A holiday atmosphere.

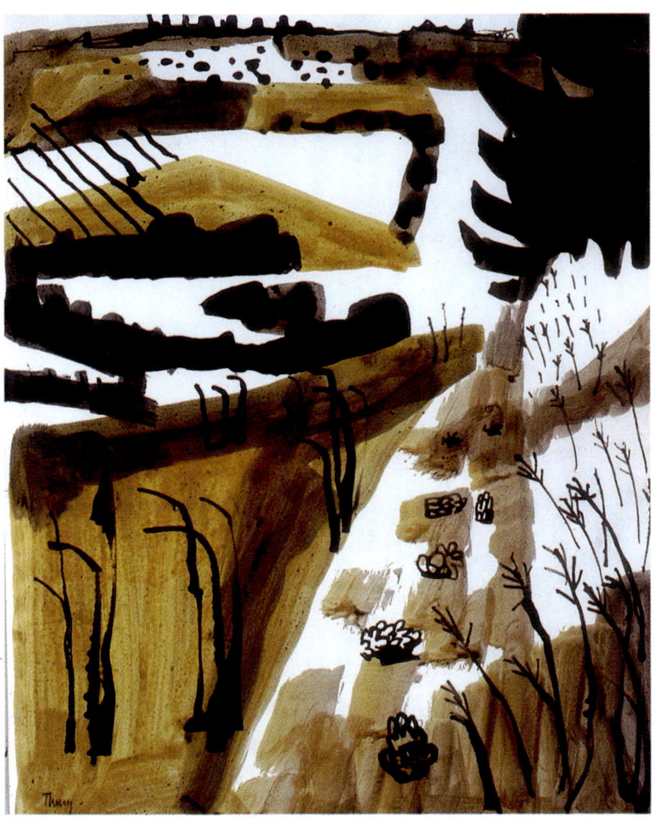

170
Landscape (Thury), undated
Pen, ink and wash
26.7 x 22.8 cm (10½ x 9 in)
Credit: The Artist

171
African Village, c. 1963
Pen and wash
Dimensions unknown
Credit: The Artist

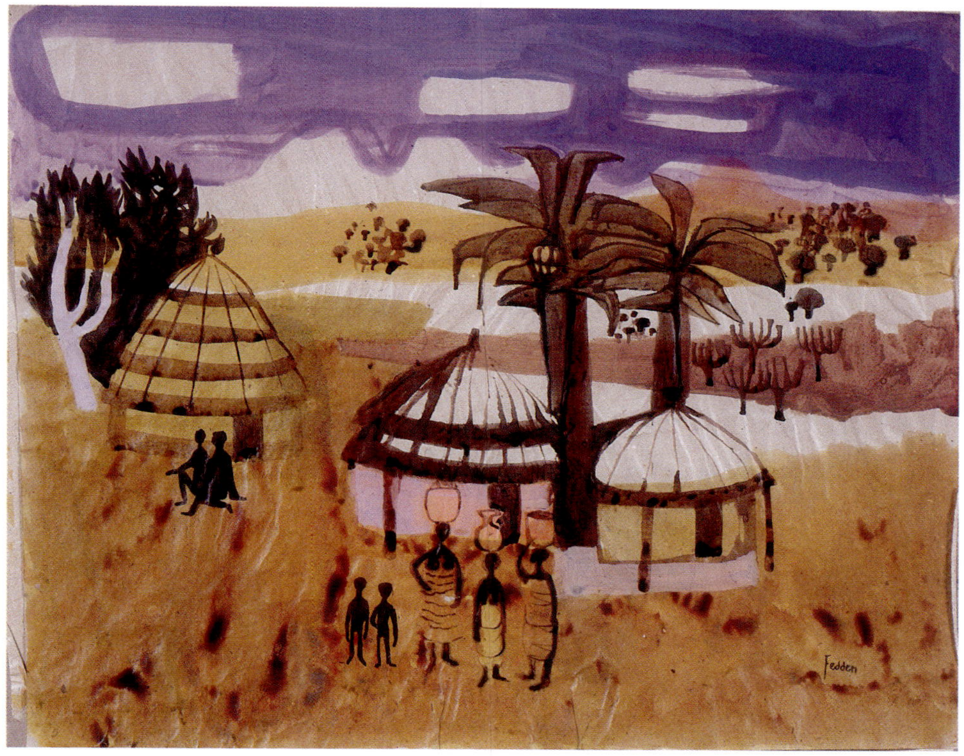

On four trips she wrote diaries (also peppered with drawings) that are funny and engaging, conveying her ebullient enjoyment and curiosity. She is a born storyteller, and her trips propagate stories almost as much as paintings. How much fruitful fictionalising takes place in either genre is anyone's guess. After all, art simplifies and tidies up experience and sometimes idealises it. I have heard stories of one or two events on past trips and have then read Mary's diary-description written at the time, and there are subtle differences! What makes a good story or a good painting is the same in principle, and a good punch line is hardly to be spoiled by over-finicky verisimilitude.

An entry in Mary's diary for 13 April 1969, during a trip to Turkey, records:

We decide that if the weather doesn't improve today & the road become possible, we must abandon Goreme (our chief reason for coming to Turkey) & drive sorrowfully back to Istanbul & home. But we wake to brilliant sun & fast thawing snow – Really Turkish weather is more unpredictable than anywhere.
We pack up & set off rejoicing, retrace to yesterday's impassable mountains and there is a snow plough with a jolly driver who tells us he has cleared the road to Urgup & Goreme, and so he has indeed with the help of the sun. And now we come to the most astonishing unbelievable landscape – A million smooth conical volcanic peaks stretching away forever over the mountainous landscape. They are soft & easily hollowed out, & from the Xth to the XIVth centuries Byzantine monks lived here at Goreme building inside the cones houses & marvellous painted churches … decorated with Christian Symbols & patterns … The later ones have all the Byzantine themes – the life of Christ … Last Judgment, Saints on Horseback, angels & so on. But alas they are outrageously & systematically defaced by Byzantine iconoclasts who disapproved of images in Christian art. Deep scores and pitmarks on all the faces. But some are less damaged & ravishing.

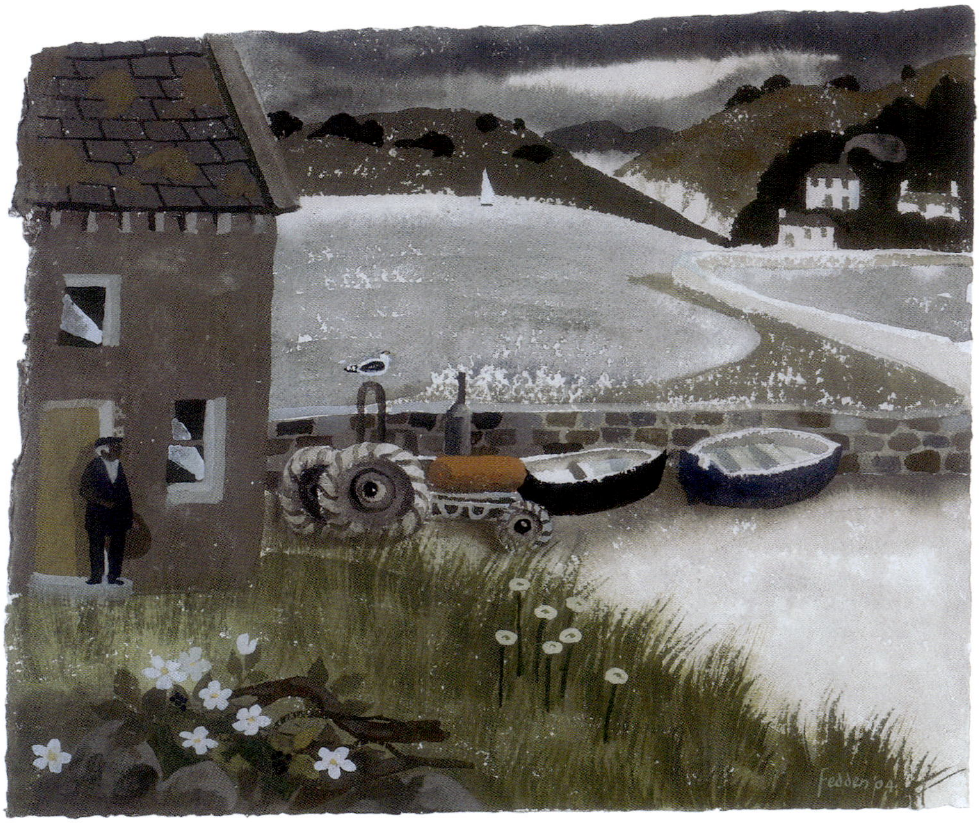

172
Myross Bridge, 2004
Gouache
28.7 x 34.3 cm (11¼ x 13½ in)
Private collection

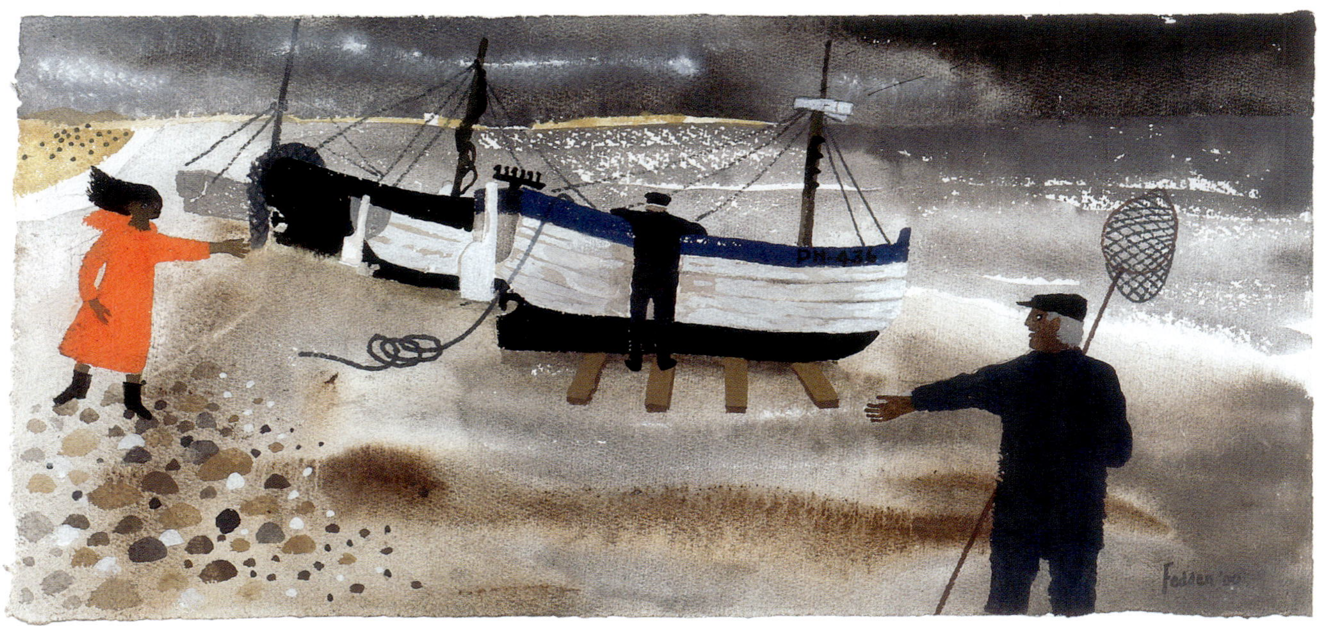

173
Dunwich, 2000
Gouache
19 x 44.5 cm (7½ x 17½ in)
Private collection

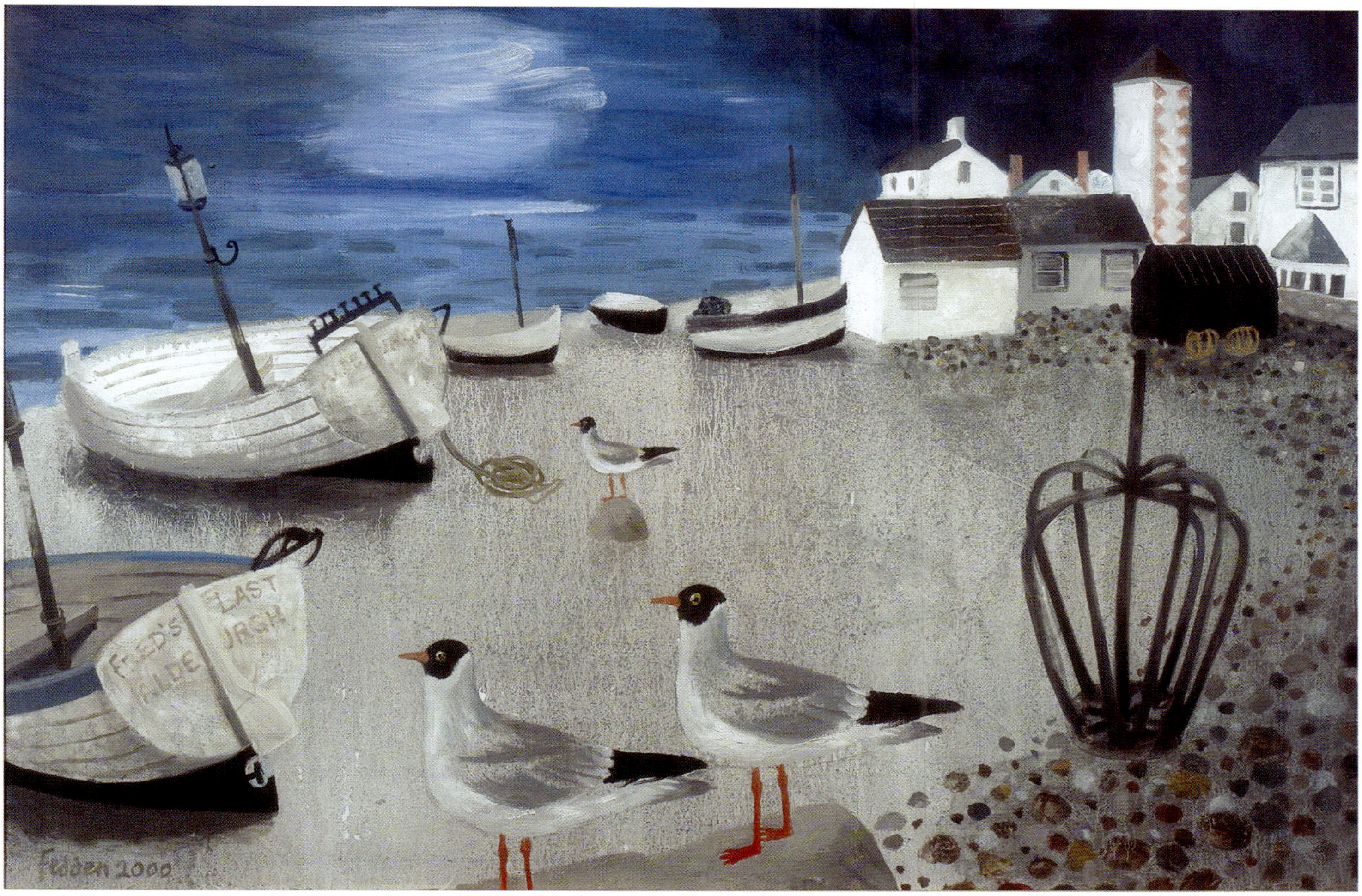

174
Aldeburgh Beach, 2000
Oil on canvas
50.8 x 61 cm (20 x 24 in)
Private collection

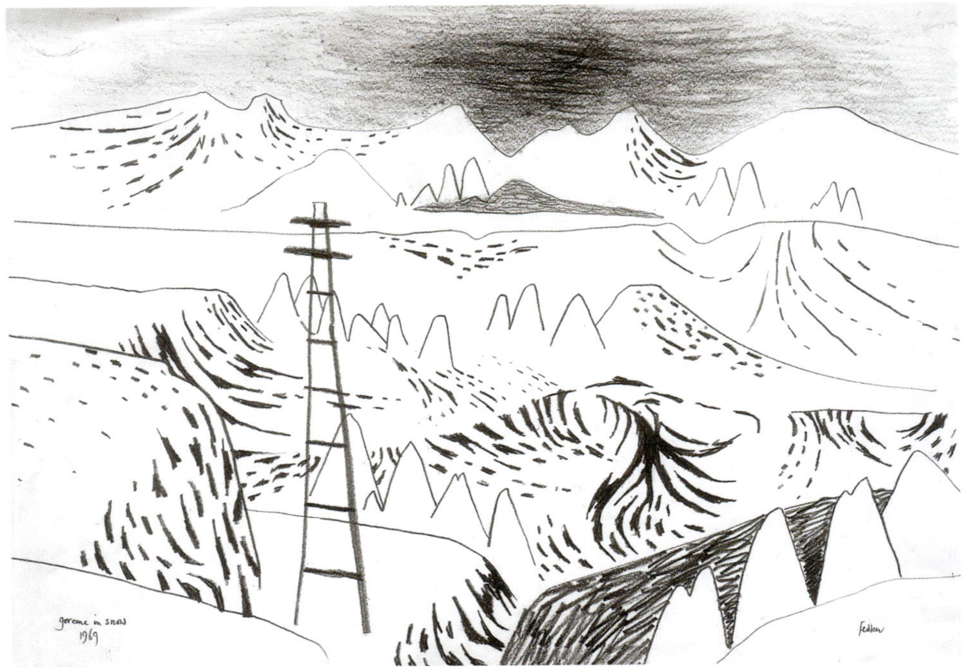

175
Goreme in Snow, 1969
Pencil
38.5 x 54.4 cm (15⅛ x 21½ in)
Credit: The Artist

A page in the diary at this point is taken up with a drawing of a decorated church, *St Barbara Goreme*, but she also made a pencil sketch in her sketchbook, *Goreme in Snow* (1969) (Ill. 175), a wonderfully schematic record of the eccentric formations confronting her, and the mountains beyond. It shows in direct terms the snow melting and the underlying forms emerging, like stripes along the back of a tiger. Fedden is a *quick* artist (she says she can never understand how some artists spend six months on one painting), and this is one of the delights of her sketches on her travels. They go straight to the point, leaving out anything she does not need to remember.

A trip to India took place in 1967–8 (Ill. 176). Fedden found it difficult to stop writing jubilantly in her diary. On 1 January 1968:

> *on to Agra at sunset, just in time to get our first sight of the TAJ MAHAL with a rosy sunset glow on the celestial white marble. It is one of the great non-disappointments of the world. Far better, bigger, purer & more beautiful in every way than I imagined. It stands on a high perfect white marble platform with a lighthouse shape at each corner & and is flanked on a lower level at each side by two perfect mosques in marble & pink sandstone; & behind drops away hundreds of feet to the broad beautiful Jumna River in a great crescent with the vast sandstone fort of Akbar in the distance.*

Next day, Julian and Mary went to see the Taj Mahal again, at 8.30 a.m. The sun was just up. Because it was the Muslim festival marking the end of Ramadan, and the mosque that flanks the Taj was besieged, the Taj itself was more or less deserted. Mary has never forgotten having it virtually to the two of them. She records: 'We wandered about for two hours … & could happily have stayed all day'. (Ill. 177)

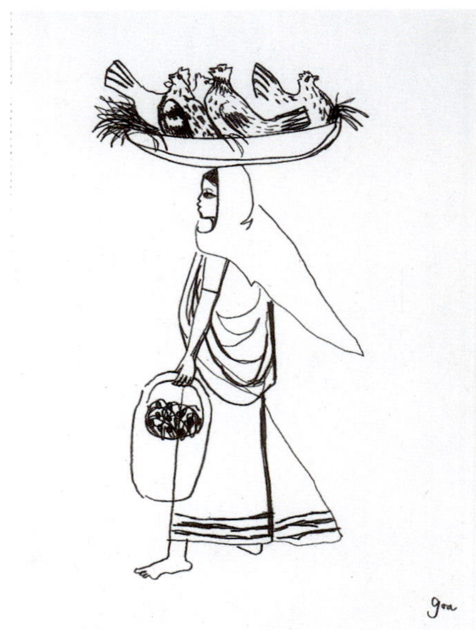

176 (above)
Goa, 1967
Pen and ink
26.7 x 22.8 cm (10½ x 9 in)
Private collection

177 (opposite)
Taj Mahal, *c.* 1968
Oil on canvas
73.2 x 59.8 cm (28¾ x 23½ in)
Private collection

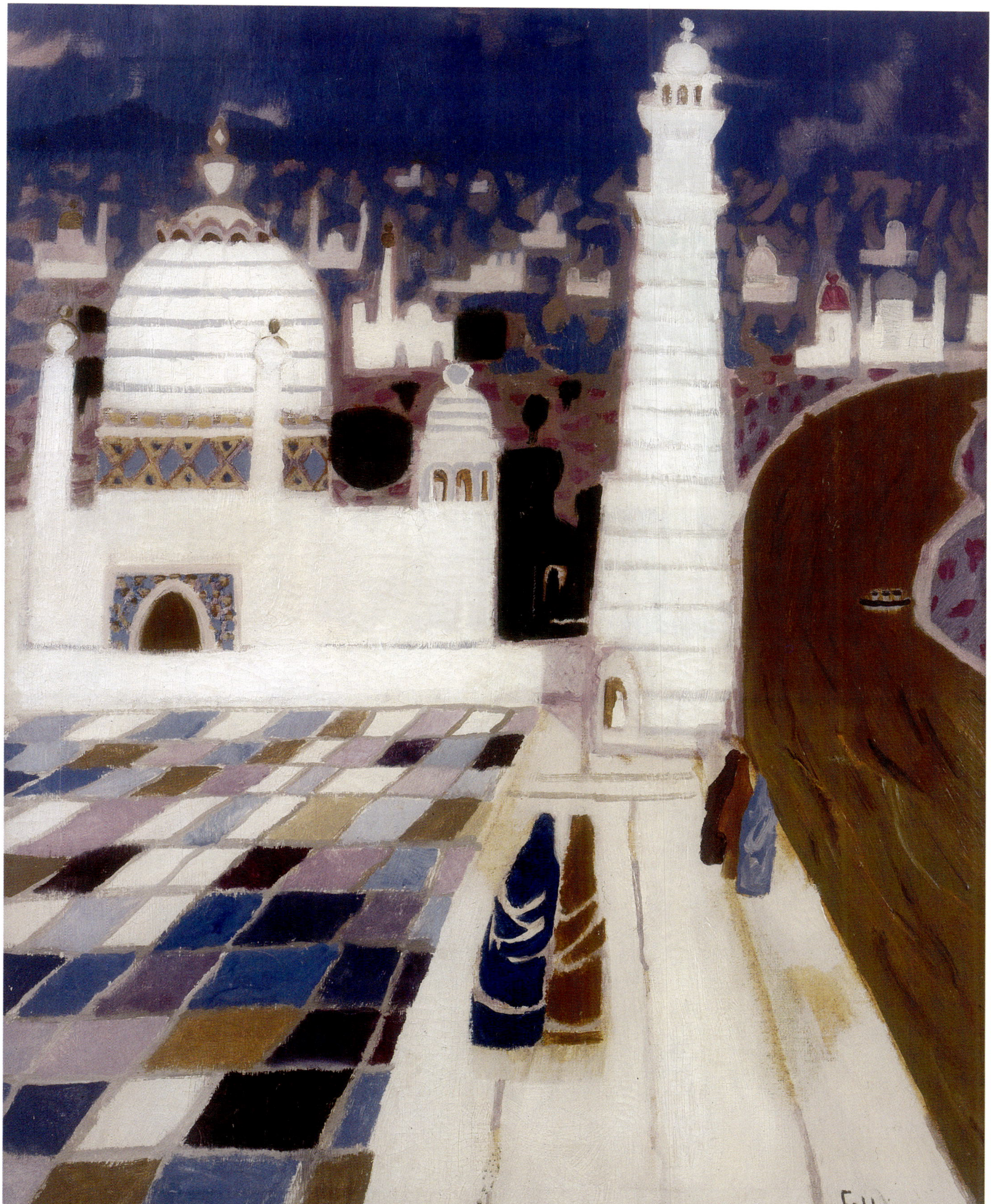
Fedden

CHAPTER NINE

Sidelines

A fair glimpse of Mary Fedden's work is not possible without mention of two aspects that she really considers sidelines. She was for a period a sought-after muralist (sometimes working with Julian). And on four occasions, she was inveigled into illustrating books.

Today she feels that her murals were not her best work. Perhaps like theatrical scene painting, they required too much compromise and teamwork, or perhaps they were too much 'public art', slightly reminiscent of the propaganda painting she worked on during World War II. She has chosen to be basically an easel painter, and this means canvases that are not vast and a scale that is domestic. Although some of her paintings in the 1950s, 1960s and 1970s are much larger than today's, even they could not be described as public-gallery paintings. Also, her favourite subject, still life, seems more comfortable in paintings of a private size – paintings that might hang happily over a mantelpiece. Her gouaches, including *Fruit and Flowers by an Open Window* (1998) (Ill. 179), suit even more intimate places.

Some of her murals still exist. One, *Children's Games* (1956) (Ill. 180), is in Highridge Infants' School in Bristol, her hometown. Another that she designed and painted – a whole roomful of murals in a children's nursery – was in the P&O liner, *Canberra*. This, too, still exists, having been conscientiously saved by P&O when the liner was eventually scrapped. It is in storage, but all of it has been painted over, except a bird that happened to be hidden by a basin. It is probably perfectly preserved, however, since it was bonded to melamine by a special Scandinavian process and is virtually indestructible. One day, perhaps, it will re-emerge, thanks to some interested conservationist or other, and see the light of day again. A study for part of it exists and suggests that Fedden, with typical professionalism, actually had a ball with her theme of fantastic animals and birds. (Ill. 181)

She was commissioned to paint another mural, once more linked to children, for the 1951 Festival of Britain (Ill. 182). She produced a highly detailed, compartmented work, which today she may feel is too stylised. It was elaborate and delightfully energetic.

Inevitably, her forte, still life, was not much represented in her murals. Figures in action were their main feature. In fact, these murals were full of inventive fun and must have served their purpose well. They also demonstrate the fact that she wasn't at all fazed by working at a large scale, even if it has not turned out to be her preference.

178
The Green Man, 1998
Gouache
30.2 x 25 cm (11⅞ x 9⅞ in)
Private collection

This picture for a Christmas story by Jane Gardam appeared in *Country Life*. It is a spin-off from *The Green Man*, a book Gardam wrote and Fedden illustrated. Here the Green Man cycles rapidly to bring the baby to the Christmas crib. '"Here you are then," said a woman. "Hurry up. Bring the Jesus. The children are waiting."'

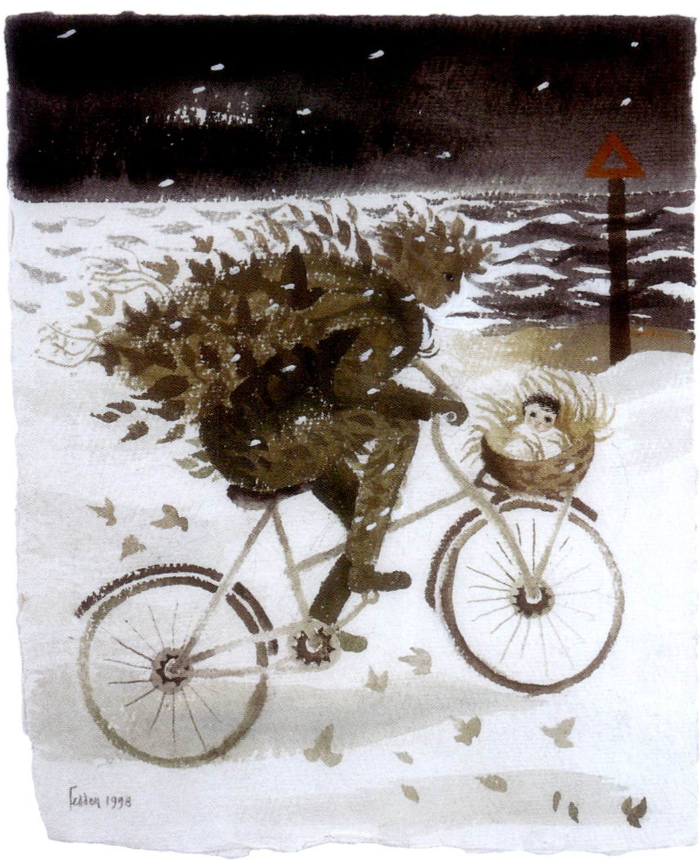

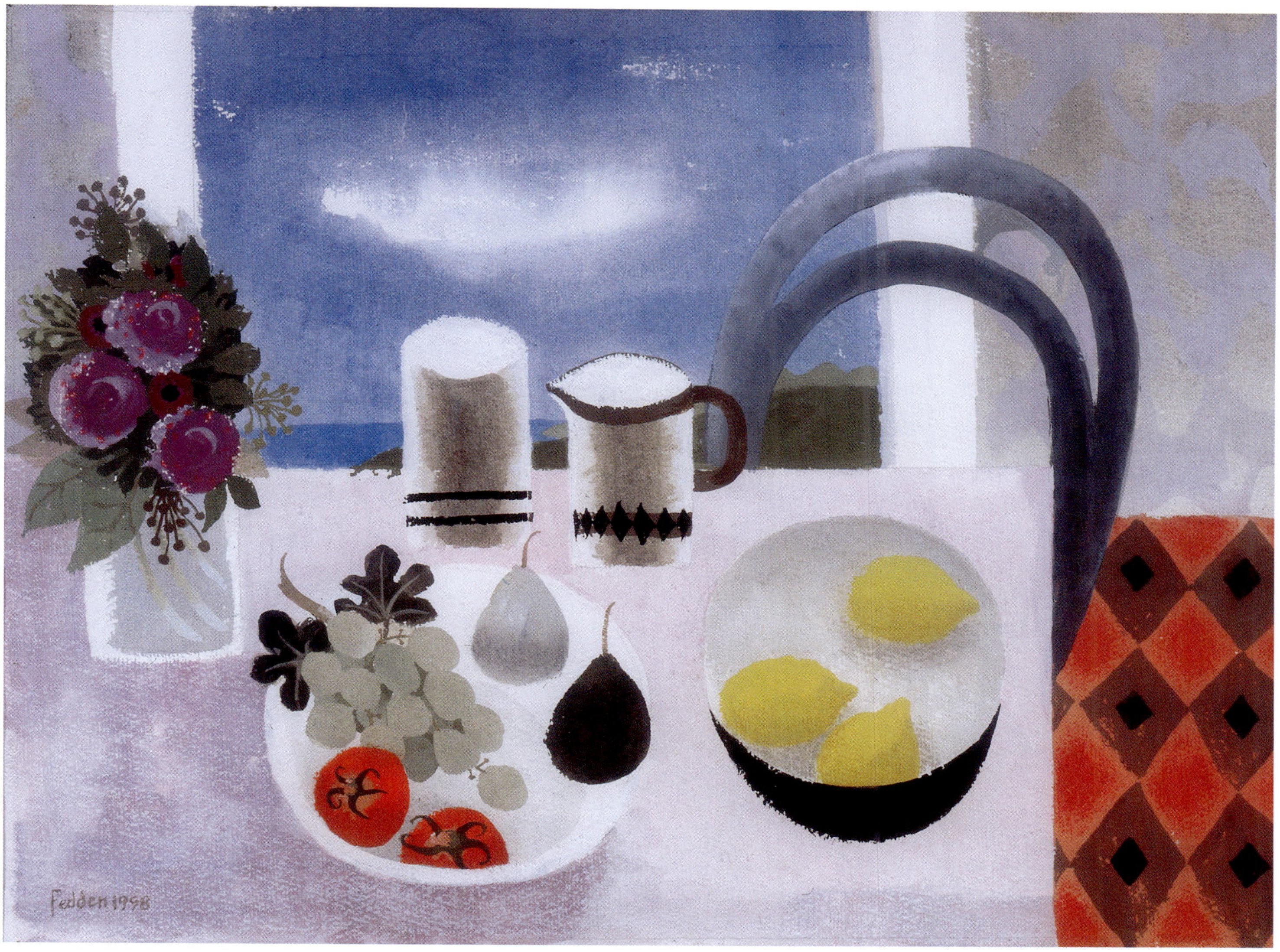

179
Fruit and Flowers by an Open Window, 1998
Gouache
38.4 x 53 cm (15⅛ x 21⅞ in)
Private collection

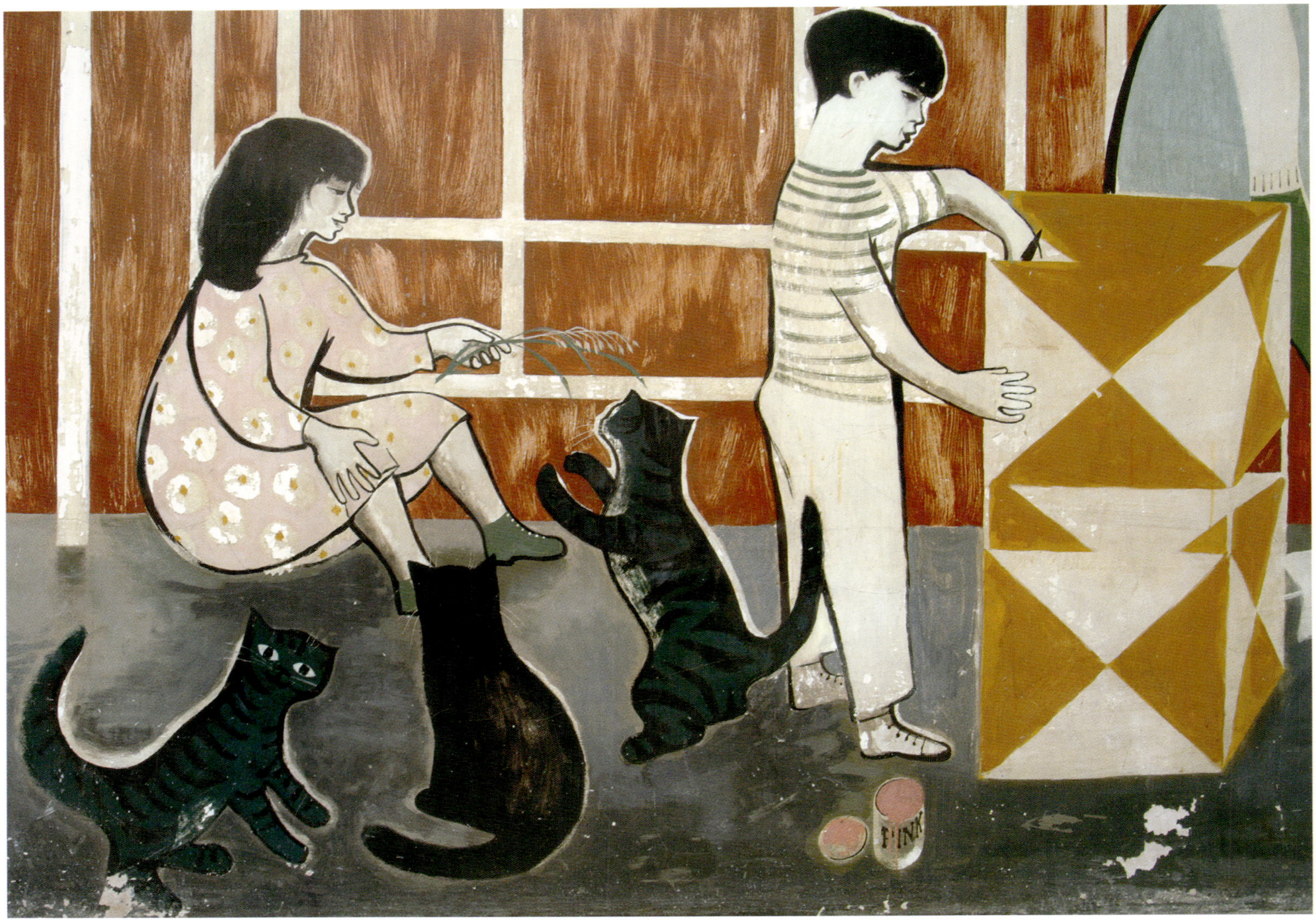

180
Children's Games (detail), 1956
Mural
Dimensions unknown
Highridge Infants' School, Bristol

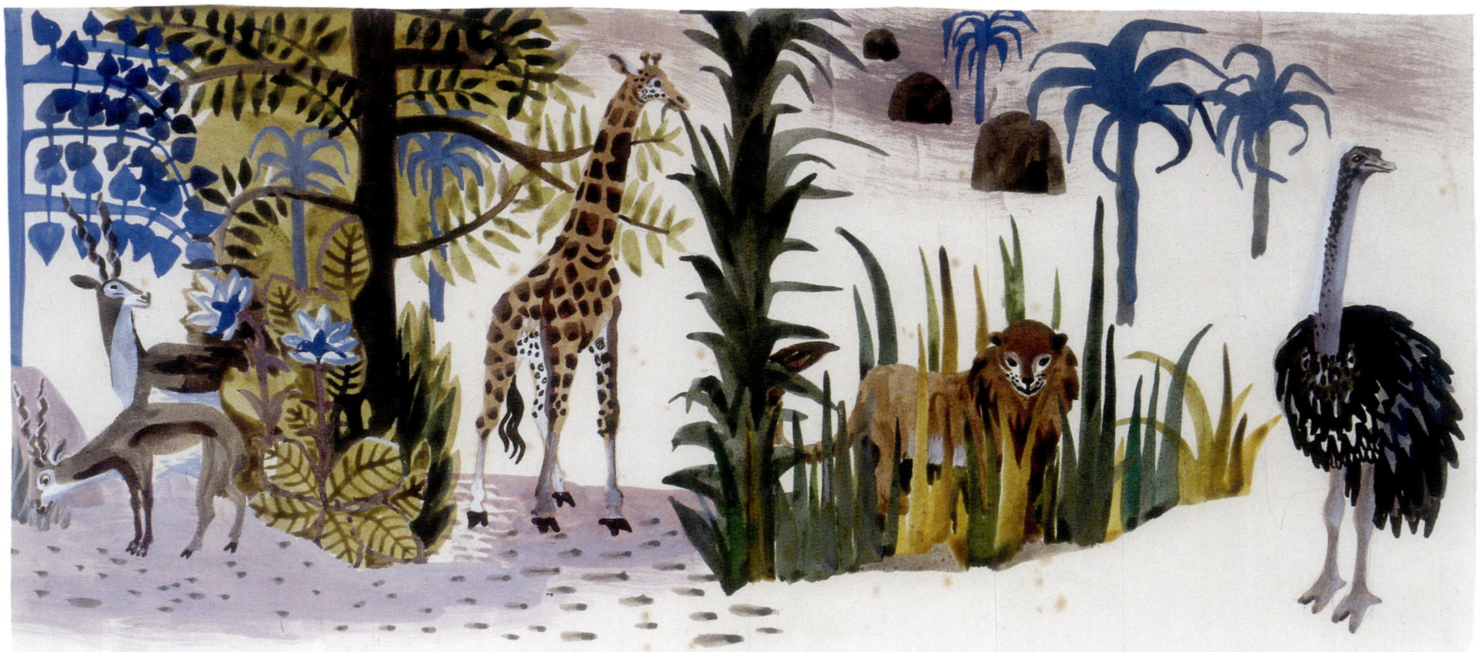

181
Wild Animals, c.1960
Gouache (study for mural)
25.7 x 58.5 cm (10 x 23 in)
Credit: The Artist

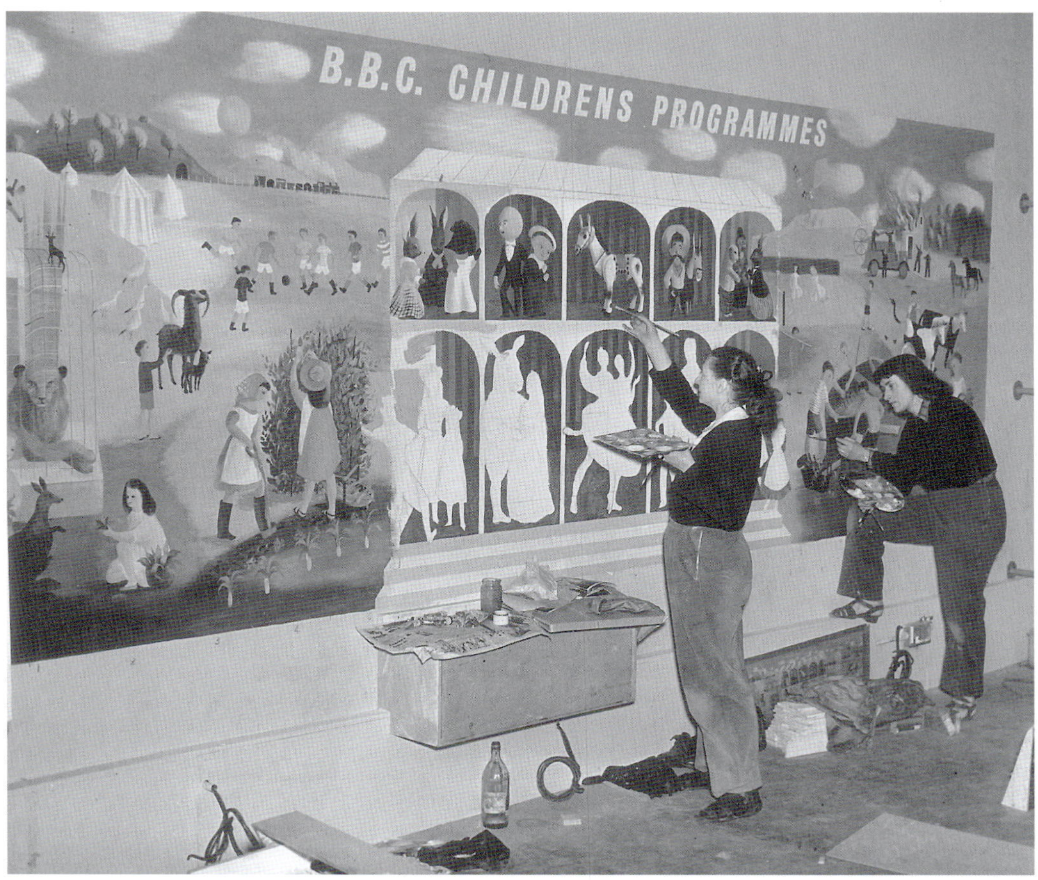

182
Mary Fedden painting her Festival of Britain mural, 1951

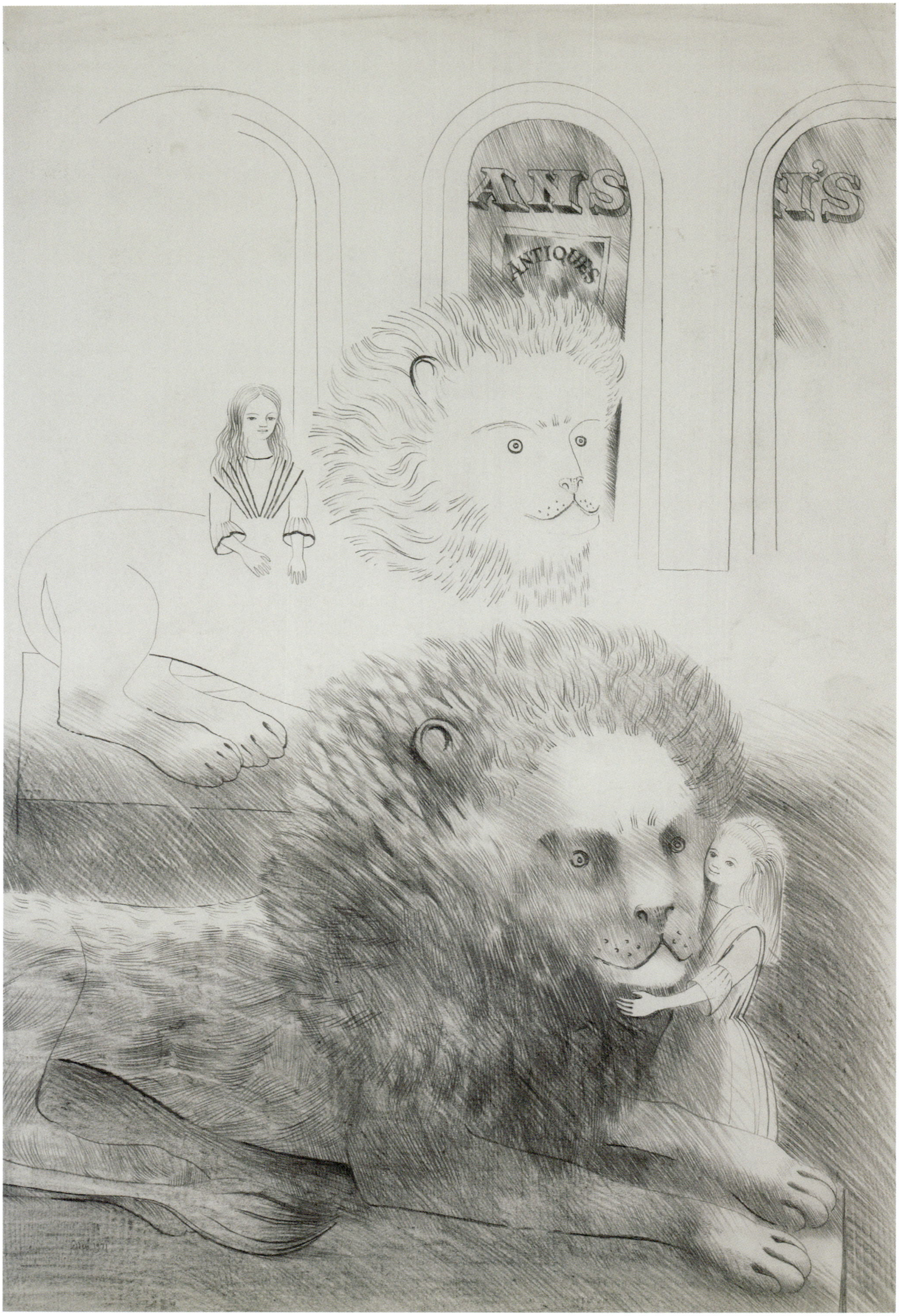
ANS
ANTIQUES

183 (opposite)
The Carved Lions, 1971
Pencil (for book illustration)
69 x 48 cm (27¼ x 18⅞ in)
Private collection

More suited to her sense of scale, perhaps, are her three published illustrated books. The fourth, for which she produced drawings of outstanding finesse and narrative sensitivity, was not, in the event, published. Had it been, it might well have rejuvenated the reputation of a good Victorian children's classic, *The Carved Lions* by Mrs Molesworth (Ill. 183).[1] Both the writing in this book and Fedden's interpretation of it see the world poignantly from a little child's viewpoint. Mary still remembers her keenness, as a girl, on Victorian children's books. 'They were so romantic!' she says. She took this commission very seriously and in good faith that her illustrations would be published. Her drawings for the book disappeared, however, until four of them re-emerged recently at auction. She had never received a penny for them.

Her three published books, each quite different from the others, all show how appropriate her painting in gouache is for book reproduction, and how aptly her imagination works as an illustrator. This is in spite of her coming from a generation when artists rather pooh-poohed 'illustration' and 'illustrators'. *Serious* artists were presumed to avoid such sidelines.

However, she is nothing if not willing to oblige persuasive friends, and so – to her credit – her three books exist: *Motley the Cat* by Susannah Amoore;[2] *The Green Man* by Jane Gardam;[3] and *Birds*.[4]

Birds gathers together gouaches of one of her favourite and long-standing subjects. Featuring an introduction by Mel Gooding, it is, in fact, a book of paintings rather than an illustrated book. As with her flowers, Fedden's birds, sourced as unselfconsciously from bird books as from snapshots or first-hand observation, are so unpretentious and straight forward that one scarcely notices their subtlety. The birds just seem to have hopped (or swum) into view (Ill. 184). These pictures make no effort to be ornithological: scientific accuracy takes second place to affection. It is as if she is familiar with Walt Whitman's observation that 'you must not know too much, or be too precise or scientific about birds and trees and flowers. A certain free margin … helps your enjoyment of these things'.[5]

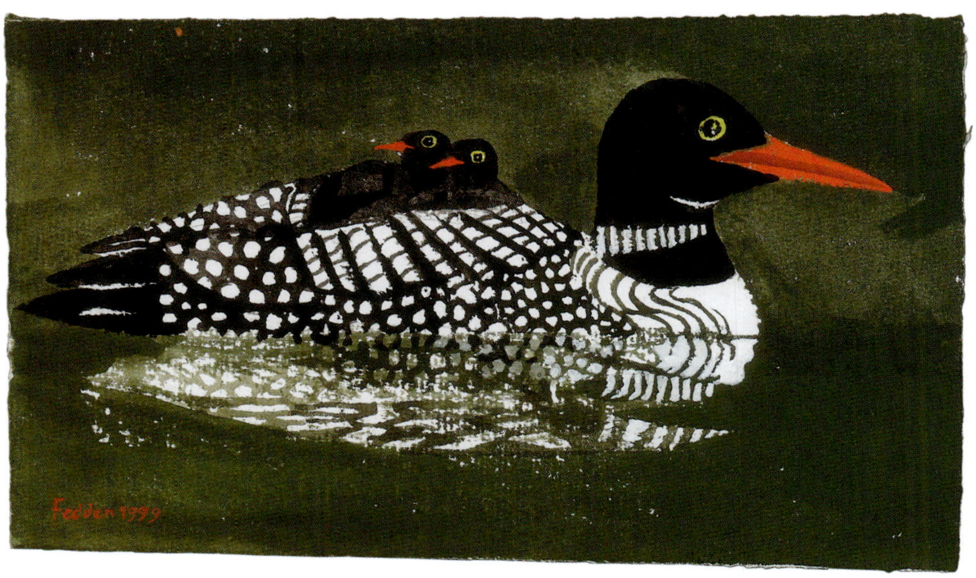

184
Loon, 1999
Gouache
13.8 x 24.8 cm (5⅜ x 9¾ in)
Credit: The Artist

This gouache, used as a book illustration, was painted 'from a photograph sent from America by Humphrey Spender'.

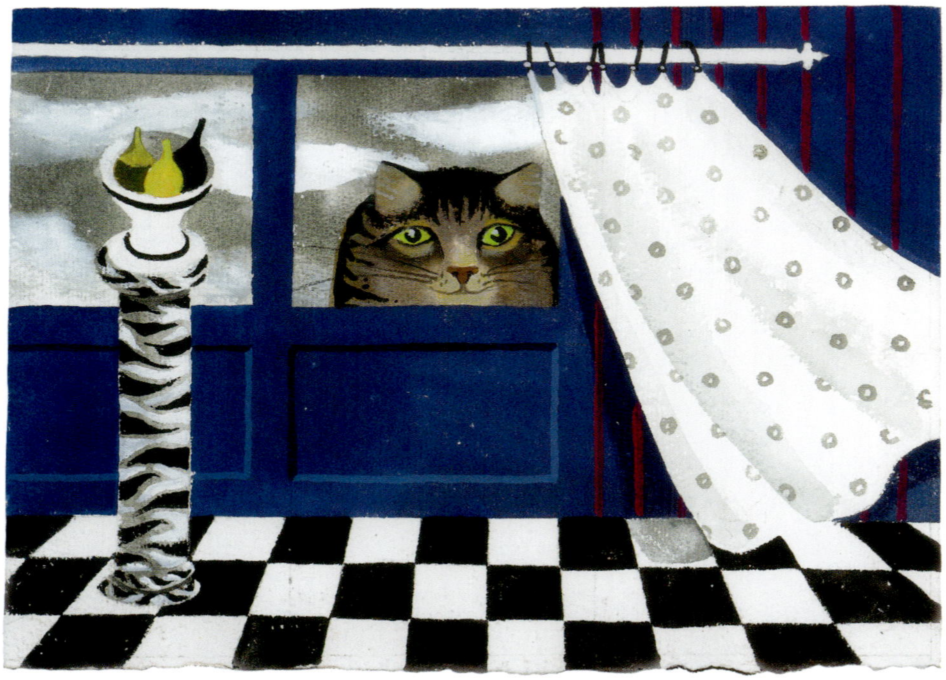

185
Motley the Cat, 1997
Gouache (for book illustration)
24.2 x 34.3 cm (9½ x 13⅜ in)
Credit: The Artist

Illustrating Susannah Amoore's children's book *Motley the Cat*, the neighbouring text reads: 'One of the girls cried "Look!" … They looked where she pointed, and there, pressed to the glass of the window, was that face, that unforgettable face … An enormous beautiful-ugly striped-like-a-tiger face.'

In *Motley the Cat,* Fedden walks a tightrope between supplying images that brilliantly express the text, depicting an appealing and moving story, and being true to the vision and quality of her own paintings (Ill. 185). Each illustration *is* a Fedden painting, while also more than serving its context. Beautifully luminous still lifes appear where they can, but the children and the cats rule. The illustrations display Fedden's understanding of both.

The Green Man is the book out of the three that, I think, exercised her ingenuity and imagination most. Her illustrations really *are* illustrations to a mystical, poetic book. The challenge of conveying a myth took this artist into unfamiliar realms, in response to the story's changing seasonal narrative and the enigmatic passage of time. She also contributes momentary touches of light-heartedness and humour. Her illustrations are not in the least subservient. They are more like a strongly visualised commentary on the words. (Ill. 186)

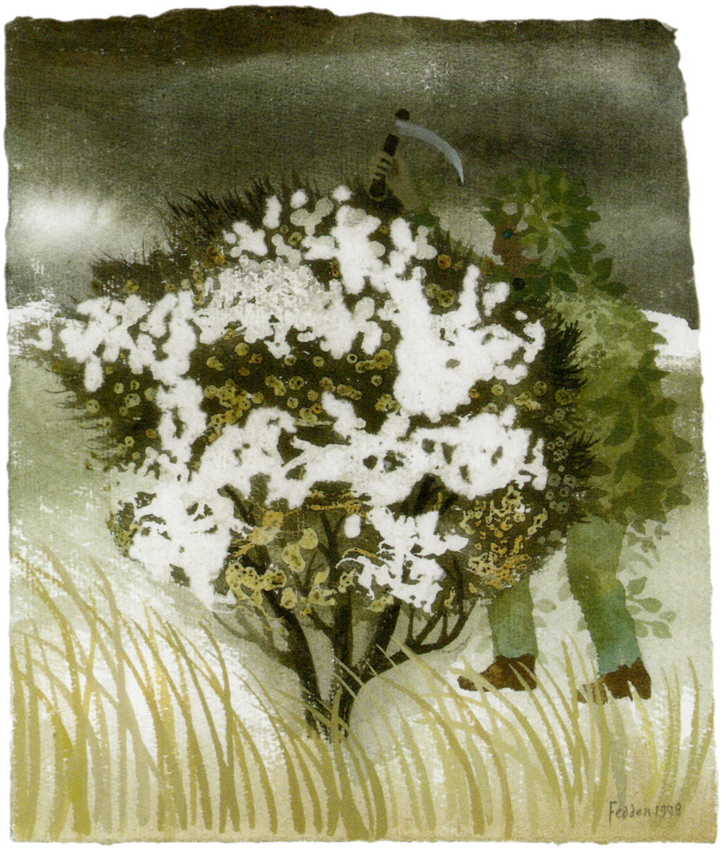

186
The Green Man ('Now you see him, now you don't'), 1998
Gouache (for book illustration)
25.6 x 21.8 cm (10 x 8½ in)
Credit: The Artist

'The field is empty,' writes Jane Gardam near this illustration in *The Green Man*, 'and you'll be lucky to catch a glimmer of a face between branches, down the coppice. Did you see a figure at work with a bill-hook by the blackthorn in white bloom? Maybe you didn't.'

There is a practicality in Fedden's conception of the artist's function. She is not averse to an artist's need to please. Her cover for one of Glyndebourne Opera House's season-long programmes is a particularly successful and charming example of her willingness to do what is required, so long as it does not compromise her art. This cannily composed design, summery in mood, also happens to be a brilliant wraparound for the magazine. (Ill. 187)

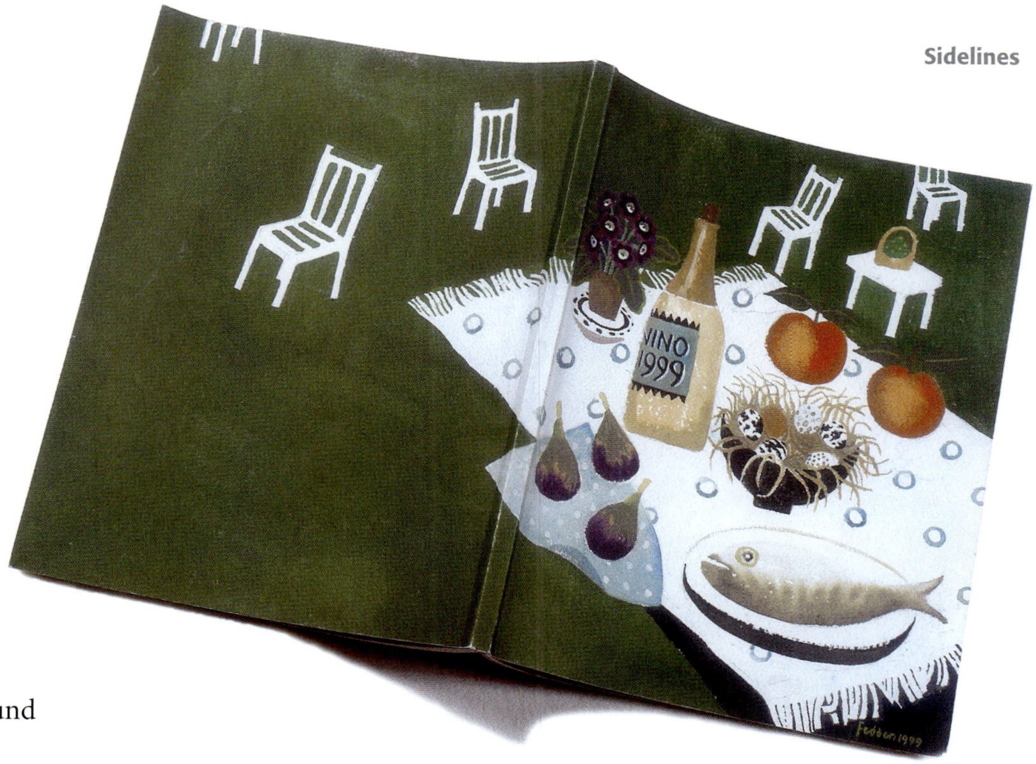

187
Cover for Glyndebourne Opera summer programme, 1999
Photo-lithography
31 x 50 cm (12½ x 19¼ in)
Courtesy of Glyndebourne Opera

One should not forget her Christmas stamp designs for the Royal Mail. *Good King Wenceslas* (1997) (Ill.188), rich in colour, bold and simple, catches the cheery chilliness of the carol and the nursery-rhyme nature of the story it tells. Fedden still feels a bit cross that the Royal Mail turned down her stamp designs. Perhaps she could take solace from the fact that she is in good company. The prestigious institution also rejected designs for stamps by Graham Sutherland. Mary at least saw hers used later as Christmas greetings cards – even if they had to be posted with someone else's stamps on the envelope.

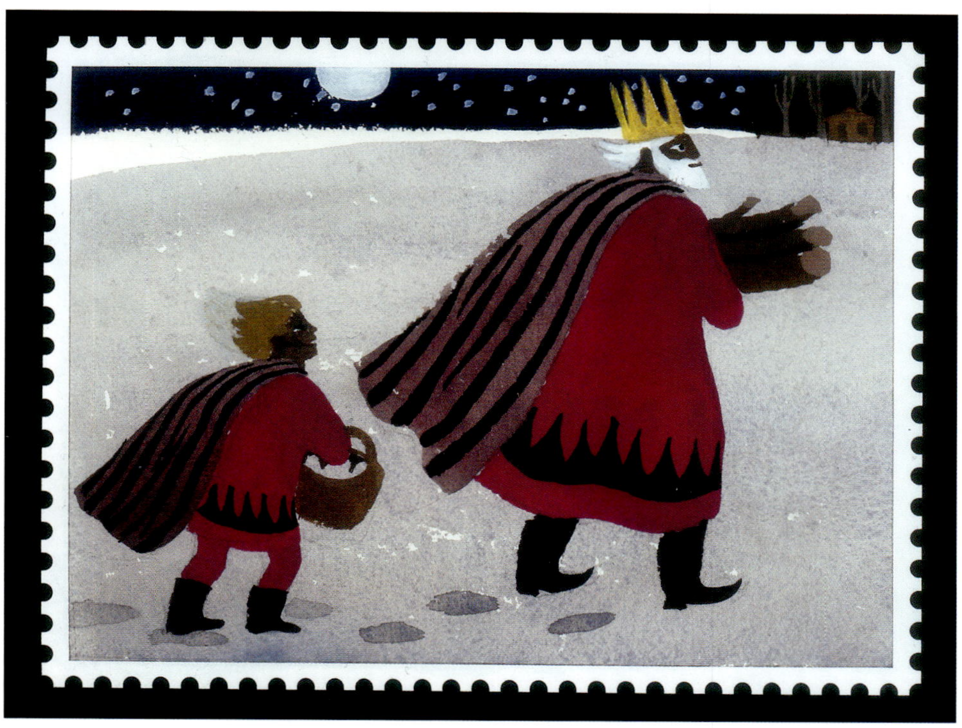

188
Good King Wenceslas, 1997
Gouache (for postage stamp)
Dimensions unknown
© Royal Academy of Arts, London

Notes

1. *The Carved Lions* by Mrs Molesworth, Macmillan (London), 1895
2. *Motley the Cat* by Mary Fedden and Susannah Amoore. Viking (London), 1997
3. *The Green Man* by Jane Gardam and Mary Fedden, Windrush Press (Moreton-in-Marsh, Gloucestershire), 1998
4. *Birds* by Mary Fedden, foreword by Mel Gooding, Windrush Press (Moreton-in-Marsh, Gloucestershire), 1999
5. *Complete Prose* by Walt Whitman, G.P. Putnam's Sons (London), 1898, p.175

I·N·T·E·R·L·U·D·E
Familiarity Breeds Contentment

Joanna Carey is a writer and children's book illustrator. She and her husband are close friends of Mary. Joanna writes so authentically about living with a Fedden painting (she actually lives with several) that what she says needs no comment:

Three Red Poppies by Mary Fedden, 2003

This painting hangs over our kitchen table. I look at it every day: it's a bold composition and with the poetic, often deceptive simplicity that imbues so much of Mary Fedden's work, it brings together landscape and still life with a natural, unforced magic that invites and rewards contemplation.

In the foreground is a round table whose curves are echoed throughout the composition, not just in the things that sit on the table, but also in the background, in the hills that fold so comfortably into one another. A harmonious rhythm leads the eye back and forth from the immediate accessibility of the still-life objects to the mystery of the world beyond. The lighting is crepuscular, the atmosphere is meditative, romantic, and against a brooding sky three clouds drift across the hills like passing thoughts.

On the table there's a fruit bowl – it's a dark oval with a sickle shaped rim that recalls those crescent moons in Samuel Palmer's twilit landscapes. There's no obvious light source here and in the shady embrace of the bowl the scarlet poppies appear lit from within. Against the muted, earthy tones that prevail, the intense colour and luminosity of the flowers has a theatrical impact that reminds me – somewhat incongruously – of Walter Sickert's picture of a singer on stage at The Old Bedford in her startlingly red dress. And Fedden creates an additional sense of theatre with the curtain – a device she often uses – that hangs to the right of the picture: drawn back to reveal the landscape it seems to suggest the point at which two different worlds come together.

One of the things I enjoy in her paintings is the element of narrative they so frequently offer, with the slight suggestion that something is about to happen or has just happened. There are no figures in this painting but the eye is drawn to the hills behind – where silhouettes of trees suggest some kind of activity – a straggly procession perhaps, going up to the chapel on the hill. And, on a different scale in the foreground, the still-life objects and the table itself inevitably refer to an unseen human presence.

The still-life objects Fedden paints appear again and again in her pictures – bowls, jugs, pebbles, bottles. They are like a versatile repertory company, appearing in many guises, taking on different characters, and moving around according to her subtle choreography. She has an unmistakable, far from literal approach to still-life painting and although the objects are closely, lovingly observed, they are constantly subject to subtle changes in form, colour and decoration. In the composition too, she takes liberties with reality, tilting the table-top towards the picture plane and creating a flattened perspective that offers multiple viewpoints – the jug here, for example, has a typically uncompromising flat bottom, and a three-dimensional elliptical top while the fruit bowl is seen from above. But if viewpoints chop and change, there's a stillness here, there's no overlapping, no jostling for position, and each object has a significance, a quiet dignity that creates an almost visionary atmosphere, a mysterious combination of tranquillity and suspense.

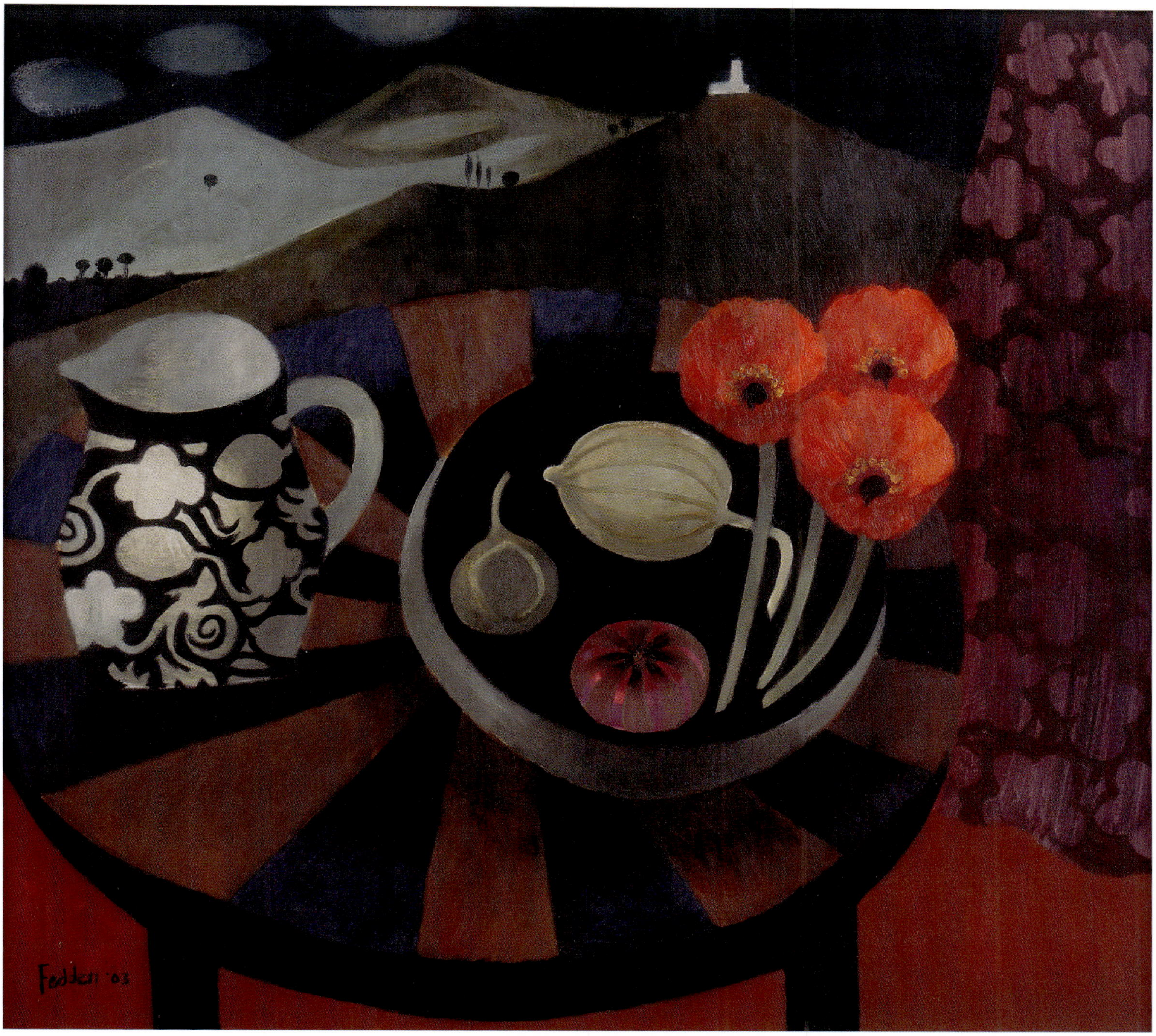

189
Three Red Poppies, 2003
Oil on canvas
69.2 x 79.4 cm (27¼ x 31¼ in)
Private collection

CHAPTER TEN

Repeats, Replications and Re-explorations

An art dealer friend said to me, 'Oh, Mary Fedden, she repeats herself, doesn't she?' And a collector of her earlier work explained that she felt Mary's work today had become 'formulaic'. Having spent months looking closely at her work, and knowing it somewhat for years before that, I find these criticisms a misapprehension to say the least.

Many of her collectors, actually, do not care a jot if she chooses to paint a close variation on a theme that has taken hold of her imagination. Mostly, they see little problem, even when she deliberately makes a virtually exact copy of a painting, thereby giving birth to twins. After all, both paintings are directly from her hand.

The *Three Red Poppies* (Ill. 189) that Joanna Carey writes so eloquently about is actually a case in point. Fedden was reluctant to sell her a different painting hanging in her studio, which she very much wanted to keep. In the end she struck a compromise with Joanna by letting her buy *Three Red Poppies* instead. 'I didn't actually want to part with that one either,' Mary says, 'so I immediately borrowed it back to make a copy for myself!' Not only that, but she made a gouache version of it that the Curwen Studio turned into a lithograph of compelling beauty (Ill. 192). No wonder the edition (of 95) proved to be a rapid sell-out. Then she also made a particularly strong finished drawing after the original painting (Ill. 193). Her compulsion to 'repeat' that image – in different media – is a matter, I think, of assured enjoyment, like continually singing a song you love and can't get out of your head!

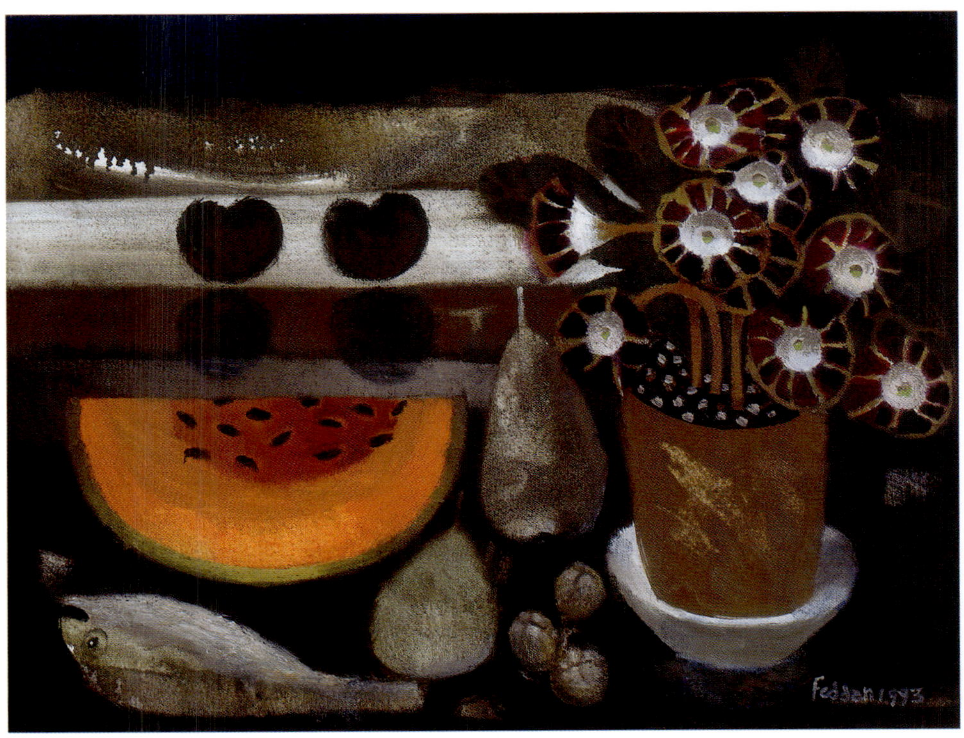

190
Auricula and Melon, 1993
Oil on canvas
29.5 x 39.5 cm (11⅝ x 15½ in)
Private collection

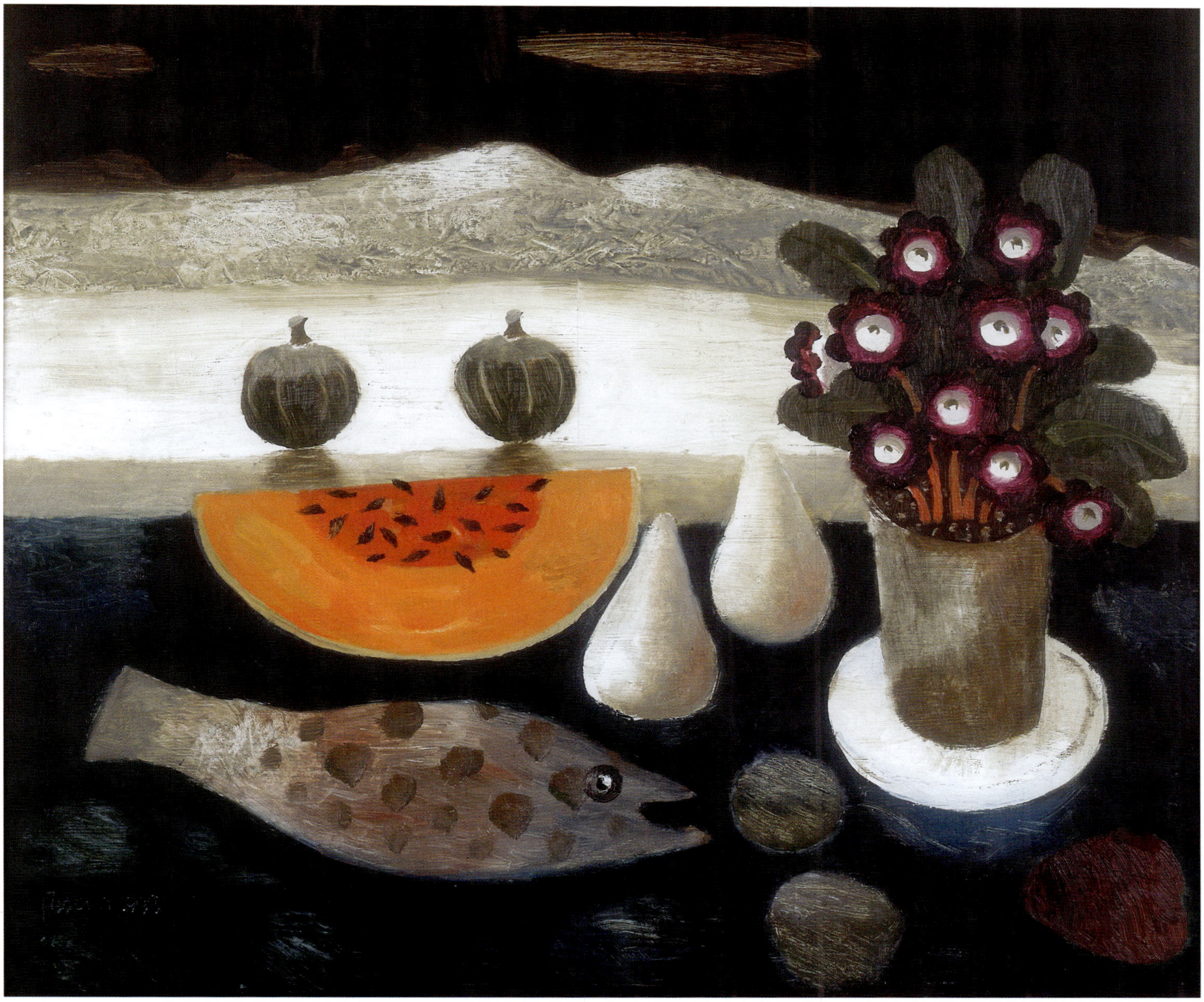

191
A Fish and a Slice of Melon, 1999
Oil on canvas
48.1 x 58.2 cm (19 x 23 in)
Private collection

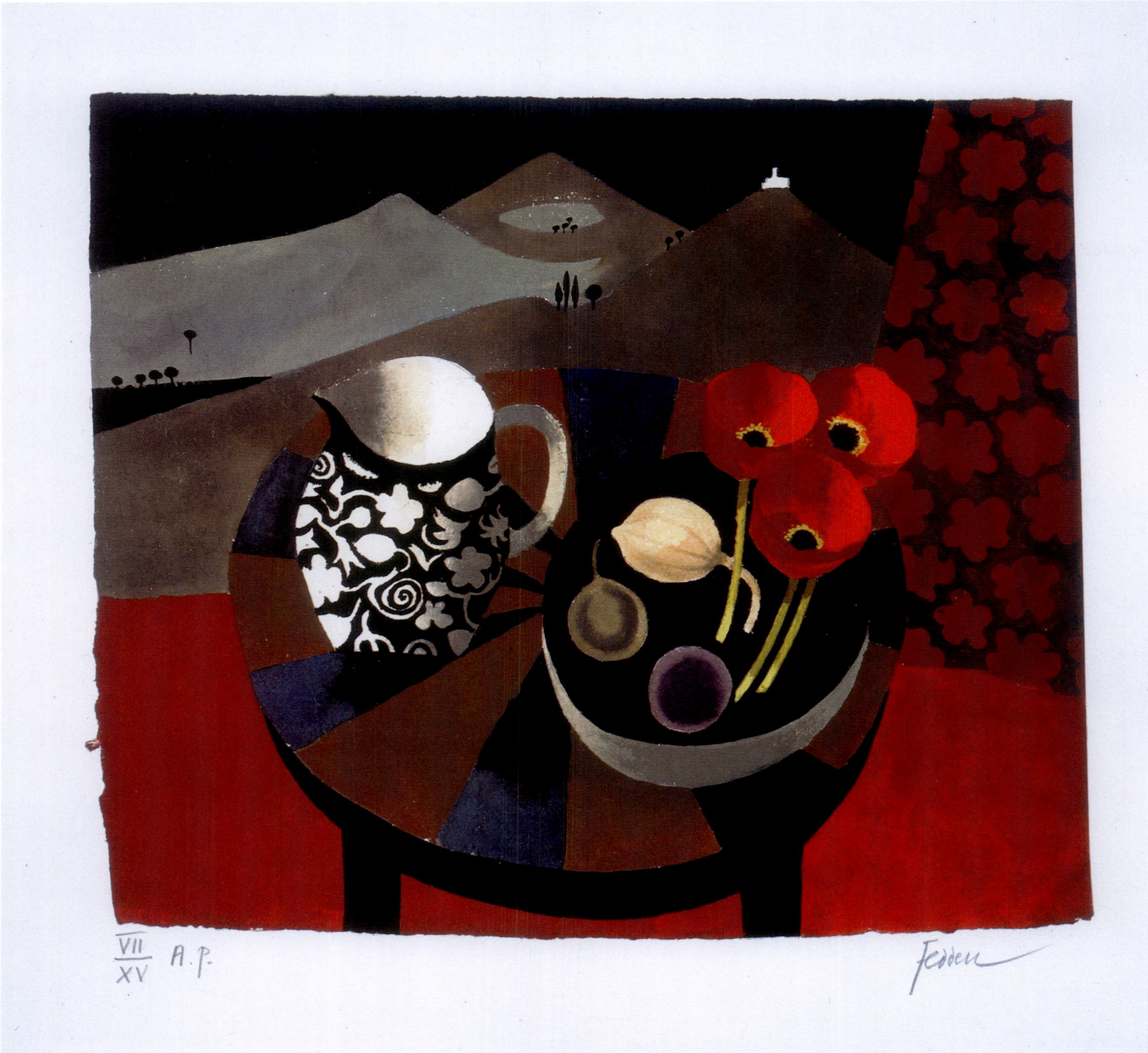

192
Three Red Poppies, 2003
Lithograph
56 x 63.5 cm (21⅞ x 25 in)
Credit: The Artist
Published by the Curwen Studio

It might be relevant that Mary lived and worked with an artist who devoted much of his time to making original prints. Prints are 'editioned', meaning that a fixed number of more or less exact replicas are printed. They are signed and numbered, and even though there may be 50 or more of them, each is considered, rightly, to be an original work of art.

Why shouldn't painters paint several versions, or even replicas, of their paintings, then? Painters in past centuries have sometimes made exact copies of their paintings for patrons and have thought nothing of it. But the notion of the almost magical authenticity of the artist's hand slowly took such firm root that self-copying or replication became virtually unacceptable. There have been

193
Three Red Poppies, 2004
Pencil on board
60 x 69.5 cm (23⅝ x 27¼ in)
Credit: The Artist

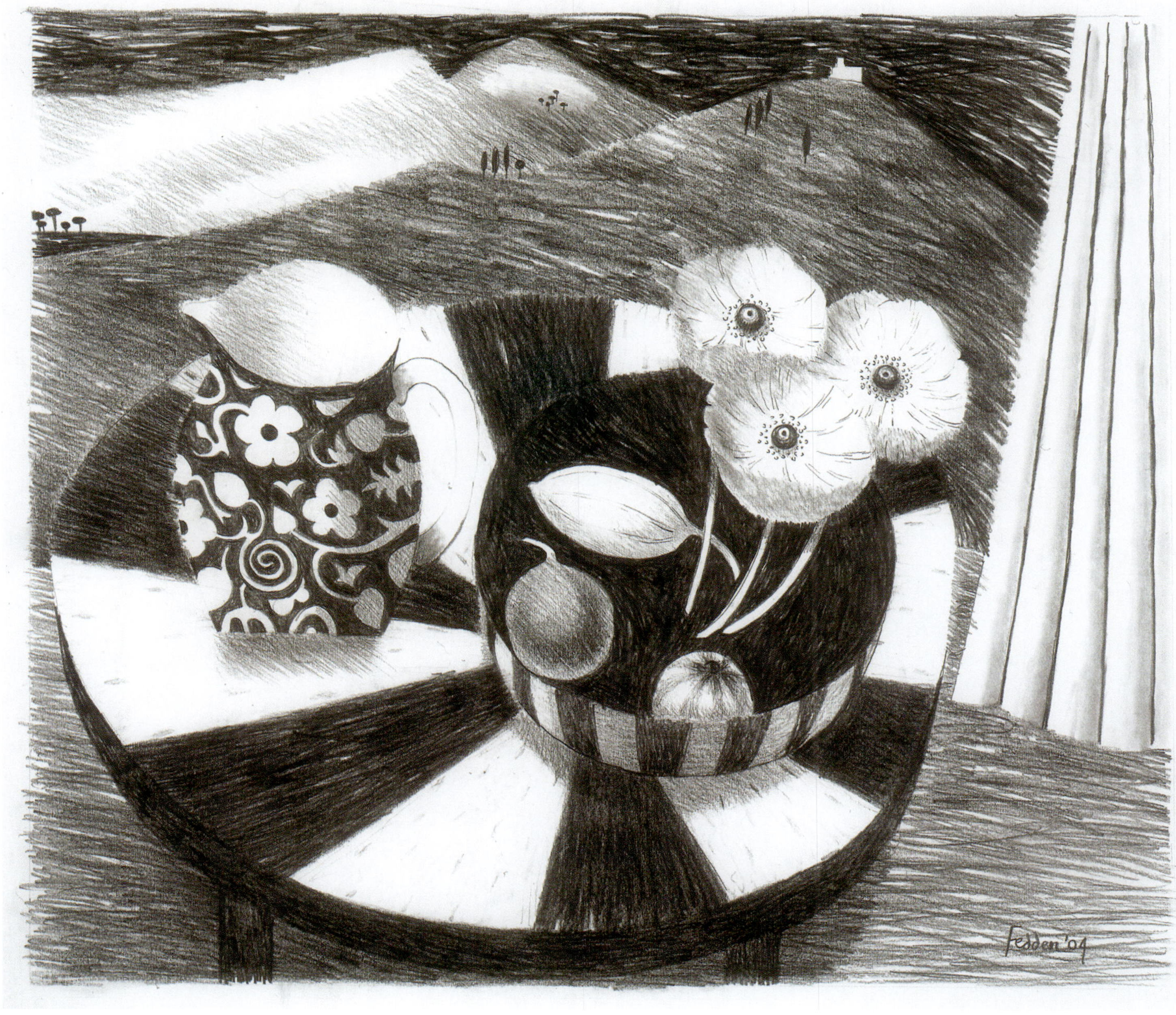

honourable exceptions in spite of this. Van Gogh painted his sunflowers several times with no guilt, but Picasso, so avid for discovery, for once voiced a conventional point of view: 'Copying others is necessary, but what a pity to copy oneself!'[1]

Fedden admitted to me, anyhow, that making a copy of one of her own paintings 'never really works. It's never quite the same as the first painting'. But there are no *rules* in art, and she clearly feels no qualms about a degree of self-copying if there is a good reason for it.

Far more frequently, anyway, she re-explores a favourite image, looking for different emphasis, different spacing, a more satisfactory balance of colours, improvement. *The Basket of Grapes* (Ill. 194) of 1999 (another painting she refuses to sell) and *The Indian Plate* (Ill. 195) of 2003 are just two variations on a still-life theme that she has found utterly absorbing for years now. Both derive

194
The Basket of Grapes, 1999
Oil on canvas
75 x 100 cm (29½ x 39⅜ in)
Credit: The Artist

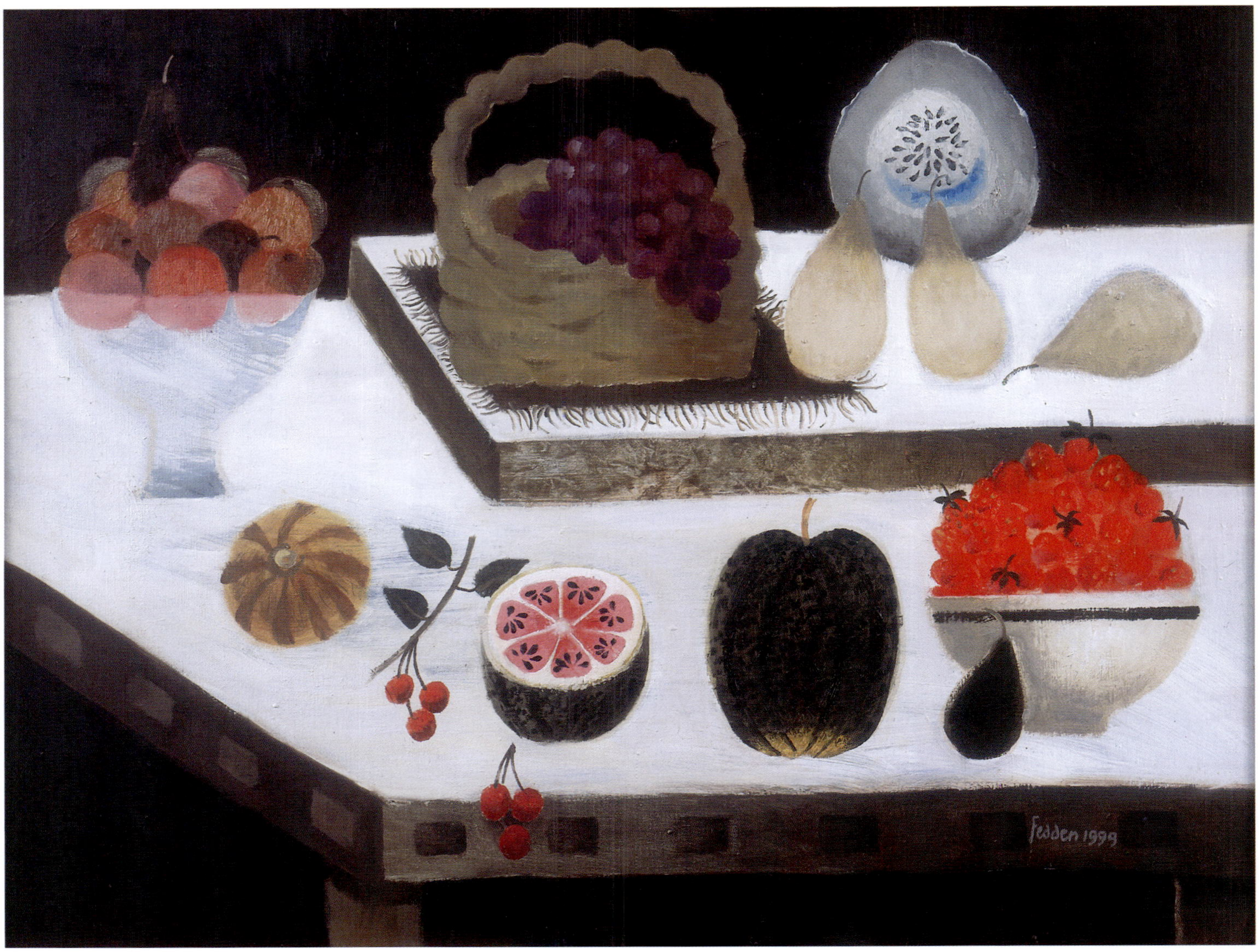

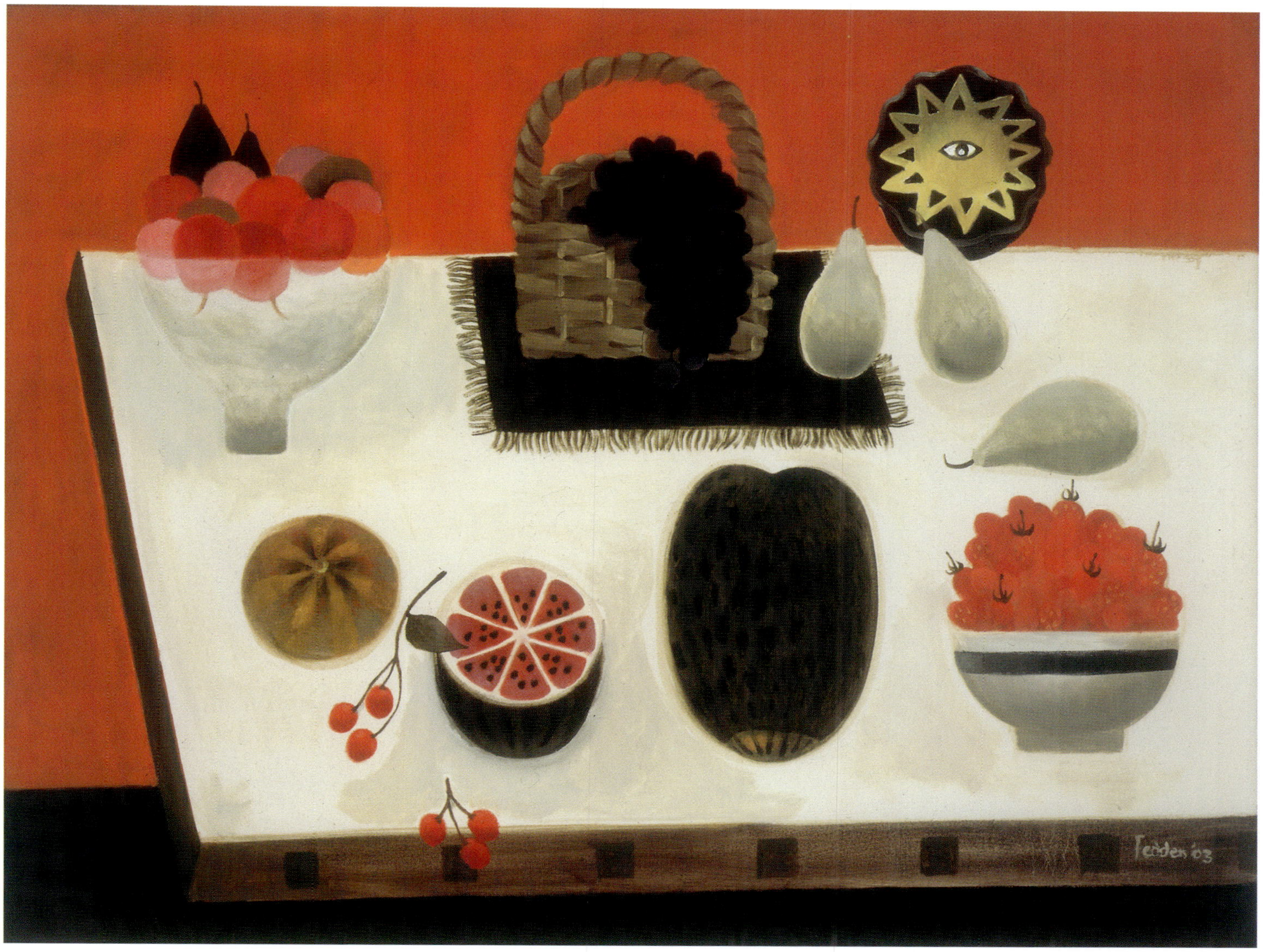

195
The Indian Plate, 2003
Oil on canvas
89.5 x 120 cm (35¼ x 47 in)
© Royal Academy of Arts, London

initially from an anonymous nineteenth-century American primitive painting called *Still Life of Fruit*, belonging to the National Gallery of Art, Washington D.C., though Fedden knows it only as a greeting card that she has long treasured in her box of inspiring postcards. She raids this box when in need of ideas for a painting. The card was sent to her in 1997 by Joanna Varcoe, who wrote on the back: 'I thought it was you!' Mary must have agreed. Her variations on it come close to the spirit and manner of this primitive painting, itself a kind of displaced folk memory or attempted imitation of European, probably Dutch, Old Master still lifes.

There is no doubt she feels that she needs to defend her strong desire to 're-explore'. 'Look at Cézanne,' she says, 'endlessly painting Mont Saint Victoire. Or Monet and his water lilies. Or what's his name – the bottle man – yes, *Morandi*.' (She likes Morandi so much she has a line of bottles gathering dust on a high shelf in her studio: 'my homage to Morandi'.)

Fedden might mention another Italian painter, Giorgio de Chirico, who, like Morandi, is associated with the 'metaphysical' artists. She certainly likes his work. His determination to repeat himself with small differences, over and over again, comes close to Fedden's practices. There are numerous versions of his haunting

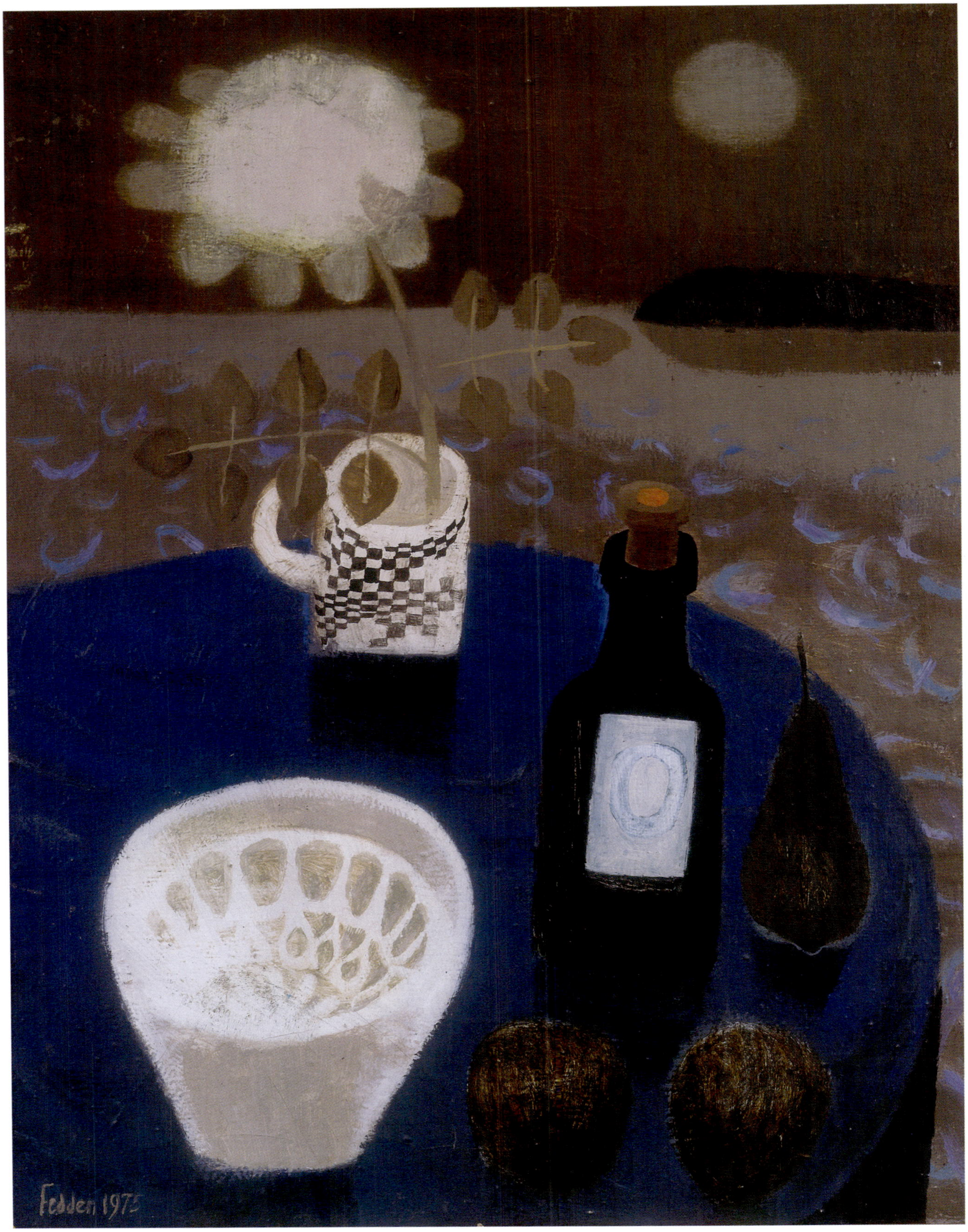

196
Jelly-Mould + Black Bottle, 1975
Oil on canvas
76 x 61 cm (30 x 24 in)
Private collection

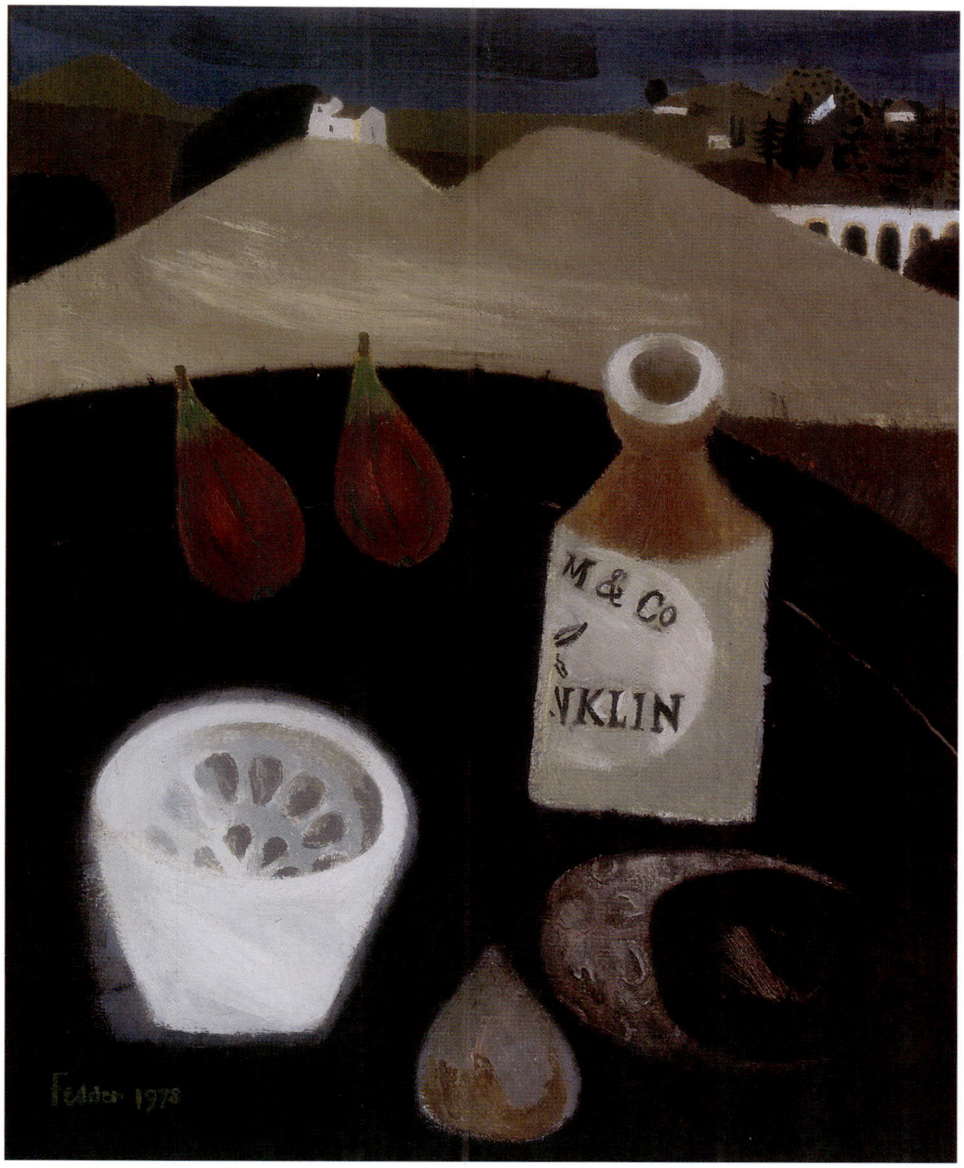

197
Jelly-Mould (2), 1978
Oil on canvas
61 x 51 cm (24 x 20 in)
Private collection

dream-piazzas. They look alike and they all have a similar feeling – and one is no 'better' or 'worse' than another just because he was obsessed with the subject. They are all de Chiricos.

It is interesting that some collectors of Fedden's work derive pleasure from owning paintings by her that are very close to each other in theme and composition. They sometimes even hang them next to each other, so they can grow intimately familiar with their similarities and differences. (Ills 196 and 197)

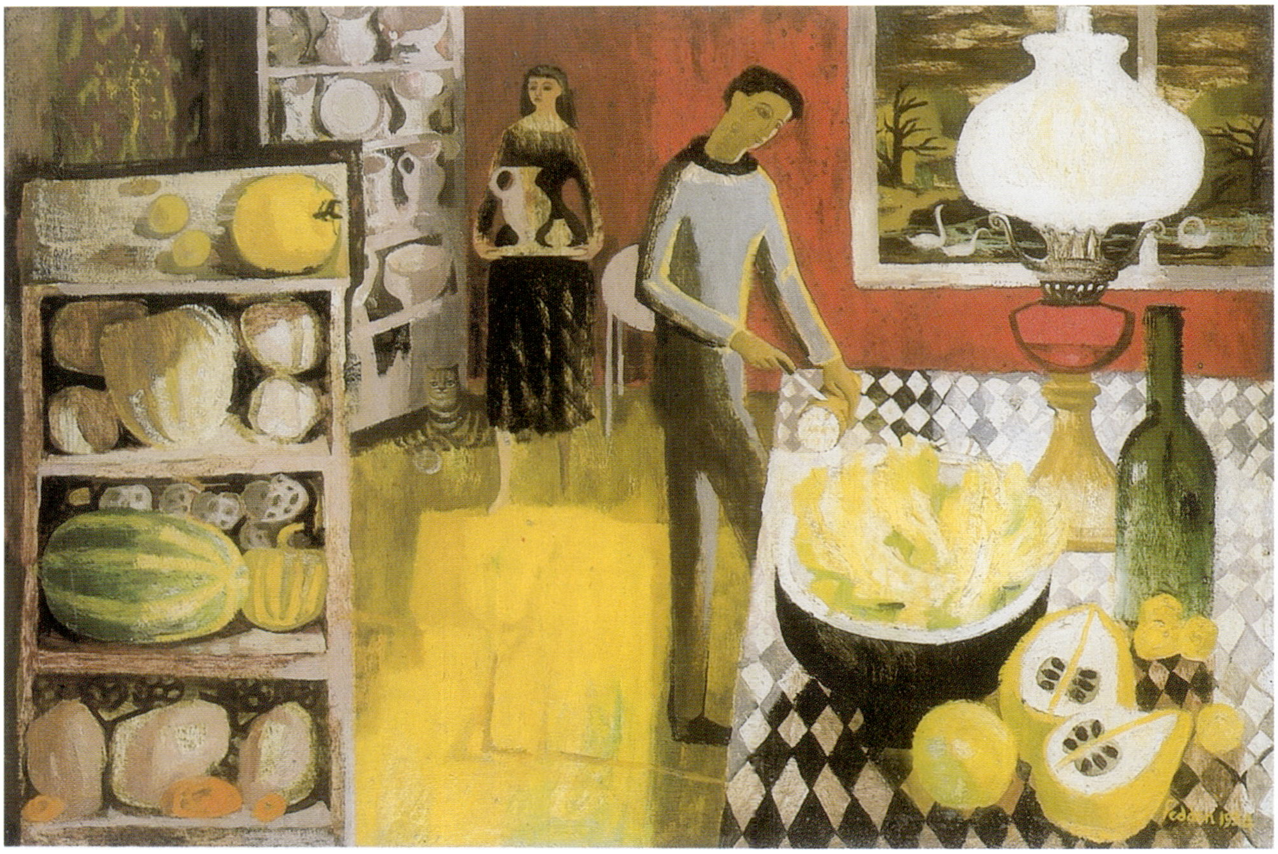

198
Julian and Mary at Durham Wharf, 1954
Oil on canvas
71 x 106.5 cm (28 x 42 in)
Private collection

Sometimes Fedden has repeated today a subject she painted years ago. Two versions of *Julian and Mary at Durham Wharf* – one painted in 1954, the other in 1997 – are a remarkable instance of this (Ills 198 and 199). Reiterating in such a way, or, as Mary herself puts it, 'having another go at it', makes the viewer, and presumably the painter, consider how her style has altered: her sense of composition, balance, light and relationships have changed. The reiteration also shows how she has achieved an economy of means in today's rendering, more than 40 years after she first painted this most personal of subjects, which is mellower and more dreamlike. It now belongs much less to a recognisable period.

Another way in which Fedden's images have been propagated is through prints such as that of *Basket of Lemons* (1971) (Ill. 200). Undoubtedly they reach people in ways that paintings do not. 'But,' she says, 'I never think: oh I really WANT to do a print!' These days, at least, she only does them because other people want her to. Sometimes a print is in answer to the appeal of a charity. She signs and numbers the prints, but her main participation is to provide a painting on which the print is to be based.

The Curwen Studio, which has over many years printed the majority of Fedden prints, now uses photo-lithography for the work. From this comes a print as near to the original as possible. Fedden's contribution at this stage is of the 'a-little-

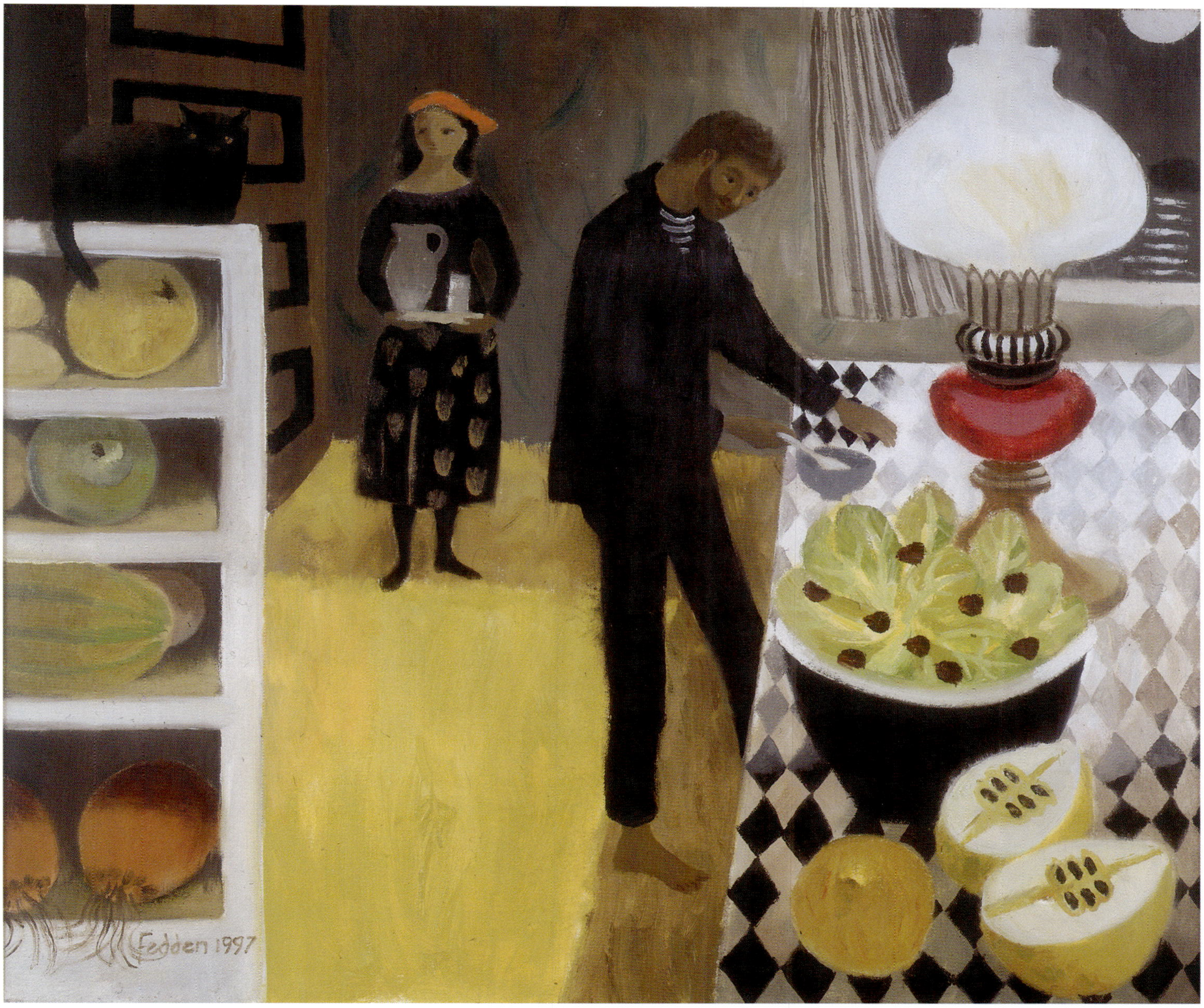

199
Julian and Mary at Durham Wharf, 1997
Oil on canvas
50.8 x 61 cm (20 x 24 in)
Private collection

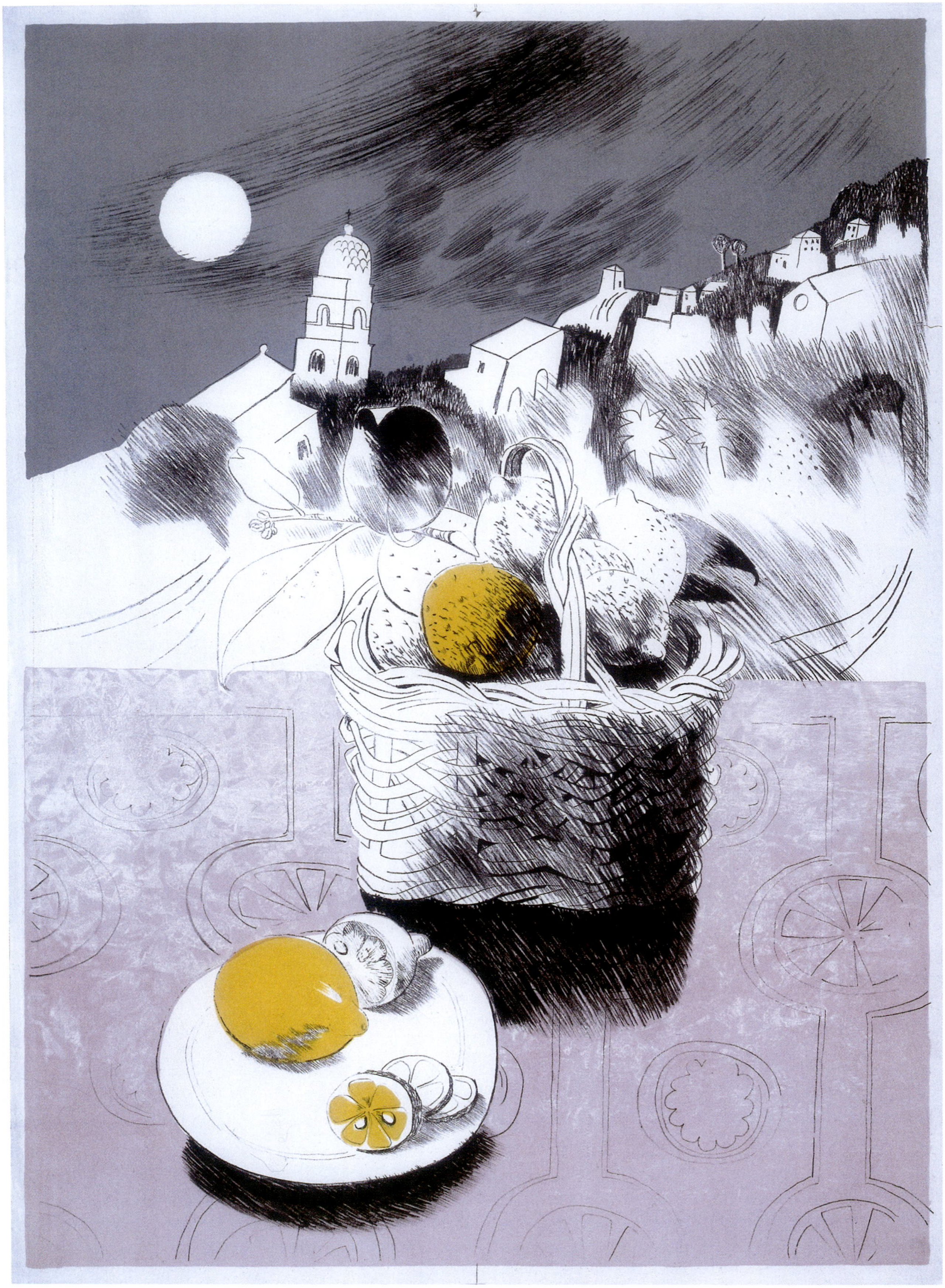

200 (opposite)
Basket of Lemons, 1971
Lithograph
74.9 x 54.9 cm (29½ x 21⅝ in)
Credit: The Artist
Published by the Curwen Studio

less-here, a-little-more-there' variety. She may want a highlight softened or an edge modified. The colour of a distant hill may need to be slightly more blue or green, and another part less yellow. She collaborates very effectively with the studio by word of mouth and letter. Usually she has no criticism, and wants nothing changed.

Only for some of the earlier prints did she show up at the workshop, but at that time Curwen was in London. Today it is in Cambridgeshire and she feels no urge to supervise *in situ* or play any kind of 'hands-on' role. She lets Curwen's expert and very sensitive printers make the adjustments. In this part of the process, they are using inks directly, mixed by hand and judged by eye. The subtlest of alterations are made until Fedden is happy with the print. Her final approval – or disapproval – is, of course, crucial. She has the ultimate sanction. Sometimes she considers the print to be better than her original!

Her prints are published in limited editions and are certainly classed as 'original prints', but she still feels that she is somehow 'cheating' by not becoming more closely involved. Her prints, in her view, are unquestionably peripheral, whether they are superbly printed like the *Three Red Poppies* or not. (Ill. 192)

She has also allowed at one time a quite different kind of printer to make what are essentially posters of her paintings, some of them of a reasonably high standard. The editions for these are far larger. They make her work available to a wider clientele, repeating images in a way she could never do herself, however hard-working, prolific and skilful she is. But in fact these posters are only reproductions.

Fedden is not a snob in such matters. Posters have their place. She *is* fussy about the quality of the prints made after her works and they certainly contribute to her popularity. However, she would much rather be at her easel, painting, than at a printing press, printing.

Note
1. *Picasso on Art, a Selection of Views* edited by Dore Ashton, Thames and Hudson Ltd (London), 1972, p.53

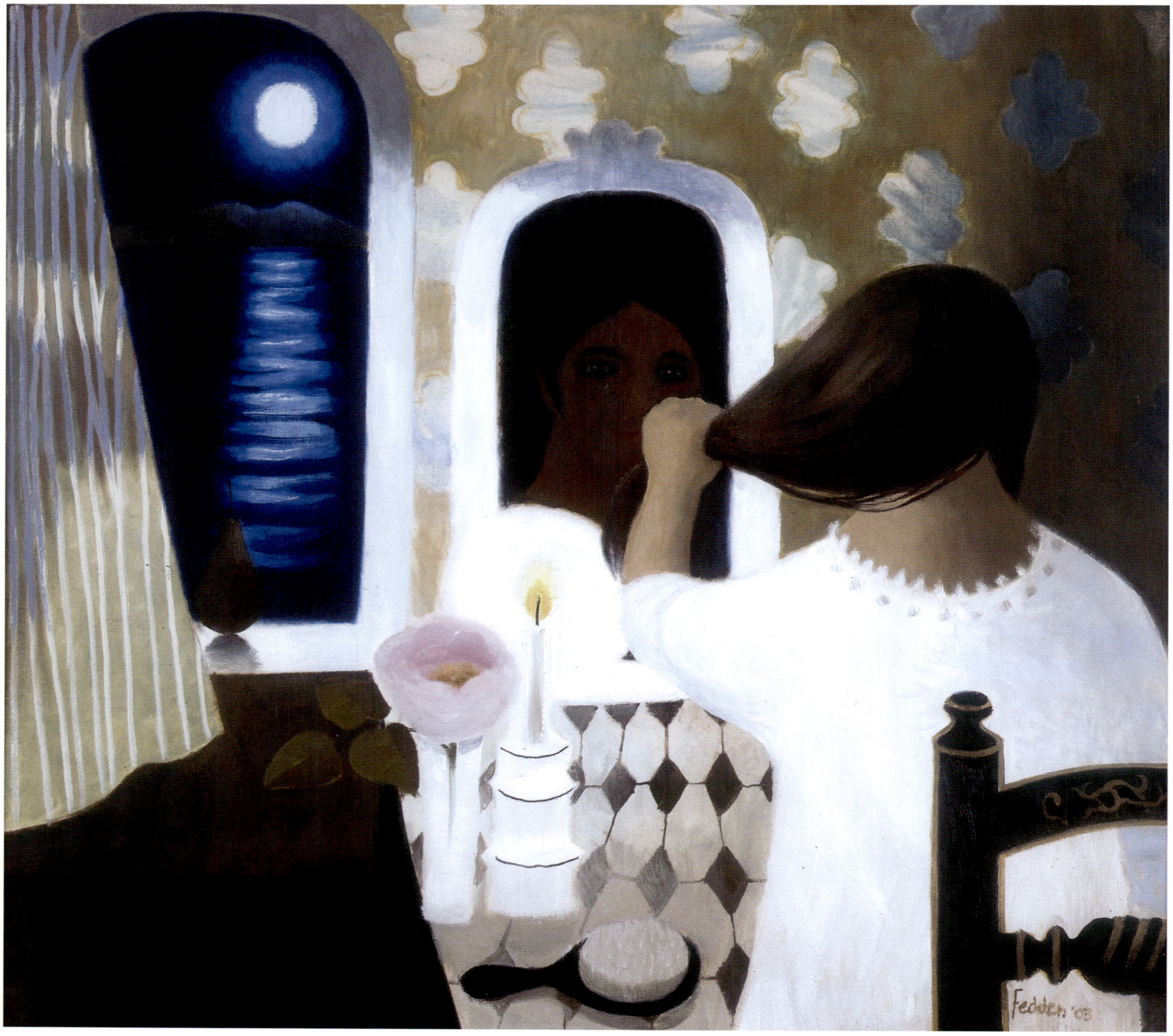

201
Girl at the Mirror, 2003
Oil on canvas
68.6 x 81.3 cm (27 x 32 in)
Credit: The Artist

Final Thoughts

While this book about her was in preparation, Mary Fedden often came out with lines from two favourite poems. One is: 'Much have I travelled in the realms of gold', the first line of Keats' 'On First Looking into Chapman's Homer'. The other lines that keep coming to her mind are the last four of Robert Frost's 'On Stopping by Woods on a Snowy Evening':

The woods are lovely, dark, and deep,
But I have promises to keep,
And miles to go before I sleep,
And miles to go before I sleep.[1]

In one sense, Mary Fedden is a survivor. She has outlived so many of her contemporaries that, perforce, she stands somewhat alone, continuing things that were started long ago yet are still exciting. In assessing her contribution, one looks back over more than five decades. Yet it is her energy today, and her productivity, together with her pleasure in unfailing powers, that strike much deeper.

Collectors and appreciators of her work tend to divide into three camps. The first camp is composed of those who like her traditional (though quite strange) work before Julian Trevelyan started to bring her into the modern art world. The second camp believes (in some case quite vocally) that she was 'at her peak' from the early 1950s to about the 1980s, painting with surges of feeling and a potently apparent compulsion. The third camp, which includes her younger fans of today, disagrees and finds her current work her most original.

One thing is arguably true: her paintings in the decades immediately after 1950 look now, for all their power and individuality, as if they are somehow typical of that period. On the other hand, it is impossible to say to whom, what, where, or when she belongs today. She simply belongs to herself. She is certainly different from many of today's artists in still being very much a *painter.* She is no conceptualist. For collectors, she positively presents a heart-warming alternative to the trends and tactics of many artists who leave them either cold or baffled.

In some ways she is comfortably old-fashioned, but she is also modern enough to be often referred to as 'a modern artist'. She is a modern artist, perhaps, in the sense that Giorgio Morandi was a modern artist, painting regardless of either tradition or Modernism, but not in opposition to either. She is not iconoclastic, not an avant-garde shatterer of conventions. She accepts without demur the traditional tools of the painter's trade. She has no 'Modernist' axe to grind. Yet her paintings (from 1950 to 2007) could never be mistaken for paintings of another time. This balance of old and new in her make-up reminds me of a moment in *The Horse's Mouth*, Joyce Carey's novel about another (but fictional) Thames-side artist, the outsider Gulley Jimson. ('Julian and I *loved* that book', she remembers.) Gulley describes a visit from a lawyer hired to defend him in court. However, they agreed that defending such an old renegade as he is would be tricky.

'I see, Mr Jimson, we'll have to concentrate on character.' 'No you haven't,' I said, 'Remember I'm an artist. And you know what that means in a court of law. Next worst to an actress.' 'That's what I mean,' he said. 'And I believe you are a modern artist.' 'Very nearly,' I said. 'Yes,' he said. 'It's a difficult case ...'[2]

Fedden might also be characterised as 'very nearly' a 'modern artist'. Her work certainly strikes traditionalists as quite modern enough, yet her net of appreciation is broad. She fishes in the waters of old art as well as modern.

Her history with regard to the Royal Academy of Arts is telling. She and Julian, in contrast to many other Royal College teachers, staunchly refused to join the Royal Academy in the 1950s, considering it totally out-of-date, beyond the pale and fuddy-duddy. The then President, Sir Alfred Munnings, presumably knowing it would strike a chord with most of middle England, had launched a vitriolic and rather silly attack on Picasso in an after-dinner speech at the Academy. Mr and Mrs Trevelyan, profoundly involved in what the auction houses now call 'Modern British' art, objected strongly. Much later, when they felt the Academy had completely changed, they were not invited to join. Julian only became an R.A. right at the end of his career and Mary not until the 1990s.

There is no doubt that Mary Fedden is a modern artist in certain ways. She paints with unstinting disregard for the tastes or opinions of others and paints fast and often. She paints 'through the bad times' and paints on because continuing to paint is what she chooses and loves to do, and it is what drives her. Stopping is just not part of the plan.

202
Little Soft Lion
Fabric and embroidery
Private collection

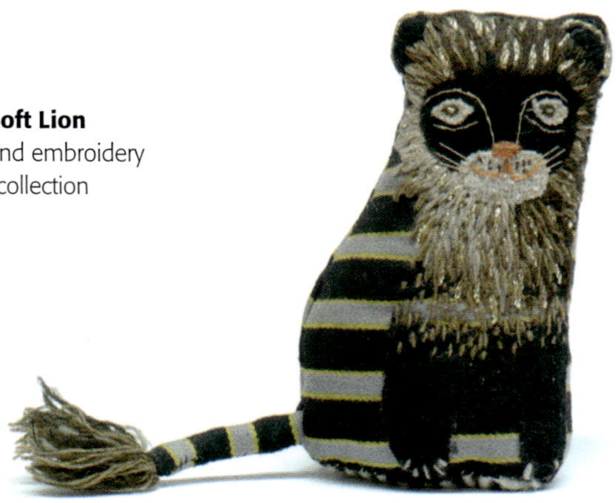

Notes

1. *The Poetry of Robert Frost,* edited by Edward Connery Lathem, Vintage (London), 2001, pp 224–5
2. *The Horse's Mouth* by Joyce Cary, Penguin (London), 1948, p.77

Index of Mary Fedden Works

Illustrated works by page number

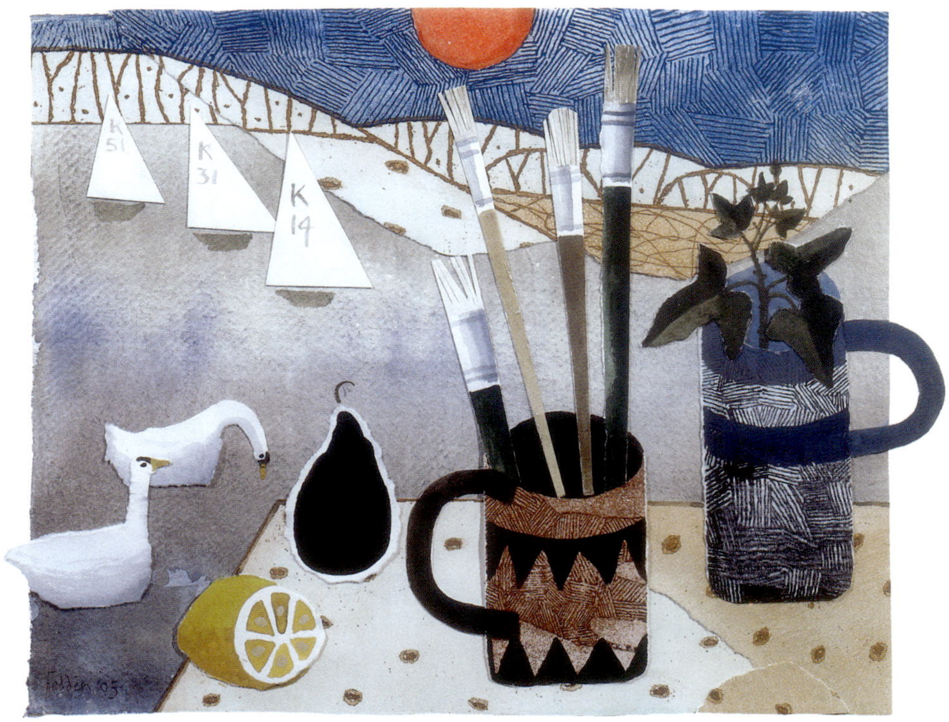

See Ill. 126, p.113